MORTAL
SECRETS

MORTAL SECRETS

Freud, Vienna, and the Discovery of the Modern Mind

Frank Tallis

ST. MARTIN'S PRESS
NEW YORK

Human kind cannot bear very much reality.

—'Burnt Norton', from *Four Quartets*
by T. S. ELIOT

Contents

Preface

Few major thinkers have been attacked and vilified more than Sigmund Freud. His ideas have been dismissed as offensive and ludicrous. He has been accused of being a child rapist, incestuous, a plagiarist, over-controlling, an unfaithful and tyrannical husband, a liar, a fraud, money-obsessed and ruthlessly ambitious. On one occasion, he is said to have come very close to committing a murder. A comprehensive census of Freud's alleged flaws, indiscretions and misdeeds would fill a book. Indeed, there are weighty critical works that consist almost exclusively of character assassination. Some allegations are true, some are partially true, many are based on hearsay, and a minority – for example, that Freud came close to committing a murder – are frankly absurd.

'Freud bashing' is the term commonly used to describe immoderate and personal criticism of Freud. Comparable figures, such as Karl Marx, for example, have 'vociferous critics', but only Freud has 'bashers'. The designation is unique because Freud has attracted singularly dyspeptic critics who habitually denounce the man along with his ideas. Freud believed, quite reasonably, that much of the hostility he encountered during his lifetime was attributable to antisemitism. He had Jewish critics as well as gentile critics, but his Jewish critics were less inclined to associate his theories with sewage and degeneracy.

By the 1930s, a distinction was being made between Aryan science and Jewish science and Freud's books were being burned by the Nazis.

Extreme Freud bashing is offset by an equally unhelpful opposite. Freud's loyal followers have treated his works like scripture. His authority is accepted without question, and he is venerated as an oracle – a conduit of timeless truths. After Freud's death, he became the subject of effusive eulogies. He was remembered as wise, witty, compassionate, principled and courageous, a lone genius who had overcome enormous obstacles and laboured tirelessly for the benefit of 'mankind'.

Because Freud polarises opinion, it is very difficult to assess his significance. He is obviously important, but how important? Biographies and commentaries are typically biased (either negatively or positively) and Freud's original publications are problematic for several reasons. He was unquestionably a great writer, but he was also a very uneven writer. His opinions changed over time, he contradicted himself, and sometimes he misleads. He is a master of arresting metaphors and literary flourishes, but he can also test the reader's patience with lists, telegraphic notes and long passages of opaque, nomadic prose. The task of evaluating Freud is further complicated by a standard text that is – in places – very loosely translated from Freud's German. Moreover, subsequent attempts to improve on the standard text have solved some problems while creating others.

Freud bashing can sometimes resemble an academic bloodsport. Nevertheless, criticism of Freud is often justified. He wasn't a reliable reporter, particularly when writing up his case studies; he overemphasised the importance of sex as an aetiological factor in mental illness; and his ideas are generally not original. But such criticism – and there is much of it – is usually in need of qualification. It would be unwise to dismiss all of psychoanalysis because Freud's case studies are capricious. We

don't reject Copernicus, Kepler and Galileo because they produced horoscopes and believed in astrology. Freud may have
accentuated sex immoderately in the consulting room; however,
his assertion that sex configures the mind and influences many
aspects of behaviour is supported by the relatively new science
of evolutionary psychology. Almost all of Freud's ideas are borrowed; nevertheless, he was extremely good at gathering them
together and using them to construct exciting new theories.

There is broad agreement with respect to Freud's greatest
contributions. His writings about the unconscious and the
structure of the mind; his account of defence mechanisms; his
commentaries on religion, culture and civilisation; his recognition of the impact of early experience on adult mental health;
and his invention of an innovative talking cure – psychoanalysis.

Freud wasn't the only doctor experimenting with psychological treatments at the end of the nineteenth century. There were
others, most notably Pierre Janet and Paul Dubois. However, it
was Freud's method (requiring analysands to lie on a 'couch')
that became the most famous. The iconic coupling of a bearded
therapist and a reclining patient is recognised all over the world.
The *New Yorker* magazine printed its first psychoanalytic cartoon in 1927 – and it has been printing them ever since. As with
almost everything associated with Freud, opinions vary wildly
on the value of psychoanalysis. There are some who argue that
Freud helped none of his patients and that psychoanalysis is
fundamentally harmful, and there are others who claim that
psychoanalysis is the most profound and life-changing of all psychological therapies. Psychoanalysis is certainly not a panacea.
Freud never said that it was. But psychoanalysis was certainly
more benevolent than many of the treatments offered to patients
in Freud's time, which were either inhumane (for example, an
electrified metal brush thrust down the throat to treat a nervous
cough) or ridiculous (rectal massage to treat homosexuality).

Twentieth-century psychiatric interventions have included painful shocks, induced comas, protracted restraint and isolation, extreme sedation, narcosis (keeping patients asleep for months) and lobotomy. By contrast, psychoanalysis is predicated on the formation of a consensual, collaborative relationship and symptoms are judged to be meaningful (as opposed to meaningless epiphenomena caused by putative chemical imbalances and structural defects in the brain). Psychoanalysis also catalysed the development of all forms of modern psychotherapy. Even those that came into being as a reaction against it. Cognitive behaviour therapy, for example.

Although psychoanalysis began as a treatment method for certain mental illnesses it evolved into something closer to a world view, a way of thinking about every aspect of human behaviour. Freud compared psychoanalysis to electricity. Electricity can be used in medical settings, for example to power an X-ray machine, but it can also be used more widely – in the home, on roads and in the air. Psychoanalysis is not exclusively 'medical'. Freud used psychoanalysis to understand mental illnesses; however, he also used it to illuminate creativity, religion, the *Mona Lisa*, jokes, mythology and politics; he used it to generate intriguing speculations about prehistoric societies and to explain strange experiences. Psychoanalysis has been enormously influential. Many works of art, music, drama and cinema have been inspired by the psychoanalytic world view. There are psychoanalytic feminists, anthropologists and 'big data' analysts. Even advertising owes a debt to psychoanalysis. Freud's American nephew, Edward Bernays, revolutionised advertising by devising successful marketing campaigns informed by his uncle's understanding of symbols and desire. Freud's ideas have been so thoroughly assimilated into our culture that even those who reject Freud still think, occasionally, like Freudians. We accept that parts of the mind operate unconsciously; that when people intend to say one

Gado/Getty Images

thing, but say another, it is revealing. The term 'Freudian slip' has become part of everyday speech. When we wake up after a night filled with vivid dreams, we wonder if those dreams mean anything. We accept that people *repress* difficult feelings. If a friend described a superior at work as *anal*, we would smile knowingly.

One of the most enduring myths about Freud – a myth Freud himself manufactured – is that he developed psychoanalysis in splendid isolation and that his most creative years were his wilderness years. In fact, during this period he had many professional friends and associates, his early publications were generally well received, and he gave lectures at the university and a Jewish lodge where he was most welcome. More importantly, his wilderness

years were spent in the world's most glamorous and intellectually exhilarating capital. Today, Vienna is sometimes referred to
as the city of dreams because it is associated with Freud and his
masterpiece, *The Interpretation of Dreams*. Freud's fame encourages us to view Vienna's golden age through a Freudian lens.
Vienna certainly *did* respond to Freud – with new art, music and
scholarship – but Freud also responded to Vienna. Psychoanalysis
was well nourished by its remarkable ambience. The mutually
beneficial dialogue between Freud and his 'hometown' has been
somewhat disregarded to better serve the lone-genius myth. Yet,
it is almost impossible to imagine the discovery of psychoanalysis
happening anywhere other than Vienna.

For twenty-five years, from 1890 to 1915, Vienna became a
dazzling beacon, powered by an unprecedented number of world-
class intellects, all of whom lived within a few square miles of
each other. They met and exchanged ideas in Vienna's famous
coffee houses, where the sensual (coffee and cake) and the cerebral

(heated debate) were pleasingly combined with billiards, gossip and newspapers. Chemists and violinists, novelists and biologists, theatre directors and mathematicians were all at ease sharing the same table. Vienna's coffee houses were intellectual melting-pots, and it is commonly supposed that the exchange of ideas between disparate disciplines was the secret of Vienna's success.

The furious creativity of Vienna's golden age eventually became feverish. Nervous disorders and decadence followed, as did the affectation of amused indifference to warnings about the future. Viennese society carried on waltzing, the couples revolving faster and faster, perversely eager to meet their so-called 'joyful apocalypse'. Many years before Archduke Franz Ferdinand's assassination, escalating tensions within the Habsburg Empire were already feeding millennial anxieties. Yet, the characters depicted in the literature of the time typically show combinations of torpor, frivolity, nostalgic yearning and resignation. As the end of their world drew closer, the Viennese responded by having more sexual liaisons, going to more balls and ordering more champagne. An enormous number of young men simply pushed a gun barrel into their mouths and pulled the trigger. The First World War blighted Vienna's cultural supremacy. Nevertheless, many of Vienna's gifted thinkers and artists remained active well into the twentieth century. The beacon of Viennese genius continued to shine – particularly in America, where many Viennese intellectuals emigrated between the First and Second World Wars.

Vienna's golden age, despite its brevity, exerted a dispro-portionate influence on the course of history. A young Adolf Hitler learned the rudiments of what was to become National Socialism in Vienna, and it was also in Vienna that Theodor Herzl (the father of modern political Zionism) first suggested that a Jewish state should be established in Palestine. The intel-lectual life of Vienna influenced global events throughout the

twentieth century, and it continues (albeit at a remote temporal distance) to influence political developments in the Middle
East. The massive shock waves that followed Vienna's cultural
detonation were complemented by a variety of smaller tremors
that are equally compelling in their own way, because their
displacements can still be detected in our day-to-day existence.

Vienna 1900 was the birthplace of modernity and the modern
mind. The term 'modern' is usually employed to describe the
post-industrial world and 'modernity' is associated with 'modernist' thought and art. Aspects of modernism were prefigured
in the nineteenth century, but true modernism is a largely
twentieth-century phenomenon. Abstract paintings, atonal
string quartets and stream-of-consciousness short stories are
all (in this sense) typically 'modern'. Modernity is not only
associated with elevated thinking and high art. Modernity also
describes how we live in the modern world. Long coffee menus,
croissants and celebrity interviews are all Viennese inventions.
The chatty, conversational style of many newspaper columns
was pioneered by golden-age Viennese journalists in pieces
called *feuilletons*. Modern buildings were appearing in Vienna
long before they started to change the skyline of New York.
And the idea of modern design for the home (practical, stripped-
down, clean and without ornament) didn't originate with IKEA,
but with the aesthetic sensibility of Viennese architects and
designers. Viennese influences can be identified every time we
enter a café, read a newspaper, look out of the window or examine the furniture in our homes; however, the place where we can
find the most profound evidence of Viennese influence is inside
our heads. How we think about ourselves has been largely determined by Vienna's most illustrious resident: Sigmund Freud.

Freud's reputation grew in the first half of the twentieth century but shrank in the second half. Successive waves of criticism
reduced confidence in psychoanalysis as a treatment – and by

association, psychoanalysis as a world view. From the 1970s onwards, archival research showed that Freud was considerably more flawed as a person than his hagiographers had suggested. Even so, Freud never disappeared from the cultural landscape. As far as the general public was concerned, his well-known face still represented all things psychological, and his books have always been available on the high street – an exceptional accomplishment for an author whose ideas were originally debated in nineteenth-century coffee houses.

After the 1950s, psychoanalysis was rejected by mainstream scientists. They argued that psychoanalysis is non-empirical and could not be falsified. It was, at best, a pseudoscience, and at worst, a practice comparable to fortune-telling. Then, in 1976, the biologist Robert Trivers used an evolutionary argument to legitimise the idea of the unconscious, and soon after several 'Freudian' concepts – for example, repression and inner conflict – were favourably re-evaluated from an evolutionary perspective. These developments appeared to confirm a prediction made by Charles Darwin in 1859, that one day, in the 'distant future', psychology would be based on a 'new foundation'. Freud's scientific rehabilitation continued. In the 1990s, the neuropsychologist Mark Solms coined the term 'neuropsychoanalysis' to describe a nascent discipline that aims to integrate psychoanalysis and neuroscience. The International Neuropsychoanalysis Society was founded in 2000 and speakers at the first congress included, in addition to Solms, distinguished luminaries such as Oliver Sacks, Jaak Panksepp and Antonio Damasio. The Nobel Prize-winning neuroscientist Eric Kandel – a great admirer of Freud – joined the editorial board of the society's journal. At around the same time, V. S. Ramachandran (described by Sacks as 'one of the most interesting neuroscientists of our time') was undertaking clinical research that strongly suggested Freudian defence mechanisms have neural correlates. In 2010, the world's most influential neuroscientist, Karl Friston, in collaboration with Robin Carhart-Harris, published an article in the prestigious journal *Brain* in which the most forward-looking models of brain functioning were used to explore possible connections between Freudian constructs and neurobiological substrates. In 2021, another *Brain* article, by Diego Centonze and Mario Stampanoni Bassi, was tellingly titled 'Time for a new deal between neurology and psychoanalysis'.

This book has four principal objectives: to provide an account of Freud's life; to summarise his key intellectual contributions; to locate Freud and his ideas in their cultural context – that is, Vienna's golden age; and to show how psychoanalysis has colonised how we think about ourselves and the world we live in.

The great physician, progressive and sexologist Havelock Ellis said of Freud that he sometimes strings his arguments on a very thin thread, but however thin the thread, Freud never neglects to string a few pearls. Even if the thread sometimes snaps, Ellis reminds us, we still have the pearls. It is important to be aware of Freud's broken threads. There are many of them. But it will be to our immense detriment – as individuals and as a culture – if we fail to pick up the pearls.

Chapter 1

Destiny's Child

We begin in a pastry shop. A young mother, Amalia Freud, is accosted by a strange old peasant woman who declares that Amalia has brought a great man into the world. The air is fragrant with gingerbread and poppy-seed cake, and the old woman's smile is enigmatic. It is a prophecy that Amalia should dismiss. After all, peasant women are always dispensing charms and predicting the future, but this prophecy deserves notice, because Amalia's little son has already been dignified by an auspicious sign. He was born with a translucent hood covering his head, a caul, believed by many to be a portent of fame and good fortune. The old woman's body sinks a little as she executes a barely perceptible genuflection. Her eyes are bright with triumphal visions. Amalia takes a deep breath and her chest expands with pride and happiness. She can feel the truth of this prophecy in her bones.

Sigmund Freud was happy to share this story with others, but at the same time he made it plain that as far as he was concerned his mother had been persuaded by nothing more than superstitious nonsense. Even though he was keen to preserve his reputation as a committed sceptic, this didn't stop him from telling his followers about another prophetic incident that, unlike his mother's encounter in the pastry shop, he could remember very clearly. When he was eleven or twelve, an entertainer in a restaurant predicted that Freud would 'probably' become a cabinet minister. The entertainer was of course wrong, because Freud didn't pursue a career in politics. But not wholly wrong, insofar as the prediction still suggests that a measure of greatness was, in some sense, preordained.

A remarkable nativity and encounters with prophets are narrative staples that have been used to authenticate heroes since ancient times. Reflecting on the caul and the pastry shop, Ernest Jones (Freud's principal British disciple and biographer) wrote 'Thus the hero's garb was in the weaving at the cradle itself'. In mythology, omens can also be credentials. The gods distinguish champions and conquerors with signs. Freud's life-story would contain many of the key ingredients of a perfectly constructed classical myth: humble origins, portents of greatness, struggles against adversity, banishment, descent into the underworld and a triumphant return with a precious gift: ascent – fame – glory. The pleasing shape of Freud's legend suggests a life that was lived self-consciously and alert to the narrative potential of situations and chance.

Although Freud feigned dismay that it should have fallen upon him, of *all* people, to battle with demons and discover ultimate truths, there are occasional unguarded passages in his autobiographical writings that expose the unmistakable self-assurance of a man who appears always to have had one ear straining for the call of destiny. By the end of the nineteenth century he saw himself as someone fated with the responsibility of disturbing the 'sleep of the world'. Yet, apart from the caul and the peasant woman, there really was nothing promising about Freud's early life. It was far more likely that a person with his parentage and background would end up managing a moderately successful textile business. Disturbing the sleep of the world shouldn't have been any concern of his.

Freud was born in a rented room above Zajíc the locksmith's shop at 117 Schlossergasse, a two-storey house in the town of Freiberg, Moravia at 6.30 p.m. on 6 May 1856. Schlossergasse has since been renamed Zámečznická, Freiberg is now Příbor, and Moravia is now a region of the Czech Republic. Zajíc's house is still there (the only building to survive street demolition in 1975) and in 2006 it opened its doors to visitors as the Freud birthplace museum. Amalia's baby had a full head of black hair which prompted her to call him (disconcertingly for us) her 'little blackamoor'. A week later, on 13 May, the baby 'entered the Jewish covenant', or more explicitly, was circumcised. His given names were Sigismund (derived from the German word for victory) and Schlomo (Solomon in English), although his family called him Sigi. He became a 'lively' infant who liked going downstairs to play with scraps of metal, which he made into small toys.

In the mid-nineteenth century, Freiberg had a population of between four and five thousand inhabitants, of which only a hundred or so were Jews. The rest were almost entirely Catholic. It was a typical Moravian town, with little to distinguish it apart from a church with an impressive steeple and chimes. Beyond the outskirts of Freiberg were farms, woods and hills, and beyond these hills the distant Carpathian mountains.

Moravia was part of the Habsburg Empire. The Habsburgs had ruled Austria from the thirteenth century and over the course of six hundred years their sovereignty extended across vast areas of Europe. The nineteenth-century Habsburgs are credited with having created an empire of bureaucrats, but behind this façade of functionaries, paper shuffling and red tape, the empire was also rather magical. The inalienable heirlooms of the royal family included a unicorn's horn and the Holy Grail;

Hector, Noah and even the god Saturn were all, at one time or another, implicated in Habsburg genealogy. In addition to securing power by conventional means, such as advantageous marriages, Habsburg rule was also buttressed by symbolism, the acquisition of special objects, and ritualistic ceremonies. They seemed to have discovered public relations in the sixteenth century. The pastry shop in which Amalia encountered the strange peasant woman (already evocative of a Grimms' fairy tale) was located in a much larger landscape of wonder and imperial enchantment.

Freud's immediate ancestors were from Galicia (a Habsburg border province, now western Ukraine). His maternal relatives were from Brody and his paternal relatives were from Buchach and Tysmenytsia. In *An Autobiographical Study*, Freud states that his family were originally from Cologne (where medieval pogroms had preceded the expulsion of Jewish residents in 1424). He supposed that his ancestors had fled eastwards in the fourteenth or fifteenth centuries because of persecution, and that they had eventually made their way back to German-speaking territories in the nineteenth century via Lithuania and Galicia. Regardless of what Freud had been told or believed, it is much more likely that his distant ancestors fled Lithuania at the end of the seventeenth century and settled in Galicia.

Freud's father, Jacob, was an impecunious wool merchant. He purchased wool from local peasants and after the wool had been dyed he sold 'finished' batches to manufacturers. Freud likened him to Charles Dickens' amiable but incompetent Wilkins Micawber, who, in *David Copperfield*, is always over-optimistically expecting something to turn up. Jacob had grown up in a Jewish Orthodox shtetl and spoke Hebrew and Yiddish, although business was always conducted in German, and as a Jewish merchant he was obliged every year to apply to the authorities for permission to trade. He was mindful of his heritage, but not religious – and he certainly didn't want to be regarded as an outsider.

Jacob's first wife, Sally Kanner, bore him two sons, Emmanuel and Phillip; however, there is some confusion surrounding whether Jacob did or didn't marry a woman called Rebecca after Sally's death. Some biographers avoid the issue by simply omitting her. Others question whether she even existed. In 1852 a woman called Rebecca *was* listed as Jacob's wife in the register of Jews maintained by the Catholic authorities. Unless the entry is incorrect, she certainly did exist and probably died prematurely like her predecessor.

Amalia Nathansohn – Freud's mother – was from north-east Galicia, near the Russian frontier, and twenty years younger than Jacob. Indeed, Jacob was already a grandfather when he married Amalia, so Sigmund was born an uncle – and one of Sigmund's half-brothers was older than his mother. After Sigmund, Amalia gave birth to another boy, Julius, who died in his first year after contracting an intestinal infection. Then, in quick succession, she produced five daughters – Anna, Rosa, Mitzi, Dolfi, Pauli – and her second surviving son, Alexander.

Jacob's young bride has been variously described as slender, pretty, beautiful, amusing, alert and sharp-witted. She seems to have retained her vital energies until the very end of her life – those who knew her in old age repeatedly emphasise her vigour, with one of her grandsons even comparing her to a tornado. Ernest Jones wrote that she possessed 'a lively personality' and enjoyed 'card parties at an hour when most old ladies would be in bed'. At the age of ninety she refused the gift of a shawl because she thought that it made her look old. Five years later, she expressed disapproval when her photograph appeared in a newspaper. 'A bad reproduction,' she said. 'It makes me look a hundred.'

When Sigi was three years old, Jacob and Amalia moved to

Leipzig. The reasons given for their departure from Freiberg were, firstly, a financial crisis that ruined the Moravian textile industry and, secondly, antisemitism; however, in 1859, many wool merchants were prospering in a relatively benign local economy and antisemitism, although ever present, was not getting any worse. It is far more likely that the Freud family had to move because of Jacob's ineptitude and the collapse of his business.

The train to Leipzig passed through Breslau, and it was there that Freud saw gas jets for the first time. These flames made him think of souls burning in hell. This isn't quite as implausible as it sounds because, even though he was only three, his Catholic nanny had spoken to him about hellfire and damnation. He had accompanied her to church with some regularity and he could imitate a priest delivering a sermon. The gas jets of Breslau were so sinister that they created anxieties surrounding train travel that lasted well into Freud's adulthood.

After a year in Leipzig the Freud family moved to Vienna. Once again, Freud saw something during the journey that made a lasting impression. He spent the night with his mother, presumably in a sleeper carriage, glimpsed her naked and experienced sexual arousal. The incident is described in a candid letter written on 3 October 1897 to his friend and colleague Wilhelm Fliess: 'libido towards *matrem* was aroused; the occasion must have been the journey with her from Leipzig to Vienna, during which we spent a night together and I must have had the opportunity of seeing her *nudam*'. Freud's coy use of the Latin words *matrem* and *nudam* suggest that he was easing his embarrassment by using 'medical' language. A few weeks later he wrote another letter to Fliess, proposing that love of one's mother and jealousy of one's father might be a universal phenomenon of early childhood. He added that this combination of feelings, reawakened in playgoers, might underlie the 'gripping power' of the Greek drama *Oedipus Rex*. 'Every member of the audience was once a budding Oedipus in phantasy, and this dream-fulfilment played out in reality causes everyone to recoil in horror, with the full measure of repression which separates his infantile from his present state.' The 'recoiling' audience that Freud had imagined was composed entirely of men, and in years to come he would struggle to make the 'Oedipus complex' a truly universal phenomenon, relevant to both men and women. These reflections, inspired by the memory of his mother's nudity, would eventually become central to his understanding of human sexual development.

The Freuds lived first in Weissgerberstrasse, then moved to Pillersdorfgasse, and finally settled in Pfeffergasse, a narrow street in Leopoldstadt, which was once a Jewish ghetto; in the 1860s it was still home to nearly half of Vienna's fifteen thousand Jews. Some migrant families had to share a single room with their respective areas separated by a chalk line on the floor. Outbreaks of tuberculosis were common. However, Leopoldstadt wasn't a slum district. There were prosperous enclaves, and it was also where the Prater was situated: a very substantial park with restaurants, cafés, a racecourse and spectacular amusements. In 1895, for example, one of the attractions was a recreation of Venice, with mock palazzos, canals and gondola rides. The apartment the Freud family occupied had two living rooms, a dining room, three bedrooms and a 'cabinet' (a small chamber set apart from the other rooms). There was no bathroom, but every fortnight a large wooden tub and barrels of hot and cold water were carried into the kitchen by porters (and collected the following morning). Personal hygiene could also be maintained by using the local bath house. The family endured several years of hardship before charitable relatives came to the rescue. And although it is unclear how Jacob got by, his Micawberish optimism wasn't *so* misplaced. Every now and again something must have turned up. Perhaps in the form of counterfeit rubles. In 1865 Josef Freud – Jacob's brother – would receive a ten-year jail sentence after being exposed in the press as a 'Jewish forger'.

Freud retained few memories of his first years in Vienna, apart from the curious exception of having once deliberately urinated in his parents' bedroom. He remembered being seven or eight at the time, but he was probably younger. 'One evening before going to sleep I disregarded the rules which modesty lays down and obeyed the calls of nature in my parents' bedroom while they were present.' Jacob Freud, understandably annoyed, is said to have declared: 'The boy will come to nothing.' Even as an adult, Freud had recurring dreams about this incident. Not because he was ashamed, but rather because his father's words had wounded his pride. He later supposed that his father had delivered 'a frightful blow to my ambition'.

It soon became evident, however, that Jacob's verdict was wrong. Freud started reading Shakespeare at the age of eight and he was 'top of the class' with such regularity it became an expectation. His school record was blemished only once, in 1869, when he was questioned about fellow pupils who had visited prostitutes. Knowledge of their behaviour was enough to reduce his conduct grade.

Freud retreated into the 'cabinet' – the long narrow room that contained his bed, chairs, a shelf and a writing desk – and applied himself to schoolwork with extraordinary diligence. His admiring parents became indulgent. They bought him an oil lamp, while the rest of the household had to make do with candles, and his sister's piano was removed because her playing disturbed him. He would even eat meals in his room to maximise study time. He mastered Latin and Greek, became fluent in French and English, and taught himself Italian and Spanish. Although he was never very good at mathematics, he was interested in science (particularly evolutionary biology), and after briefly flirting with the idea of becoming a lawyer he resolved instead to become a doctor. This conversion occurred after he had heard an essay on Nature (attributed to Goethe but actually the work of a Swiss theologian) read aloud at a public lecture. It portrayed Nature as a bountiful Mother with tantalising secrets. Freud, even at the age of seventeen, was stirred by an invitation to probe beneath the surface of observed reality.

A photograph of Freud taken around this time shows a slim, well-dressed young man with thick dark hair and a slight

GL Archive/Alamy Stock Photo

moustache. He is leaning, casually, against a piece of furniture, but his expression is resolute. He looks assured and quietly determined; however, his sobriety is diluted by a dash of dandyism. His mother – who doesn't look very much older than her son – is sitting next to him. They make a very handsome pair.

As Freud's school days came to an end, the promise of the caul and the pastry shop prophecy must have been playing on his mind. He was even beginning to experience presentiments of his own. 'I seem to remember', he later wrote, 'that through the whole of this time, there ran a premonition of a task ahead, till it found open expression in my school-leaving essay as a wish that I might during the course of my life contribute something to our human knowledge.' After taking his final examination before leaving school, Freud wrote to his friend Emil Fluss: 'People who fear nothing but mediocrity, you say, are safe. Safe from what? I ask. Surely not safe and secure from being mediocre?'

Freud began studying medicine at the University of Vienna in the autumn of 1873.

Paintings of the Viennese medical establishment in Freud's time create a strong impression of an advanced and scientifically respectable culture: venerable professors demonstrate new surgical procedures; steeply tiered lecture theatres are crowded with serious young men in wing-collar shirts (it wasn't until 1903 that the first woman graduated in medicine); laboratories are filled with complicated contraptions and microscopes. Around 1900, Vienna certainly was a cutting-edge research centre; however, healing wasn't a priority. In 1850 the only treatment available at the Vienna General Hospital was cherry brandy because doctors were much more interested in understanding diseases than eradicating them. The administration of active remedies was inconvenient. They interfered with the occurrence of symptoms and made nosology impossible. When questioned about treatment, one professor responded: 'Treatment, treatment, that is nothing; it is the diagnosis that we want.' Wards were managed by untrained nurses, many of whom were former housemaids and washerwomen. Their duties included selling coffee, and they ignored patients who didn't tip. It wasn't until 1882 that a nursing school was established to attract 'girls' from so-called 'good' families.

Although patient care was perfunctory, the medical school in Vienna produced a continuous stream of outstanding scientific accomplishments: the systematisation of dermatology, the foundation of modern urology, the introduction of the eye chart to standardise spectacle prescriptions, advances in anaesthesia, revolutionary gastric and laryngeal surgery, the identification of blood types, and the utilisation of blood pressure as a diagnostic tool. The gulf between academic distinction and clinical indifference typical of hospital medicine in Vienna from the mid- to late nineteenth century can be attributed to the influence of Carl von Rokitansky, who became head of the medical school in 1844. His ambition was to make medicine more scientific by matching symptom clusters with pathological findings. Estimates vary, but he may have conducted or supervised as many as eighty-five thousand autopsies. Eventually, his labours did result in a deeper understanding of many illnesses and better patient care, but only after a protracted period of therapeutic nihilism.

Underlying Rokitansky's method was an idea that can be traced back to Anaxagoras, a pre-Socratic Greek philosopher who asserted that 'phenomena are a visible expression of that which is hidden'. Freud had encountered the same idea in the essay that inspired him to study medicine. Nature 'is incessantly speaking to us, but betrays not her secret'.

Rokitansky became a public intellectual and his conviction that truth hides behind phenomena was discussed and debated in salons where scientists and artists mixed. Subsequently, the

idea acquired general currency. To discover the 'truth' behind
the outward form of the human body, the artist Gustav Klimt
observed Emil Zuckerkandl, the professor of anatomy at the
medical school, dissecting corpses.

When Freud arrived at the medical school, five years before
Rokitansky's death, he would have been encouraged to interro-
gate appearances, and this attitude became, much later, typical
of his approach to understanding the mind. Eventually, he
would assert that, as physical symptoms arise from concealed
atrophies and ruptures, so it is that thoughts, dreams, impulses
and emotions are the product of invisible biological and psychological processes.

In the 1870s, qualifying as a doctor in Vienna involved five
years of course work followed by three examinations. Freud took
six years to complete his course work and then he delayed taking
his finals for another two years. It took him a full seven and a
half years to qualify. This was because he took numerous extra
classes, including philosophy, zoology, physics, Aristotelian
logic, spectrum analysis and plant physiology – and then dedicated even more of his time to non-essential research projects.

Jacob Freud began to wonder whether his son's academic
monasticism was really in the boy's best interests. His solution
was to propose an arranged marriage; however, the match he
had in mind was his granddaughter, Pauline, Sigi's childhood
playmate and the daughter of Sigi's half-brother Emmanuel.
Clearly, such a marriage would be considered somewhat incestuous by contemporary standards. Emmanuel had emigrated
to England in 1859, his business was profitable, and he agreed
with his father that a fresh start and married life might be good
for his bookish half-brother. So, at the age of nineteen, Sigi
was taken to Manchester to see Pauline. But passions failed
to ignite. Ernest Jones reflected that if Pauline had aroused
Freud's amorous instincts, 'much might have been different in

our world'. Apparently, Freud often thought about his trip to Manchester and how his life might so very easily have taken an entirely different course: Mr Freud, the enterprising president of a local business association, ensconced with his family in a fine house near the new Town Hall – a relatively untroubled existence – functions – anonymity – peace and quiet. He supposed that this imaginary incarnation would have been a much more contented version of himself. He was almost certainly being disingenuous. The idea of obscurity would have made his blood run cold. Although Freud wasn't impressed by Pauline, he was impressed by England. Without a trace of sentiment, he wrote to a friend that 'in spite of fog and rain, drunkenness and conservatism' and the 'Many peculiarities of the English character' he much preferred England to Vienna. He remained an Anglophile all his life.

Shortly after returning to Vienna, Freud resolved the long-standing issue of what name he wished to be known by. Even when Freud was a schoolboy, he occasionally shortened Sigismund to Sigmund. After his second year at university, however, he always employed the abbreviated form. The last time he used Sigismund was when he inscribed his German translation copy of Darwin's *The Descent of Man* in 1875. Thereafter, he was always Sigmund. The subject of his name change was never discussed with his family or followers, so we don't know his precise reasons; however, the dupe or stooge in contemporary Viennese antisemitic jokes was usually called Sigismund and it is likely that he didn't want to be identified with an offensive stereotype. Freud had joined the Reading Society of Viennese German Students as soon as he had enrolled at the university. Although ostensibly a literary society, it was politically nationalist and had to be dissolved in 1878 when significant tensions arose between Jewish and non-Jewish members. Nationalists believed that Jews, even German-speaking Jews, were not really

'German'. Freud would later write that one of his greatest dis-
appointments with academia was that he was expected to feel
inferior because of his heritage: 'I have never been able to see
why I should feel ashamed of my descent or, as people were
beginning to say, of my "race".'

Freud's non-essential research projects took him some distance from the medical curriculum. He made two trips to a
Zoological Experimental Station in Trieste where he dissected
four hundred eels to find their testicles. The gonads of the eel
had proved mysteriously elusive, and a candidate organ had been
identified only two years earlier by a Polish scientist. Freud's job
was to check the Polish scientist's results. It was a curious assignment and one destined to raise eyebrows retrospectively given
that Freud would one day write extensively about the 'castration
complex'. He evidently enjoyed being in the south, and when he
wasn't dissecting eels his principal pastime seems to have been
observing beautiful Italian women walking around the town.
The first cracks were beginning to appear in his ascetic veneer.

After the second trip to Trieste and at the age of twenty
Freud became a research scholar at the Institute of Physiology.
This rather grand appellation is deceptive because the reality
consisted of a professor and two assistants who occupied the
stinking ground floor and basement of a former gun factory.
There were microscopes in a large room where lectures took
place and a large number of windowless cubicles that served as
laboratories. Water had to be drawn outside in a yard and carried into the building by a caretaker. There was no gas supply,
so chemicals had to be heated using a spirit lamp. Experimental
animals were kept in a shed.

The professor who presided over the Institute of Physiology
was Ernst Brücke, a small, laconic man with red hair and striking blue eyes. His manner was stern, yet he was also benevolent
and admired by his students. Freud liked him a great deal but

claimed that he never became indifferent to those 'terrible blue eyes' that could reduce him 'to nothing'. The first task Freud undertook in Brücke's laboratory was an investigation of the large nerves in the spinal column of the larval form of the brook lamprey. This ostensibly dull and routine piece of lab work was more consequential than it appears.

From the 1840s onwards, Brücke had been a leading advocate of mechanistic physiology. This was a reaction against vitalism, which supposed that all living things are animated by a 'life force' that is qualitatively different from known energies like electricity. Mechanistic physiologists respected Newtonian principles and believed that ultimately, everything in the universe, including the behaviour of living things, could be understood as the outcome of physical processes. The mechanistic agenda overlapped considerably with Darwinism. If life arises from observable processes, then the nervous system of a man and a mollusc can be compared and failure to discover essential differences can be interpreted as a challenge to religious doctrine. Correspondences suggest that human beings are neither special nor divinely favoured, but simply animals on a continuum that connects simple and complex organisms.

Freud continued investigating the nervous systems of creatures such as the crayfish and water crab until he was drafted for the first of two periods of military service. Medical students spent most of their time getting bored in military hospitals before being allowed to go home in the evening, and Freud was no exception. He found the experience tedious, and on his twenty-fourth birthday he was arrested for being absent without leave.

On returning to university, Freud decided to sit the examinations that would qualify him to practise medicine. He spent very little time revising because he was confident that his photographic memory would compensate for any motivational

shortcomings, and he managed to pass his papers with a mixture
of excellent and satisfactory grades. After which he went straight
back to Brücke's institute where, in due course, he was promoted
to demonstrator – an unpaid position that involved preparing
slides and some teaching responsibilities. He also managed to
find a part-time post at the Chemical Institute analysing gases.
He was much more interested in discovering nature's secrets
than in curing illnesses. Having published several scientific
articles, he was hoping to pursue a career in biological research.
Unfortunately, he didn't have much money and he was dependent on dwindling parental support and occasional loans from his
solvent friends. His situation was unsustainable.

Brücke was aware of Freud's circumstances. Moreover, his
two assistants were still relatively young, so there was no prospect of Freud being able to step up in the foreseeable future.
Brücke decided to offer the impoverished young man some
friendly advice. 'The turning point came in 1882,' Freud later
recalled, 'when my teacher, for whom I felt the highest possible esteem, corrected my father's generous improvidence by
strongly advising me, in view of my bad financial position, to
abandon my theoretical career. I followed his advice, left the
physiological laboratory and entered the General Hospital as an
Aspirant [Clinical Assistant].' Freud certainly needed to become
financially independent and working at the General Hospital
was the obvious solution; however, money had suddenly
become a matter of extreme urgency for another reason. It was
in 1882 that Freud fell madly in love.

When Freud came home after work, he usually exchanged
a few words with his family before rushing off to his 'cabinet'.
This habit was broken on an evening in April when he discovered that one of his sisters had invited a guest – a woman in
her early twenties with long dark hair pulled back to reveal
a narrow, pale face. She was peeling an apple and chatting.

To his family's surprise, instead of making his usual excuses, Freud sat down and seemed strangely keen to participate in the conversation.

The visitor's name was Martha Bernays. She was originally from Hamburg and her family had been living in Vienna for thirteen years. Her late father had been secretary to a famous Viennese economist and her brother Eli was now the head of the Bernays family. She also had a younger sister called Minna (who might have been present when Freud saw Martha for the first time). The Bernays family were not as wealthy as they once were, but they were respectable. Martha's grandfather had been a distinguished chief rabbi and she was also a distant relative of the German Romantic poet Heinrich Heine.

Apart from a single episode of infatuation in his adolescence, Freud had never been in love. But as soon as he saw the pale young woman sitting with his family, he was smitten and transformed. Suddenly, the bookish young man who had previously shown more interest in crabs than women became the world's greatest romantic. Every day he sent Martha a red rose and a visiting card inscribed with a motto. He compared her to a fairy-tale princess. He sent her a copy of his favourite Charles Dickens novel, *David Copperfield*, and started writing her letters. Eventually they would number around fifteen hundred. Martha responded with a few lines of thanks and then with tokens of reciprocal feeling: a cake she had baked herself and a sprig of lime blossom. On 17 June, only two months after seeing Martha for the first time, Freud proposed marriage – and Martha accepted. They decided to keep their engagement a secret because they feared that Martha's mother Emmeline would object. Freud was in no position to provide a home for a new wife and start a family.

The following day, Martha had to leave Vienna for an extended holiday with relatives near Hamburg. And the day after that, Freud wrote her a slightly delirious letter in which he addressed her as his 'precious', his 'darling', his 'beloved little bride'. Their romance, he said, had seemed to him like 'a beguiling dream'. He couldn't believe his good fortune. Separation proved too painful, and he was soon on a train to Hamburg carrying an engagement ring in a matchbox on which he had written the words of a folk poem titled 'When my sweetheart is married'.

As soon as Martha returned to Vienna, Freud continued seeing her regularly. He was mindful of his chivalrous obligation to protect her virtue and conducted himself accordingly. The couple touched hands under the table at social gatherings, and when alone, they kissed and embraced. Any further intimacies were forbidden. They didn't tell Martha's mother about their secret engagement for six months and only found the courage to do so after Martha's brother, Eli, had announced his engagement to Freud's sister, Anna. Emmeline responded somewhat unhelpfully by deciding to move back to Hamburg with Martha and Minna. The train journey from Vienna to Hamburg took two days and the return ticket was very expensive. Emmeline's decision put an end to Sigmund and Martha's dalliances and the couple compensated by writing to each other almost every day. Thereafter, Freud's relationship with his mother-in-law was never a very happy one.

Falling in love did not distract Freud from his appointment with destiny. Love brought it closer. If he was going to provide for Martha, he would have to enter private practice and start seeing patients who were wealthy enough to afford substantial consultation fees. Searching for eel gonads and dissecting primitive fishes was intellectually satisfying, but activities like these were never going to finance a household in a desirable district of Vienna. He already knew a great deal about nerves and the nervous system, so it was logical to consider psychiatry and neurology as potential specialisms.

Even when Freud was at his most romantic, the promise of greatness was never far from his thoughts. In 1885, he wrote to Martha and told her that he had destroyed all his papers (with the exception of her love letters) to confound future biographers. He imagined them struggling to piece together 'The Development of the Hero'. He was only twenty-eight years old, and although cultured, intelligent, and the author of some academic articles, he had achieved very little. Yet, somewhere deep in his mind, the story of the caul and the pastry shop prophetess, and the favouritism of a young, beautiful mother, must have been endowing him with supreme confidence.

Chapter 2

Love and Madness

The engagement of Sigmund and Martha lasted four and a half years. At least three of them were spent apart. Emmeline Bernays' decision to move back to Hamburg with her daughters infuriated Freud, because establishing himself as a doctor with enough money to support a wife and family would take a long time. There would be no more regular meetings, no more weekend walks, no more secret kisses. Minna, Martha's sister, was engaged to Freud's friend Ignaz Schönberg, and early in 1883 Freud wrote her a letter in which he expressed his frustration: '[Emmeline] wants to move to Hamburg at the behest of some extraordinary whim, oblivious of the fact that by so doing she would be separating you and Schönberg, Martha and myself for years to come.' He tried his best to maintain a dignified tone, but it is obvious that he thought his future mother-in-law was being selfish.

Many years later, Freud wrote: 'It is well known that the relationship between son-in-law and mother-in-law is one of the most awkward aspects of family organization, even among civilized peoples.' Mothers are reluctant to hand their daughters over to a 'stranger' and their physical appearance shatters romantic illusions. A mother-in-law will remind a husband of his wife, 'through so many common features', and yet she will lack – he added somewhat ungallantly – 'all the charms of youth, beauty and psychological freshness that make his wife precious to him'.

Although Freud objected to Emmeline's decision to interpose 460 miles between him and his 'Princess', he shared her views concerning the importance of solvency. He was determined not to repeat his father's mistakes and he accepted that his marriage would have to be postponed indefinitely until his prospects improved; however, in much the same way that Freud, the medical student, was distracted by all manner of non-essential enthusiasms, so it was that Freud, the young doctor, took a roundabout route to the wedding canopy. During this extended period of betrothal, Freud gave Martha ample reason to entertain doubts concerning his suitability as a future husband. He had fits of sexual jealousy, he demanded that she abandon religious observances, and he started taking cocaine (the new 'wonder drug' that he was researching). Although Freud's love letters contain many instances of neuroticism and male chauvinism, they are also eloquent, tender and spontaneous. In one of them, dated ten days after his proposal of marriage, he tells his 'sweet girl' that he is sitting in a laboratory writing with a pen that he has just stolen from Professor Brücke's desk, on paper that he has torn from a notebook. 'Outside there is fog and drizzle.' He is waiting for an experiment to run its course. Gas bubbles 'sizzle' in his apparatus, and he confides, with a touch of superior amusement, 'people around me think I am computing my analysis'. A random melancholy thought flows directly from his mind to the page: 'two-thirds of chemistry consists of waiting, it is probably the same with life'. Time dragged when Martha was absent.

The couple agreed to destroy their correspondence on their

wedding day. When that day arrived, Martha couldn't bear to watch the history of their romance consumed by flames. After Freud's death, Martha was again about to burn their correspondence when, thankfully, her daughter intervened.

Freud's jealous feelings were stirred prior to his engagement, and they continued to disturb his mental equilibrium for some time after. He discovered that Martha had enjoyed some songs composed and performed by her cousin, Max Mayer. He

adoc-photos/Getty Images

insecurely asked Martha to stop using the musician's first name, but he subsequently apologised for being unreasonable. Another of Martha's admirers, the womanising painter Fritz Wahle, roused less manageable feelings. Wahle was an acquaintance of Freud and engaged to one of Martha's cousins. When Freud learned, from Schönberg, that Wahle had kissed Martha after he, Freud, had started courting her, he was consumed with rage. Schönberg, who was a mutual friend, arranged a meeting in a coffee house where he hoped Freud and Wahle would resolve their differences in a civilised manner. Wahle declared that if Freud failed to make Martha happy, he would shoot him, and then end his own life by shooting himself. He then composed an intimate letter to Martha that Freud read and immediately tore up. Wahle stormed out of the coffee house and, overcome with emotion, burst into tears. Martha claimed that her relationship with Wahle was entirely innocent. After further correspondence and face-to-face discussion, Freud issued an ominous-sounding ultimatum. If Martha didn't reject all of Wahle's future overtures, then he would settle the affair finally.

Freud's jealousy could be apocalyptic. He admitted that when he thought about Martha and Wahle he wanted to 'destroy the whole world'. Martha may have exacerbated matters by being more flirtatious than is commonly supposed. In one of Freud's letters to Martha, he wrote: 'Do you remember how in our walk with Minna along the Beethovengang you kept going aside to pull up your stockings? It is bold of me to mention it, but I hope you don't mind.' Obviously, Martha's attempts to conceal her wardrobe malfunctions were not so thorough as to preclude the possibility of being surreptitiously observed.

Only a month after his engagement to Martha and with the long-term goal of being able to provide for a wife and family uppermost in his mind, Freud moved into quarters at the Vienna General Hospital and began working as a junior doctor.

He would spend the next three years acquiring experience in a range of medical disciplines: surgery, internal medicine, dermatology and, more significantly, psychiatry and nervous diseases. The General Hospital occupied twenty-five thousand acres and provided care for more than three thousand patients, but when Freud arrived, conditions were still fairly primitive. There weren't enough gas lamps so many patients had to spend much of the day in darkness and some operations were undertaken by candlelight. Clouds of dust made breathing difficult for patients suffering from lung disease. After five months of psychiatry Freud decided to specialise in neurology. He spent over a year working in the department of nervous diseases, during which time he lectured visiting doctors on a particular structure in the brain, wrote a dissertation, and was made temporary superintendent (a position which came with considerable responsibilities) when two colleagues were transferred to the Austrian frontier during a cholera epidemic.

Overall, these were very lean years for Freud. His salary was a pittance and he had to supplement his income by writing summaries for a medical journal, coaching pupils and seeing the occasional private patient referred to him by sympathetic patrons. But he was still earning barely enough to support himself, let alone a family. He was forced to borrow money from friends, and he accepted a monthly stipend from a generous colleague, Josef Breuer (an arrangement that lasted for six years).

Freud had first encountered Breuer in Brücke's laboratory. He was a scientist and a trusted family doctor with an excellent reputation. Images of him show a man with a receding hairline, full beard and pouched, sad eyes. The two men became close friends and Breuer assumed the role of a kindly uncle. Breuer had already told Freud something that would, some years after, set him on the path to fame and fortune – his eagerly anticipated appointment with destiny. It concerned a new treatment for hysteria that Breuer had developed, based on the systematic recovery of traumatic memories. Freud had listened with polite interest, but he hadn't really appreciated its significance. And anyway, he was about to be distracted by his next enthusiasm.

While reading a weekly German medical publication, Freud had found some interesting research conducted by a doctor who had reinvigorated Bavarian troops by giving them a stimulant derived from coca plant leaves. Freud wondered whether such a tonic might have medical uses. He ordered some of the substance, cocaine, and on 30 April 1884 – Walpurgisnacht, the most auspicious night of the year for concocting magical potions and signing pacts with the devil – he imbibed 0.05 grams in a 1 per cent water solution and within minutes felt 'light and exhilarated'. Four weeks later, probably under the influence of cocaine, he was writing to Martha in a feverish way which, although light-hearted, seems to show that Freud was fantasising about the aphrodisiac possibilities of his new wonder drug. 'Woe to you, my Princess, when I come. I will kiss you quite red and feed you till you are plump. And if you are forward, you shall see who is the stronger, a gentle girl who doesn't eat enough or a big wild man who has cocaine in his body.'

Within months of discovering cocaine, Freud published an essay, *On Coca*, in which he prematurely reported the successful treatment of a morphine addict. Cocaine had allegedly alleviated the man's withdrawal symptoms. The patient was Freud's companion Ernst Fleischl Edler von Marxow, a gifted scientist who had been appointed as a professor at the medical school when he was only thirty-four years old. Unfortunately, while conducting an autopsy in 1871, 'Fleischl' had contracted a potentially life-threatening infection that had necessitated the amputation of part of his thumb. The ensuing nerve damage and tumours were the cause of extreme pain and he became addicted to morphine. In reality, Freud's cocaine treatment was an abysmal failure. Fleischl's condition deteriorated over time and eventually he became addicted to both morphine *and* cocaine.

Despite this worrying outcome, Freud continued to overestimate the beneficial powers of cocaine. He used it himself and recommended it to others, including Martha. Although Freud's 'cocaine episode' is usually dated from 1884 to 1887, throughout the 1890s his mood swings, vivid dreams and the occasionally giddy prose of his letters all raise the possibility that he took the drug until the end of the century.

In 1885, after an oral examination and the delivery of a public lecture, Freud became a lecturer in neuropathology at the university. He also received permission to work for three weeks at a private mental hospital. The elderly director employed only pretty housemaids and catered for an exclusive clientele of shabby and eccentric aristocrats. When conducting ward rounds, Freud had to wear a silk hat and white gloves.

Earlier in the year, Freud had applied for a travel grant of 600 gulden which would enable him to study abroad. There were only two other applicants and one of these withdrew. On 19 June he was informed that his application had been successful. He resigned from his post at the General Hospital, visited Martha, and then set off for the Salpêtrière in Paris. The ostensible purpose of his trip was to learn more about neuropathies in children. But Freud had an ulterior motive. He hoped that he would return to Vienna as a more credible specialist in nervous diseases. He would be better placed to start a private practice and, finally, have enough money to get married.

The medical director of the Salpêtrière was Jean-Martin Charcot. History has judged him to be less consequential than his legend, but he was, at that time, a man of colossal reputation and influence. He was 'A prince of science' and his showy medical demonstrations earned him further monikers such as 'the Paganini of hysteria' and 'the Napoleon of the neuroses'. He spoke several languages, was fond of quoting Dante and Shakespeare, invited celebrities and statesmen to his dinner parties, and commanded very high fees, sometimes the equivalent of thousands of pounds for a single consultation. He usually collected the money himself and arranged his earnings into piles on his desk. His fondness for watching his wealth accumulate is difficult to understand, because his wife was one of the richest women in Paris. His residences were full of Renaissance furniture, art works, stained glass, baroque prayer stools, Chinese antiques, Louis XI and XII tapestries and collections of rare books. He counted Jesus Christ as a personal enemy, but in his favour he adored animals, and allowed his predictably mischievous pet monkey to wreck expensive household fruit decorations with patient good humour.

In the 1880s, Charcot's lectures were so entertaining they attracted not only doctors but also writers, actors, artists, social commentators and public officials. They were delivered in a cavernous hall in which a low stage was bedecked with statues of contorted figures, plaster casts of deformities, organs in jars and spotlighted anatomical drawings on poster stands. Attendees could also marvel at luminous images produced by an early slide projector. Even more theatrical were Charcot's medical demonstrations, which often involved the summoning and removal of a patient's symptoms using hypnotism. A well-known painting by André Brouillet shows Charcot, in his clinic, surrounded by doctors, students and various prominent Parisians, presenting a swooning 'hysteric' who is about to fall back into the ready arms of an assistant. The woman's blouse has slipped off her shoulders, and her abandonment suggests that the male spectators might be showing keen interest for more than just professional reasons.

Charcot's showmanship made him a public figure, but it also

overshadowed his actual accomplishments. In some medical histories his theories and interventions are treated almost like footnotes. Yet he correctly judged hysteria to be a condition worthy of scientific study and he differentiated hysterical symptoms from those arising from known nervous diseases; he demonstrated that hysteria wasn't (as some thought) a condition that affected only women and he recognised that hypnosis could be used as a research tool. Implicit in much of Charcot's work is the notion that unconscious 'fixed ideas' can seed disturbed states of mind.

Before starting work at the Salpêtrière, Freud spent a few days being a tourist. He visited the Place de la Concorde and the Louvre, and attended a theatre performance that went on until midnight – 'disgraceful pigeon-hole boxes, in a corner of the highest gallery . . . there is no music, no orchestra, and the signal for the play to begin consists of three blows with a hammer behind the curtain'. His description of the Champs-Élysées is vivid: 'Elegant ladies walk here with expressions suggesting that they deny the existence in this world of anyone but themselves and their husbands or are at least graciously trying to ignore it; one side of the avenue is formed by an extensive park in which the prettiest children spin their tops, ride on merry-go-rounds, watch the Punch-&-Judy show, or drive themselves about in little carriages drawn by goats.' He was impressed by the exceptionally good coffee, appalled at the price of toiletries – 'just think, for 3 toilet articles (some talcum, tar and mouthwash) I had to pay 3.50 francs' – and thought the newspaper vendors were far too loud. Eventually he would discover 'Chocolat Marquis', a dessert that he found so delicious he promised to bring some home for his sister-in-law to taste: 'that you shall have'. For a young man drifting through a decadent city full of carnal temptations, his later claim that he found Parisian women to be very ugly is, frankly, a little unconvincing.

In a letter to Martha dated 21 October, Freud recorded his first impression of Charcot: 'a tall man of 58, wearing a top hat, with dark, strangely soft eyes (or rather one is, the other is expressionless and has an inward cast), long wisps of hair stuck behind his ears, clean shaven, very expressive features with full protruding lips'. Charcot's entry obviously overwhelmed Freud because the great neurologist wasn't tall, but short and stocky. 'He sat down', Freud continued, 'and began examining the patients. I was very much impressed by his brilliant diagnosis and the lively interest he took in everything . . . ' Freud's description of what happened next is filmic. He creates dramatic tension by employing the literary equivalent of close-ups and long-shots: 'I gave my card to the *Chef* who handed it to Charcot. The latter fingered it for a while and after the consultation asked where I was.' Silence – inquisitive looks – some shuffling? 'I came forward and gave him my introduction. He recognised Benedikt's handwriting, stepped aside to read it, said *"Charmé de vous voir"*, and invited me to accompany him. He advised me to make my working arrangements with the *Chef de Clinique*, and without any further ado I was accepted.' Freud thought that Charcot had the appearance of 'a worldly priest from whom one expects a ready wit and an appreciation of good living'.

After this initial meeting, Charcot hardly acknowledged Freud's presence for over a month. The young 'German' was just another face in a large crowd of foreign students, and easily overlooked. But in December, Freud succeeded in drawing attention to himself by offering to translate Charcot's lectures, and thereafter he was admitted into Charcot's inner circle.

Freud was invited to one of Charcot's parties for the first time in January 1886. He bought a new shirt and white gloves, had his beard trimmed in the French style, and decided to wear a black tie and tailcoat. He shared the cost of the carriage with a nervous colleague, but was 'quite calm' himself, because he'd taken 'a small dose of cocaine'. As expected, Charcot's other guests were highly distinguished. They included a member of the Academy of Science, a professor of forensic medicine, the novelist Alphonse Daudet and the artist Edoardo Tofano (whose work was reproduced and sold all over the world). Freud reported to Martha that he had accepted a coffee, then some beer, and had 'smoked like a chimney'. He described Madame Charcot as 'small, rotund' and 'vivacious' and declared that if he wasn't already in love, he would have tried to court Charcot's 'buxom' daughter. Two weeks later Freud had become quite nonchalant about hobnobbing with Charcot and his eminent friends, but he still needed a fortifying dose of cocaine to set him up for the evening. There was a tricky moment when Gilles de la Tourette (of Tourette's disorder fame) predicted a ferocious Franco-German war. Freud disingenuously declared his neutrality by pointing out that he was Jewish. Charcot's daughter was dressed in a flattering Greek costume and Freud incautiously informed Martha that Mademoiselle 'looked quite attractive'.

Alcohol was flowing freely, although on this occasion he wisely limited his drinking to a cup of chocolate.

During his stay in Paris, Freud mentioned Josef Breuer's new treatment to Charcot. Given that Charcot had been studying traumatic paralysis for at least two years, he should have wanted to hear more. Breuer had established a connection between the recovery of traumatic memories and the relief of symptoms. 'But the great man', Freud wrote many years later, 'showed no interest in my first outline of the subject, so that I never returned to it and allowed it to pass from my mind.' Freud's appointment with destiny was delayed yet again.

Freud's personal contact with Charcot lasted from the end of October 1885 to the end of February 1886 – roughly four months, minus a week's holiday at Christmas. Charcot was also absent for two weeks because of illness. This brief exposure was enough to affect Freud profoundly. In 1889, he would name his son Jean-Martin. On the day of Freud's departure, Charcot gave Freud a gift: an inscribed photograph of himself. In this image, the Napoleon of the neuroses stands with his right hand in his coat and his left hand behind his back – a pose so obviously modelled on portraits of the great military leader and statesman that its ostentation invites ridicule (German doctors called him 'Napoleon head'). Freud never saw Charcot again.

On returning to Vienna, Freud announced that he would be setting up in private practice by placing an advert in the daily newspapers and medical periodicals:

Dr Sigmund Freud, Docent in Neuropathology in the University of Vienna, has returned from spending six months in Paris and now resides at Rathausstrasse 7.

He earned over 1,000 florins in three and a half months and for the first time ever marriage started to feel like a

realistic prospect. However, even at this very late stage there
was another postponement. He had to complete his compulsory
military service.

Freud reported for duty on 11 August 1886 and was posted to
Moravia. He served as regimental chief physician, then battalion head physician, and succeeded in gaining a promotion from
Lieutenant to Captain. He was complimented by his superiors
and judged to be a 'good influence'. Superficially, it appeared that
Freud had matured and that his second stint in the army would
be endured with greater equanimity than the first. Privately,
however, he was just as cynical and dismissive. On 1 September,
Freud wrote to Breuer from Olmütz and complained: 'We continually play at war.' While his battalion was making a mock
assault with 'blank cartridges', he was stretched out with his
orderlies on 'some old stones'. A mounted General arrived and
informed them that under real combat conditions they would
all have been killed. Freud hated military authoritarianism:
'I deeply dislike having my value written on my collar'. He
declared that the only thing that made Olmütz bearable was a
'citified café' where he could find 'ice-creams, newspapers and
good pastry'. The letter ends abruptly with an apology for 'stupid
chatter' and mention of a patient who had rather surprisingly
been 'deriving unmistakable benefit' from arsenic injections.

When the military manoeuvres were completed, all obstacles
to the happy union of Sigmund and Martha had been removed –
with the exception of one complication. The wedding was to take
place in Germany and Freud wanted a civil ceremony. Austrian
law, however, required a religious ceremony. Unhappily, Freud
had to learn the groom's responses in Hebrew. He was tutored
by Martha's Orthodox uncle, who was, apparently, singularly
unimpressed by his student's lack of respect for Jewish custom.
The civil ceremony took place on 13 September and the religious ceremony the following day. The wedding party, totalling

fourteen guests, dined in a Hamburg hotel restaurant. On the table were napkin rings, each one showing an oval portrait of the young couple. The guests were served vegetable soup, pâté, fish salad, beef fillet, peas, asparagus, roast goose and compote.

Sigmund and Martha embarked on a two-week honeymoon. They travelled to the Baltic coast before returning to Vienna, via Berlin, Dresden and Brünn. Their first home was in a building known as the House of Atonement. It had been built on the site of a tragic fire, and prospective tenants were reluctant to move in for superstitious reasons. The arrival of a happy young couple encouraged others to overcome their qualms; however, behind closed doors, Sigmund and Martha weren't as happy as they appeared. Martha found Sigmund's insistence that she must abandon all Jewish ritual deeply upsetting. There would be no more Sabbath candles, no more prayers. It was something she would have to get used to, because her husband would never compromise. He thought that belief in scripture was as irrational as refusing to rent an apartment because of burning ghosts.

Like most private doctors, Freud received patients at home. On his first day he discovered that he didn't have enough chairs, so Martha had to borrow some from the porter.

Curiously, Freud chose to treat his patients using the most conventional 'nerve' remedies of his day: electrotherapy (mild currents passed through affected areas), rest, massages and advice on where to go for water cures. The results were disappointing, and he suspected that those patients who reported improvements were simply the most suggestible. It wasn't electrotherapy that was helping, but rather *belief* in electrotherapy. Towards the end of 1887, Freud tried to exploit the clinical possibilities of suggestibility with the aid of hypnosis. In Paris, he had witnessed Charcot hypnotising patients and commanding symptoms to appear and disappear. Freud tried doing this with his own patients, but once again, the results were mixed.

In addition to using hypnosis to maximise the therapeutic potential of suggestibility, he was also using it to explore his patients' histories. When in a hypnotic trance, patients were able to answer his questions about the origin of their symptoms more readily than when they were 'awake'. They could better remember half-forgotten incidents that coincided with the onset of their problems. Freud had learned this technique from Breuer, who had discovered it (more or less by accident) while he had been developing his new treatment for hysteria. Freud wasn't using this technique to alleviate symptoms. He was simply curious about the circumstances surrounding the appearance of symptoms.

Around the same time that Freud began experimenting with hypnosis, he became acquainted with a Berlin-based doctor called Wilhelm Fliess. Breuer had advised Fliess to attend some

of Freud's occasional lectures. The two men subsequently met and started a lengthy correspondence which allowed them to share and develop their thoughts on various aspects of biology and psychology. The bulk of these letters were written between 1887 and 1900. More letters were written after 1900 but by that time their creative partnership had effectively come to an end. Only Freud's half of the correspondence survives.

In 1928, Fliess's widow sold Freud's letters to a Berlin bookseller on condition that they would never be sold on to Freud himself. She suspected that he would probably destroy them. After the Nazis came to power in 1933, the letters were smuggled to France and purchased for 12,000 francs by Freud's disciple Princess Marie Bonaparte. She informed Freud of her acquisition in 1936. Freud attempted to get the letters back, but without success – although Bonaparte did allow Freud to inspect some of them. Bonaparte then deposited the letters with the Rothschild Bank in Vienna. At a later date they were returned to Paris (to avoid confiscation by the Gestapo). In due course, the letters were packaged in waterproof and buoyant material and sent on a perilous voyage across the English Channel, which, by that time, was heavily mined. The fate of Fliess's half of the correspondence is unclear. Freud, whose memory was photographic, couldn't remember. Perhaps he'd destroyed them, or lost them – it was all very hazy.

Until the 1980s, it was generally accepted that Fliess was Freud's intellectual stooge, a fringe practitioner who offered Freud support at a time when he was labouring in isolation to create a revolutionary new science of the mind. Uncharitable commentators have repeatedly caricatured Fliess as something of a mad scientist, and it is true that many of his ideas *do* sound ridiculous. They have been described as 'a farrago of nonsense' and 'downright silly'. He asserted that there is a close relationship between the nose and sexuality and that certain sexual problems should be treated by operating on 'genital spots' within the nose. He believed that 'periodicities' underlie all physiological processes and that the numerical values associated with these cycles could be used to calculate events such as the age at which a person is likely to die. Less contentious, given current attitudes to sexual fluidity in liberal democracies, was his supposition that all human beings are fundamentally bisexual.

None of his views were regarded as being especially outlandish by his peers. Many distinguished academics had been writing about precisely the same topics for decades. Darwin, for example, had commented on a range of phenomena germane to Fliess's principal scientific preoccupations. Furthermore, irrespective of Fliess's partiality for wayward speculation, his theorising often contained a grain of truth. The sense of smell is connected to mating behaviour in animals, biorhythms (such as the sleep-wake cycle) are related to health, and sexual ambiguity can be observed in the womb – the reproductive organs are initially undifferentiated during normal embryonic development. While developing his ideas on periodicity, Fliess seems to have anticipated what would later become the rhythm method of contraception (a discovery attributed to the Austrian gynaecologist Hermann Knaus).

It is clear, then, that Fliess wasn't the crackpot physician described by many of those who had a personal investment in preserving Freud's legend. On the contrary, Fliess's colleagues were typically impressed by his breadth of knowledge, and Freud almost certainly owed him a greater intellectual debt than he was prepared to admit – which is probably why he destroyed or conveniently mislaid Fliess's letters. Freud was also anxious to keep his half of their correspondence out of the public domain in the 1930s for another reason. His letters contain affectionate salutations, declarations of love and references to his 'feminine side'. Ernest Jones was convinced that Freud's attraction to Fliess was, at least in part, homoerotic.

The appearance of Fliess in 1887 completes a quartet of medical men – the other three being Brücke, Charcot and Breuer – who are understood to have exerted the greatest influence on Freud's thinking. Freud had been eager to make Fliess's acquaintance because he had recognised a kindred spirit, someone with comparably grandiose ambitions. Fliess was, in fact, edging towards unifying biology and medicine within an evolutionary framework.

Five years had elapsed since Breuer had first told Freud about his new therapy technique and they still discussed it occasionally, regardless of Charcot's indifference. Freud was even using Breuer's technique to recover memories that his patients had temporarily forgotten. Nevertheless, Freud still failed to appreciate the magnitude of Breuer's achievement. Stolid, dependable Breuer had discovered the prototype of psychoanalysis.

Chapter 3

Hysteria

Establishing a medical practice in late nineteenth-century Vienna was no easy matter for a young doctor, largely because it was a city of extraordinary class consciousness and snobbery. All societies are hierarchical, but the boundaries that separated the various levels of Viennese society were preserved by strict etiquette, status symbols and the observation of rigid protocols. A person's *exact* position in the social hierarchy could be determined as soon as he or she started to speak. Aristocrats close to the Emperor used their own nasal-sounding court dialect, *Schönbrunnerdeutsch*. Even in coffee houses it was possible to hear customers affecting the same intonations to create an impression of eminence. The status of passengers travelling in an imperial carriage could be ascertained by observing the angle at which the coachman was holding his whip. Any Habsburg subject, however humble, could apply for an audience with the Emperor, but soldiers had to be in uniform, civilians in formal evening suits, and peasants in their folkish national costume. It is said that when the Emperor was dying, his personal physician disregarded court etiquette and dashed to the palace in his ordinary clothes. The unconscious Emperor opened his eyes and uttered his final, scolding words: 'Go home! And dress correctly!'

Freud existed in a sub-culture obsessed with appearances. In 1885, he had to attend an oral examination wearing a top hat, white gloves and morning suit. His letters contain many references to the clothes he owned: 'beautiful' black ties from Hamburg, 'new boots ... with laces and English soles'. He listened carefully to fashion advice given to his colleagues: 'his tailor ... told him that for a party it is quite unnecessary to wear a tailcoat and that he could go in a redingote'. Freud's son, Martin, recalled seeing his father carelessly dressed only once. 'This happened when I was six years old.' It was such an astonishing sight that he remembered it for the rest of his life. Freud preferred conventional suits, rather than evening dress, but his jackets, waistcoats and trousers were always made from the best materials and they were perfectly cut. He took pains to ensure that he was impeccably groomed and visited the barber every day.

As well as maintaining a stylish wardrobe, a young doctor also had to hire a smart carriage and pair, otherwise he wouldn't be deemed worthy of respect. Arriving at a patient's house in a one-horse carriage was professional suicide, while taking a bus was a public declaration of unfitness to practise.

For Freud, all of these costly obstacles to progress were relatively minor compared to the more fundamental problem of his race. In 1889, the coalition of Christian Socialists published a manifesto calling for the complete elimination of Jews from the medical profession. For many Viennese, the idea of being examined by a Jew was repulsive.

A culture of fellowship and patronage developed among Jewish doctors. Senior physicians would offer their juniors advice; they would arrange introductions, give financial assistance and, most importantly, provide work. Describing the situation many years later, Freud said Jews had 'no choice, but to band together'. Freud was lucky to have Josef Breuer as his patron because Breuer was well connected. He referred educated, affluent patients to Freud, and after Freud had returned from Paris – having benefited from an association with Charcot – Breuer encouraged his colleagues to consult his young friend concerning the care of their own patients. Even with Breuer's support, Freud couldn't assume that he would receive a steady stream of referrals – or get paid. In 1887, nine days after the birth of his first daughter, Mathilde, Freud wrote to his mother and sister-in-law: 'Almost simultaneously with her birth my practice underwent a revolution which couldn't be more radical. The previous six weeks had been the quietest of the whole year; then, when Martha's labour started, I was asked to attend a joint consultation with Chrobak at Frau L's on Monday . . . Yesterday evening there was a consultation with Kassowitz, a few days ago I put Frau Dr. Z on a fattening cure – in short, activities galore. My consulting room is full of new faces, more than I usually see in 2 months. I have to admit that none of this has earned me anything as yet, nor will every contact lead to something, but things are picking up as if the birth of a daughter were equal to a certificate of qualification for the medical profession.'

By the end of the 1880s, Freud was itching to make his mark. He had spent a decade seizing opportunities, pursuing enthusiasms and working hard, but it was still unclear how he would eventually distinguish himself and achieve greatness. He had translated the British philosopher John Stuart Mill into German; he had discovered a (not very *reliable*) procedure for staining brain sections with gold chloride solution to improve the microscopic study of nerves; he had rubbed shoulders with celebrities in Paris, and made the acquaintance of many worldly and philanthropic Jews in Vienna. He was building a reputation, certainly, but his many achievements were inconsequential when measured against the massive scale of his ambition. In a letter dated 14 February 1884, he wrote to Martha telling her about a lecture he had given in front of Theodor Meynert – the intimidating professor of psychiatry at the University of Vienna – and 'an assembly of psychiatrists and several colleagues'. It was a resounding success. 'I haven't had such a triumph for a long time,' Freud wrote, with a hint of swagger. Yet almost immediately he is fretting about the challenge ahead. 'Oh, but now comes the worry about holding one's own, finding something new to make the world sit up and bring not only recognition from the few but also attract the many ... ' It wasn't enough that he had made Meynert, arguably the greatest living brain anatomist, sit up, he wanted *the world* to sit up.

Private practice wasn't Freud's only source of income. He also accepted a part-time appointment as the director of a new neurological outpatient clinic at a children's hospital – the Kassowitz Institute. His association with this clinic would last for ten years, during which time he became a leading authority on paediatric cerebral paralyses and made major contributions to the extant literature. Another of his neurological interests was aphasia – disordered speech production or comprehension attributable to brain damage.

In 1891, Freud published a monograph titled *On Aphasia*. It is a work of much greater significance than its pithy title suggests. Freud's contemporaries supposed that specific speech problems were caused by well-circumscribed areas of brain damage. Freud, on the other hand, advocated a more complex view. He emphasised the effects of local damage on the whole brain.

Freud's holism was influenced by the English neurologist John Hughlings Jackson. Jackson had proposed that recently evolved higher regions of the brain regulate or inhibit lower (and more primitive) older regions. Thus, a phenomenon like aphasia might be understood as the consequence of higher brain centres failing and control being progressively ceded to lower brain centres. The idea that primitive aspects of the person are held in check by inhibitions is a central tenet of psychoanalysis. For this reason, some commentators have described *On Aphasia* as the first Freudian book. Although *On Aphasia* has several distinctive Freudian elements – indeed, the whole subject of disordered speech anticipates Freud's subsequent fascination with linguistic blunders – it is *Studies in Hysteria*, co-authored with Josef Breuer, that is usually identified as the first of Freud's books that contains incontestably Freudian content.

Hysteria (grouped in Freud's time among the neuroses) had become an extremely common condition across the whole of Europe by the end of the 1890s. An English 'lunacy commissioner' wrote: 'Every large city [is] filled with nerve-specialists and their chambers with patients.' This was partly due to poorly defined diagnostic criteria. Even something as trivial as an aching arm might be enough to attract a diagnosis of hysteria. Symptoms could be physical, such as paralysis and pain, or mental, such as mood disturbances and hallucinations. Although no organic cause was ever found, most doctors assumed that, ultimately, all hysterical symptoms were attributable to inherited neurological defects.

Hippocrates believed that hysteria was caused by the womb travelling periodically to the brain and he recommended early marriage as a remedy. Clitorectomy was offered as a treatment until the 1860s. Charcot was fully aware that men, even vigorous artisans with 'no signs of effeminacy', could also exhibit the same symptoms. Nevertheless, women were diagnosed with hysteria very much more often than men. This gender discrepancy has led many feminist historians to recast hysteria as a form of protest. They suggest that by adopting the 'role' of the 'hysteric', many women were able to challenge and transcend suffocating social impositions. Although the diagnosis of hysteria was ostensibly undesirable, being 'ill' allowed some women to express themselves more freely and to postpone, or even escape, over-controlling husbands, serial pregnancies and domestic drudgery.

We tend to think of hysteria as a redundant historical curiosity, but it still exists. Today, when patients present with 'hysterical' symptoms they receive a diagnosis of conversion disorder or functional neurological disorder (FND). The word 'functional', in this context, is roughly equivalent to 'psychosomatic'. Occasionally, dramatic outbreaks of hysteria attract media interest. Resignation syndrome, for example, which was first identified in Sweden in the 1990s, and was associated exclusively with young asylum seekers enduring a long wait to be granted citizenship. Typically, an episode of depression would intensify, progress through apathy to stupor, and finally lead to a total lack of responsivity. Affected patients would lose consciousness, become incontinent, and need to be fed through a tube. Like late nineteenth-century women, these disenfranchised refugees may have been 'staging' a protest.

In fact, there are many contemporary common ailments, such as irritable bowel syndrome (IBS) and chronic fatigue syndrome (CFS), with largely unidentified organic causes, that might be functionally equivalent to hysteria; that is, they are conditions that are at least partly a reaction to the stress of modern living. It is possible that the frustration, suppressed anger and anxiety that troubled women in the late nineteenth century is still widespread – and 'psychoactive'. Recent research has shown that up to 50 per cent of primary care patients present with symptoms that have no 'medical' explanation.

Breuer had developed the 'cathartic method' – his new treatment for hysteria – by June 1882, but he didn't share his discovery with Freud until November. They discussed the new treatment intermittently, but it wasn't until 1889 that Freud, having just returned to Vienna after visiting Nancy to perfect his 'hypnotic technique', gave Breuer's cathartic method the serious consideration it deserved. By that time he had been seeing patients with hysteria long enough to realise that standard physical treatments and hypnotic suggestion were, at best, unreliable, and at worst, completely ineffective. Freud began to conduct some therapeutic experiments of his own, based on Breuer's model, and he became increasingly convinced that the cathartic method represented a major breakthrough in the understanding of hysterical phenomena. He proposed that they work together on a joint publication. Breuer 'objected vehemently'. Freud was insistent, Breuer gave way, and in 1893 they issued a preliminary statement which, two years later, became the introductory thesis of *Studies in Hysteria*.

In November 1880, Breuer had been called to a third-floor apartment in a white stone building on Liechtensteinstrasse in order to treat an educated twenty-one-year-old woman whose name was Bertha Pappenheim. The Pappenheims were a strait-laced *haute bourgeois* Jewish family with Orthodox origins. After this initial house call, Breuer continued to visit Bertha every day for eighteen months. Summarising her presentation in the 1950s, Ernest Jones described her as having developed 'a museum of symptoms'. These ranged from minor physical ailments, for example cough and headache, to more troubling afflictions, such as paralysis and anorexia. Her psychological symptoms were equally varied and often quite remarkable. They included mood swings, agitation, confusion and stupor, as well as idiosyncratic peculiarities such as speaking exclusively in foreign languages, slipping backwards in time, and hallucinating skulls and skeletons. The ostensible cause of her hysterical illness was the stress she had experienced while nursing her father, who eventually died in April 1881. But it is also possible that some of Bertha's symptoms were produced by the morphine she took to control her neuralgic pain.

Every evening, Bertha would enter an altered state of consciousness (probably autohypnosis) and recite stories in the style of Hans Christian Andersen. These spontaneous creations relieved her symptoms, albeit temporarily, and she dubbed this procedure her 'talking cure'. Even though Bertha's first language was German, she spoke these words in English. They encapsulate a radically modern idea: that illness can be talked away.

A critical juncture in Bertha's treatment occurred during a hot spell of weather in 1882. Despite the heat and her terrible thirst, she refused to drink water for six weeks. She survived by eating only moist fruits. Under hypnosis, Bertha recalled seeing her English lady-companion's 'revolting' dog drinking out of a glass. She hadn't expressed her irritation at the time because she didn't want to appear impolite. Having remembered the incident under hypnosis and having vented her feelings, she was able to drink once more. Breuer was able to treat Bertha's other symptoms in the same way: 'hysterical phenomena disappeared as soon as the event that had caused the symptom was reproduced under hypnosis'. It should be noted that Breuer was not employing hypnosis as a tool to enhance the power of suggestion. He wasn't commanding symptoms to disappear. Instead, he was using hypnosis to retrieve disturbing memories that had been inhibited or repressed. Trapped feelings were being released, which is why he called his new treatment the cathartic method.

The history of Bertha's illness and treatment became the first of five detailed case studies reported in *Studies in Hysteria*. Although Breuer acknowledged that it was a considerable time before Bertha regained her 'mental balance', he also stated that she subsequently enjoyed 'complete health'. In fact, Bertha experienced several relapses. Indeed, her last hospital admission was in June 1887 – five years after the 'successful' completion of her treatment.

Breuer chose to conceal Bertha's true identity with a strangely alluring alias: Anna O. The feminist historian Elaine Showalter, psychoanalysing Breuer, has suggested that the 'O' represents 'the symbolic circle or cipher of feminine sexual mystery'. It is a plausible hypothesis if we accept the content of a letter written by Freud to the author Stefan Zweig in 1932 as factual.

According to Freud, Breuer had terminated Bertha's treatment after he, Breuer, had found her simulating childbirth. 'Now,' she had cried, 'Dr. B's child is coming.' Fearing accusations of professional misconduct, Breuer referred her to a sanatorium near the Swiss-German border. In his letter to Zweig, Freud added that Breuer had 'held in his hand the key . . . but he let it drop'. Breuer's reaction to Bertha's phantom labour had exposed Breuer's unwillingness to acknowledge the importance of sex in psychopathology. Consequently, Freud had been obliged to press on with the work they had started together, alone – a solitary and fearless explorer of the darkest recesses of the human mind.

Freud's dramatic account of the end of Bertha's treatment is problematic because it is uncorroborated, and Freud could be very creative when presented with opportunities to gild his own legend. He was particularly fond of the lone genius motif. Many commentators have confidently described Bertha's phantom labour as a myth; however, there are good reasons for giving Freud the benefit of the doubt. In *Studies in Hysteria*, Breuer awkwardly confessed to having 'suppressed' many interesting details of the case of Fräulein Anna O. Is this an oblique reference to Bertha's phantom labour? It is generally agreed that Bertha was beautiful and accomplished, that Breuer and Bertha had become exceptionally close, that Frau Breuer had become sick with jealousy, and that when Breuer eventually wrote up the case he was keen to emphasise that 'the element of sexuality was remarkably undeveloped' in his former patient. For many years, salacious rumours about Breuer's 'treatment' of Bertha circulated among physicians who were later involved in her care. And why did Breuer do nothing with his case notes for over a decade? Why was he so reluctant to publicise his fascinating discoveries?

Bertha's phantom labour might have been one of Freud's self-serving inventions. But then again, it might not. We simply don't know. What we do know, however, is that Bertha and Breuer's relationship, irrespective of imputed sexual undercurrents and possible improprieties, was an astonishingly productive collaboration. The cathartic method was as much Bertha's discovery as Breuer's. Bertha experimented with her own consciousness and employed language that influenced Breuer's thinking. Her whimsical substitute term for describing the 'talking cure' was 'chimney sweeping', which, by analogy, implies an underlying therapeutic process which involves the clearing out of pathogenic memories. Ultimately, this idea of clearing out was distinguished by the technical term 'abreaction'. Breuer was impressed by Bertha's 'considerable intelligence' and her 'rich poetic and imaginative gifts'. Metaphorically they *did* produce a 'child' together, and that 'child' was the cathartic method.

To what extent, however, was Freud correct when he judged the cathartic method to be a breakthrough? In 1924, he wrote that Breuer's case study had 'accomplished more towards an understanding of neuroses than any previous observation'. But the cathartic method was only modestly successful. When Breuer terminated Bertha's treatment, she was still quite 'ill'. Although it is true that Breuer didn't discover a lasting cure for hysteria, he certainly *did* advance 'understanding of neuroses' commensurate with Freud's estimation. Breuer connected Bertha's symptoms with her experiences, and this connection made her symptoms meaningful. They could be understood as somatic memories or symbols; they could be *interpreted*. This might strike some readers as logical and obvious. But in the 1880s and 1890s the connection between symptoms and experiences was largely unacknowledged. And although the cathartic method didn't prevent Bertha's subsequent hospital admissions, it did provide her with temporary relief when her symptoms were particularly distressing.

Anna O's true identity wasn't revealed until 1953. She had been dead for seventeen years. After recovering her 'mental balance', Bertha had channelled her 'considerable intelligence' and 'imaginative gifts' in many directions. She had become a famous translator, writer, campaigner and women's rights activist; she had waged war on the 'white slave' trade and travelled across Europe to rescue sex workers and orphans. She was a founder member of the German League of Jewish Women, she stood up to the Gestapo, and she counted Albert Einstein among those who admired her zeal for justice. In 1954, the German government honoured her by issuing a commemorative postage stamp bearing her image in a series titled 'Benefactors of Mankind'.

Breuer might not have cured Bertha, but perhaps his treatment was ultimately enabling. Unlike many of his colleagues (especially those practising in England and France) he was never contemptuous of his patient. On the contrary, he was attentive and respectful. He allowed Bertha to express herself and he listened carefully to what she had to say. It is possible that these experiences altered her sense of self-worth and her expectations of what she might achieve in a world dominated by men – even if the realisation of those achievements was somewhat delayed.

The remaining cases in *Studies in Hysteria* were all written by Freud. Although Freud had adopted Breuer's cathartic method (at least to the extent that his therapeutic formula had become the systematic retrieval of memories) he was still employing electrotherapy, baths, massage and hypnosis, simultaneously. Evidently he was not ready to abandon established procedures. He did, however, develop a new way of encouraging patients to make fuller disclosures based on a procedure originally used

by the French neurologist Hippolyte Bernheim: 'pressure technique'. Freud would lay his hand on a patient's forehead, apply
pressure, and give assurances that important memories would
'come to mind' at the point when the pressure was released.
Apparently, it was very effective. But it is also reminiscent of
Charcot's dubious theatricality and not very different from
hypnotic suggestion. Both pressure technique and hypnotic
suggestion have in common the exploitation of authority as a
means of manipulating expectations.

Case number two in *Studies in Hysteria* is Frau Emmy von N –
real name, Fanny Moser – a woman described as a forty-year-old
widow from Livonia. Like Anna O, Frau Emmy suffered from
many symptoms: twitches, agitation, pains in the face, arms
and legs, hysterical delirium, insomnia, hallucinations, and
the production of a curious clicking or clacking noise. During
otherwise coherent conversations she would suddenly break
off, appear horrified or repulsed, and call out fearfully, 'Keep
still – don't say anything – don't touch me!' She would then
continue talking, seemingly unaware that her speech had been
interrupted. Frau Emmy reported many traumatic experiences
associated with death. At the age of seven she unexpectedly
saw her sister in a coffin; at the age of nine she saw her aunt
in a coffin and was unlucky enough to be present when her
deceased relative's jaw dropped open; at the age of nineteen she
returned home and was shocked to discover her mother's body.
Her mother's face was contorted. Frau Emmy even witnessed
her husband's death: he had risen from a breakfast table at the
end of the bed, looked at her strangely, and collapsed. In addition
to these traumatic events, she was also distressed by unhappy
family relationships.

Following Breuer's example, Freud discovered chains of
association that connected Frau Emmy's symptoms with her
traumatic memories; however, he wasn't convinced that these

memories provided a complete and satisfactory explanation of her hysteria. He was troubled by certain questions. A traumatic experience might cause a symptom, but why did that symptom persist? And were their other causal factors, perhaps more fundamental, that should be considered? After reflecting on these questions, he reached a speculative conclusion concerning Frau Emmy's symptoms that became central to his general thinking: 'I am led to suspect that this intense woman, who was capable of such strong feelings, had not conquered her sexual needs without a hard fight, and had sometimes reached a point of severe exhaustion in her attempt to suppress this most powerful of all drives.' Ultimately, Frau Emmy's essential energies had been sapped by the demands of maintaining sexual abstinence. There isn't a great deal of evidence in the case study to merit this conclusion and Freud was undoubtedly attempting to make the facts fit his hypothesis. This hypothesis, however, was shaped not by *one* case but by *many* cases. The traumatic memories of Freud's hysterical patients tended to have something to do with sex. Today we are inclined to think of sexual trauma as rape or sexual abuse, but in Freud's day erotic thoughts or fantasies might also be experienced as traumatic, depending on the individual's moral code and circumstances.

Frau Emmy continued to relapse under stress and Freud attributed this unsatisfactory outcome to his own shortcomings, having failed to account for 'the connections between the phenomena more thoroughly'. In 1924 he added a footnote explaining that some years after treating Frau Emmy he had encountered a distinguished colleague (actually the eminent psychiatrist Auguste Forel) who had also been unable to treat her.

The third case study is Miss Lucy R, an English governess employed by a wealthy widower to care for his children. Her general psychological symptoms were relatively minor – fatigue and depression; however, she also reported an olfactory hallucination of 'burnt pudding'. Miss Lucy was unwilling to acknowledge that she had fallen in love with her employer. Sadly, her ardour was never reciprocated. Her olfactory hallucination was connected to smelling a real burning pudding while contemplating separation from the children, to whom she had become attached. Freud's treatment seems to have clarified her feelings and her symptoms subsequently disappeared. The doctor–patient dialogue, reported in some detail, shows that Miss Lucy had become quite philosophical about her situation. Four months after her treatment came to an end, Freud met her at a summer resort: 'She was in good spirits and assured me that her good health had been maintained.'

Case number four, Katharina, is something of a curiosity. The introductory paragraphs contain some of the most vivid and engaging descriptive prose ever to appear in a medical report. Freud was on holiday in the Alps, and he had climbed to the top of a mountain. While enjoying the view, he heard the words: 'Are you a doctor, sir?' He had been followed by a young woman whom he recognised. She had served him his meal and he inferred that she was a relative of his landlady. The young woman then disclosed several alarming symptoms: breathlessness, suffocation, a feeling of pressure on her chest, and a recurring hallucination of a horrible face. Freud linked these symptoms to a history of molestation by her 'uncle' – although in reality the abuser was her father, a drunk who would get into bed with her whenever the opportunity arose. Researchers have since identified Katharina as Aurelia Kronich, and the encounter Freud described took place in August 1893 on the Rax. Freud exercised considerable and perhaps unacceptable licence with the chronology of this case study to make it consistent with his views on 'delayed trauma' – his observation that the onset of symptoms and the original traumatic event or events that caused them can be separated by a period of dormancy. Was Freud's conversation with Aurelia helpful? She got married in 1895, had six children, and as far as we know she lived a happy life. But whether we can attribute any of this to Freud's minimal intervention is extremely doubtful.

Fräulein Elisabeth von R (real name Ilona Weiss) is the fifth and final case study reported in *Studies in Hysteria*. She was a woman in her mid-twenties who complained of leg pain and difficulty walking. A peculiarity of her condition was that when her legs were pinched or pressed during examination, her expression suggested that she was experiencing pleasure. Freud wrote: 'I couldn't help thinking that it was as if she were being tickled voluptuously – her face became flushed, she threw back her head and closed her eyes, her trunk bent backwards.' Fräulein Elisabeth confessed that when her sister had died, she had thought of her widowed brother-in-law: 'Now he is free again and I can become his wife.' Desire conflicted with conscience, and she struggled to prevent the idea from returning. The result of her self-censorship was that her emotional pain was converted into physical pain. Freud encouraged her to acknowledge her feelings, and by doing so he gave her opportunities to 'discharge the store of excitation that had been accumulating for a long time'. In the spring of 1894, Freud attended a ball, and he was gratified to see Fräulein Elisabeth 'fly past in a lively dance'; however, the relief that she experienced was temporary. She married, and according to her family she continued to experience leg pain and consult specialists for the rest of her life. In 1935, reflecting on her treatment with Freud, she said: '[Freud] was just a young, bearded nerve specialist they sent me to. He wanted to persuade me that I was in love with my brother-in-law, but that wasn't really so.'

Critics have pointed out that the 'talking cure' wasn't really a cure – or, as cures go, not a very good one. However, Breuer and Freud's book is titled *Studies in Hysteria*, not *Treatment of Hysteria*. It is a work that is as much concerned with theory as it is practice and should be judged accordingly. Moreover, *Studies in Hysteria* is unabashedly experimental. Novel treatment strategies are being employed and results are being reported, even when they are patchy. *Studies in Hysteria* was never intended to be read as a definitive treatment guide. It was a bulletin, an update concerning work in progress.

Freud was perfectly aware that the talking cure was not a panacea. Indeed, in the final chapter he openly acknowledges that the procedure has limitations, and he lists its 'negative aspects'. Finally, he concedes that the cathartic method is ultimately constrained by the human condition and modestly accepts that psychotherapy can only ever turn 'hysterical misery into common unhappiness'. This is quintessential Freud: a refusal to offer comforting reassurances and resolute insistence on unsentimental realism.

In the preface of the first edition of *Studies in Hysteria*, Breuer and Freud state that, although they agree on the facts, their 'interpretations and conjectures do not always coincide'. It is a curious way to introduce a collaborative project. Freud always stressed that their failure to 'coincide' was, for the most part, a failure to agree on the importance of sex. As we have already discovered, Freud was still stressing that Breuer had been reluctant to acknowledge the importance of sex when he wrote to Stefan Zweig some thirty-seven years later. Shortly after *Studies in Hysteria* was published, Freud's views on the relationship between sex and mental illness became such an obstacle to collaboration that they could no longer work together. Eventually they became completely estranged.

This was Freud's version of events, and it was accepted in psychoanalytic circles for decades. The truth is more nuanced. Breuer was never as prudish as Freud suggested. In 1924, Freud

declared that Breuer 'shrank from recognizing the sexual aetiology of the neuroses'. Yet, in *Studies in Hysteria*, Breuer affirms
that the 'sexual drive' is the 'most powerful source' of the neuroses. He couldn't have been clearer: 'I do not believe that I am
exaggerating when I claim that *the great majority of severe neuroses
in women originate in the marital bed.*' Breuer did not agree with
Freud's assertion that sex was implicated in *all* cases of hysteria,
but to suggest that he shrank away from a sexual theory of neurotic illness is misleading. Sex wasn't the only subject that they
couldn't quite agree on. They also had differences of opinion
concerning the role of 'hypnoid states', treatment methods and
treatment length. Perhaps Freud overstated their 'disagreement'
over sex because it served his preferred narrative. It made him
look bold and heroic.

What, then, was the real reason for Freud and Breuer's
estrangement? Breuer always treated Freud as an equal; however, it is highly likely that Freud was growing tired of being the
junior partner. He was all too aware that the cathartic method
had been Breuer's breakthrough, not his own. By 1897, Freud
confided to Wilhelm Fliess that the mere sight of Breuer made
him want to emigrate. He even started avoiding Breuer's neigh-
bourhood to reduce the risk of a chance encounter.

Breuer and Freud might not have discovered a cure for hysteria, but while attempting to treat the illness they had developed
an impressive theoretical account of symptom formation.
Traumatic experiences, sexual or otherwise, are related to
intolerable thoughts and feelings that become separated from
consciousness and converted into symptoms. These symptoms
are usually, but not always, symbolic. For example, a rebuke that
felt like 'a slap in the face' might be repressed and consequently
produce numbness or stinging pain in the cheek. Recovering
traumatic memories can be therapeutic, insofar as recollection
facilitates the release of dammed-up or 'strangulated' emotions.

Thus, memories that had been, in a sense, split off are reintegrated and unity of mind is restored. The self, having been divided by trauma, is healed, and made whole again. Inner conflicts caused by disturbing experiences and desires are resolved by disclosure, insight and self-acceptance.

Several concepts and assumptions had come to acquire special significance. Firstly, past experiences provide a better understanding of symptom formation than invoking a speculative and inherited neurological defect. Freud still acknowledged constitutional vulnerabilities, insofar as a pre-existing physical problem might serve as a path of least resistance for the expression of hysterical symptoms. Even so, forensic exploration of past experiences had demonstrated that hysteria has its own internal logic. Secondly, the idea that parts of the mind are inaccessible or can become inaccessible was widely accepted; however, Breuer and Freud's work demonstrated that, at least in the context of hysteria, the contents of the unconscious have enormous explanatory power. What patients don't know about themselves is much more informative than what they do know. Freud in particular stressed the importance of digging down into the mind by comparing psychotherapy with 'excavating a buried city'. Thirdly, when emotions like anxiety and guilt threaten to overwhelm the person, a defence mechanism, repression, pushes associated memories into the unconscious. This was very much Freud's idea rather than Breuer's. He didn't know how such a mechanism might work, but he assumed that something analogous to physical forces must be operating in the mind. Something must be doing the pushing and holding down.

The idea of repression makes Freud's interest in sex logical. Sexual impulses are arguably the strongest and most primitive. Indeed, they can be conceptualised as a 'weak point' in the functioning of 'civilized' beings. Therefore, sexual thoughts and feelings are more likely than non-sexual thoughts to

require strict control. Sexual feelings are more likely to be
repressed, and once they are in the unconscious they can convert into symptoms.

Studies in Hysteria is a landmark 'medical' publication, but its
influence has extended well beyond psychiatry and neurology.
It can be read as 'literature' and it has inspired generations of
writers whose stories have explored themes relating to mental
illness, altered states of consciousness and female sexuality.
Case reports in the 1890s were typically short and written in a
'telegraphic' style. Many consisted of only a few lines. The case
reports of Breuer and Freud are, by contrast, extended and full
of fascinating details. Breuer deserves credit for setting a high
standard in this respect with Anna O, but Freud's contributions
show genuine literary flair. After an introductory paragraph,
Freud begins the case of Frau Emmy: '*May 1, 1889.* I find a woman
who has distinctive, finely cut features and an appearance that
is still youthful lying on the couch with a leather bolster under
her neck. Her face bears a tense, pained expression.' The sense
of drama is palpable. We are reading a 'private' clinical diary,
eavesdropping on intimate disclosures, and we experience a
transgressive thrill. The opening of Katharina is reminiscent
of Hitchcock: a doctor, impatient for solitude, walks off 'the
beaten track' and climbs to a remote hut, only to discover that
he has been followed by a mysterious young woman. The case
of Lucy R is the prototype of countless 'Gothic' tales in which
prim English governesses are haunted by strange phenomena.
Psychological thrillers and psychological ghost stories found
new directions after Breuer and Freud.

Freud was worried that the case histories might lack 'the serious stamp of science'. They were too enjoyable. He subsequently
defended his work by arguing that the kind of writing used by
novelists to describe the inner life of characters was exactly the
kind of writing necessary to illuminate the inner life of patients.

There is, Freud asserted, an intimate relationship between 'the story of the patient's suffering and the symptoms of their illness'. Hysteria is a disguised narrative. It will only be truly understood if traumatic experiences are ordered, like chapters in a book.

Alfred von Berger, professor of history and literature at the University of Vienna and director of the Court Theatre, wrote a glowing review of *Studies in Hysteria* titled *Surgery of the Soul*. 'We dimly conceive the idea that it may one day become possible to approach the innermost secret of human personality.' Freud had borrowed the techniques of poets and novelists in the service of science. This meant that poets and novelists could borrow scientific ideas in the service of art. Soon, *Studies in Hysteria* was being discussed by writers such as Hermann Bahr and Hugo von Hofmannsthal. It became a reference work, not only for doctors but for authors, playwrights and theatre directors.

Although von Berger and other significant writers were impressed by *Studies in Hysteria*, Ernest Jones tells us that Breuer and Freud's achievement was largely unacknowledged. Eight hundred copies of the book were printed and thirteen years later only 626 had been sold. Breuer and Freud shared earnings of 425 gulden, which when Jones was writing converted into £18 each; however, Jones was simply reinforcing Freud's legend – unrecognised greatness, social exclusion and the lonely pursuit of truth. In 1924, Freud wrote that one of the main reasons why Breuer had abandoned their joint project was because he had been hurt and discouraged by severe criticism. Freud had soldiered on, marching into the wilderness. 'For more than ten years after my separation from Breuer I had no followers. I was completely isolated. In Vienna I was shunned.'

Studies in Hysteria might not have sold many copies, but its readership was select, distinguished, influential and predominantly appreciative. The eminent Swiss psychiatrist Eugen Bleuler, for example, regarded *Studies in Hysteria* as one of the most important books on the subject in recent years. Moreover, Freud's driving ambition and social networking were finally yielding results. In 1893, his name was included in a Viennese *Who's Who* of celebrities. *Studies in Hysteria* didn't damage his reputation; on the contrary, it enhanced his reputation. He was seeing the wives of bankers, the daughters of industrialists and baronesses. As his ideas about the mind and treatment evolved, he decided that the term 'cathartic method' no longer described what he was doing. He needed another term. In 1896, he chose 'psychoanalysis'.

Chapter 4

Dark Glamour

Something very odd happened in Vienna during the 1890s and early years of the twentieth century. Mental illness, or 'nerves', became fashionable. Today the term 'nerves' is usually applied to individuals with a nervous disposition, but in Freud's time it was the colloquial term for a range of neurological and psychiatric conditions. A 'weak' nervous system could cause symptoms directly, by not functioning properly, or indirectly, by amplifying the adverse effects of stress – particularly the stress of modern city living. Bizarrely, as the century turned, indications of strain or fatigue began to acquire an aura of modish desirability. A new set of aesthetic values emerged as artists captured 'the allure of nerves' on their canvases. This shift of perspective was the result of a complex set of influences: serendipity, individual personalities, the prevalence of the neuroses, and developments in art and literature. Nerves would become a defining feature of Vienna's golden age, and thereafter a permanent feature of the modern cultural landscape. The after-effects of this aesthetic revolution are still with us. They are discernible in contemporary glossy magazines and in art galleries, on billboards, catwalks and album covers.

The Empress Elisabeth, affectionately referred to by her adoring public as Sisi, was the first major figure to embody the allure of nerves. She combined melancholy with sex appeal, and in doing so presaged a modern phenomenon exemplified by tragic figures such as Marilyn Monroe and Lady Diana Spencer. The Viennese were obsessed with royalty. So much so that reproduction portraits of the Emperor, Franz Josef, were inescapable in public spaces and official buildings. When his engagement to 'Her Serene Highness, Princess Elisabeth Amalie Eugenie, Duchess of Bavaria' was announced in the *Wiener Zeitung*, it was sensational news; however, even before her arrival in Vienna, royal genealogists were apprehensive about the Princess's tainted Wittelsbach bloodline. Her grandfather was a feeble-minded 'cripple' who had once been held in police custody after a brawl.

Irrespective of her hereditary shortcomings, Sisi was tall – at least in comparison with her peers – elegant and exceptionally stylish. Her bridal trousseau consisted of twenty-five trunks filled with jewellery and outfits suitable for every conceivable occasion. Her extensive wardrobe included items such as a blue velvet cloak with sable trimmings and a sable muff, four ballgowns, seventeen 'fancy gowns' with trains, nineteen summer frocks, twelve headdresses of feathers, rose petals, apple blossoms, lace, ribbon and pearls, sixteen hats and 168 pairs of stockings. Her collection of underwear and nightwear was equally impressive: 144 camisoles, seventy-two petticoats of piqué, silk and flannel, sixty pantalettes, ten bed jackets, twelve embroidered night caps – and so on. In addition to the 113 pairs of shoes that she brought to Vienna, mostly fragile footwear made of velvet, taffeta and silk, Sisi was supplied with a new pair of practical shoes every day, because it was considered improper for the Empress of Austria to wear the same pair of shoes twice. The only non-glamorous items listed in her trousseau inventory were three pairs of rubber galoshes. A famous portrait of Sisi, completed when she was twenty-eight, shows her posing in an off-the-shoulder dress with her remarkably abundant hair constellated with diamond stars. She was reputed to be one of the most beautiful women in the world, perhaps even *the* most beautiful.

Sisi's figure was unfeasibly slender. Even after having four children, her waist measurement was only twenty inches (fifty-one centimetres). A man with large hands could have enclosed her waist in a circle produced by touching the tips of his fore-fingers and thumbs. She maintained an average lifelong weight of forty-seven kilograms (103lb) by following draconian diets – for example, eating nothing but oranges (and occasionally ice flavoured with violet). Sometimes she didn't eat anything at all. Before going to bed, her hips were wrapped in dressings soaked with vinegar. Her hair had to be combed for three hours every day and, every fortnight, it was washed with cognac and egg yolks (a ritual that lasted from morning till night). She used face masks of crushed strawberries or raw veal for her complexion, although it was rumoured that, like a vampire countess, she remained youthful by drinking blood. This aspersion is proba-bly connected with her occasional consumption of a fortifying broth produced by boiling shank juices. Her palace dressing room was converted into a gymnasium with monkey bars and ropes. One observer, finding her hovering above the ground in a silk dress and train, described the Empress as resembling 'a creature somewhere between snake and bird'. She was fifty-four years old at the time.

Clearly, Sisi was suffering from an eating disorder with marked obsessional features. But she also exhibited a number of other symptoms: fits of nervous laughter, tearfulness, anxiety about descending staircases, suicidal thoughts and numerous behavioural oddities. She was never happy in the Viennese court, which she hated because of its strict protocols and hide-bound formality. Consistent with feminist accounts of hysteria, Sisi's symptoms might be understood as a form of rebellion; a response to feeling trapped and frustrated. She was denied self-determination and the only control she could exercise was control over her own body. Sisi was certainly a natural non-conformist; she smoked, even though it was considered unseemly for women to indulge in the habit, and she had an anchor tattooed on her shoulder, like a 'common' sailor.

After the death of her son, Crown Prince Rudolf, she dressed in black and developed the habit of hiding her face behind an umbrella or a raised fan. She became an inveterate traveller, crossing Europe – somewhat aimlessly – in a luxuriously appointed carriage, or cruising to remote locations in the Mediterranean. Austrian diplomats were bemused when she declined invitations to official functions and instead requested introductions to Arab snake charmers, conjurors and soothsayers. When the imperial yacht encountered violent storms, she had herself tied to a chair on deck. Court aids and socialites gossiped about her amorous adventures, although there is no evidence to suggest that she formed anything other than platonic relationships. It seems highly unlikely that Sisi, having finally won her freedom, would have wanted to tether herself to a man.

On 10 September 1898, Sisi was assassinated by an Italian anarchist in Geneva. An unsolicited photograph of her was taken in the preceding week. It is an early example of the kind of photography we often find in contemporary tabloid news-papers: a slightly out-of-focus image of a celebrity captured in an unguarded moment. She is standing in front of a brasserie, accompanied by Baroness Rothschild. If Sisi had noticed the camera pointing in her direction, she would almost certainly have opened her umbrella and shielded herself from view. The photograph is affecting, because it shows not an icon but a real woman who seems deep in thought. Even so, she still looks exceedingly elegant in her ankle-length coat and neat feathered hat.

Over the course of her life and in common with many aristocrats, Sisi visited several spa towns. She was fond of exotic locations, such as the Baths of Hercules in the Carpathian mountains. Her husband, on the other hand, preferred the more familiar ambience of the Salzkammergut. Wherever the aristocracy went, the fashion-conscious Viennese bourgeoisie were sure to follow. Thermal baths were recommended for a wide variety of ailments; calming immersion in hot spring water was judged to be excellent for nerves frazzled by noisy thoroughfares and electric lights. Thus, the 'allure of nerves' was made even more alluring by so-called 'health tourism'. Wealthy neurasthenics could reserve suites in 'Grand Hotels' and sunbathe on south-facing balconies; they could socialise with other guests, play card games in the casino, attend zither concerts, circumnavigate lakes on pleasure boats, and spot celebrities.

The strengthening associations between luxury, leisure and illness began to shape the Viennese vision of what a mental hospital might look like and what services such an institution should offer. The Am Steinhof asylum, opened in 1907, wasn't so much a hospital, but rather a beautifully landscaped town that tumbled down verdant parkland. The community was overlooked – then, as it is now – by architect Otto Wagner's extraordinary and glorious Church of St Leopold, a kind of modernist Taj Mahal with a spectacular golden dome and lantern. Although Am Steinhof was a state institution, it also had its own sanatorium, which provided care to fee-paying patients suffering from nervous conditions. Contemporary posters and adverts show a collection of pristine façades, rolling hills and sunlit uplands in the distance. At the centre of the sanatorium complex was the Kurhaus, designed in the voguish Jugendstil style, which had, in addition to conventional treatment rooms, its own ballroom, music room, billiard room, writing room, winter garden and swimming pool. The wealthiest patients could pay for their own residential Jugendstil pavilions.

Reflecting on his early years in clinical practice, Freud informed his patient and friend Princess Marie Bonaparte that he had 'treated only poor people'. Although this is true, at least up until 1887, thereafter his clientele became increasingly well-to-do. It has been estimated that three quarters of his patients were wealthy.

Freud's first case report in *Studies in Hysteria*, Frau Emmy von N, was reputed to be the richest woman in Europe. She was born Baroness Fanny Louise von Sulzer-Wart of Winterthur, and when she was twenty-three she married a much older man, the spectacularly prosperous industrialist Heinrich Moser. Four years after marrying Fanny, Moser died – as described by Freud in *Studies in Hysteria*. Fanny (and her daughters) inherited most of his fortune. The children of Moser's previous marriage were convinced that Fanny had poisoned their father. Moser's body was disinterred, autopsies were undertaken, and Fanny's name was cleared. Freud only refers to these events obliquely in his case report: 'Her fear of strangers, and fear of people in general, proves to be left over from the time when she was exposed to the persecutions of her family.' Irrespective of the evidence, society gossipmongers were never going to allow such a delicious rumour to fade away over time. The possibility, however minuscule, that the richest woman in Europe might also be a murderess was simply too exciting. Fanny maintained a 'novelistic' lifestyle. She entertained distinguished guests, made extravagant donations, and developed a penchant for medically qualified lovers. Later in life she fell in love with a young man who divested her of a substantial part of her fortune. She died in 1925, still very rich, even though she had been heinously fleeced.

Frau Cäcilie M, who is introduced to us as a mere footnote in *Studies in Hysteria*, was really Anna von Lieben. Like Fanny Moser, Anna was born a baroness. Her father and her husband were both bankers, and her mother threw parties attended by composers such as Brahms, Liszt and Johann Strauss. Freud got to know Anna very well, but (he coyly confides) he was unable to expand upon her case details due to 'personal circumstances'. He provides only a sketchy account of a woman whose hysteria 'took a variety of different forms'. In fact, Anna was a larger-than-life character who possessed the qualities of a prima donna. She was a gifted musician, highly literate, and extremely good at chess. Indeed, she could play two opponents at once. A professional chess player was paid to keep vigil outside her bedroom door, just in case she was seized by the competitive urge at an unsociable hour. Her appetites were excessive. She was overweight (so much so that she needed a lift to travel between floors), addicted to morphine, and enjoyed after-hours shopping sprees. Fine fabrics were a passion. When staying at her family villa, south of Vienna, she had her favourite breakfast, lamb cutlets, delivered every morning from the city. Anna visited 'slimming spas' and occasionally attempted to lose weight by restricting her diet to caviar and champagne.

The subject of Freud's *The Psychogenesis of a Case of Homosexuality in a Woman* – 'a beautiful and clever girl of eighteen' – was Margarethe Csonka, the daughter of an oil magnate (and business partner of the Rothschilds). In 1917, Margarethe fell in love with Baroness Leonie von Puttkamer, a demi-mondaine and member of the Prussian nobility who dressed flamboyantly, wore fabulous hats and glided down avenues with a giant wolfhound straining at the leash. In the early 1920s, the Baroness had a scandalous affair with a nude dancer and spent time in a cell of the regional courthouse after her husband suspected her of trying to poison him. Margarethe visited the Baroness while she was being detained, provided her with considerable assistance, and remained totally besotted.

Many of Freud's affluent patients were of the same class as the women who appear in Gustav Klimt's famous society portraits. These arresting, opulent masterpieces could easily serve as illustrations for a sumptuously produced book of imaginary psychoanalytic case studies. Almost all the subjects show signs of nervous agitation, delicacy and exhaustion. Their faces are pale, or at best artificially enlivened by dabs of rouge that do not disguise their underlying pallor.

Klimt's most celebrated society portrait is the first of two he

produced of Adele Bloch-Bauer. Her face, shoulders and hands are suspended in a gold plane that is textured with abstract shapes and spirals. Adele's heavy eyelids and parted lips are redolent of languid eroticism, but her twisted hands are deformed by nervous tension. She is hiding a crooked finger. In reality, she was moody, introspective, tired all the time, and prone to headaches and nebulous ailments.

Adele was married to an honourable, older and rather dull sugar magnate who collected porcelain. She, in stark contrast, was an avid reader of French, German and English literature, studied works of medicine and science, mixed with well-connected and brilliant women (such as Alma Mahler), entertained a former chancellor (who used to talk politics with Leon Trotsky in Café Central), and developed socialist sympathies. It is supposed that Adele's marriage was not very exciting, which has led some to conclude that, while she was sitting for Klimt, she probably allowed the great painter to seduce her. Klimt was a compulsive philanderer and society women who sat for him risked a certain amount of reputational damage; however, Adele and Klimt may have already been intimate. Klimt's 'orgasmic' portrait *Judith*, unveiled some years earlier, is an uncanny double of Adele. Art historians have interpreted its overt sexuality as incriminating evidence. The writer Felix Salten came perilously close to indiscretion. He saw in Klimt's *Judith* a 'present-day figure', 'a beautiful hostess', 'whom men's eyes follow at every premiere as she rustles by in her silk petticoats'.

Adele's portrait made her a celebrity at the age of twenty-six, an icon of modern womanhood whose nervy imperfections contribute to her desirability. Viennese slang for the vagina was 'jewellery box'. The journalist and author Ludwig Hevesi described Adele's portrait as 'a dream of bejewelled lust'. Like Freud, Klimt was interested in truth: 'Truth is fire; and to tell the truth means to glow and burn.' Adele's portrait mines truth, all the way down to its lowest stratum. Klimt had read Darwin and was acutely aware that he was painting not only a society beauty but also an animal with reproductive potential. The shapes on her dress are not decorative fancies, but symbols of fertility: the rectangles represent sperm, the ovals represent eggs.

Klimt isn't portraying Adele as a sex object. He is simply acknowledging the reality of female sexuality, at a time when women from 'good' families were expected to have only pure thoughts and be quick to blush. Klimt recognises that Adele's sexuality is an aspect of her being. She is not limited or defined by her desirability. Her face isn't beautiful in a bland way. It is a face full of character. The inspiration for Adele's portrait was a Byzantine mural of the Empress Theodora. Theodora was a concubine who, on marrying the Emperor Justinian, used her power to improve the legal status of women in the Eastern Roman Empire. Adele's nerves are, at least in part, enabling. Her restlessness is aspirational. Her sensitivities are complemented by intellect and humanity. She is a twentieth-century *Mona Lisa*.

Adele and the women in her circle were very fashion conscious, not only because they could afford to be, but also because fashion was becoming more intellectually relevant. Around 1900, couture was increasingly recognised as an industry that had much in common with high art. In Vienna, Jugendstil decoration started to appear on the latest styles emerging from Paris. Furthermore, the idea that clothes could say something about a person's beliefs and politics started to gain currency. Fashion could make a statement.

Dresses that declared one's support for experimental art and female emancipation could be purchased at the Flöge Sisters boutique on Mariahilfer Strasse. Emilie Flöge was Klimt's sister-in-law and over time they became not only friends but also a creative team. Whether or not they became lovers is still open to debate. It has been suggested that Klimt's painting *The Kiss* shows the couple in a passionate embrace – and Klimt's last words were 'Send for Emilie'. At its height, the boutique employed eighty seamstresses and only the wealthiest society women could afford to shop there. The interior was designed by Josef Hoffmann and Kolomon Moser, founders of the arts and crafts collective known as the Wiener Werkstätten (Vienna Workshops). The walls were lacquered white, the mirrors were adjustable, and the floors were covered with grey felt so that nervy customers could try their dresses on without getting cold feet. Furniture was geometric – cuboid and rectangular – and everything from the door sign to collar-labels was stylistically consistent.

Getting dressed was something of an ordeal for most well-to-do women in fin de siècle Vienna. Stefan Zweig described the process in his autobiography: 'First a countless number of hooks and eyes had to be fastened in the back from the waist to neck, and the corset pulled tight with all the strength of the maid in attendance. The long hair ... was curled, brushed, combed, flattened, piled up, with the aid of a legion of hairpins, barrettes, and combs and with the additional help of a curling iron and curlers, by a hairdresser who called daily, before one could swathe and build her up with petticoats, camisoles, jackets and bodices like so many layers of onion skin, until the last trace of her womanly and personal figure had fully disappeared.' A future husband had no idea whether his fiancée was 'fat or lean, short-legged, bow-legged, or long-legged' until all was revealed on the wedding night. It must have come as something of a relief, therefore, when the *haute bourgeois* women of Vienna were offered a less taxing alternative.

The Flöge sisters sold clothes consistent with 'reform move-ment' values. 'Reformers' had campaigned to make female clothing more comfortable, which was a political as well as a practical objective, because comfortable clothes would allow women to compete with men in the workplace. Emilie Flöge recruited Klimt as a fellow couturier and together they created a collection of loose-fitting dresses, inspired by an unprepossessing reform movement favourite: the simple 'sack dress'.

Emilie modelled the collection in a series of outdoor photographs, taken by Klimt, that were later published in an arts and design magazine. The idea of modelling garments in a landscape was an innovation. One of these photographs, which was taken in the summer of 1906, could easily have been taken in the 1960s. Emilie is standing in front of some trees, her hair cunningly arranged to suggest casual disarray, looking down, her head turned slightly to the left. She seems to be wearing not one but several necklaces which suspend assorted baubles and beads. Her dress is long, with frilly sleeves, and patterned across the chest with interlocking triangles. She could be on her way to Woodstock.

Terms such as 'sack dress' suggest formlessness and asceticism; however, the Viennese reimagining of the basic shift was visually exciting and sexually provocative. It could be worn without a corset, which made it, paradoxically, more revealing. As Zweig pointed out, traditional Victorian encasements could completely obscure a woman's figure, but an intent observer could very easily get a sense of the physical reality beneath a loose-fitting 'chiton'. High fashion was introducing an additional sexual charge into society gatherings. When fabrics stretched to accommodate movement, they now did so against fleshy contours, rather than whalebone cages. Klimt's 1902 portrait of Emilie Flöge shows her wearing an exquisite reform-style dress decorated with split ovals – his symbol for the vulva.

We can be fairly certain that the nervy, intellectual women of Vienna who, like Adele Bloch-Bauer, regularly met to discuss art, literature and social justice were all wearing loose-fitting reform-style dresses.

The year before Adele's portrait was unveiled, Klimt met a seventeen-year-old artist who he invited to his studio. The young man brought some drawings and asked the master if, in his opinion, he possessed any talent. 'Much too much,' Klimt replied. The hopeful teenager was Egon Schiele, and during his short life Schiele would take Klimt's subtle allusions to nerves as the starting point of an artistic journey characterised by extremity. In Schiele's portraits it is as if the tension locked in Adele Bloch-Bauer's hands is released, and spreads through entire bodies. Schiele was given permission by a physician,

Erwin von Graff, to attend his clinic, and Schiele's friend, the painter and stage performer Erwin Osen, studied the inmates of the Am Steinhof asylum.

In many of his self-portraits, Schiele presents himself naked or partially clothed, with his limbs awkwardly twisted. These angular portraits resemble widely circulated photographs of hysterics taken when Charcot was medical director of the Salpêtrière. Sometimes, Schiele shows himself masturbating, which was in his day believed by many doctors to be a cause of insanity. The neuroscientist Eric Kandel has asserted that Schiele's self-portraits are not crude exhibitionism, but 'an attempt at full disclosure of the self, a self-analysis, a pictorial version of Freud's *The Interpretation of Dreams*'.

Schiele's ability to find concupiscence in sickness is truly extraordinary. His oeuvre is full of emaciated, cadaverous women – dressed minimally, usually in little more than a pair of stockings – whose seductive magnetism might pull admirers not into bed but into the grave. Yet even Schiele's most anorexic models, such as the skeletal vamp depicted in his 1910 pencil drawing *Nude in Front of the Mirror*, are indisputably alluring. Her eyes smoulder and her calculated posture is intended to arouse. Her hip is thrust to the side and her bony arm encourages the eye to drop down its length towards her buttocks and genitals. It is a way of standing that we have seen reproduced in the fashion sections of countless contemporary magazines – and it is still imitated by supermodels when they pause at the end of catwalks.

Schiele's 1914 *Crouching Blonde Nude with Extended Left Arm* shows a near naked woman on her knees. Nerves and the bestial overlap. Unlike Klimt, who alluded to Adele's reproductive potential with subtle symbols, Schiele forces us to confront Darwinian realities directly. The blonde's haunches swing as her weight is transferred to her left arm and she moves forward like

© Christie's Images/Bridgeman Images

a feline predator. Yet Schiele's atavistic subject is glamourised by luxurious tangles of pre-Raphaelite hair, red lips and black stockings. She is crawling out of prehistory – the dark cave of ancestral memory; however, Schiele's touches of glamour suggest that she is also emerging from the unconscious and into a dream. She is a fantasy figure whose disordered nerves have broken down her inhibitions.

According to Hermann Bahr, the only meaningful response to the modern age was nerve-art. In an essay published in 1891, he underscored his faith in neuroticism as a creative tonic: 'When nervousness becomes completely liberated and man, especially the artist, becomes entirely subordinate to the nerves, without regard for the rational and sensuous, then the lost joy will return to art.' He stresses his thesis with thumping repetitions of 'nerves, nerves, nerves'.

There were many talented writers living in Vienna who

shared Bahr's vision, but it was Peter Altenberg who became the most celebrated incarnation of nervous genius. Born Richard Engländer, the son of middle-class Jewish parents, he abandoned legal and medical studies and reinvented himself by combining the moniker of a girl he had loved in his youth with the name of a small town on the Danube. He was diagnosed with neurasthenia in his twenties, but his condition was never successfully treated, even though he visited several sanatoria and spent time in psychiatric institutions (where he unwisely bribed hospital porters to bring him large quantities of alcohol). Aspects of his mental illness were explored in his writing, and he called himself, with candid relish, the 'Fool of Vienna'. In one of his autobiographical pieces two young men invite him to join them for champagne. The first words out of Altenberg's mouth are 'Gentlemen, I am very ill.' He exaggerated his eccentricities and incorporated them into a round-the-clock 'performance' that exploited preconceptions of 'mad genius'. He cultivated a very distinctive appearance – pince-nez, enormous walrus moustache, check coat and cane – that made him eminently recognisable. Eventually, it became quite difficult to determine how much of his odd behaviour was attributable to nerves and how much was simply affectation. He lived in hotels, renounced underwear, and championed nudism – especially when prac-tised by women.

Altenberg's output consisted almost entirely of short works. He typically observed and recorded scenes from everyday life: drifters in a coffee house, a snatch of conversation, the 'aristo-cratically delicate hands' of a female cashier. He was, like Freud, a connoisseur of those things usually overlooked or ignored: 'For a long time now I have been judging people on the basis of *minute details*.' Inspired by the economy of postcard writing, he produced exquisite literary miniatures. Examples of his concise poetry were set to music by Alban Berg. Two of these 'songs'

were premiered in 1913 but the audience rioted. There were
calls for the composer to be locked up in Am Steinhof – where
Altenberg had already been admitted. It wasn't until 1952 that
Berg's *Five Songs on Picture Postcard Texts by Peter Altenberg* was
finally heard without interruption. Igor Stravinsky described it
as one of the most perfect compositions of the twentieth century.

Nerves, sex and celebrity are still closely connected in the
popular imagination. Exclusive rehab clinics may have replaced
the Grand Hotels of spa towns, but they essentially provide similar services for a similar clientele. And Schiele's brand of erotic
emaciation continues to exert a strong influence on fashion.
Even in a health-conscious world in which the consumption
of vitamins and weight training are commonplace, painfully
thin models twist their limbs and stare blankly into camera
lenses. Modern life is stressful; it strains the nerves and alters
appearances. Anxiety, depression, addiction and exhaustion
are the new normal. 'Heroin chic', a look promoted by major
fashion houses in the 1990s, glamourised drug abuse. The ideal
'grunge' model was skinny, angular and pale, with red lips and
dark pouches under her eyes. For the cover of his *Heroes* album,
David Bowie (an artist who incorporated elements of sexual
'transgression' into his stage act) was photographed imitating
a Schiele self-portrait. The Turner Prize-winning ceramicist
Grayson Perry has created a public persona around what was
once considered a sexual perversion – cross-dressing.

Human beings are animals who exist in social hierarchies.
And it is individuals at the top of social hierarchies who set
cultural agendas. As such, the Viennese preoccupation with
the allure of nerves was not a trivial phenomenon. It was a
glimpse of the future. A prophecy concerning the shape of the
modern mind.

Chapter 5

The Royal Road

Professionally and domestically, the final decade of the nineteenth century was the most important in Freud's life. He moved to a spacious apartment where he established what would become his fixed, daily routines. His clinical reputation grew. His friendship with Wilhelm Fliess intensified and stimulated a period of concentrated intellectual activity during which ideas were developed, rejected and replaced by superior ideas. He began work on a grand neuropsychological theory of mind which was then summarily cast aside. But by the turn of the century he had not only outlined the basic principles of psychoanalysis he had also published *The Interpretation of Dreams*, a book which is now widely regarded as his masterpiece.

Sigmund, Martha and their three children Mathilde, Martin and Oliver moved into Berggasse 19 in September 1891. It was a relatively new building and would be Freud's base for forty-seven years. Three more children followed: Ernst, Sophie and Anna. Although Martha had given birth to six children in eight years, it was Sigmund who named them. Mathilde, after Josef Breuer's wife; Martin, after Jean-Martin Charcot; Oliver, after Cromwell; Ernst, after Brücke; and Sophie and Anna, respectively, after the niece and daughter of Samuel Hammerschlag (Freud's old schoolmaster). Minna, Freud's sister-in-law, became part of the Freud household in the mid-1890s. Ignaz Schönberg, to whom she had been engaged, had died in 1886 after contracting tuberculosis – and Martha needed plenty of help. Like most middle-class families, the Freuds employed a cook (who was rarely seen out of the kitchen), a housemaid (to serve dinner and let in visitors), a governess (for the older children), a nanny (for the younger children) and a charwoman (to perform chores).

In his autobiography, Martin Freud wrote that when he was two years old he was woken up by an explosion. The cause was a gas supply problem affecting the watchmaker's apartment below. Martin saw light coming through the window, the nanny carrying a baby, and a 'Bedouin' standing in the doorway. The Bedouin asked 'Are the monkeys all right?' before being trans-formed into his father wearing a large white bath robe. The watchmaker, who must have had unusually quick reactions, survived the explosion by jumping out of a window. Freud, who had been seeing patients in his private quarters, took over the watchmaker's apartment in November 1896 to make more room for his family. It was in his downstairs study that he would eventually finish writing *The Interpretation of Dreams*.

Freud was a creature of habit. He began his working day at eight o'clock in the morning, usually with a couple of profes-sional visits. Then he saw more patients at home before breaking for lunch at one o'clock. All the family assembled at the dining table and waited for Freud to enter, after which he would take his seat at one end, facing Martha at the other end. Dishes were served by the maid: soup, meat and vegetables, followed by a sweet. Freud was exceedingly fond of artichokes and boiled beef, but he despised cauliflower, and he didn't really like chicken. Lunch was followed by a brisk walk around the ring road, which was sometimes shortened by a dash across the inner city to collect or deliver proofs. Being an enthusiastic walker, Freud owned two walking sticks, one for his daily walks and another for hiking. He also carried a folding magnifying glass. Freud saw patients again in the afternoon, ate an evening meal, and then went downstairs to write. Often he was still at his desk at two or three o'clock in the morning.

When Freud had finished writing, he would climb the stairs – 'several steps at a stride' – and make his way to bed. His ascent was recapitulated in a dream that he included in *The Interpretation of Dreams*. 'Very inadequately dressed, I am making my way from a ground-floor flat up the stairs to a higher floor . . . Suddenly I see a maid descending the stairs towards me . . . I feel ashamed and try to hurry.'

By the standards of his day, Freud would have been judged if not exactly handsome then attractive and distinguished. He was five foot seven inches, and had brown, greying hair and brown eyes. His beard, which had been quite full when he was younger, was tidier in middle age. He spoke in a measured, low voice, and was remarkably articulate. Even so, he had a habit of making small gestures that obviated the need to talk. When he shook hands, he pulled people closer. When conversing, his manner was a little reticent, yet his gaze was disturbingly direct. People felt that he could read their minds.

In the mid-1890s, a telephone was installed in Freud's apartment. He hated it. Indeed, he had a deep mistrust of all mechanical and electrical devices. He was also suspicious of bicycles and typewriters.

On Saturday nights he met with friends to play the four-hand card game *tarock*. He joined a Jewish lodge where he attended social and cultural events. Occasionally, he went to the theatre or the opera. Although Freud is sometimes characterised as a man who actively disliked music, this is almost certainly an exaggeration. He enjoyed Mozart and he once dreamed that he was standing in a train station singing an aria from *The Marriage of Figaro*. He also attended public lectures, most notably those given by Mark Twain. The famous American author, depressed after the death of his daughter, moved to Vienna in 1897 for a much-needed change of scene.

Freud's favourite pastime was collecting art objects. This avocation became immensely important to Freud, not only because he found antiquities aesthetically pleasing, but also because they were a source of inspiration. His books and essays are full of references to classical civilisation and archaeology. His first acquisition was in 1886 – a reproduction of a Roman bust of the Oceanid Clytie. He thought that it looked like Martha. Further purchases, one of which was a plaster copy of Michelangelo's *Dying Slave*, were made in December 1896. In due course he stopped buying replicas and amassed hundreds of authentic artefacts that he arranged on his desk and displayed in cabinets.

Every summer, Freud and his family embarked on an extended holiday. The family would usually leave ahead of him in May or June and Freud would follow at the end of July. After spending a few weeks together, Freud would journey (accompanied by his wife, brother or sister-in-law) to more distant destinations. He was always back at work in Vienna by mid-September.

Outwardly, Freud was a happy man, particularly when he was with his children. In their company he 'threw aside all his professional worries and was all laughter and contentment'. He amused them with fairy stories and ritual repetitions of the same jokes. He wasn't particularly involved in overseeing their education, but two adjoining studies in Berggasse 19 were equipped with maps, little desks, bookshelves and a trapeze hanging over a mattress in the doorway.

The decade that preceded the publication of *The Interpretation of Dreams* is biographically puzzling, because we are presented with two quite different Freuds. On the one hand there is the good-humoured, sociable family man, and on the other the neurotic, ambitious, introspective doctor (revealed in his letters to Wilhelm Fliess) who later admitted to feeling profoundly isolated. It is also possible that during this period Freud, the ostensible ideal husband, was emotionally overwrought because he was having a sexual relationship with his sister-in-law.

Minna Bernays had always been close to Freud. Their early correspondence contains playful expressions of affection and admiration. Unlike Martha, Minna was interested in Freud's work. Indeed, the first indication that Freud wanted to write a book about dreams appears in a letter to Minna. She was also witty and elegant. She liked music, collected cactuses and enjoyed playing cards. Freud addressed her using pet names. From 1897, Freud and Minna became travelling companions, and they were often away for weeks. On one occasion Martha had to send them a telegram demanding their return. Minna developed the unusual habit of calling herself 'Frau Professor Freud', a misappropriation of title that irritated Martha, but which she tolerated without complaint. In Berggasse 19, Minna was obliged to walk through Sigmund and Martha's bedroom to get to her own adjoining bedroom. These sleeping arrangements were very cosy – to say the least.

Gossip about the nature of Freud and Minna's relationship remained uncorroborated until 1957, which was when Carl Gustav Jung, by then Freud's estranged disciple, made an explosive revelation in an interview. Apparently, back in 1907, Minna had told him that Freud was in love with her and that she was feeling guilty about their assignations. Jung and Freud's friendship had ended so badly, Freudian loyalists viewed Jung's 'shocking' revelation as the final attempt of a bitter old man to slur his enemy. Less compelling evidence for the affair was subsequently collected by historians of psychoanalysis who discovered incriminating material in Freud's contemporaneous writings. Then, in 2006, an 1898 Swiss hotel register was found showing that Freud had booked himself and Minna into a double room for two nights as husband and wife. Superficially, this looks like conclusive proof. But posing as spouses might have been an unavoidable necessity. A prudish hotelier would have refused to accommodate an unmarried couple. Martha was aware that her husband and sister sometimes pretended to be espoused. It was never a secret.

Freud wrote about infidelity in his books. He supposed that its frequency demonstrated that social disapproval was not only ineffective, but also hypocritical. In his 1908 essay *'Civilized' Sexual Morality and Modern Nervous Illness*, he wrote: 'The "double standard" that applies to the men in our society is the plainest admission that society itself, which has laid down the rules, does not believe it possible to comply with them.' He also recognised that women, having been forced to submit more than men to the 'requirements of civilization', are likely to be proportionally more conflicted. They will experience greater stress created by the oppositional demands of sexual need and 'sense of duty'. While discussing these ideas, Freud said something startling: 'the cure for nervous illness arising from marriage would be marital unfaithfulness'. A little illicit sex might be 'medicinal'.

Freud's critics maintain that the evidence for his affair with Minna is overwhelming, and their charges have become increasingly dark. Minna is now alleged to have terminated a pregnancy and consequently suffered health problems. Loyalists describe such allegations as novelistic. The truth of the matter is that we can never know what really happened. How can we? It is certainly possible that Freud and Minna had a sexual relationship – they had ample opportunity – but whether they did or not probably matters less today than when Jung made his revelation in the 1950s. Attitudes have changed. There is no longer a need to assert, like Freud's early disciples, that he was a perfect human being with few flaws. Clearly, he had many flaws. Moreover, 'reputational damage' of this kind is seen as less consequential now. Intellectual achievements are not devalued because of adultery. The affair (if it did happen) is important only because it is likely to have affected Freud's mental state during the most creative period of his life.

On 23 October 1896 Freud's father, Jacob, died. Soon after, Freud started to experience a range of symptoms: breathlessness, mood swings and difficulty concentrating. He also experienced regret because he had often judged his father unkindly in the past. Yet only a year after his father's death, Freud was judging Jacob in the harshest possible terms. He suspected that Jacob had sexually molested his neurotic brother and several younger sisters. This was because at that time Freud believed that neurotic illness was attributable to sexual abuse in childhood; however, he quickly disowned the 'seduction theory'. It seemed increasingly implausible to him that so many parents and older siblings were molesting younger family members. Nevertheless, the troubling fact remained that most of his neurotic patients claimed they could remember being sexually abused. Freud's solution to this problem was to suggest that his patients were not recounting real memories, but fantasies. Freud did not deny the reality of sexual abuse. He just couldn't make it the basis of a universal theory. Freud's interest in fantasy and dreaming were complementary, insofar as they both reflected his increasing interest in the non-objective causes of neurotic illness.

In addition to making theoretical advances, Freud was also consolidating the essential details of the practice of psychoanalysis. As a neurologist, Freud would have had a daybed or divan (what we now incorrectly call a 'couch') in his office. He would have used his couch when physically examining patients, during hypnotic procedures and electrotherapy, and when practising his pressure technique. Much of his day-to-day practice would have involved ministering to recumbent patients, so it must have felt quite natural for him to ask his neurotic patients to lie down before he 'examined' their minds. The idea of using an otherwise standard piece of office furniture for psychotherapy might have first occurred to him in the preceding decade. His patient Anna von Lieben was so overweight that she found walking difficult and spent most of her time reclining on a divan.

Once Freud had started using a 'couch' for psychotherapy, he stopped sitting at the foot-end of the couch and repositioned himself at the head-end. Many years later he explained why this had been necessary. He had found that making eye contact with

Everett Collection/Bridgeman Images

supine women emboldened would-be seductresses. The couch that Freud used in Berggasse 19 was given to him as a present around 1890 by a patient, Madame Benvenisti. He used it for the rest of his life, and it can now be admired – covered with a Qashqai carpet – in London's Freud Museum.

Between 1892 and 1895, Freud developed the technique of 'free association'. Patients were told to say whatever came to mind and to resist the urge to censor thoughts and memories, even if those thoughts and memories seemed unimportant or nonsensical. The English translation of Freud's German term, *freier Einfall*, is somewhat misleading. Firstly, the German *Einfall* – literally a 'fall-in' – was intended to suggest something much closer to 'uncontrollable intrusion' than free association. Thus, relaxing mental control allows unconscious material to 'fall into' or interrupt the stream of consciousness. Secondly, the term 'free' suggests a degree of chance at odds with Freud's determinism. Ultimately, when free associating, the material that enters consciousness is *determined* by unconscious mechanisms.

Freud claimed that he had discovered free association by 'following an obscure intuition'. Ernest Jones thought otherwise. He thought that Freud had based free association on advice to aspirant writers given in an 1823 essay by the political philosopher and satirist Ludwig Börne. Börne had suggested that writers wishing to produce original work should jot down whatever entered their heads 'without any falsification or hypocrisy'. Freud was given the collected works of Ludwig Börne when he was fourteen years old, and they were the only books in his early library that he kept as an adult. When Freud visited the Père Lachaise cemetery in Paris, he searched for only two graves: one was the resting place of Heinrich Heine (a distant relative of his wife who was in fact buried in the Cimetière du Nord) and the other belonged to Ludwig Börne.

Like most doctors, Freud was aware that the intimate atmosphere of the consulting room could very easily become sexually charged. It wasn't unusual in the nineteenth century for female patients to confess that they were attracted to their physicians. Freud explained this phenomenon with reference to repressed sexual feelings. For example, a woman who had once repressed the urge to kiss an elegantly outfitted suitor might be overcome with a desire to kiss her well-attired doctor. Freud called this kind of emotional displacement 'transference'. Over time, he realised that transferences could be discussed and used to demonstrate the effect of past relationships on present relationships. The concept of transference didn't feature greatly in Freud's early writings. Indeed, when he reflected on how he had analysed Ida Bauer – the case study we now know as Dora – he chastised himself for not paying enough attention to her transferences. Analysing transferences became increasingly central to the practice of psychoanalysis.

By the end of the 1890s, Freud had developed his essential practice procedures and he had invented a name to describe what he was doing. He ended the decade, the most significant and transformative in his life, with the publication of his magnum opus, *The Interpretation of Dreams*, in which he revealed how the chaotic narrative of dreams could be made meaningful. He famously called dream interpretation the 'via regia, the royal road to knowledge of the unconscious in the life of the mind'.

Freud said that he became interested in dreams because they were frequently described by his free-associating patients; however, when he was a young man, he kept a dream diary and wondered whether dreams could predict the future. Unfortunately, these notebooks have been lost. His mature interest in dreams began around 1894. In 1895, he attempted to develop a model of the mind based on his knowledge of the nervous system. His *Project for a Scientific Psychology* was abandoned, but while he was writing it he supposed that dreams might be nocturnal hallucinations produced by residues of 'energy' in an otherwise inactive brain. It was also around this time that Freud became interested again in his own dreams. After his father's death (and the onset of what he called his 'little hysteria') he decided that he needed to see a psychoanalyst. The problem, however, was that he was the only one. Freud's solution was to put himself on the couch and much of his self-analysis was achieved by interpreting his own dreams, many of which are reported in *The Interpretation of Dreams*.

Freud's first complete analysis of one of his own dreams was accomplished on Wednesday 24 July 1895. The method he employed had evolved through repeated attempts to analyse both his dreams and those of his patients. Freud was holidaying with his family at Schloss Bellevue, a hotel situated in the hills close to Vienna. His dream, now known as the dream of Irma's injection, was prompted by a perceived reproach (delivered by a visiting colleague and friend) concerning the unsuccessful treatment of one of his patients. Freud believed that his dream represented a wish: that Irma's current condition – 'not entirely well' – was neither his fault nor his responsibility. This interpretation confirmed a pre-existing suspicion that dreams are motivated by wishes.

Irma (in the dream) was in fact Emma Eckstein, a young 'hysteric' with gastric problems and painful periods. In the mid-1890s Freud was still enthusiastic about Wilhelm Fliess's theories linking hysteria to nasal pathology. In 1894, Freud had invited Fliess to travel from Berlin to operate on Emma's nose. Two weeks after the operation, Emma's nose started to hurt, suppurate and produce a foul odour. A piece of bone came loose and she started to bleed. The cause of Emma's symptoms was a half-metre strip of gauze that Fliess had neglected to remove after operating on the turbinate bones. When the gauze was removed the patient haemorrhaged. For several weeks it was unclear whether Emma would survive. Remarkably, neither Emma nor her family blamed Freud for recommending Fliess (or Fliess for his appalling incompetence). Emma remained in Freud's care and eventually became his first student of psychoanalysis. After interpreting the dream of Irma's injection, Freud asked Fliess whether he thought his achievement – the unlocking of the secret of dreams – would ever be commemorated with a marble tablet. Many years later, while dining with Ernest Jones at the Bellevue restaurant, the marble tablet was discussed again. A commemorative plate was finally unveiled at the Bellevue in 1977: 'In this house on July 24, 1895, the secret of dreams was revealed to Dr. Sigm. Freud.'

German readers in Freud's day would have been disconcerted by his choice of title: *Die Traumdeutung*. It would have reminded them of astrology (*Sterndeutung*) and the cheap 'dream books' (containing 'keys' to dreams) that were consumed by gullible members of the public. *Deutung des Traums*, which corresponds with the original English translation by James Strachey, would have sounded more respectable. One can only assume that it was Freud's intention to be provocative.

Freud's preface to *The Interpretation of Dreams* was preceded by an epigraph from Virgil's *Aeneid*: 'If I cannot bend the higher powers, I will move the infernal regions.' The original Latin can be translated in a variety of ways; however, Freud's intention was that the epigraph should presage his conclusion that in dreams, desires that are frustrated by the upper, censorious levels of the mind are forced to find satisfaction in the netherworld of the unconscious. The epigraph also invites us to consider the perilous nature of Freud's endeavour. He was necessarily exposing himself to the 'infernal' contents of the unconscious, both directly and indirectly, through self-analysis and by analysing his patients' dreams. We are being promised an epic. Many years later, reflecting on his achievement, Freud wrote in the preface to the third (revised) English edition: 'Insight such as this falls to one's lot but once in a lifetime.' *The Interpretation of Dreams* is groundbreakingly modern, insofar as it subverts classical hero-ism. Freud's descent into the underworld, unlike that of Virgil's Aeneas, doesn't begin in a mysterious cave. It begins in a hotel.

Freud's assertion, that every dream is an attempt to fulfil a wish, applies to all dreams, even anxiety dreams and night-mares. A good example of this is the dream of the burning child. A father was lying on his bed with an unobstructed view into the next room. Through the doorway he could see candles around the body of his dead child and an old man engaged to sit and pray as part of a bedside vigil. The father went to sleep and dreamed that his child was pulling his arm and whispering, 'Father, can't you see I'm burning?' The father woke up and became aware of a flickering light. He discovered that the old man had fallen asleep, a candle had fallen on to his child's bed, and the sheets were on fire. There are some pedestrian reasons (such as sensory stimulation) that can explain why the fire might have encouraged the father's sleeping brain to produce this particular dream. These, Freud readily admits; however, in addition, he points out that in this dream the dead child is alive again. Thus, a wish was fulfilled.

Pure wish fulfilment dreams need no interpretation because the motive is obvious. A person who is hungry might dream of attending a banquet. However, the relationship between motive and appearances can be obscure. Complex or confus-ing dreams require psychoanalytic interpretation to reveal the underlying wish.

Freud distinguished between the manifest and latent con-tent of dreams. The manifest content is what is remembered on waking: locations, people, narrative, thoughts and feel-ings. These might at first seem nonsensical, but successful interpretation of these elements will reveal a deeper, true meaning – the latent content. Freud suggested that the manifest content is like a hieroglyphic script that must be translated, character by character, to be fully understood.

Freud observed that the manifest content of dreams is frequently linked with impressions from the previous day. These daily residues will not produce a dream, however, unless they are organised by a wish. He suggested that such residues are a little like an entrepreneur in search of capital for an enterprise. If the enterprise in this analogy is the dream, then the capital is an unconscious wish. Even if the entrepreneur has an excellent idea, the enterprise will not be launched without the necessary investment. Ultimately, many unconscious wishes can be connected to (or are prefigured by) wishes first experienced in childhood. Thus, a dream can be motivated by current wishes, past wishes, or a combination of the two.

Dreams, Freud suggested, are the guardians of sleep. The manifest content of a dream is obscure for a purpose. It disguises underlying wishes which, if explicitly fulfilled in a dream, might jolt sleepers wide awake. Many of our wishes are disturbing, particularly those that have been repressed. They are likely to offend or shock our civilised sensibilities, even when we are slumbering. Dreams, like every aspect of mental life described by Freud, are overdetermined and highly complex. Any single dream can be analysed at different levels, and each of these levels might conceal a different wish. However, the deeper one descends, the more likely it is that one will encounter imagery that represents the fulfilment of infantile wishes, and at the very lowest levels, wishes that resemble primal appetites more closely than wants. This is the principal reason why Freud supposed that ultimately, almost all dreams are sexually motivated.

A dream, like a neurotic symptom, is a compromise. Repressed and sometimes disturbing wishes find easy expression when we are asleep, and mechanisms come into play that disguise wishes in order to preserve sleep. The manifest content is suspended between the acceptable and the unacceptable.

The means by which the latent content of a dream is disguised Freud termed the 'dream work'. He identified several mechanisms. Condensation or 'compression' occurs when two or more images are combined without loss of meaning or implication. A figure might appear, for example, who is simultaneously the sleeper's mother and wife. Displacement occurs when meanings or emotions that belong to one dream element or memory are transferred to another dream element. Thus, an ostensibly benign scene, such as a walk in the park, might be imbued with inexplicable feelings of sadness that actually belong to an unconscious memory of loss. Representation is a mechanism that modifies unconscious thoughts so that they can be realised in visual, verbal and conceptual forms. For example, a young man wishing to oppose his father might dream that he is an officer sitting opposite an emperor. The dream work also makes use of symbols; a symbol isn't created during a dream, but rather 'borrowed', because it already exists in the unconscious. Freud's work has become strongly associated with sexual symbolism. He suggested, for example, that 'sharp weapons' represent the male member and boxes represent the female genitalia. However, it should be noted that Freud issued 'an emphatic warning against overrating the importance of symbols'. They are only instructive if they can be meaningfully contextualised. After the latent content of a dream has been translated into the manifest content, the dream narrative might be subject to secondary revision. The logical part of the mind is still functioning, and it attempts to make the dream more intelligible. It acts like a newspaper editor making last-minute changes to an article before publication.

The Interpretation of Dreams contains Freud's first published

account of how the emotional development of children recapitulates the plot of Sophocles' play *Oedipus Rex*. Oedipus, the King
of Thebes, gradually learns, step by painful step, in a drama that
unfolds with successive revelations like psychoanalysis itself,
that he has murdered his father and is married to his mother.
Freud suggested that desire to possess the opposite-sex parent
and rivalrous feelings towards the same-sex parent are part
of normal sexual development. Parents serve as prototypes
for lovers. This is supported, Freud believed, by the relatively
common phenomenon of children declaring that they intend
to marry their mothers or fathers when they have 'grown up'.
Repressed vestiges of infantile wishes to possess the opposite-
sex parent can influence the content of dreams. Somewhat
overconfidently, Freud declared: 'The dream of having sexual
intercourse with one's mother is ... a dream that many men
share – and recount in outraged amazement.' A footnote was
added to this section in 1914: 'None of the findings of psychoanalytic research has provoked such embittered denials, such
fierce opposition – or such amusing contortions – on the part
of critics as this indication of the childhood impulses towards
incest which persist in the unconscious.' Little has changed since
1914. Today, the Oedipus complex remains the most controversial precept of psychoanalysis.

Freud's technique for interpreting dreams was very straightforward. When a patient recounted a dream, Freud would isolate
thoughts, feelings, conversations and images, and use each of
these elements as a starting point for exploratory discussions
and free association. Repressed material was then likely to 'fall
in' to the flow of the patient's speech. Attending a play during
a dream might be associated with a memory of seeing a play
in real life called 'Step by Step'. Step by step suggests a ladder,
which Freud believed was a symbol for sexual intercourse. A
ladder is ascended 'in rhythmic stages, coupled with increasing

shortness of breath'; 'a person attains a high point' and is quickly 'back down' again. Thus, by determining associative links, Freud worked out the latent content from the manifest content.

The method Freud employed to interpret dreams was original, but his general theory of dreams and dreaming was anticipated by many physicians and psychologists. For example, in 1893, the English psychologist James Sully suggested that repressed desires 'work themselves out' the next night. Dreams are revealing, and 'bring up from the depths of our subconscious life the primal, instinctive impulses'. A dream might at first appear to be 'balderdash', but it is 'like some letter in cipher' that if carefully examined will yield a 'serious, intelligible message'. Freud acknowledged Sully, but only in the fourth edition of *The Interpretation of Dreams*, which was published in 1914. In 1861, the psychiatrist Wilhelm Griesinger suggested that dreams frequently represent 'the imaginary fulfilment of wishes'. Many ideas that are now attributed to Freud were not his. Even so, *The Interpretation of Dreams* was uniquely detailed, complex and textured. Freud's theory is underpinned by 'scientific' concepts such as associative memory, preconscious processing and evolved drives, and these concepts are skilfully integrated. Freud was exceptionally adept at amalgamating ideas and his dream theory is impressive beyond the sum of its parts. In fact, it is an astonishing synthesis.

Freud might have claimed dreaming as a phenomenon fit for scientific study, but his dream theory is not robustly scientific. Truly scientific theories must be testable. The core of Freud's dream theory is almost impossible to test because his instructions for interpreting dreams allow considerable latitude with respect to subjective judgement. When is a Zeppelin in a dream an airship rather than a disguised penis? Detailed knowledge of the dreamer and the dreamer's circumstances might help to determine the answer to such a question, but definite proof – supporting one or other possibility – will always be elusive. Even more problematic is that Freud posits the operation of mechanisms that allow interpretations to be revised. For example, he suggests that if a dream is proving difficult to interpret, 'one can try reversing specific portions of its manifest content, whereupon everything, quite often, will become clear immediately'. Permission to adopt a contraposition allows psychoanalysts so much licence, desired results are almost guaranteed.

The philosopher Ludwig Wittgenstein found Freud's dream theory logically inconsistent. How can a wish be fulfilled in a dream if the dreamer isn't aware of having had that wish in the first place? And how can a symbol function as a symbol if the dreamer doesn't know what it is supposed to be symbolising? The simple answer to these questions is that unconscious knowledge, even if confined in the unconscious, can still influence conscious mental events. As soon as the mind is divided, contradictions are easily accommodated.

Modern dream theories tend to focus on the function of dreams. In other words, they seek to answer the question: Why do we dream? Dreams might help us to 'dissolve' unpleasant emotions which would otherwise overwhelm us; they might consolidate and reconsolidate memories, or offer us opportunities to rehearse coping in simulated, threatening situations; they might expedite problem solving and promote creativity. A representative example of a contemporary account of dreaming is the NEXTUP (Network Exploration to Understand Possibilities) model, initially developed by Robert Stickgold and later by Antonio Zadra. They propose that 'dreaming is a unique form of sleep-dependent memory processing that extracts new knowledge from existing memories through the discovery and strengthening of previously unexplored weak associations'. The sleeping brain begins with a new memory and searches for other weakly associated memories that are then combined in a dream narrative. The function of this narrative is to explore unusual associations. Thus, 'novel, creative, insightful, and useful associations [are] discovered and displayed in our dreams'. Freud's answer to the question of why we dream is that we dream to protect sleep. He is interested in answering supplementary questions concerning the meaning of dreams because his theory suggests that most dreams are encrypted.

Curiously, the modern 'dream theory' most strongly associated with opposition to Freud is neither modern nor, strictly speaking, a theory. Even in Freud's day there were those who believed that dreams are produced by lingering activity in the sleeping brain. Indeed, Freud was one of them for a while. He referred to this notion as 'dreams are froth'. During the 1970s new physiological evidence appeared to confirm the dreams-as-froth approach and confidence in Freud's theory was undermined. If dreams are the result of disorganised, low-grade brain activity then they can only ever be meaningless. But if dreams *are* neurological froth, then patterns of brain activity associated with dreaming should be random. Contemporary research has proved otherwise. Since the invention of brain-scanning technology, stable patterns of activation have been identified. These relate to visual perception, initiating movement, autobiographical memory and emotion. At the same time, regions controlling rational thought are deactivated. A less sophisticated but even more powerful refutation of 'dreams as froth' is the well-documented phenomenon of recurring dreams. Once again, if dreams are truly random then recurring dreams should be exceptionally rare, rather than relatively common.

Freud's observation that dreams incorporate memories from the previous day has gained some experimental support. Subjects taught how to play the computer game Tetris – which involves falling blocks – experience game-related imagery in dreams sampled just after the onset of sleep. The so-called Tetris

effect is robust and can be detected even when subjects are suffering from amnesia: amnesic subjects who have no memory of
playing the game will still report seeing Tetris-related imagery
in their dreams. Regardless of the Tetris effect, the existence of
Freudian 'daily residues' remains contentious and real incidents
are probably not repeated in dreams to the extent that Freud
suggested; however, there are marked emotional continuities.
Emotions felt during the day certainly *do* seem to shade the
affective 'tone' of dreams that occur the following night.

The idea that repressed material returns in dreams has fared
better. Sleep researchers have found convincing evidence for
a dream rebound effect. If a particular thought is suppressed
prior to sleep it is likely to bounce back in a dream and the
effect is stronger if the thought is unpleasant; however, there is
no evidence to suggest that these thoughts are transformed or
disguised.

Freud's suggestion that dreams contain symbolic (or at least
metaphorical) representations is difficult to demonstrate experimentally. There is, however, abundant anecdotal evidence.
Anxiety dreams are frequently transparent in this respect. A
dream of being naked in front of an audience might be readily
connected with worries about being 'exposed' as inadequate
or ill prepared. Many famous scientists and artists have made
breakthroughs after being inspired by metaphorical representations in dreams. Friedrich August Kekulé discovered
the benzene ring after seeing a snake seizing its own tail in a
dream; Albert Einstein gained insights into relativistic physics
during a dream in which he was descending a mountain in a sled
and observing the stars; Niels Bohr recognised a fundamental
principle of quantum mechanics after having a dream about a
horse race.

It is certainly the case that we dream about things that we
desire. Wanting and dreaming are associated in everyday

language. We follow our dreams and hope that our dreams will come true. In addition, problem-solving dreams – of the kind reported by Kekulé, Einstein and Bohr – are clearly the outcome of 'wishing' for a solution. But these kinds of wishes aren't forbidden or repressed. Quite the contrary. After the First World War, even Freud began to doubt the propriety of wish fulfilment. He came to accept that some bad dreams might have nothing to do with repressed wishes and a great deal more to do with traumatic experiences. Contemporary sleep researchers like Zadra and Stickgold agree that dreams can be 'driven' by repressed desire, but only rarely. Mark Solms, however, has pointed out that 'wishing' might be subserved by the mesocortical-mesolimbic dopamine circuitry of the brain. This circuit has been variously called the brain's 'reward', 'wanting' and 'seeking' system. Solms concludes: 'It is also the circuit that drives dreaming.'

If, when we dream, the rational and largely inhibitory areas of the cortex become less active and subcortical structures become more active, then one would expect dreams to be shaped – in part, but consistently – by basic instincts and urges, as Freud suggests. Animals rehearse predatory behaviours in dreams. Cats that have had the neural fibres that normally suppress movement during dreams surgically cut will stalk, pounce and act out a 'kill' while remaining asleep. Similarly, humans have a very high incidence of violent dreams or dreams that involve attempting to escape from an aggressor. Sexual dreams are also very common. Men have elevated levels of testosterone, become erect, and sometimes ejaculate while dreaming. Galen described erections during sleep in the first century. Women exhibit clitoral swelling when they dream and roughly a third of women have nocturnal orgasms.

In sum, support for the various elements of Freud's dream theory is inconsistent and the central feature – interpretation of the manifest content – is essentially untestable. This does not, however, mean that Freud was necessarily wrong. It can be argued that conventional scientific methods (and measures) are simply ill suited to the task of proving Freud's dream theory. Psychoanalysts have always maintained that the appropriate test of Freud's dream theory is psychoanalysis. Unless one spends hours and hours discussing dreams with patients one will never become acquainted with the numerous and subtle proofs that arise from the process. In addition, neuroscientists have made increasingly favourable judgements about Freud's dream theory in recent years. In 2019, Sidarta Ribeiro concluded: 'The Freudian proposition that desire is the motor of dreams is much more factual than its critics would acknowledge.' Commenting on Solms – and contradicting traditional, received opinion – he added: 'The involvement of the dopaminergic reward system' demonstrates that 'psychoanalytic theory is testable, definitely'.

Freud continued revising *The Interpretation of Dreams* for much of the rest of his life. In total there were eight editions, and the final version was published in 1929. When asked which book among his writings was his favourite, Freud nominated two: *Three Essays on the Theory of Sexuality* and *The Interpretation of Dreams*. He couldn't choose between them. This is curious, because dream interpretation became less central to the practice of psychoanalysis in Freud's later years. He became more interested in how patients resist psychoanalytic insights and the role of transferences.

Why, then, was Freud so proud of *The Interpretation of Dreams*? And why is it his best-known work? How has it come about that a rambling nineteenth-century medical treatise can still be purchased in most high-street bookshops?

The Interpretation of Dreams is not only a medical treatise, it is also a work of literature. Unfortunately, many readers never get to discover its literary merits because they abandon the book early on, discouraged by its turgid introductory chapters. Read as a literary work, *The Interpretation of Dreams* is so unique that it creates its own hybrid genre. It is simultaneously a work of science and autobiography, a travelogue of the unconscious, a meditation on the human condition and a collection of short stories told in the language of dreams. Alongside Marcel Proust's *À la Recherche du Temps Perdu* and James Joyce's *Ulysses*, it completes a trilogy of modernist masterpieces all of which, in their different ways, succeed as explorations of mental life. In fact, it is possible to read *The Interpretation of Dreams* as a first-person, experimental novel; a book about a late nineteenth-century bourgeois doctor's obsessive search for the solution to an ancient mystery. His single-mindedness is vaguely reminiscent of Ahab's obstinate pursuit of the great white whale in *Moby Dick*. As the quest proceeds, we intermittently slip into the world of dreams – dreams that preserve some fascinating historical trivia. Where else could you find out that Viennese sex workers tended to wear earrings with blue stones?

Freud is remarkably candid about his autobiographical dreams. He once dreamed that he was riding a horse. In reality, he had only ridden a horse once in his life and he hadn't enjoyed it at all. Freud explains that his dream was triggered by a painful stimulus. He had developed a boil at the base of his scrotum that had grown 'as large as an apple'. Indefatigably industrious, he still put in 'a hard day's work'. The dream fulfils a wish, because in the dream, Freud was riding as if the boil didn't exist. Given that riding with a scrotal boil the size of an apple would have been unimaginably painful, the dream was the ultimate negation of his suffering. Freud's willingness to discuss an embarrassing physical problem is significant because it reflects his complete engagement with corporeality. He never shies away from embodiment – the first condition of being human. He never attempts to minimise or conceal the awkwardness and indignity of having a body that excretes waste, leaks fluids and is vulnerable to disease.

Many authors had written about dreams before Freud, but none of them in quite the same way. When we read Freud's summaries, we experience a frisson of recognition. We know this dreamworld because we have been there. Unlike the fantastic and exotic dreamworlds of the Romantics, Freud's dreamworld is very familiar. It has sitting rooms, busy streets, train stations, theatres and restaurants – all the trappings of modern life. And Freud, better than any of his predecessors, really captures the atmosphere and peculiarity of dreams; the way in which odd things happen but are accepted as normal, or everyday scenes are imbued with a sense of terror. We recognise the dissociations and the disjointed narratives, the way in which single locations can somehow be two places at once – the impossible paradoxes, the magical realism. Freud also records dreams that contain some wonderfully uncanny images. When he was six or seven, he had an anxiety dream that he analysed some thirty-seven years later: his mother asleep, being carried by people with bird beaks – sparrowhawk gods from an Egyptian tomb relief – and laid upon a bed. This brief dream, little more than a fragment, was charged with so much power that young Freud woke crying and screaming before rushing to wake his parents.

Occasionally, there is humour. One of Freud's patients revealed that he had dreamed of a friend grabbing his penis – a dream that could be traced back to a childhood memory. At the age of twelve, the patient was visiting a bedridden friend who accidentally exposed himself while changing position. For reasons that remain obscure, the patient reciprocated by exposing himself and then grabbing his friend's penis. The friend, understandably speechless, assumed a look of indignation that encouraged his visitor to release his grip. Freud, comically deadpan, explains that this dream demonstrates the class of transformations that involve opposites. The original scene was repeated in the dream twenty-three years later but with roles reversed.

The pleasure of recognition is heightened when Freud describes typical dreams – for example, being naked in public, not being able to move, flying, or sitting an examination. These familiar dream scenarios suggest significant underlying commonalities that connect us, not only to the citizens of fin de siècle Vienna but to all of humanity. Indeed, Freud supposed that in addition to mundane commonalities, we share universal experiences, such as being born, that are also represented in dreams. One of his complete and elegantly compressed transcriptions of a birth dream has the quality of haiku poetry: *In her summer holidays on Lake —— she plunges into the dark water at the point where the pale moon is reflected in the surface.* Freud is even prepared to consider the possibility that dreams connect us to a collective ancestral past: 'we are then promised a glimpse into phylogenetic childhood, into the development of the human race, of which that of the individual is in fact an abbreviated replay shaped by the accidents of life'. By analysing dreams, we can obtain knowledge of 'archaic inheritance, what is innate in man's mind'. Freud concludes that psychoanalysis is unique among the sciences, as it has at its disposal the means of reconstructing 'the earliest, most shadowy phases of the dawn of mankind'. This is intoxicating speculation. If we excavate our dreams, to the lowest level, we will find the remains of our ancestors. Freud's evolutionary psychology comes perilously close to mysticism: 'Every dream has at least one point where it eludes explanation – a sort of umbilicus linking it to the unknown.'

Ernest Jones informs us that six hundred copies of *The Interpretation of Dreams* were printed, and eight years elapsed before all of them were sold. Twenty-three copies were sold in the first six weeks and 228 over the next two years. Freud was paid 522.40 gulden – the equivalent of £41 16s in Jones's time. 'Seldom', Jones laments, 'has an important book produced no echo whatever.' Once again, Jones is exaggerating the degree to which Freud's intellectual accomplishments were overlooked. *The Interpretation of Dreams* was written for a small, professional readership. Sales figures may have been disappointing, but they were not catastrophic. Busy colleagues with little time to spare would have probably opted to read Freud's excellent precis – *On Dreams* – rather than his weighty tome.

Irrespective of initial sales figures, *The Interpretation of Dreams* gradually reached more and more readers. Like its predecessor, *Studies in Hysteria*, it was admired, not only by neurologists and psychiatrists but by individuals working in the arts.

Writers responded to *The Interpretation of Dreams* by either including dreams in their novels or, more interestingly, depicting dream-like realities. Franz Kafka is perhaps the pre-eminent example of the latter. His oddly dissociated characters find themselves in disorientating and disturbing situations that we now describe as Kafkaesque. Yet the terms 'Kafkaesque' and 'Freudian' (when applied to dreams) are almost interchangeable. Novels set within dreams or in worlds that have become dream-like are now a recognisable literary genre; authors such as Hermann Hesse, Anna Kavan, Angela Carter, Kobo Abe, Kazuo Ishiguro, Haruki Murakami and Vladimir Sorokin have all produced outstanding examples. Maurice Sendak's celebrated children's book *Where the Wild Things Are* is about a boy who is sent to bed early without his supper and whose bedroom is magically transformed into a landscape populated by strange beasts. Infantile rage is 'worked through' in a dream – and consequently survived. Sendak was in analysis – his partner was an analyst – and he counted psychoanalysts among his closest friends. Although stories have always had morals and underlying purposes (as in fairy tales and fables), the explicit requirement of codebreaking is very much a post-Freudian, modern phenomenon. We are being asked to read novels in a novel way.

J. G. Ballard, the most modern of modern writers, said that his characters follow the logic of their dreams: 'That's what my fiction is all about: people following their obsessions and their private mythologies to the end, whatever the cost.' Acknowledging Freud's influence, he added: 'Well, I've always thought of Freud really as a great novelist.'

In 1909, the Viennese composer Arnold Schoenberg completed a nightmarish monodrama (an opera for one singer) titled *Erwartung*. A woman wanders through a dark wood and finds the body of her lover. Yet, we cannot help but suspect that she is the murderer. The libretto was written by the poet and medical student Marie Pappenheim, who was possibly related to Bertha Pappenheim (the patient Breuer called Anna O in *Studies in Hysteria*). Schoenberg described the text as an 'anxiety dream', and it is easy to construe the libretto as words spoken by a patient on Freud's couch. The concept of an opera that is effectively set in the unconscious was so revolutionary that it forced Schoenberg to explore an entirely new approach to composition. No themes are repeated, so the listener is deprived of any musical 'landmarks'. The listener is constantly moving forward into unknown territory. The Freudian dreamworld continued to inspire composers, even those eager for audiences to leave theatres whistling memorable tunes. The hit musical *Lady in the Dark*, by Kurt Weill and Ira Gershwin, is divided into three acts titled 'Glamour Dream', 'Wedding Dream' and 'Circus Dream'.

After the First World War, artists associated with the surrealist movement specialised in producing dreamscapes. Indeed, from the 1920s and 1930s paintings such as René Magritte's *The Difficult Crossing* and Salvador Dalí's *The Persistence of Memory* became emblematic of the unconscious. But the surrealist vision

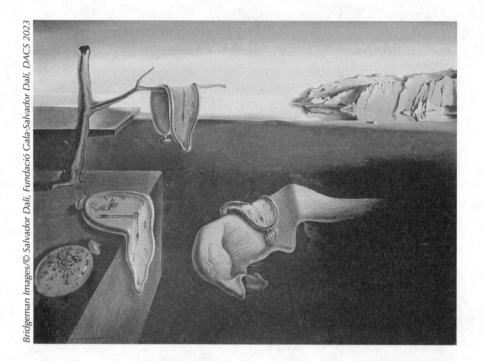

of the unconscious is essentially Freud's vision. *The Interpretation of Dreams* was, in many respects, the original surrealist manifesto, pre-dating André Breton's by over twenty years.

The cinematic potential of the Freudian dreamworld was swiftly realised by film makers. Not only do early 'German' expressionist films explore Freudian themes, but the techniques employed by directors such as Fritz Lang and Robert Wiene resemble Freudian 'dream work'. Décor, lighting and symbols – that is, the manifest content of the film – frequently allude to a deeper, latent content. Alfred Hitchcock's psychoanalytic thriller *Spellbound* includes a dream sequence designed by Salvador Dalí. Since then, dream sequences – and specifically Freudian dream sequences – have become a standard feature of film and television. We no longer require visual and auditory cues to signal departures from reality. When we see dream-like imagery it is automatically assumed to be interpretable. The music video that accompanied rap artist Childish Gambino's

2018 song 'This Is America' was immediately understood to be 'symbolic' by an internet audience of millions, prompting a worldwide debate concerning its deeper meanings. The video ends with one of the most common nightmare scenarios – the protagonist being chased.

Attempting to evaluate the significance of *The Interpretation of Dreams* is instructive, because the exercise reveals something very interesting about Freud's intellectual legacy. Freud's 'dream book' was ostensibly written for doctors. Its objectives were precise and narrow. Yet it is consequential beyond its stated ambitions, and this is true of psychoanalysis in general. Freud set out to develop a medical specialism but succeeded in producing a complex system of thought, a new way of understanding the mind, relationships, history and culture.

Even Freud's fiercest critics will grudgingly refer to Freud's dream theory as ingenious. For sceptics, it is perhaps comparable to a fourteenth-century orrery, which reproduces the motions of the planets inaccurately but can still be appreciated on its own terms as an intricate, well-crafted mechanism.

Chapter 6

Dora

On 31 December 1900, one of Freud's patients, an eighteen-year-old woman called Ida Bauer, began her treatment session with a surprising question: 'Doctor, did you know that today is the last time I'll be coming here?'

Freud's response was measured: 'I couldn't have known. You haven't said so before.'

'Yes,' Ida agreed. 'I'd decided to stick it out until the New Year, but I'm not going to wait any longer to be cured.' After eleven weeks of psychoanalysis, she was clearly unimpressed by both Freud and his method.

'You are free to leave at any time,' Freud reminded his patient. Then he added, 'But for today, let's continue with our work. When did you reach this decision?'

'Fourteen days ago. I think.'

Fourteen days sounded to Freud like the standard period of notice usually given before leaving a job.

They continued talking in much the same way as they had on previous occasions. The session was very productive. As the end approached, Freud adopted a manner reminiscent of a detective revealing a murderer's motive on the final pages of a crime novel. 'So, you must have been bitterly disappointed when your accusation failed to provoke renewed advances from Herr Zellenka, but instead only denials and slanders. You will agree, that nothing makes you so angry as when people think that you simply imagined the scene by the lake. I know now – and this is what you don't want to be reminded of – that Herr Zellenka's declaration of love was serious, and he wouldn't have stopped declaring his love until you had married him.'

Freud was expecting Ida to respond with a blunt contradiction. He had grown used to her prickly personality and waspish remarks. Instead, she said nothing. His words had moved her. Ida swung her legs off the couch and stood up. Freud informs us that she 'said goodbye as sweetly as anything, with warmest wishes for the New Year and – never came back'. Although fifteen months later she *did* return. But only to make a point.

After Freud had been dismissed by Ida, he immediately started work on her case study. It was originally titled *Dream and Hysteria* but was translated into English as *Fragment of an Analysis of Hysteria (Dora)*. Dora was the name Freud chose to disguise Ida's true identity, which remained a well-kept secret until 1978. Ida's case study was written from memory. Freud was reputed to have an uncanny ability to remember what was said during treatment sessions; however, he admitted that some of his dialogue should be regarded as dependable rather than faithful. Which invites the question: to what extent can we really depend on an account that lacks fidelity? The case study was published in 1905, five years after Ida discontinued her therapy, and three years after her final meeting with Freud.

For loyal Freudians, *Fragments of an Analysis of Hysteria* is an ingenious and insightful inquiry into the mental life of a young woman. Ernest Jones thought it was a thing of beauty. But for Freud's critics, it is nothing less than an abomination, an ill-judged vanity project that exposes his worst personal flaws and the perversity of psychoanalytic thinking. There is no other work in the Freudian canon that divides opinion so strongly – and for good reason. *Fragments of an Analysis of Hysteria* is often described as Victorian melodrama, but today, its readers are more likely to be reminded of a modern psychological thriller, the kind that probes the dark undercurrents of family life. It is a disturbing exploration of what happens when the thin veneer of bourgeois respectability cracks and primitive desires become too strong to control. As usual, Freud is completely aware of the literary qualities of his material. So much so, he expresses faint irritation that, unlike a writer working on a novella, he is obliged to document a clinical reality which complicates his protagonist's motivation.

Ida was born in 1882, on the same street where she would one day attend her treatment sessions with Freud. She was the daughter of Filipp Bauer and Katherina Gerber, Bohemian Jews who, like Freud, were brought to Vienna by parents who wanted a better life. Filipp became a successful businessman and acquired several textile mills located in the north-western regions of the empire. In 1888, Filipp moved his family – Katherina, Ida and her brother Otto (a precocious boy destined to be a leading Marxist politician) – to the Tyrolean spa town of Meran. Filipp was suffering from tuberculosis and Meran was renowned for its tubercular cures. From the age of six, Ida nursed her father and they became very close. Unfortunately, Filipp's recuperation was mired by setbacks. He was already blind in one eye, so when the retina of his functioning eye became detached, blindness seemed inevitable; however, within a matter of months his sight was miraculously (if incompletely) restored. Two years later he experienced an episode of confusion and paralysis caused by meningeal inflammation – a delayed consequence, like blindness, of having contracted syphilis in his youth.

Filipp and Katherina Bauer became acquainted with another Jewish couple: Johann 'Hans' Zellenka, the handsome branch director of a large luxury textile business, and his pretty but 'nervous' young wife Bela Giuseppina – or 'Peppina' (the daughter of a prosperous bank manager). It was Hans who advised Filipp to make an appointment to see Freud. Filipp subsequently travelled to Vienna where Freud administered a 'vigorous anti-syphilitic cure'. During Filipp's periods of infirmity, he came to rely more and more on the ministrations of Peppina Zellenka. His wife, Katherina, suffered from an obsessional illness and her time was fully occupied performing household chores and cleaning. Peppina ousted Ida from Filipp's bedside, assumed the role of primary caregiver, and the two friends became lovers. They did little to conceal their relationship. Filipp lavished gifts on Peppina, and when the Bauers and the Zellenkas went on holiday together, Filipp and Peppina took separate 'end rooms' in a hotel suite so that they could continue meeting without interruption. It is likely that both Katherina and Hans, for their own quite different reasons, were tacitly consenting: Katherina because she was avoidant of sex and suffering from what Freud called her 'housewife's psychosis', and Hans because he was a serial philanderer and immediately alert to how he might exploit the situation to his advantage.

Ida was a sensitive child with a history of bedwetting and breathing difficulties. From the age of twelve she developed a number of worrying symptoms, most notably severe headache, cough and loss of voice. She was subsequently taken to see specialists who may have subjected her to painful and invasive electrical treatments. Consequently, she formed a dim view of the medical profession.

As Ida matured, she became increasingly attached to Peppina and the two Zellenka children. Peppina was inappropriately candid. She talked to Ida about sex and marriage, and when Ida spent nights at the Zellenkas' residence, Hans left the bedroom so that Peppina and Ida could sleep together. It was also about this time that Hans started to buy Ida gifts and send her post-cards – a development completely ignored by Ida's parents.

When Ida was thirteen, Hans invited her to watch a religious ceremony from what Freud referred to as his 'shop' (in reality, more likely his office) in the town square. She was surprised to discover that he had dismissed his assistant and she was his only guest. Hans asked Ida to wait for him while he lowered the awning, and when he returned, he pulled her towards him and kissed her on the lips. She was disgusted and rushed out of the building. Ida didn't mention the assault to her parents and thereafter she avoided being alone with Hans.

In 1898, when Ida was fifteen, she travelled to Vienna with her father for a consultation with Freud. Her headaches had become less frequent, but her cough and loss of voice had persisted. Freud diagnosed hysteria, recommended psychother-apy – and Ida declined. She had had enough of doctors. From Vienna, father and daughter travelled to the Zellenkas' summer residence which was situated by an alpine lake. Filipp booked himself into a nearby hotel and planned to go home after a few days. Ida was to stay on.

Ida noticed that the Zellenkas' young governess was being extremely rude to Hans. When the two 'girls' were alone, the governess confided that Hans had begged her 'to be nice to him' because 'he got nothing from his wife'. The governess had 'yielded' to Hans's sexual advances, but he had lost interest in her almost immediately. She intended to remain in her post a little longer and if Hans's ardour failed to reignite she would hand in her notice.

A few days later, Ida and Hans took a boat trip on the lake and went for a walk while the boat was docked. Hans made 'a declaration of love' and repeated his weak seduction line: 'You know I get nothing from my wife.' Ida slapped Hans's face and fled. She decided to make her way back to the Zellenkas' residence by walking around the lake. When she learned that it would take her two and a half hours, she abandoned the attempt and returned to the boat. She was approached by Hans who begged her to forgive him and not to mention his behaviour to anyone. Hans's gauche propositioning was the 'scene by the lake' referred to by Freud in the last moments of Ida's 'final' therapy session.

Ida tried to carry on as normal. She took her usual afternoon nap, but when she woke up she was astonished to find Hans standing next to her bed. Naturally, she asked him what he was doing. His response was defiant. As far as he was concerned, he could do whatever he liked. When Filipp announced that he was ready to leave, Ida said that she was coming with him. Her behaviour must have seemed odd, because she didn't explain why she was suddenly anxious to return home.

Fourteen days later, Ida told her mother about the 'scene by the lake' and after some preliminary correspondence a meeting was arranged in which Filipp challenged Hans – who was dumbfounded. He hadn't done anything wrong; he was completely innocent. Nevertheless, Hans thought he could explain how it was that he had come to be wrongly accused. His wife had informed him that Ida had been showing an unhealthy fascination with sex. The girl had been reading books likely to excite amorous fantasies. Her story was simply the product of an inflamed imagination. Filipp and Katherina were completely won over by this defence and no further questions were asked. The two families continued socialising as if nothing had happened and they even spent Christmas together. Hans was free to continue molesting Ida.

In the autumn of 1898, Filipp moved his family to Reichenberg, the location of one of his factories. Only a year later he decided to move again, this time to Vienna. Soon after, Hans was promoted, and the Zellenkas followed the Bauers to the capital. When Ida went for a walk, she often saw her father with Peppina. Worse still, she would also see Hans, who had evidently started stalking her. On one occasion, Hans followed Ida for a considerable distance to discover if she had taken a lover. Ida's health suffered. She became depressed and irritable. She felt no affection for her father, and her relationship with her mother, which had always been poor, deteriorated. Ida wrote a suicide note and left it where she knew her parents would find it. Then she had a fainting fit followed by amnesia. Although Ida didn't want to see any more doctors, Filipp was insistent. She had to see someone, and soon. She was still only seventeen.

In October 1900, Filipp Bauer left the apartment building where he lived with his family on Liechtensteinstrasse and walked the relatively short distance to Berggasse 19. He explained to Freud that he had returned once again because of his daughter's illness. In his opinion, Ida's current symptoms were connected to her false memory of Hans Zellenka's lakeside declaration. Since that time, Ida had demanded that the Bauers break off all relations with the Zellenkas. But this was unthinkable. Filipp was bound by ties of honest friendship to Frau Zellenka and he couldn't possibly do anything to hurt her feelings. She was in an unhappy marriage and suffered from nerves. He was her sole support. 'In view of my own state of health I probably do not need to assure you that there is nothing forbidden in our relationship. We are two poor human beings comforting one another as best we can with friendship and sympathy.' Then, curiously, he echoed Hans's embarrassing seduction line: 'You know that I get nothing from my own wife.' Freud thought it wise to suspend judgement until he had heard what Ida had to say first.

Ida had been used as a sexual bargaining chip, an offering, a means of appeasing Hans so that Filipp and Peppina could continue their affair. She had been neglected by her mother, betrayed by Peppina, and gifted to a paedophile by her father. She had been trapped in an intolerable situation for years and it is hardly surprising that by the time she was approaching her eighteenth birthday she was ready to write a suicide letter. Yet Freud believed that Ida's symptoms were caused not only by traumatic experiences but also by internal conflicts. She wasn't battling with Hans's demons, she was battling with her own.

Ida had told Freud that being kissed by Hans was repulsive. But Freud asked: what if she was aroused by Hans's kiss? Perhaps she *did* have sexual fantasies, and some of these may have been explicit – such as performing oral sex? Was her subsequent self-disgust represented symbolically by an expulsive, persistent cough? Was her secret attraction to Hans, an older man, presaged by the close father–daughter relationship that had developed when she had acted as Filipp's nurse? And how hurt had she been when Peppina dislodged her from her father's bedside? Was Ida jealous? Did she want to be compensated? Did she now want Hans's affection in exchange for Filipp's? Moreover, what was the nature of Ida's attachment to Peppina? Beautiful, confiding Peppina, with whom she had shared a bed and who possessed a body she admired for its 'delightful whiteness'? Was guilt, associated with her sexual awakening, being intensified by homoerotic longing?

Explanations that link a single cause to a single symptom are satisfying and easy to follow. But Freud posits one potential cause after another. This can be frustrating for some readers who feel overwhelmed. Critics have suggested that the relentless enumeration of causal factors is Freud's crude way of proving a point. He silences dissenters by burying them under an avalanche of speculative 'evidence'. To some extent, this is true.

He is indefatigable when seeking to link a particular symptom with sexual experiences, fantasies and memories. Nevertheless, his insistence that symptoms are usually 'overdetermined' is almost certainly correct.

Uncovering a straightforward cause-and-effect relationship is a relatively rare occurrence in clinical practice. Given how the mind works, it is much more likely that the causes of a symptom will be convergent and complex. Many experiences (in childhood, adolescence and adulthood) will create memories (accessible, partially accessible or inaccessible) which will then influence an individual's mental life and determine his or her reactions to day-to-day events.

Unlike Filipp and Katherina, Freud never questioned the veracity of Ida's account of the 'scene by the lake'. Therefore it seems odd that he wasn't particularly interested in exploring the probable traumatic effects of Hans's molestation. Even more so given that he had been investigating the psychological consequences of traumatic sexual experiences for some time. Ida had said that when, aged thirteen, she was kissed by Hans, she had found it repulsive; however, Freud believed that the kiss had excited her. Freud doesn't – as some critics have suggested – disqualify Ida's feelings, because, for Freud, it is possible to feel both repulsed and excited simultaneously. Minds are complex and can accommodate many contradictions.

Fragments of an Analysis of Hysteria contains one of Freud's most frequently quoted passages. It is a description of how human beings inadvertently disclose their innermost thoughts with small, seemingly random actions: 'He that has eyes to see and ears to hear may convince himself that no mortal can keep a secret. If his lips are silent, he chatters with his finger-tips; betrayal oozes out of him at every pore.' Freud supplies us with an arresting and erotically charged example. One day Ida arrived wearing a purse around her neck and she 'played with it as she lay there, opening it up, inserting a finger, closing it again, and so on'. After categorically denying that she could remember masturbating as a child, her dextrous manipulations suggested otherwise. Thus, through keen observation, 'the task of making conscious the most hidden recesses of the mind is one which it is quite possible to accomplish'. The idea of unconscious self-betrayal is fascinating, but this passage seems to reveal more about Freud's mental processes than Ida's. His soft-core language – *as she lay there, opening, inserting* – suggests an erotic daydream. Something is being betrayed, certainly, but it is far from clear whether it is Freud's or Ida's unconscious that is doing the betraying.

Ida's case study presents Freud's apologists with a considerable challenge. He makes many sweeping generalisations that are completely unsupported. For example, 'Women take a special pride in the state of their genitals'. And crucially, he never succeeded in winning his patient's trust. Therapy sessions were more like a battle of wills than a constructive dialogue. Even if we accept that Ida was ill disposed towards doctors, Freud's failure to establish a therapeutic alliance with his patient was a significant shortcoming. Some have suggested that, over time, Freud grew to despise Ida, which, if true, would have compromised his ability to function as a competent therapist.

Ida was certainly a testing patient. She frequently questioned Freud's interpretations and could be sarcastic. After Freud proposed that a jewellery box in one of her dreams represented the vagina, she responded sharply: 'I knew *you'd* say that'. Freud appended a haughty footnote: 'A very common way of rejecting an item of knowledge arising from the repressed'. He obviously felt it necessary to embrocate her stinging remark with a statement that feels very much like *esprit d'escalier*.

Freud's analysis of Ida's jewellery box dream culminated in a major deductive coup. He put it to Ida that she wasn't really frightened of Hans Zellenka. She was frightened of *herself* – or, more accurately, her own sexual desires. It is a moment of high drama that Ida instantly deflates. 'Of course,' Freud reports, exhausted by her recalcitrance, 'she would not go along with this piece of interpretation.'

Ida's refusal to meekly accept Freud's authority has made her something of a feminist heroine. Her advocates have argued that Freud, smarting from her keen retorts, meanly portrays her as uncooperative and disrespectful, rather than shrewd and scep- tical. And if Ida was prickly, we should be sympathetic. Being 'handed over' to Freud – another older man – probably felt much the same as being handed over to Hans Zellenka.

There is, however, a less obvious feminist reading of *Fragments of an Analysis of Hysteria*. Freud insisted that sexual matters should be discussed with women using proper terms rather than euphemisms. In effect, women and men should be treated the same. 'One can talk to girls and women about all kinds of sexual matters without doing them any harm, first if one adopts a particular way of doing this, and secondly if one can convince them that it is unavoidable.' According to Freud, Ida masturbated, had explicit sexual fantasies, thought about oral sex and was probably bisexual. Irrespective of whether Freud was correct about Ida's predilections and inner life, he cannot be accused of denying or shying away from female sex- uality. Ida is nothing like the giggling, blushing and sexually naive (or even sexless) 'girls' described by Stefan Zweig in his autobiography. She is not pitiful and doll-like. Ida is composed of flesh and blood and her carnality is *modern*. She is intelligent, assertive, and has sexual needs.

The standard criticisms of *Fragments of an Analysis of Hysteria* are still valid. Ida was undoubtedly the victim of sexual and emotional abuse; however, by at least acknowledging the *reality* of female sexuality, Freud sides with the women's movement of his day, for whom sex had become an important issue. Only ten years earlier, Richard von Krafft-Ebing – a psychiatrist with a global reputation – had declared that women had little 'sensual desire'. If women were not sexually passive, he warned, 'the whole world would be a bordello, and marriage and the family unthinkable'. At precisely the same time, the American physician Clelia Duel Mosher was undertaking research that revealed about three quarters of married women enjoyed sex with their husbands on a regular basis. Mosher was also one of the first doctors to point out that tight corsetry interfered with breathing. Freud's acceptance of Ida's sexuality doesn't redeem him, but it adds momentum to twentieth-century liberalism. *Fragments of an Analysis of Hysteria* would have been read enthusiastically by many women eager to establish sexual equality, not only in the workplace but also the bedroom.

When Ida terminated her therapy, she said that she had reached her decision fourteen days earlier. This period – also the period of notice given before quitting a job – was a recurring motif in her history. Freud thought that it represented the period Ida had been prepared to wait for Hans to make a second declaration of love after the 'scene by the lake'. If Hans had made a second declaration, she would have known that he was serious, that he wasn't going to toy with her as he had toyed with the unfortunate governess. The fact that Ida had, in a sense, given Freud 'fourteen days' notice suggested that she had also been waiting for him to make some sort of declaration.

Had her feelings for Hans been transferred to Freud? Had she given *him* fourteen days to demonstrate he wasn't toying with her? Employing bullish rather than persuasive reasoning, this is what Freud concluded. He had already supposed that Ida wanted to kiss him. Hans was a smoker, and somewhat simplistically, Freud argued that because *he* was a smoker, Ida wanted to kiss him too: 'If I finally bring together all these clues, which suggest a transference to myself, since I am also a smoker, I come to the view that it probably occurred to her during a session between us that she desired a kiss from me.' Once again, this feels more like another instance of 'self-betrayal' – wishful thinking rather than clinical insight.

On reflection, Freud regretted that he had paid insufficient attention to the degree to which Ida's past relationships, particularly with her father and Hans, had interfered with the 'therapeutic' relationship. This phenomenon, which Freud called 'transference', was something he had encountered before. Attitudes and emotions associated with a historically important individual frequently contaminate a patient's perception of his or her therapist. Thus, Ida's putative desire to kiss Hans had been transferred, with the helpful mediation of smoking as an associative link, to Freud. By the time Freud had started thinking about Ida's transferences, it was too late. She had avenged herself on him as she had avenged herself on Hans Zellenka. He wrote, she 'left me, just as she believed herself deceived and abandoned by him'.

Fifteen months after terminating her therapy, Ida returned to consult Freud, on April Fools' day. He was immediately suspicious. She had ostensibly made the appointment because she wanted him to treat her facial neuralgia. Freud asked Ida how long she had been in pain. She replied: 'Fourteen days.' Of course, for Ida, the words 'fourteen days' always signified more than 'fourteen days'.

Ida confessed that since her last appointment she had been feeling better. Freud attributed this improvement to the insights she had been afforded during her brief (and admittedly incomplete) psychoanalysis. This could be true, or at least partially true; however, it is equally likely that other factors, such as increased maturity and empowerment, had also had a beneficial effect – especially so given what she was about to disclose.

In May 1901 (the preceding year) one of the Zellenka children died. Regardless of all that had happened, Ida wanted to pay her respects, so she arranged to visit them. Typically, Ida was received by Hans and Peppina as if nothing unusual had ever passed between them. Perhaps the Zellenkas were somehow diminished by their grief and Ida recognised that she could take advantage of their vulnerability.

It was certainly an odd moment to start pressing for admissions. Ida told Peppina that she knew about her affair with Filipp. She forced Hans to admit that he had propositioned her by the lake. Then she went home and reported Hans's admission to her father.

After confronting the Zellenkas, Ida was free of symptoms until mid-October when she once again lost her voice. This coincided with witnessing a road accident. She was somewhat evasive about the details until she 'finally admitted' to Freud that the victim of the accident had been Hans. Ida had been walking along a busy street when she had spotted Hans coming towards her. He had stopped and he had appeared confused. While he was in this distracted state he was hit by a carriage, although he survived without serious injuries.

What was going through Hans's mind? Had he been paralysed by the unexpected appearance of the woman he loved? Or was he fearful because Ida now represented vengeance? Did he see a vision of unattainable beauty, or a terrifying revenant? It is also possible that Hans was overwhelmed by shame and had attempted to end his own life.

Freud's explanation of Ida's 'fourteen days' of neuralgic pain prior to her consultation is somewhat self-aggrandising. The pain had started after Ida had read about Freud's academic promotion in a newspaper. The doctor whom she had rejected was now a distinguished professor, lauded by his colleagues, and her regret had been converted into pain. She was, Freud argued, punishing herself. Freud also suggested that mixed up in the conversion was regret that she had slapped Hans in the face by the lake. Whatever the actual explanation, Ida's neuralgia had given her a good excuse to see Freud one last time, to prove that she really hadn't fantasised the 'scene by the lake'. Telling Freud about Hans's admission must have given her some satisfaction – although Freud had never doubted her.

Freud's egotistical explanation of Ida's neuralgia is typical of much of the Afterword of *Fragment of an Analysis of Hysteria*. It often feels like Freud is having to work very hard to make the evidence fit his theories. The task of persuading the reader is made even more difficult by the fragmentary nature of the material. Why did Freud choose to write up an incomplete analysis when, instead, he could have chosen one that had been successfully concluded?

Having already published *The Interpretation of Dreams*, which is largely theoretical, he wanted to show how dream interpretation works in practice. A very substantial proportion of Ida's case study is indeed devoted to decoding two of her dreams. In addition, a fragment of an analysis is more tractable than a completed analysis. Freud explains that, at the time of writing, he hadn't been able to 'fully master' the large amount of case material that he would have collected over the course of a year.

Yet, Freud's justifications are not compelling, and the tone and content of the Afterword suggest that his reasons for writing up the troubling case of Ida Bauer were more personal. In several passages he seems to be writing the case for himself rather than an academic readership. It is as though he is reassuring himself that he did the right thing and didn't make any serious errors of judgement. He reminds himself that Ida was a testing patient, the kind who engages doctors, sabotages treatment, then despises their incompetence. He resolves self-doubt by making increasingly dogmatic statements: 'I can only repeat it over and over again, because I never encounter anything else: sexuality is the key to the problem of psychoneuroses and neuroses in general. No one who scorns this idea will ever be in a position to solve this problem.' We can imagine Freud, sitting at his desk late at night or in the early hours of the morning, the atmosphere dense with cigar smoke, his pen nib scratching out words that when spoken aloud sound alarmingly reminiscent of articles of faith. There is a note of desperation in his insistent inflexibility and his unwillingness to entertain alternatives.

Ida had nettled Freud. So much so that he started to analyse himself.

He wondered why he had given Ida the clinical alias 'Dora'. The name had popped into his head, and it had felt remarkably appropriate – almost perfect. His explanation was disappointingly anodyne. His sister Rosa had employed a maid who shared her name. To avoid confusion, the maid had called herself Dora. Freud couldn't use Ida's real name in his case study and the maid couldn't use her real name in Rosa's home. This similarity had linked the maid with Ida in Freud's unconscious. Thus, the name Dora had struck Freud as being exactly right for Ida.

Freud was seeking to understand an underlying associative process, so perhaps he can't be blamed for failing to pursue this line of inquiry further; however, the name Dora was much more meaningful to him, both personally and culturally, than his explanation suggests. *David Copperfield* was Freud's favourite Dickens novel. Copperfield married Dora Spenlow, who asked him to think of her as his 'child wife'. Theodora, the Byzantine empress whose image inspired Klimt's nervy and erotic portrait of Adele Bloch-Bauer, was a courtesan who eventually used her power to free women from sexual slavery. In *The Secret History*, Procopius describes Theodora's penchant for sexual marathons with relish: 'Often she would go to a bring-your-own-food dinner party with ten or more youths, all at the peak of their physical prowess and with sex their trade, and she would lie with all her fellow-diners the whole night through; and when she had worn them all out she would turn to their servants, as many as thirty on occasion, and copulate with every one of them – but even so could not satisfy her lust.' Pandora, the Greek equivalent of the Judaeo-Christian Eve, possessed a box (or jar) which, once opened, spread doleful cares among humanity. Freud had been quick to interpret the jewellery box that featured in one of Ida's dreams as a symbol of the female genitals. Dora was also the name of Josef Breuer's daughter. The name Dora therefore knots together several ideas: precocious sexuality, lust, sexual politics, 'betrayal', the mystery of the feminine and the lure of the forbidden.

In the final paragraph of the Afterword, Freud briefly mentions that Ida married a young man who had featured in one of the dreams she had reported. He then concludes on an optimistic note, implying that Ida was poised to free herself from her complicated past and embark on a new and more satisfying existence.

The man in Ida's dream was Ernst Adler. He was, supposedly, an 'engineer', although there is little evidence to suggest that he ever did much engineering. His uncle was a famous actor, he is reputed to have been a 'playboy', and he hobnobbed with aristocrats. He was also a keen amateur musician who aspired to be a composer. Ida met Ernst on a tennis court at an expensive holiday resort. He was nine years older than Ida and probably seemed very glamorous. By that time Ida was desperate to leave home and a romantic adventure presented an obvious, perhaps even irresistible, escape route. The couple were soon engaged. They married on 6 December 1903 in a fashionable reform temple located in central Vienna. This was two years before the publication of *Fragments of an Analysis of Hysteria*. Ida's parents were suspicious of the bridegroom, who was still living with his parents in Leopoldstadt. Even so, Ernst was welcomed into the family. Filipp gave Ernst a job and on one occasion hired an orchestra so that his son-in-law could hear his own music.

Sixteen months after the wedding, Ida gave birth to a baby son. Two months later, Ida and Ernst converted to Protestantism. Neither Ida nor Ernst had been raised in religious households and conversion to Christianity was an easy way of circumventing obstacles to social progress. Like many Viennese Jews, Ida wanted to integrate and be accepted. She became rather conventional. She decorated her home in the traditional Victorian style, attended the opera, and had high hopes for her musical son who was taught to play the piano by a pupil of the composer Arnold Schoenberg and at the age of seven could sit through a complete performance of Wagner's *Lohengrin*. Eventually he became a conductor and opera director who worked with musical colossi such as Arturo Toscanini and Georg Solti.

After the First World War and the collapse of the Austro-Hungarian Empire, the Bauer family fortune was lost. There would be no more hiring of orchestras. Ernst wasn't a very good businessman. Nor, as it turned out, was he a very good husband. He spent a great deal of time gambling at the Automobile Club and accrued significant debts.

In 1923, Ida's otolaryngologist referred her to Felix Deutsch, one of Freud's disciples. She had developed vertigo and tinnitus, but the specialist could not identify an organic cause. She was also suffering from many other symptoms, including headaches and a persistent cough; however, unlike the coughing of her youth, her current affliction was readily explained by the fact that she had become a heavy smoker. Deutsch's account of his contact with Ida is fascinating but, unfortunately, unreliable. Nevertheless, the general impression that he gives us can probably be trusted, regardless of many doubtful details.

Ida told Deutsch that she was unhappily married and that she was considering divorce. Ernst was unsupportive and she suspected him of being unfaithful. Men were 'selfish, demanding, and ungiving'. Her son, whose future success and prosperity meant so much to her, was now a rebellious teenager and not particularly interested in pursuing a dull, reliable career path. He had discovered 'girls' and had taken to staying out late. Although his behaviour wasn't at all unusual, Ida was finding it hard to cope with his newfound independence and inaccessibility. Deutsch believed that her tinnitus, the ringing and noise in her ears that prevented her from sleeping, was connected with her continuous straining to hear her son returning from his 'nightly excursions'. Ida found Deutsch's insight very helpful. Indeed, she started feeling better almost immediately.

The picture we have of Ida in her middle years is rather sad. Unloved and chain-smoking cigarettes; prone to obsessional cleaning; deprived of her inheritance by circumstance. But things were about to get a great deal worse.

Ida acquired her husband's taste for gambling. In 1932, she was playing bridge for money when news reached her that Ernst had collapsed. She dismissed the suggestion that it might be serious and finished her game. When she arrived home, Ernst was already dead.

Even though Ida hadn't been happily married, Ernst's death still caused her distress. The following year Hitler was appointed chancellor in Germany, and after the Anschluss in 1938, Ida's life took on the qualities of a nightmare. The Nuremberg racial laws of 1935 became applicable to Austria, and Ida, a convert to Christianity, was declared a Jew, her citizenship revoked, and her right to vote removed. Suddenly, a Jew could be arrested for something as innocuous as greeting a friend.

During Kristallnacht (9 to 10 November 1938) – the Nazi rampage which involved the desecration of synagogues, the closure of Jewish businesses and the confiscation of property – Ida was taken to a public building where she was starved and forced to do gymnastics. We can't be certain, but it is highly likely that she was then sent to Dachau concentration camp for a month before being permitted to return to her ransacked apartment. It was imperative that she leave Vienna. Getting a passport was a complex and exhausting process involving paperwork and humiliating encounters with the police and the Gestapo. Not many countries were willing to accept Europe's dispossessed Jews. Even so, Ida and her son managed to escape Nazi persecution and travel to America.

Ida settled in New York. Her son lived in the Midwest, then worked for an opera company on the west coast, before finally accepting a position in New York in 1945, most probably to be near his mother. Sadly, Ida had developed colon cancer and she died only a matter of months after his arrival.

How strange it must have been for her in those last days, lying between starched sheets in a Manhattan hospital bed, remembering the past, the distant world of her childhood. The spa town promenade along which prosperous invalids strolled. Bands playing waltzes and polkas, peasants in traditional dress, vineyards and castles; Hans Zellenka's office on the square, imperial Vienna, portraits of the Emperor, gas lamps and carriages. Her father taking her to see a well-tailored doctor who lived at Berggasse 19.

When Ida consulted Felix Deutsch, she mentioned with some pride (if we can believe him) that she had once been a patient of Freud – 'a famous case in psychiatric literature'. It seems unlikely that she understood the extent and durability of that fame. She was Freud's most controversial case study – and hence the subject of countless academic commentaries. Biographers have written books about her. She has inspired novels and an opera. And how surprised would she have been to learn that many readers today encounter her not as a famous hysteric or an unhappy, traumatised widow in her sixties, but primarily as a self-possessed eighteen-year-old, an iteration of a Byzantine empress, a Pandora – a new Eve. Modern woman. Unintimidated by authority, even when that authority was Sigmund Freud.

Chapter 7

Secrets and Lies

Sigmund Freud and Wilhelm Fliess met for the last time in August 1900 at Achensee, a lake in the Tyrol. As they walked together, the tone of their conversation became querulous. Fliess pointed out that, ultimately, his ideas about periodicity contradicted psychoanalysis. If mental states are influenced by fundamental biological cycles, then psychological treatments could only ever have marginal effects. Freud and Fliess also engaged in a dispute concerning which one of them had been the first to think of universal bisexuality – the idea that all men and women share opposite-sex attributes and attitudes. Universal bisexuality was a concept that could be used to explain sexual diversity. For example, during sexual development, the female traits of a bisexual man might become dominant, leading to homosexuality. Freud would eventually reject such thinking as simplistic and conclude that universal bisexuality owed less to biology and more to early identifications with male and female parents.

Fliess blamed Freud for the tense, belligerent atmosphere of their final meeting. He believed that Freud had begun to covet his, Fliess's, discoveries. Six years later, Fliess stated, somewhat ambiguously, that Freud had showed 'violence' towards him at Achensee. Privately, he was less reticent. He told his friends and relatives that Freud had lured him off the beaten track with murderous intent. His erstwhile colleague had meant to push him over a precipice and into the lake below. Fliess couldn't swim and he supposed that Freud was strong enough to overpower him.

The so-called 'murder plot' was sensationally revealed by Peter Swales in the 1980s. Fliess never said that Freud had attempted to murder him, only that he had suspected this was Freud's intention. Yet Fliess's paranoia was presented like an exposé. Swales' research is interesting, not because it proves that Freud was a would-be murderer, but rather because it shows the degree to which Fliess had come to mistrust Freud. After Achensee, Fliess decided to stop sharing his scientific findings with Freud and to terminate their correspondence. Nevertheless, they continued to write to each other for another two years and Freud's letters were often quite 'chatty'. He still signed off with 'cordial thanks' and 'greetings'.

Freud wrote a thinly disguised account of the Achensee altercation in his book *The Psychopathology of Everyday Life*, and he accepts that he was in the wrong with regard to the priority dispute. Without mentioning Fliess by name, but rather a 'friend' with whom he 'used to have lively exchanges of scientific ideas', Freud admits that their quarrel was caused by his own memory lapses and that these were unconsciously motivated by self-interest: 'Over the next week I did in fact remember everything just as my friend had tried to remind me of it.'

A contrite Freud tried to make amends by suggesting to Fliess that they write a book together. This would allow them to clarify priorities publicly. But Fliess supposed that Freud's invitation was a ruse, a sneaky attempt to link their names and thereby share credit. Fliess refused to meet Freud in 1902 and their correspondence ceased.

Fliess's mistrust of Freud was immoderate, but not unjustified. Freud wasn't a homicidal maniac, but he was certainly capable of manipulation and deceit.

In 1903, a book was published by a young philosopher called Otto Weininger containing ideas about bisexuality that were more or less identical to Fliess's. Fliess wrote to Freud and asked him if he knew anything about Weininger's book. Freud's initial response was evasive; however, in due course he was forced to acknowledge that he had been indiscreet. He had divulged Fliess's ideas to a one-time patient and pupil who had in turn divulged those ideas to Weininger. He had even read Weininger's book before its publication. Freud followed his frank admission with a haughty flourish of condescension: Fliess would just have to accept that he couldn't patent his ideas. Besides, the whole incident was 'a trivial matter'. On that wounding note, their correspondence was brought to its bitter and this time definitive conclusion. Reflecting on Freud's behaviour, even the perennially steadfast Ernest Jones conceded that Freud hadn't been 'completely straightforward'.

Freud's offhand dismissal belies the depth and longevity of his complicated feelings for Fliess. In 1912, Freud was lunching at the Park Hotel in Munich with five followers, including Jones, Carl Jung and Franz Riklin. Suddenly, Freud rebuked the two Swiss psychiatrists for omitting his name from their publications. Jung and Riklin were understandably perplexed. Everyone was perfectly aware that psychoanalysis was Freud's discovery. But Freud continued castigating them, lost consciousness, and fell to the floor. Jung carried Freud to the lounge and laid him on a couch. As he revived, he spoke the curious phrase 'How sweet it must be to die'. Later, Freud told Jones that he had had similar attacks in the same room at the Park Hotel in 1906 and

1908. He believed that this was because he associated Munich with Fliess: 'There is some piece of unruly homosexual feeling at the root of the matter.'

Freud and Fliess's interest in bisexuality was probably more than academic. In 1898, Freud wrote an ardent letter to Fliess in which he declared 'it was necessary for me to love you in order to enrich my life'. And in 1900, even as their association was nearing its end, Freud conceded: 'No one can replace for me the relationship with the friend which a special – possibly feminine – side demands.'

If Freud and Fliess had 'unruly' homosexual feelings for each other (as seems to be the case) then Fliess's allegation of murderous intent and Freud's subsequent betrayal of trust are more readily understood. The two men were like unhappy lovers – hurt, angry and upset – incapable of negotiating a civil separation.

A few months before the publication of *The Interpretation of Dreams*, Freud published a paper titled *Screen Memories* in which he argued that many seemingly trivial recollections from childhood – often inexplicably vivid and preserved for no obvious reason – screen (or cover) significant, deeper memories of disturbing or emotionally charged events. Although screen memories are not a 'record' of real events, they are composed of parallel, figurative elements. A screen memory is related to a real memory in much the same way as the manifest content of a dream is related to the latent content of a dream. Thus, unacceptable or discomfiting memories are converted into less troubling (and more accessible) memories by anodyne distortions and inoffensive transformations.

Freud first explained how screen memories can be decoded with the aid of a clinical example: the childhood recollections of his patient, Mr Y. He described Mr Y as 'a man of thirty-eight, with a university education, who has maintained an interest in psychological questions'. In the 1940s, psychoanalyst and philosopher Siegfried Bernfeld demonstrated that Mr Y never existed. He is Freud's invented doppelganger – which is why his biographical details are almost identical to Freud's. It is curious that it took so long for Freud's chicanery to be discovered, because the exchanges between Mr Y and Freud read precisely like someone talking to himself.

Mr Y obligingly volunteered a distant memory for Freud to deconstruct. 'The scene seems to me fairly inconsequential, and I can't understand why it should have become fixed in my memory. Let me describe it to you.' The landscape of Mr Y's childhood is rural – a sloping meadow, dandelions and a farmhouse. He is accompanied by an older male cousin and the cousin's little sister, who holds a bunch of flowers. The two boys 'fall upon her' and 'snatch her flowers'. She is upset and runs off in tears.

The older male 'cousin' was Freud's nephew, John, and the girl was John's sister, Pauline (Sigmund's childhood playmate whom Jacob Freud had hoped Sigmund would marry). Through Mr Y, Freud acknowledges, 'to take away a girl's flower – that means to deflower her'. Some of Freud's critics have implied that *Screen Memories* is in fact a confession of infant sexual sadism. We know that Freud and John treated Pauline 'shockingly' because Freud said so in a letter to Fliess dated 3 October 1897; however, we should bear in mind that he was referring then, as in *Screen Memories*, to a time before his family settled in Vienna. Whatever misdeeds were perpetrated, it seems unlikely that the two boys, aged three and four, would have been capable of 'deflowering' a two-year-old – although it is entirely possible that their games might have been sexualised and coercive.

The insinuation that Freud was a child rapist serves as yet another example – like the 'murder plot' – of the extreme eagerness with which Freud bashers seize any opportunity to cast him in the worst possible light. The feverishness of such accusations undermines their purpose. Freud wasn't a monster or malevolent or Faustian (as many have suggested). He could be grandiose, dogmatic, inflexible, indiscreet, controlling and unforgiving, but all these personal defects are irrelevant with respect to his intellectual legacy. Freud's most *consequential* failing was his cavalier attitude to the truth. He had a marked tendency to misreport life events to enhance his 'legend' and he undoubtedly adulterated case reports to support his theories.

A very notable example of Freud's unreliable testimony can be found in *An Autobiographical Study*. He describes delivering a paper before the Viennese Society of Physicians on male hysteria in 1886. He informs us that the conservative audience received the new ideas he had brought back to Vienna from Paris with dismay. The physicians responded with hostility, and he was made an outcast. Freud's account is completely dishonest. His paper contained nothing that the senior physicians who attended his lecture would have considered 'new' and the minutes of the meeting record a debate that was much more sophisticated and rational than Freud suggests. He wasn't shunned by the Viennese medical establishment, and nobody objected to his presence at various local societies. He attended two more meetings of the Viennese Society of Physicians in 1887 and only a year and a half after his male hysteria presentation he was elected as a member. It is of course possible that in the forty years that separated his Viennese Society of Physicians presentation and writing *An Autobiographical Study* his memory had failed him. But given what we know of Freud's fondness for romanticising his past, we can be fairly certain that his account of rejection and exile was knowingly crafted. Likewise, when he wanted to make the results of his own self-analysis sound more objective, he simply invented Mr Y.

The degree to which Freud indulged in narrative embellishment and opportunistic misrepresentation wasn't fully appreciated until the 1970s and 1980s. Psychoanalysis, particularly in its early years, wasn't nearly as effective as Freud would have us believe; Breuer didn't break with Freud because he was a timid prude; Freud wasn't ignored by his colleagues for over a decade; Fliess wasn't a passive admirer of Freud's genius – and so on. Freud's outstanding feat of manipulation was to convince his devotees that he had no interest whatsoever in recognition and posterity. Anxious to compensate for his modesty, they trumpeted his preferred narrative and emphasised his stoic qualities.

Freud's selective memory and inaccurate autobiography are highly problematic. His critics assert that his dishonesty was so habitual that he can't be trusted. He was a fraud. But this isn't a very measured response. We should certainly approach his autobiographical writings and the recollections he shared with his disciples with extreme scepticism. We should also exercise caution with respect to his case studies. They are so pliant they can accommodate almost any of his preconceptions. However, Freud's intellectual legacy requires more nuanced consideration. Otherwise, we risk oversight. Dismissing Freud because of his shortcomings is like dismissing Sir Isaac Newton because he was a disagreeable misanthrope whose personal papers reveal a gullible fascination with alchemy and esotericism. Our loss will be greater than our gain.

Freud was so convinced that he was discovering fundamental truths that he wasn't overly concerned with the quality of his evidence. This is hardly what we expect from a man of science, but it *is* possible to be right about something in the absence of evidence. The ninth-century Persian chemist Jabir ibn Hayyan suggested that a split 'atom' might produce enough energy to obliterate Baghdad, and Albert Einstein formulated special relativity after imagining what it would be like to ride on a beam of light. Freud's mendacity is regrettable. It should not be glossed over – a common dereliction in hagiographic biographies. Science is a collective undertaking that relies on accurate reporting to progress. It is vital to know when and where Freud's work fails to meet expected standards.

Freud was human. He was right about some things and wrong about others. This banal observation, which applies to every person who has ever lived, becomes a necessary corrective when discussing Freud, because he has attracted so much hostility. Clearly, he had a bad side – but he had a good side too.

In 1905, the young and impecunious Swiss poet Bruno Goetz was studying Hinduism in Vienna. He was suffering from facial neuralgia and his professor advised him to visit Freud for a consultation. To stimulate Freud's interest, the professor forwarded some of Goetz's poetry. Goetz subsequently presented himself for an assessment and Freud took his history. Goetz talked about his father, his unfortunate love affairs and his attraction to a sailor. When Freud had completed his assessment, he informed Goetz that he didn't think psychoanalysis would be very helpful. Even so, he wrote a prescription and asked, 'When did you eat your last steak?' It had been four weeks. 'I rather thought so,' said Freud. He dispensed some dietary advice and handed Goetz the prescription and an envelope. 'A small honorarium for the pleasure you have given me with your verses and the story of your youth.' Goetz returned to his room. He opened the envelope and found 200 kronen inside. Freud's kindness made him weep.

On his way to lecture in America in 1909, Freud realised the extent of his fame for the first time when he found his cabin steward on the *George Washington* reading a copy of *The Psychopathology of Everyday Life*. It was the kind of book a cabin steward could enjoy – short, accessible and engaging. Published eight years earlier, the book had gained a wide readership. During Freud's lifetime it was his 'bestseller'.

The Psychopathology of Everyday Life is an inquiry into the psychology of simple mistakes, such as removing the wrong item from a drawer, forgetting something on a shopping list, or tripping over a word in a sentence. What Freud had to say about slips of the tongue was so fascinating, it changed not only the way we think about our articulatory mishaps but the language we use to describe them. After the publication of *The Psychopathology of Everyday Life*, people started to use a new colloquialism: 'Freudian slip'. Although slips of the tongue were universally recognised before Freud – after all, they happen all the time – it was Freud who first suggested that they are more than just hiccups in speech production. He insisted that verbal slips merited analysis because they have meaning. They can tell us something about the person. We have all made Freudian slips, and when they occur, we are usually aware that they are not due to our tongues slipping, but rather our guard slipping. The popular appeal of *The Psychopathology of Everyday Life* is largely explained by the familiarity of its subject matter. We recognise ourselves.

It was probably around 1898 that Freud started to connect mistakes and blunders with unconscious interference. Before that time, errors were judged to be the result of random factors such as poor concentration or coordination failures. Freud found such explanations superficial and unsatisfying. In *Introductory Lectures on Psychoanalysis*, he exposed the weakness of such accounts with an analogy. A man is robbed in a dark lonely spot and he doesn't see the thief's face, so he tells the police that he was robbed by loneliness and darkness. Of course, in reality the man's remote situation and the cover of darkness only *facilitated* the robbery. He was robbed by the thief. Fatigue, excitement or absent-mindedness are merely conditions under which errors are likely to occur. They are not ultimate causes. Freud maintained that to establish the ultimate cause of an error we must first understand its general context and connect it with an unconscious wish or intention. Only then will the thief of his analogy be apprehended.

Freud's German word for revealing mistakes (verbal or other-wise) is *Fehlleistung*. It can be translated as faulty function, faulty achievement or faulty act. In the standard English edition of Freud's works, James Strachey uses 'parapraxes' – a neologism that combines two Greek words. Ordinary English terms such as slip, blunder, lapse, error and mistake are more serviceable although they lose some of the implied meaning of the German original – the notion of 'accomplishment', for example, which is less passive and suggests that the mistake was caused by a disruptive agency. Unfortunately, 'parapraxes' remains the accepted term in the anglophone world, even though it always feels wrong in an English sentence: 'This was a parapraxis.'

Slips of the tongue are members of a cognate group that includes slips of the pen, misreading and mishearing. A second group subsumes memory lapses: forgetting objects, proper names, foreign words, intentions and impressions. A third group unifies a variety of bungled actions: losing or mislaying and accidents such as dropping.

Freud argued that parapraxes are caused by interference that can be linked to suppressed or repressed urges, wishes, feelings and thoughts. These are usually repressed because they are at variance with a person's self-concept (how they see themselves) and self-image (how they want others to see them). Mental content of this kind is discomfiting. It is likely to epitomise unattractive qualities – enviousness, egocentricity or hostility. Repressed sexual desires, particularly inappropriate or unac-ceptable sexual desires, are also likely to produce parapraxes.

Unconscious interference is essentially the result of conflict between conscious and repressed content. It is fundamentally the product of mutually opposing intentions.

A man who promises to help his exceptionally talented friend by mentioning him to a superior at work, and then forgets, is not just forgetting but demonstrating his insecurity and the fact that he really sees his friend as a competitor. His conscious intention to help is negated by a deeper, semi-conscious or unconscious intention to obstruct. 'Forgetting' provides a convenient cover for shirking his obligation. The man isn't generous-spirited (as he likes to believe) but threatened and envious.

Freud's favourite example of a verbal slip was supplied by a president of the Austrian Parliament. The president once opened a session by declaring it 'closed' instead of 'open'. Since it was generally expected that the session wouldn't be productive, he obviously wished that he could end the session before it had started. Another amusing example provided by Freud concerns a professor of anatomy who said: 'The study of the female genitals, despite many temptations – I beg your pardon, experiments . . . ' The unconscious sometimes behaves like an uncooperative twin who is eager to disclose what we are trying hardest to conceal. A dramatic example of a slip of the pen is included in Freud's *Introductory Lectures on Psychoanalysis*. Posing as a bacteriologist, a murderer was obtaining lethal germs from a biological institute. When one of the cultures was ineffective, he wrote a letter of complaint to the directors and instead of writing 'in my experiments on mice' he wrote 'in my experiments on men'. Perhaps the most notorious self-incriminating Freudian slip to make headlines in recent years was provided by George W. Bush. In 2022, during a speech intended to condemn Vladimir Putin's invasion of Ukraine, Bush declared that one man had initiated a 'wholly unjustified and brutal invasion of Iraq'. Shocked pause. 'I mean of the Ukraine.'

In *The Psychopathology of Everyday Life*, Freud described a domestic 'accident' that took place in his study. He was always keenly aware of the fragility of the precious antiquities on his desk. Consequently, nothing was ever broken – except once. Freud wrote: 'My inkstand was a slab of Untersberg marble hollowed out to take the glass inkwell, which had a lid made of the same stone and with a knob. There was a row of bronze statuettes and terracotta figurines arranged in a circle behind this inkstand. I sat down at my desk to write, made a curiously clumsy, sweeping movement with the hand holding my pen and knocked the lid of the inkwell, which was already lying on my desk, to the floor.' The lid broke. How could he have been so careless? It was so out of character he felt that the incident deserved an explanation. A few hours before, Freud's sister had been in the room, looking at his 'new acquisitions', and she had been critical of the inkstand. 'You ought to have a prettier one.' When Freud returned to his desk a few hours later, he 'accidentally' swept the lid away. 'Did I perhaps conclude from my sister's words', Freud speculated, 'that next time she had occasion to make me a present she was going to give me a better inkstand, and had I broken the plain, old one to make sure that she put the plan she had indicated into practice? If so, then my sweeping movement was only apparently clumsy, and in reality was both dextrous and purposeful, since I contrived to avoid all the more valuable objects standing close to the inkstand.'

Psychoanalysis distinguishes every trip, spill and stumble with an underlying motive. We botch our tax form when we don't want to pay; we mislay our phone when we want to avoid a difficult conversation; we lose our car keys when we don't want to go to work.

The Psychopathology of Everyday Life, like so much of Freud's writing, transcends its apparent purpose and makes a super-ordinate point about self-understanding. Small things matter.

The humdrum and the mundane are as telling – perhaps even more so – as prizes, major undertakings, feats and exploits. Even something as inconsequential as dropping a pen can illuminate the unconscious. Had Freud been a film maker, he would have favoured the 'close-up'.

It is curious that a man so enchanted by the grandeur of the ancient world, so determined to ennoble his biography with epic tropes, should also be exquisitely sensitive to the minutiae of behaviour – a tapping foot, a momentary downward glance, a stumble over a threshold. But such contradictions are key to Freud's distinct approach to psychology. He picks up a clue, a mere thread, and follows it into the labyrinth. He can find in a dream of a bourgeois sitting room a royal road that descends, via the nursery, into the expanse of prehistory. Freud is constantly building bridges that connect what at first appears trivial with the profound. When we make a Freudian slip, we are also slipping backwards in time, reverting momentarily to a state before the evolution of inhibitions.

The mechanisms that produce neurotic symptoms are the same as those that produce simple errors. Hence, the 'psychopathology' of everyday life. What has been repressed returns and interrupts behaviour. For Freud, the differences between healthy minds and 'sick' minds are quantitative, not qualitative. His framework has more in common with modern, evolutionary psychiatry (which does not make a sharp distinction between healthy minds and sick minds) than traditional, medical psychiatry (which is predicated on the categorial dichotomy of normal and abnormal).

The Psychopathology of Everyday Life is fundamentally a book about deception and betrayal. We deceive ourselves and we deceive others with varying degrees of success, and sometimes a slip will expose our true intentions. We are aware that others do the same. Consequently, we monitor others for small indications of deceitfulness. It cannot be pure coincidence that Freud was thinking about betrayal at precisely the same time as his relationship with Wilhelm Fliess was becoming competitive. And if Freud had conducted (or was still conducting) a sexual relationship with his sister-in-law, his study of 'slips' might have been given additional impetus by the need to guard against them.

Freud's penchant for investigating aspects of human behaviour that others regarded as trivial continued to steer him in unusual directions. In 1905, *The Psychopathology of Everyday Life* was followed by *The Joke and its Relation to the Unconscious*. While reading a proof copy of *The Interpretation of Dreams*, Fliess had noted that Freud's manuscript contained quite a few jokes. Freud had always been interested in jokes. Indeed, he had started collecting Jewish jokes and amusing anecdotes in 1897. Fliess's chance observation seems to have had a galvanising effect.

Freud suspected that the mental processes that produce dreams, screen memories and symptoms – that is, repression and transformations – might also shape our sense of humour. The scenarios described in jokes often feature lewd or offensive behaviour. Anal, crude or sadistic content is relatively common – the kind of material that would ordinarily be subject to complete or partial repression. In much the same way as the dream work transforms unacceptable repressed material so that it can be represented consciously, so it is that the 'joke work' accomplishes comparable 'translations'. However, the joke work is less efficient. It does not produce complete transformations. Lewdness and crudity are still present in jokes, albeit in a superficially 'cleaned-up' form.

According to Freud, humour is defensive. For example, it can be deployed to reduce the anxiety and discomfort surrounding aspects of being human that make us uncomfortable. Scatological jokes are common because defecation regularly reminds us of a humbling and humiliating aspect of embodiment. Similarly, gallows humour can relieve tension in situations that confront us with the frightening prospect of death or loss. Jokes dilute reality so that it becomes more bearable.

In Freud's time, jokes about Jews featuring antisemitic stereotypes were extremely common; however, Jewish grotesques featured not only in jokes told by gentiles about Jews, but also in jokes that Jews told each other. Freud suggested that this class of Jewish jokes was protective. Anticipating mockery diminishes its emotional impact. Thus, Jews were using humour to inoculate themselves against prejudice. Humour can be cruel, but it is also necessary. Freud would almost certainly be highly critical of 'cancel culture' and all those who insist that offence – any offence – is unacceptable.

Today, *The Joke and its Relation to the Unconscious* is probably Freud's least-read book. Although the title promises a combination of light diversion and quirky insight, it delivers neither. Humour rarely survives translation without losing some of its zest and observational jokes rely on recognition and detailed knowledge of context. What people found amusing in Freud's time doesn't seem particularly funny now, and a book about jokes that doesn't make us laugh feels unsatisfactory. Our failure to 'get' Freud's jokes makes his arguments seem less persuasive. Contemporary readers are also alienated by Freud's inclusion of jokes that reflect outmoded social attitudes. For example:

PHYSICIAN to Husband of ailing wife: 'I don't *like the look* of your wife.'
HUSBAND to Physician: 'I haven't *liked the look of her* for a long time.'

Yet, for all of its problems, *The Joke and its Relation to the Unconscious* demonstrates, once again, Freud's uncanny ability to identify something important that others have inexplicably overlooked. Humour isn't trivial. From Aristophanes and Juvenal to sitcoms and stand-up, it makes us who we are. Much of the graffiti found on the walls of Pompeii is sexual and meant to make the reader laugh. Under Stalin's oppressive regime in the USSR, dissidents circulated disrespectful joke books – a 'crime' punishable by imprisonment or even death. Satirists are prepared to risk their lives for the sake of a joke. Freud recovered humour from the margins of human psychology and afforded it a more central role. Man is not only a 'rational animal', as Aristotle suggested, but also a 'funny animal'.

Formal photographs of Freud on book covers are very misleading. He is usually shown scowling at the camera, eyes narrowed to peer deeper into the soul. But he is only scowling because he didn't like being photographed. At least, that's what he told Ernest Jones. Presumably he included cameras, along with bicycles and telephones, in his category of contrivances to be mistrusted. When Freud wasn't posing for posterity, a different person emerged. Candid portraits show a man whose expression is less severe – softer. We know that he made his children laugh and that he shared jokes with his friends. His writing can be deadpan. When lecturing, he would invite criticism from the audience and then respond with witty remarks. Droll observations, puns – his finger tapping a cigar preparatory to the delivery of a one-liner: sometimes he must have resembled Groucho Marx. Woody Allen, in his film *Annie Hall*, mistakenly identifies *The Joke and its Relation to the Unconscious* as the source of Groucho's famous quip about not wanting to join a club that would accept him as a member. Like many comedians, Freud used jokes as a form of therapy. During the First World War he collected jokes about the conflict to cheer himself up. Ernest Jones wrote that, after the war, he found Freud 'somewhat greyer and a good deal thinner than before the war'. But Freud's sense of humour was still intact. He surprised Jones by mentioning that he'd recently encountered an ardent communist who had half converted him to Bolshevism. The communist had told Freud that the advent of Bolshevism would necessarily lead to years of misery and chaos, but that these difficult times would be followed by years of peace and prosperity. 'I told him I believed the first half,' said Freud to Jones.

The Psychopathology of Everyday Life and *The Joke and its Relation to the Unconscious* are books that connect the unconscious to daily existence. They bring the unconscious closer. The unconscious of German Romantic philosophy, which preceded Freud's unconscious, was a semi-numinous realm that could only be *felt* when rationality was swept away by powerful emotions. For example, being overwhelmed while communing with nature. Slips and jokes are less grandiose entry points. They dispense with the need for mountains, lakes and stars. The presence of the unconscious can be felt just as easily while sharing a joke with a friend in a coffee house.

Freud's daily routine involved a brisk walk around Vienna's ring road. And he must have been aware that although he was making only one circuit, he was in fact circumnavigating two cities. The glittering city of baroque palaces, balls and busy thoroughfares, and the dark subterranean city beneath his feet. Vienna has an extraordinary number of catacombs, cellars and tunnels, as well as an extensive sewage system – made famous as the setting for a chase sequence in Carol Reed's 1949 cinematic masterpiece *The Third Man*. The poor, the sick and the destitute of Vienna descended into the sewers to shelter and keep warm. There may have been thousands of people living on the banks of Vienna's underground canals before the First World War.

What offended polite society was hidden from view in a fetid underworld. An underworld that existed only a few feet beneath the leather of Freud's well-polished shoes.

It seems unlikely that such a potent analogy would have

escaped Freud's notice. The two Viennas, light and dark, and the two levels of mind, conscious and unconscious. Every day, just below the pomp and imperial splendour, filth and hidden horrors.

Chapter 8

Cabal

Freud's assertion that he was 'completely isolated' for 'more than ten years' during which he was shunned by the medical establishment is largely untrue. He later described this period of his life as 'a beautiful heroic era'. The solitary nature of his work – particularly self-analysis and writing long hours into the night – must have made him feel isolated, but in fact throughout his 'lonely' decade he was either corresponding with Wilhelm Fliess and meeting with colleagues or giving lectures and being reviewed. The medical elite were perfectly aware of Freud, although by 1902 official recognition of his accomplishments was well overdue. The title of 'Professor' was neither stipendiary nor a guarantee of appointment to the university professors' council, but it nevertheless conferred a high level of prestige. For the Viennese, a professor possessed god-like qualities.

Freud's work on aphasia and infantile cerebral paralysis alone should have been sufficient to earn him the title, and his neglect was probably attributable, at least in part, to anti-semitism. But his *prolonged* neglect was because of pride. For a man with Freud's background, the only reliable way to achieve social advancement in Vienna was *protektion*. This involved

enlisting the support of influential men and women – industrialists, celebrities, aristocrats – who would act as advocates.
Freud hated the idea. He thought that he should be made a
professor purely on merit. Unfortunately, that wasn't how
things worked in Vienna. He was nominated in 1897, 1898,
1899 and 1900, and year after year he was passed over by the
Ministry of Education. Eventually, Freud had to accept that he
was never going to be a professor without patrons. The time
had come to 'break with strict virtue and to take appropriate
steps, just like other mortals'. He spoke to his old physiology
professor, the wife of an eminent classicist, and finally Baroness
Marie von Ferstel (one of his patients and a distant relative of
his wife), who procured a meeting with the minister of education. Married to a diplomat and a worldly negotiator, the
Baroness ensured the success of her mission with a 'bribe' (a
painting for the minister's new art gallery). On 22 February
1902, the Emperor signed the necessary decree, and Dr Freud
became Professor Freud. Whether the bribe was critical or not
is still the subject of debate. The minister is said to have been
irritated by the Baroness's interference and it is just possible
that Freud's application would – on this occasion – have been
successful regardless.

Freud liked being called 'Professor'. Almost everyone used his
title when addressing him directly, even those who were more
like friends than colleagues. A greater number of high-society
patients came to him for treatment, and he was able to raise his
fees. When he visited Café Landtmann for coffee and cake, the
waiters were exceedingly deferential. There was much bowing
and clicking of heels. But none of these preferments were very
important to him. What he really wanted was for psychoanalysis to be accepted as a significant contribution to human
knowledge, and in this respect being called 'Professor' hadn't
changed anything. He was still the only psychoanalyst in the

world and his psychoanalytic works had had little or no effect on how his contemporaries treated their patients.

Psychoanalysis was destined to become one of the great intellectual traditions of the twentieth century. Within a timespan of thirty to forty years, it would become the dominant school in psychiatry, evolve into a 'world view', exert a profound influence on the arts, and make Freud a household name. Seeding psychoanalysis across continents was a significant organisational accomplishment. Centres of excellence had to be established, conferences arranged, publications translated, analysts trained. Yet, this massive undertaking was launched by a chance remark and a handful of men – Max Kahane, Rudolf Reitler, Wilhelm Stekel and Alfred Adler – sitting around a table in Freud's waiting room.

Kahane and Reitler were regular attendees at Freud's university lectures and both men had known Freud since childhood. Kahane had founded a sanatorium, and Reitler had established an institute that specialised in thermal therapies. Although Kahane was the author of a textbook in which he mentioned Freud's new methods, it was Reitler who became the first doctor after Freud to practise as a psychoanalyst. The first person to attempt psychoanalysis after Freud was, in fact, a former patient (and 'collaborator') – Emma Eckstein. In 1901, Kahane mentioned Freud's discoveries to another physician, Wilhelm Stekel, who subsequently consulted Freud because of his compulsive masturbation problem. It is unclear whether Freud's treatment was successful as accounts differ; however, Stekel was clearly impressed by Freud's clinical skills. Around this time Freud also became acquainted with Alfred Adler, a physician with a keen interest in socialism and workers' rights. Adler had written a book on the occupational hazards of the tailoring trade. The two men probably met for the first time after Adler asked Freud for some advice concerning the care of one of his patients.

It was Stekel who suggested to Freud that he should start a discussion group. So, in the autumn of 1902, Freud sent post-card invitations to Kahane, Reitler, Stekel and Adler, and the five men assembled at Berggasse 19 to debate the psychological significance of smoking. Thereafter, they continued to meet every Wednesday evening as 'The Psychological Wednesday Society'. Stekel, who was also a journalist, summarised their deliberations in the Sunday edition of a liberal newspaper.

The meetings at Berggasse 19 were highly ritualistic. Members of the society would gather around an oblong table and the names of those wishing to make a presentation were deposited, like lottery tickets, in an urn. The first 'ticket' to be blindly selected determined who would speak. Members were forbidden to peruse papers in advance and presentations were heard in absolute silence. A fifteen-minute interval, during which coffee and cakes were served, was followed by a discussion. Every member of the society was provided with an ashtray, and cigars and cigarettes were smoked continuously. In the early years of the Psychological Wednesday Society, it was always Freud who closed the meeting with a summation. Martin Freud recalled that afterwards, the accumulated smoke was so dense he thought it remarkable that his father and his associates had been able to breathe.

A rule of the society was that new members should only be admitted by unanimous consent – although, in reality, almost anyone who wanted to attend was welcomed. The society quickly expanded to around twenty members although less than half of that number attended meetings regularly. From the very beginning, psychoanalysis appealed to individuals whose principal interests lay outside medicine and neurology. Thus, the writer Hermann Bahr, the music critic David Bach and the publisher Hugo Heller were all early attendees.

Stekel employed Pentecostal imagery to describe the transfer of ideas from person to person: 'A spark seemed to jump from one mind to the other, and every evening was like a revelation.' Other converts used similar language and frequently compared themselves to apostles. The musicologist Max Graf said: 'There was an atmosphere of the foundation of a religion in that room. Freud himself was its new prophet who made the heretofore prevailing methods of psychological investigation appear superficial.' The men who gathered around Freud were, according to Stekel, 'brothers of an order'.

The Psychological Wednesday Society resembled a 'secret lodge': the fragrant cigar smoke, like incense; the ceremonial urn; the communal strudel – a Viennese substitute for the congregational breaking of bread; Freud, the hierophant, officiating, his authority buttressed by a collection of watchful antique figures. Occasionally he would take one of his 'idols' or 'animal-shaped gods' and hold it in his hand while talking – like a shaman channelling spirits.

In 1906, Freud's small group of followers presented him with a medallion to mark his fiftieth birthday. On one side was Freud's portrait, and on the other, Oedipus and the sphinx. Around the medallion's edge was a line from Sophocles: 'Who divined the famed riddle and was a man most mighty'.

As Freud read the quotation, the blood drained from his face and he became agitated. Apparently, when he was a student he used to stroll around the arcaded courtyard of the university, inspecting the busts of the famous professors. He had hoped that one day *his* bust would be placed among these intellectual giants and that his pedestal would be inscribed with those exact words. It was a coincidence, of course, but Freud's disquiet was enough to remind everyone present that the gods were still taking an active interest in the destiny of 'a man most mighty'. Some years later, when Freud showed the medallion to Ernest Jones, he refused to translate the Greek encomium. Jones naively attributed Freud's reticence to his exceptional modesty.

The purpose of the Psychological Wednesday Society was to develop and promote a new science; however, Freud's early devotees were peculiarly willing to embrace ritual and conduct their business in a manner suggestive of esotericism and mystery. Today, this seems rather odd. But their behaviour is completely explicable when placed in its cultural context. Around 1900, Vienna was a honeycomb of secret cells, circles and societies. Many movements, particularly political movements, had comparable 'clandestine' origins.

Vienna was teeming with coffee houses, beer cellars, sequestered dining rooms and salons – all 'private' spaces where people were free to argue, speculate and think the unthinkable. Why it was that some of these gatherings metamorphosed into secret societies is unclear.

One possibility is that the occult revival of the late nineteenth century, a phenomenon strongly associated with the practice of ceremonial magic and the formation of orders, was still gripping the imagination of many Viennese intellectuals. Seances – another form of secret gathering – were also popular. Freud may have been particularly susceptible to these influences. Psychoanalysis resembles mediumship, insofar as it involves relaying messages from the unconscious rather than the afterlife.

A second possibility is that cultish gatherings were encouraged by a prevailing sense of impending doom. Cults tend to proliferate when cataclysms are predicted, and fin de siècle Vienna, the capital of a senescent empire, was judged to be edging towards ruin. In November 1899, a leading Viennese newspaper carried the front-page headline 'Postcards from the End of the World'. An enterprising individual had produced postcards in readiness for the coming apocalypse. If the old world was about to crumble, then it was imperative to prepare for the new. Consequently, like-minded individuals assembled behind closed doors to listen to their chosen prophets.

A third possibility is repressive legislation – namely, Article 18 of the 1867 Law on Associations. The empire was extremely wary of subversion and citizens could only meet as 'associations' if they were granted a licence by a special commissioner. These licences were difficult to obtain and imposed restraints on certain activities. Freemasons, for example, were allowed to meet in Vienna as a 'friendly society', but they were forbidden to conduct any rituals. Many groups may have opted to meet surreptitiously to avoid state interference.

The most successful secret societies in Vienna were also the most toxic. They typically combined occultism and racism under the banner of pan-German nationalism – a movement underpinned by the belief that the German-speaking peoples should unite and pursue common goals. One of the most influential advocates of pan-German nationalism was Guido List, a writer and journalist whose principal interests were German history and pagan mythology. Even though his background was prosperous, he felt it necessary to distinguish himself by introducing the nobiliary particle 'von' into his name.

At the age of twenty-seven, von List celebrated the summer solstice at the 'Heathen Gate', an arch and plinths situated in the ruins of Carnuntum – the Roman legionary fortress halfway between Vienna and Bratislava. Von List and his companions toasted past Germanic heroes, lit a solstice fire, and in its embers arranged bottles in the shape of the eighteenth rune or 'hook cross' – better known after the Second World War as a swastika.

Around 1900, he became the leader of a group of pan-German 'initiates'; however, his transition from writer to prophet occurred two years later. During a period of temporary blindness, he experienced a series of revelatory visions, and thereafter he started producing works that were essentially a call to arms.

According to von List, the human race could be divided into Aryan masters and servile 'herd people'. The Aryan homeland was a continent near the North Pole which the Aryans had been forced to leave during the ice age. They had brought their advanced civilisation south, but over time their inherent nobility had been corrupted by miscegenation. In order to remedy this harm, von List argued for strict segregation and the abolition of mixed marriages. Only the master race should enjoy civil liberties and the servile races should be denied education, the right to enter a profession, participation in business, and land ownership. Selective breeding was essential in order to avert the otherwise inevitable descent into chaos. He did not believe that a Germanic utopia could be achieved without a struggle, and he predicted a great war that would end in triumph if the northern races – the Germans, English and Scandinavians – fought side by side. The main obstacle to progress was the 'enemy nomads' – von List's term for the Jews. Nomadism, he believed, should be obliterated. Von List established a 'magical' lodge in 1907, Armanship, and another mystical society in 1911, High Arman's Revelation. The so-called Arman fraternities adopted the swastika as their emblem. It represented the 'invincible', the Germanic Messiah who would reign like a god and lead his people to victory.

Von List's strain of pan-German esotericism was developed by Adolf Joseph Lanz (who later reinvented himself as Baron Jörg Lanz von Liebenfels). At the age of nineteen, Lanz joined the Cistercians of the Chapter of the Holy Cross in the Vienna woods and took the name Brother George. Like von List, he experienced a visionary awakening when he came across a depiction of a knight trapping a monkey underfoot on a gravestone. He interpreted this as a revelation: the deliverance of the German peoples would necessitate the subjugation of the 'monkey man' by the 'master man'.

In 1900, aged twenty-five, Lanz abandoned monasticism and founded the Order of the New Templars, a fellowship united by the Grail myth and pan-German sentiment. The order attracted a number of wealthy patrons, and their donations enabled Lanz to purchase a castle in the Nibelung district of the Wachau. There, the New Templars dressed in surplices emblazoned with red crosses and performed their rites. Lanz incorporated von List's swastika in a newly designed Templar's flag, which he raised above the castle tower for the first time in 1907. His main occupation was writing articles for pan-German newspapers, and in 1906 he published his most important work,

'Theozoology, or the News about the Little Sodom Monkeys and the Electron of the Gods'. He argued that the Aryan gods harnessed electrical power and demanded the sterilisation and castration of inferior races to ensure the purification of German bloodlines. He also created a journal, *Ostara* (the name of the pagan goddess of dawn and spring). Although early editions included articles by other writers, he soon became the sole contributor.

Lanz was particularly preoccupied by the role of blonde women in his eagerly awaited pan-German paradise. He proposed the establishment of cloistered breeding colonies in rural areas where Aryan brood mothers could be regularly inseminated by pure-blooded, athletic men. Lanz was also in favour of medical checks on women prior to marriage to confirm their virginity. A fine upstanding Aryan needed to be absolutely sure that his prospective wife's 'erotic taste' had not been 'spoiled' by 'Primitive-sensual dark men'. Women, Lanz opined, had been gifted to men as slaves. 'They are our property, like a tree that bears fruit is the property of a gardener.'

In 1908, a young artist, newly arrived in Vienna, became acquainted with the writings of von List and Lanz. He borrowed a copy of von List's *The Secret of the Runes* from the public library and carried it around with him for weeks. He also visited Lanz to scrounge some missed issues of *Ostara*. When this artist, Adolf Hitler, eventually turned from art to politics, he made extensive use of von List's and Lanz's ideas. One of the speeches he delivered in Munich in 1920 contains a passage taken directly from von List's *The Names of Germania's Tribes*.

Although Hitler adored Norse myths, Wagnerian opera and ritual, he didn't want to be dismissed as a 'Romantic' idealist. Secure jobs and bread on the table were more important to voters than knights and dragons. Again, the city of Vienna provided him with instructive models: the leader of the parliamentary pan-Germans, Georg Schönerer, and the Mayor of Vienna, Karl Lueger.

Schönerer, whose party members used the *heil* greeting, favoured the use of simple slogans ('Through purity to unity'), approved of gymnastics, and held rallies. Karl Lueger – an outstanding orator – staged photo opportunities with celebrities and never married so that he could be a more credible fantasy husband for his many female admirers (who dubbed him 'Handsome Karl'). His ruthless pragmatism is exemplified by his frequently quoted and chilling declaration 'It is I who decide who is a Jew'. He could overlook a man's religion if he was useful – at least temporarily.

Hitler may have prioritised practical politics, but at the same time it is impossible to ignore his early exposure to pan-German mysticism. German supremacy, eugenics, mythology, ritual and runes feature in the writings of figures like von List and Lanz and reappear thirty years later as policies, propaganda and occultism in the Third Reich. Himmler authorised expeditions to Iceland in order to find pagan relics. In the medieval castle of Wewelsburg, he and twelve Gruppenführers would sit at a round table and attempt to communicate with their Teutonic ancestors. The SS emblem was a double rune.

Mainstream histories tend to underplay the influence of von List and Lanz on the evolution of National Socialism. Many of their sophisticated contemporaries regarded them as laughable buffoons. But if they were buffoons, they were extremely dangerous buffoons. The eminent historian William M. Johnston has stressed that as soon as Hitler transplanted their ostensibly 'harmless eccentricities' to Germany, their malignant philosophy 'threatened civilization'. In his autobiography, Stefan Zweig would look back and reflect: 'We failed to see the writing on the wall in letters of fire ... Only decades later, when the roof and walls of the building fell in on us, did we realize ... the

downfall of individual freedom in Europe had begun with the new century.'

In its early days, the psychoanalytic movement looked like a typical Viennese secret society, one of many, all of which benefited from relatively benign conditions for incubation and growth. Freud's ceremonial urn and animal-gods and von List's runes and rituals have much in common. They reflect the predilections of men whose formative years coincided with the late nineteenth-century occult revival. However, the 'atmosphere of the foundation of a religion' in Freud's smoky waiting room was probably also infused with a form of esotericism much closer to home.

In Leopoldstadt, only a short distance from Berggasse 19, numerous Jewish Orthodox sects would have been assembling around their particular *tzaddik* – an intermediary between God and community. They would have sat at his table, eaten together, and asked him for advice, which was often informed by his understanding of Kabbalah – the Jewish mystical tradition. Many aspects of Kabbalah presage psychoanalytic thinking. For example, dream interpretation, close attention to language, conceptualising sexual desire as an energy, and recognition of symbols. Moreover, Kabbalistic knowledge is usually communicated orally. This resembles 'training analysis' – the psychoanalytic convention of being psychoanalysed in order to become a psychoanalyst. Freud's ancestry was Orthodox, and there is some evidence to suggest that he owned volumes of Kabbalah.

In April 1908, the Psychological Wednesday Society became the Vienna Psychoanalytic Society – the prototype of many other similar societies that would eventually become established in Europe, Russia, Scandinavia, North America, South America, India, Japan and Australia. However, psychoanalysis never quite divested itself of its cultish qualities, its patina of mysticism, its cloying fragrances – wisps of smoke curling around the feet of ancient goddesses. Freud was always revered as a prophet, always surrounded by a protective inner circle of 'initiates', and psychoanalysis continued to trespass on occult territory: dreams, ghosts, premonitions, telepathy. Freud was like the last Kabbalist – a reincarnated medieval magician intent on raising modern demons. He insisted on talking about all those things that polite society wished to ignore. And Freud did little to present his disturbing ideas in a sanitised form. Indeed, he seemed to go out of his way to emphasise aspects of psychoanalysis that could be labelled as 'degenerate'. His preoccupation with sex did not enamour him to those who were deeply suspicious of 'Primitive-sensual dark men' and 'enemy nomads'. To good Aryans, Freud's mind was like a sewer. Long before Hitler's rise to power – and the ritual burning of Freud's books – many had already concluded that the sewer was where Freud and his ilk belonged.

Chapter 9

Uncomfortable Truths

More than the unconscious, even more than dreams, the name of Sigmund Freud is associated with sex. Although sex was fundamental to his new science, psychoanalysis was more than just a branch of sexology. Psychoanalysis can illuminate subjects as diverse as the origin of religion and the behaviour of crowds. It even has something to say about small curiosities, such as why we sometimes feel uneasy when we look at the face of a doll. Yet, for well over 120 years, Freud has been typecast as either a sexual monomaniac or a sexual prophet.

In one of his letters to J. J. Putnam, the founder of the American Psychoanalytical Society, Freud wrote: 'I stand for an infinitely freer sexual life.' For many, he became a forerunner of the counter-culture champions of 'free love' in the 1960s. The French poet Comtesse Anna de Noailles was deeply disappointed when she discovered that the real Freud was less rakish than his reputation. 'Surely *he* never wrote his "sexy" books. What a terrible man! I am sure he has never been unfaithful to his wife. It's quite abnormal and scandalous!' In 1910, at a conference for neurologists and psychiatrists held in Hamburg, an attendee exclaimed that psychoanalysis wasn't a science, but rather a matter for the police. Even Martha, Freud's wife, told a visitor that she thought psychoanalysis was a 'form of pornography'.

In 1924, the Hollywood film magnate Samuel Goldwyn set sail for Europe, intending to proposition Freud. He planned to offer him $100,000 for 'a really great love story'. Freud was 'the greatest love specialist in the world'. Goldwyn was one of several entertainment industry moguls who had come to the conclusion that Freud's risqué psychology could be monetised. A few months later, the New York Times declared 'FREUD REBUFFS GOLDWYN: Viennese Psychoanalyst is Not Interested in Motion Picture Offer'. Freud responded to Goldwyn's overture with a pointed one-line letter: 'I do not intend to see Mr. Goldwyn.'

The association between Freud and sex is exemplified by a piece of pop-art that is frequently reproduced on posters and T-shirts under the phrase 'What's on a man's mind'. It shows a cartoon profile of Freud in which an embedded figure of a naked woman supplies the lines of his forehead and nose.

Terms employed by Freud in his theory of sexual development have entered everyday language. A television series featuring a difficult relationship between a father and son might be described by a critic as an exploration of 'Oedipal' conflicts; an irritatingly fastidious person might be pronounced 'anal' or 'retentive'. But how do Oedipal conflicts evolve in the context of sexual development? And how is anal retention connected with sex? Many of Freud's terms – auto-erotic, penis envy, libido – have become untethered; they float in and out of conversations, carrying little meaning beyond their dictionary definitions. It is an intriguing paradox. Freud's theory of sexual development has been extremely influential, but public understanding of his theory is at best sketchy and vague.

Freud was an early convert to Darwinism (which affords sex a central role in evolution) and he was quick to connect neurotic illness with sexual memories and fantasies. *Studies in Hysteria* and *The Interpretation of Dreams* are full of references to sex. However, Freud's first major work devoted entirely to sex was *Three Essays on the Theory of Sexuality*, published in 1905. Freud wrote *Three Essays on the Theory of Sexuality* and *The Joke and Its Relation to the Unconscious* simultaneously. The manuscripts were placed on adjacent tables and Freud chose to work on one, rather than the other, according to how he felt on the day. Along with *The Interpretation of Dreams*, *Three Essays on the Theory of Sexuality* is reckoned by psychoanalysts to contain Freud's most important work. This was, as we know, also Freud's verdict. When Ernest Jones asked him to identify which of his books were his 'favourites', Freud carried both volumes from his bookcase and 'with a quiet smile' said: 'It seems to be my fate to discover only the obvious: that children have sexual feelings, which every nursemaid knows; and that night dreams are just as much a wish fulfilment as day dreams.' Freud revised *Three Essays on the Theory of Sexuality* extensively. He was still redacting and adding to the text some twenty years after its initial publication. Originally only eighty pages long, by 1925 it had gained an additional forty pages.

Jones informs us that if *The Interpretation of Dreams* was denigrated as whimsy – 'fantastic and ridiculous' – then *Three Essays on the Theory of Sexuality* was reviled as 'shockingly wicked'. Freud had articulated uncomfortable truths that the world wasn't ready (or was too cowardly) to accept. His insights were startling, and pedestrian thinkers failed to recognise his genius. He was viciously criticised by narrow-minded colleagues and he became 'universally unpopular'. 'Odium' was 'brought down on him'. He was denounced as 'evil' and perceived as a man who had 'filled his cup of turpitude'. Jones's apostolic outrage finds expression in language reminiscent of the King James Bible.

Once again – as with *The Interpretation of Dreams*, and before that, *Studies in Hysteria* – the received history of psychoanalysis does not agree with archival research. Although it is true that certain sections of Viennese society viewed *Three Essays on the Theory of Sexuality* as degenerate filth, the majority of medical practitioners would not have been as scandalised as Jones suggested. Almost all of the ideas included in Freud's three essays had already appeared in academic publications over the preceding twenty-five years. As early as 1867, when Freud was aged only eleven, the eminent British psychiatrist Henry Maudsley asserted that those who denied infant sexuality had either never observed the behaviour of young animals or must be 'strangely or hypocritically oblivious' of their own histories. An illustration in an 1879 publication written by the Hungarian paediatrician S. Lindner shows a very young girl raising the hem of her dress so that she can stimulate her genitals with one hand while sucking the thumb of her other hand. It is a remarkable image because it subverts all that we expect a Victorian line drawing of a child to represent. There is no sentimentality, no mawkish idealisation. Her forefinger is plainly curling between her labia in search of her clitoris while she unconsciously rehearses fellatio with a substitute penis. It would not be out of place in a provocative modern art exhibition.

In reality, *Three Essays on the Theory of Sexuality* was not exceptional. It appeared at a time when interest in sex and sexology was widespread. The late Victorian era was the golden age of sexology. Yet, over time, it was Freud's theory of sexual development that achieved global recognition and almost all of his competitors were reduced to footnotes in books about psychoanalysis. How many people today have heard of Albert Moll, Magnus Hirschfeld or Iwan Bloch, the trio credited with establishing modern sexology? It wasn't until the 1970s that the task of correcting misconceptions about the originality of Freud's *Three Essays on the Theory of Sexuality* began in earnest.

Although *Three Essays on the Theory of Sexuality* was never quite as revolutionary as Jones suggested, it is still a landmark publication. Compared with his rivals, Freud's thinking was much broader in scope and more obviously relevant to clinical practice. His theory accounted not only for sexual development, but also for how aspects of sexual development related to the formation of neurotic symptoms. Consequently, it provided a rationale for therapy and clarified therapeutic objectives. Whereas sexologists tended to make isolated observations, Freud connected observations. In fact, the whole of psychoanalysis can be conceptualised not as a series of innovations, but rather a giant act of creative synthesis.

Freud's ideas concerning sex and sexual development are summarised below. Although many of these ideas appeared in his three essays, additional material is included to reflect the evolution of his theory over time.

In 1926, Freud wrote that 'the forces which drive the mental apparatus into activity are produced by bodily organs as an expression of the major somatic need ... we give these bodily needs, in so far as they represent an instigation to mental activity, the name of "Triebe"'. Somewhat mischievously, he added 'a word for which we are envied by many modern languages'. *Triebe* has no single-word English equivalent, and it is usually translated as 'instinct', 'drive' or 'instinctual drive'. In the majority of cases, instinct and drive can be used almost (but not quite) interchangeably, even though they have different (but overlapping) meanings. Sex is motivated by an instinct, an inborn inclination, that utilises a quantum of energy to drive mental and physical activity in a particular direction.

Freud made a distinction between life-preserving instincts (which motivate searching for food and avoiding danger) and sexual instincts (which motivate finding a mate). This dichotomy corresponds with Darwin's 'survival selection' and 'sexual selection'. A peacock's tail is metabolically costly, cumbersome, and a conspicuous lure to predators. Its evolution is inconsistent with the dictum 'survival of the fittest', and Darwin was obliged to explain how such anomalies arise by complementing natural selection with a second evolutionary theory, sexual selection. Peahens find large, heavy, brilliant tails attractive, so 'peacock tail genes' will be preferentially transferred from one generation to the next. In a sense, sex is more important than survival, because genes outlive individuals. As long as peahens and peacocks are mating, it doesn't matter if a certain number of peacocks get eaten by leopards. Freud agreed with Darwin. Sex is fundamental. Eventually, Freud began to think of the self-preservation and sexual instincts as part of a single 'life' instinct. Later, he created a pleasing duality by balancing the life instinct, Eros, with a death instinct (although the death instinct was never fully developed by Freud and it was always regarded with a certain amount of scepticism, even by psychoanalysts).

In his three essays, Freud undertakes a meticulous analysis of the sex drive according to its origin and qualities. Firstly, it is generated by the body. This happens when the erogenous zones become 'excited' by a stimulus. Secondly, it exerts 'pressure'. The strength of this pressure will vary according to the degree of excitation. Thirdly, it has an aim. This is usually a behaviour, the act an individual feels pressure to perform in order to release the build-up of sexual tension. And fourthly, it has an object: the thing or person required to satisfy the aim. If the aim is reproductive sexual intercourse, then the object will be an opposite-sex partner.

Freud used the concept of libido – a hypothetical energy – to describe economic aspects of mental life. Amounts of libido can be invested and withdrawn from mental representations. If a heterosexual woman is feeling sexually aroused while thinking of a naked man, her libido is being invested in this mental image. Freud's inclusion of libido in his theory reflects the degree to which he was influenced by figures such as Hermann Helmholtz and Gustav Fechner (who respectively described the mechanical and mathematical relationships underlying psychological phenomena). In fact, there is no such thing as sexual energy. Libido is merely a serviceable metaphor. Human beings might behave 'as if' their desires are fuelled by varying amounts of 'energy', but sexual attraction is complex, and the nervous system does not work on hydraulic principles. Freud, a neurologist who had undertaken a great deal of laboratory-based research, was completely aware of this. His employment of metaphor is knowing.

According to Freud, sexual feelings are present from birth. This assertion, stated without qualifications, will strike many as absurd. Clearly, neonates don't show very much interest in sex; however, Freud wasn't suggesting that babies are sexual in the same way that adults are sexual. He is referring to feelings that serve as the prototype of adult sexuality – an innate capacity to experience certain sensations, such as touch and warmth, as pleasurable. This predisposition has evolutionary advantages (more obvious in apes, perhaps, than in human neonates). Contact, incentivised by pleasure, will encourage a young animal to cling to its protective mother.

At first, the capacity for an infant to experience 'sexual' pleasure is completely generalised. Stroking any part of an infant's body will elicit signs of satisfaction or delight. Freud called this characteristic polymorphous sexual perversity. Over time, the sexual instinct becomes more particular and specific aims and objects are differentiated. Sexual development proceeds through three overlapping phases, oral, anal and phallic-Oedipal, and in each of these phases sexual interest is focused on a particular area of the body. A latency period of diminished sexual interest follows before a final pubertal or genital phase.

The oral phase extends from birth to the first year of life. During this phase, sensual pleasure is produced mostly by the mouth during breast feeding. Much of this pleasure can be attributed to the satisfaction of hunger; however, Freud pointed out that a baby will suck beyond its nutritional needs. When a nipple isn't available, it will suck a thumb instead. He detected intimations of post-coital abandon in the languor of a well-fed baby: 'If we see a child falling back into sleep, sated from the breast, with reddened cheeks and a blissful smile on its face, we cannot help thinking that this image also remains a definitive expression of sexual satisfaction in later life.' Infants are not always cheery, luxuriating cherubs. Freud understood that infants are animals, and when their teeth appear, aggressive impulses will make them bite. In a bold theoretical leap, he connected oral aggression with character. He supposed that unconscious memories of biting the nipple might promote sadistic tendencies in adulthood.

The anal phase extends from the first year to the second year. Transfer of sensual focus from the mouth to the anus occurs because bowel movements and bowel control become an increasingly salient feature of an infant's life. Freud supposed that, from the infant's point of view, evacuating the bowel must feel like a major event and relief will be experienced as proportionately satisfying. Defecation is also associated with the earliest experience of mastery. As the infant's body develops, it learns to control its bowel movements. Production of faeces is applauded by parents who frequently react as though they have been given a gift. Consequently, evacuations can come to represent 'good behaviour' and a willingness to obey. Alternatively, retention can frustrate parental expectations and become a means of showing defiance. Because the anus is an erotogenic zone, it is assumed that both evacuation and retention will be associated with a degree of 'sexual' pleasure.

As with biting during the oral phase, retention during the anal phase can gratify sadistic impulses. Parents can be punished – the faecal 'gift' withheld. Freud supposed that the conflicts surrounding potty training might shape personality. For example, if stools are like gifts, and gifts have monetary value, the habit of retention might eventually translate into parsimony. In a later paper Freud proposed a triad of traits that develop together during the anal phase: frugality, obstinacy and orderliness. Hence, the anally retentive or anal personality.

The phallic-Oedipal phase extends from the third to the sixth years. As soon as children become curious about sex differences and the mysterious provenance of babies, psychological processes are initiated that will lead to the formation of Freud's most referenced construct, the 'Oedipus complex' (a term that he did not use before 1910). A 'complex' consists of largely unconscious thoughts, emotions and impulses that amalgamate around a particular theme. In the case of the Oedipus complex, the theme is the child's relationship with its parents. Sexual entanglements within families had already been noted by doctors and explored in literature, but Freud's decision to harmonise a phase of sexual development with Sophoclean tragedy is highly distinctive.

According to the Delphic oracle, the child of the Theban king and queen, Laius and Jocasta, is destined to kill his father. When Jocasta gives birth to a child, Oedipus, he is abandoned on a mountainside and left to die. However, he is rescued and raised in Corinth. As an adult, Oedipus encounters a chariot on the road, quarrels, and kills the passenger – Laius. Oedipus liberates Thebes from the curse of the sphinx by solving its riddle and he marries the widowed queen. When he discovers that he has killed his father and married his mother, he blinds himself. Of course, Oedipus is metaphorically blind from the very beginning. His tragedy arises from unknowing. By choosing the Oedipus complex as the cornerstone of psychoanalysis, Freud is

reminding us that without self-knowledge we are psychologically vulnerable.

The purpose of the phallic-Oedipal phase is to guide object
choice. Boys are guided towards women, girls to men. Both
boys and girls begin with a common primary attachment to
their mothers, but as they mature (becoming increasingly aware
of their fathers and how the sexes differ) their developmental
courses diverge. The end point is heterosexual orientation prepared by infantile attraction to opposite-sex parents.

At the age of three, boys become sexually attracted to their
mothers. This coincides with a shift of sensual focus from the
anus to the penis. The potential for the penis to give pleasure
is discovered by accident – while being bathed, for example.
Boys are discouraged from playing with themselves by adults,
who might issue threats like 'Stop doing that or I'll cut it off'. At
roughly the same time, boys learn that girls do not have a penis.
Consequently, they begin to suffer from castration anxiety.
Because they are in constant competition with their father for
their mother's attention, they begin to fear paternal retribution.
They suspect that sexual attraction to their mother is futile and
the threat of castration causes them to repress their Oedipal
yearnings. This is the point when they enter the latency period,
in which sexual feelings subside until puberty.

Like boys, girls also experience a shift of sensual focus from
the anus to the genital area. They discover that they do not
have a penis, feel inferior, and develop 'penis envy'. Mothers
are blamed for this deficiency. They have not endowed their
daughters with 'proper' genitals, and they are even suspected
of having performed genital mutilation. Mothers are rejected
and affection is transferred to fathers (who girls suppose might
be able to give them a penis). The Oedipus complex is now the
Electra complex (a term introduced by Jung and subsequently
rejected by Freud). Normal heterosexual development proceeds

when girls replace their wish for a penis with a wish for a baby. A somewhat inconclusive entry into the latency period follows. They fear maternal retribution, but the absence of castration anxiety means that forbidden sexual desires are repressed with less vigour. Consequently, women are more likely to experience unresolved sexual feelings for their fathers than boys for their mothers.

During the latency period, sexual interest diminishes – although it is not entirely suspended. Moreover, the sex drive is put to other uses. The diversion of sexual energy during the latency period prefigures the sublimations of adulthood, the redirection or discharge of instinctual energy into non-instinctual forms of behaviour. For example, the creation of art.

On reaching puberty, boys and girls enter the final, genital stage of sexual development. The Oedipal dramas of infancy have already established opposite-sex objects. Puberty revives sexual interest, and the genitals become the focus of sexual pleasure. The sex drive can now fulfil its evolutionary destiny: reproduction. Young women must undergo one further transformation. A new wave of repressions shift sexual enjoyment from the clitoris, which resembles the male penis, to the uniquely female vagina.

Neurotic illness is largely the result of either a failure to pass successfully through the stages of sexual development or regression – slipping back to a pre-genital stage. Infantile wishes and urges will then intrude into awareness, causing levels of discomfort that will necessitate the deployment of defences, which will then produce symptoms. Freud's novel framework suggests that the neuroses are not illnesses in the accepted sense, but a consequence of incomplete development, reawakened infantile desires and unmastered childhood conflicts.

Three Essays on the Theory of Sexuality – and Freud's general thinking about sex – reveal two rather different Freuds. On the one hand we have the visionary theorist, who recognised the importance of building his psychology on firm, evolutionary foundations; the compassionate, liberal-minded doctor, whose empathic gifts allowed him to enter the sensory world of neonates and infants. And on the other hand we have the wild speculator, whose unchecked, heady assertions about female inferiority and penis envy test our patience and credulity; the author of psycho-sexual just-so stories that invite accusations of misogyny. Unfortunately, the latter Freud has attracted so much criticism that the former Freud is often overlooked. While rightly decrying the lesser Freud for his febrile guesswork and male chauvinism, critics have failed to notice the greater Freud – the rational, sensitive, liberal physician – who has exerted an extraordinarily benign influence on modern attitudes towards sex and sexuality.

Freud not only blurred the medical boundary separating mental illness and mental health, but also the moral boundary separating 'sexual perversity' from 'sexual normality'. If the evolutionary purpose of sex is reproduction, then all sexual behaviour with the exception of sexual intercourse is by definition deviant. Even 'normal' behaviour such as kissing can be considered 'perverse', because it is surplus to requirements. Since Freud's time, anthropological research has shown that there are indeed many societies who do not include kissing in their repertoire of sexual behaviours. Although Freud acknowledged that some perversions – licking excrement, for example – are so extreme that it is difficult not to view them as pathological, he still contested the supposition that such behaviour is invariably accompanied by 'serious abnormalities'. The only perversion that Freud condemns in his three essays is paedophilia.

Freud's defence of homosexuals is expansive: homosexuality was commonplace in classical civilisations, many of the world's greatest thinkers and artists were homosexual, and the majority of homosexuals are medically unremarkable. What's more, homosexuality and heterosexuality are not distinct. Homosexual men frequently seek cross-dressing partners – that is, men who make themselves look like women; and hetero-sexual men frequently engage in anal sex, a practice strongly associated (albeit from absence of choice) with homosexuality. Implicit in Freud's argument is the suggestion that homosexuals and heterosexuals aren't so very different. It is a sentiment that encourages tolerance.

Freud declares that there is 'something innate underlying perversions', but 'it is something *innate in everyone*'. Children are not born pure and corrupted by the world. In fact, they are born perverse and checked by the world's civilising influences. Freud's theory of sexual development reverses a way of thinking about children that dates back to Biblical times. Jesus advised his followers to be like children if they wished to enter the kingdom of heaven. But a baby is not – to paraphrase T. S. Eliot – a 'simple soul', issued from the hand of God. A baby is a promiscuous voluptuary with irregular tastes. Freud was writing at a time when sexual deviance was routinely explained by 'degenera-tion': neurological and moral dissolution caused by 'defective' heredity. By rejecting the notion of degeneracy, Freud placed himself in opposition to the Viennese pan-German nationalists who planned to purify the gene pool and populate the world with golden-haired, wholesomely heterosexual demi-gods. Freud's sexual theory derails pan-German Utopianism. We are all, even pan-Germans, born perverts. And we can all easily regress into states of perversity. Naturally, the Nazis were hor-rified by the implications of Freud's theory and one of their first acts of collective intellectual vandalism was to burn his books.

Three Essays on the Theory of Sexuality revolutionised child psy-chology. Although books on child rearing and education began to appear as early as the sixteenth century, the study of children was almost exclusively concerned with behaviour rather than experience. Freud's reconstruction of the inner world of the child was bold, imaginative and sympathetic. A baby isn't a blank slate. A baby is a person, and his or her character is already being formed during breast feeding and potty training. Freud's complete engagement with neonatal and infantile experience underscores another aspect of his modernity. His immersion in biology, even down to the level of the elimination of waste products, links experience – psychology – with metabolism and viscera. Embodiment, with all of its attendant limitations and indignities, is the first condition of being human. It is a funda-mental identification that has since been powerfully represented in the work of modern artists such as Francis Bacon, whose carnal figures (one famously depicting his lover dying on a toilet) endorse Freud's unwavering realism.

Freud's sexual theory changed attitudes towards sexual choices, ushered in a new approach to child psychology, and stressed the close relationship between mind and body. These are broad, almost accidental consequences of Freud's argu-ments and thinking. But to what extent are the specific details of Freud's sexual theory supported by evidence? And to what extent is his sexual theory testable?

Although neonates and infants experience pleasurable sen-sations, the degree to which these sensations correspond with adult 'sexual feelings' is impossible to establish. Other than noting superficial continuities – babies, adult men and some adult women find sucking nipples pleasurable, for example – nothing more can be added or proved. Biting the nipple during breast feeding and retention of faeces are common behaviours, but once again, demonstrating a connection between these activities in babies and infants and adult personality charac-teristics has not been proven to the satisfaction of empiricists. That young children are sexually curious and experience (albeit intermittently) feelings that approximate adult sexual arousal is now generally accepted; however, Freud wasn't the *only* doctor to write about childhood sexuality in the early years of the twentieth century and this feature of his theory was neither innovative nor unique.

The Oedipus complex was disproportionally significant to Freud as both a theorist and as an individual. He discovered the Oedipus complex through self-analysis, recognised correspondences between his own emotional history and the Greek myths (many of which feature incest and murder), then proceeded to identify Oedipal themes in the stories and customs of cultures described by anthropologists. Eventually, he became convinced that the foundations of the Oedipus complex, the underlying disposition, were inherited in the form of a 'race memory' dating back to a time when incest and violent parental retribution were, so he claimed, realities of tribal life. All of which led him to conclude that he had identified a truly universal phenomenon.

Freud's attachment to the Oedipus legend was profoundly personal. He was obsessed with the ancient world; as a child, he was sexually aroused when he glimpsed his naked mother; he strongly identified with Oedipus, the solver of riddles; as we have already learned, when he fantasised about being honoured by the university with a bust, he envisaged a quote from Sophocles on the plinth; a reproduction of *Oedipus and the Sphinx* by the nineteenth-century neoclassicist Ingres hung on his wall – just above the foot of his famous 'couch'. The Oedipus legend was so important to Freud that he seems to have projected his own Oedipal preoccupations on the entire human race, past and present. In fact, it is extremely unlikely that every human being's sexual destiny is determined by the formation and resolution of the Oedipus complex. And it is equally unlikely that the 'mental illnesses' formerly classed as neuroses – certain forms of anxiety disorder, for example – are

all attributable to unconscious, Oedipal material. There are many routes to sexual maturity and the causes of mental illness are complex and varied. Even so, it would be unwise to dismiss the Oedipus complex as a psychoanalytic delusion, a concept that only exists because of Freud's mother fixation, enthusiasm for Ancient Greece, and grandiosity.

All infants, both boys and girls, have a vested interest in

competing with fathers for maternal attention. Fathers gain genetically if they impregnate mothers; however, infants will then have to share resources with siblings. Later in childhood, competing for the attention of opposite-sex parents foreshadows competing with peers in order to win the attention of prospective mates. Big data analyses have shown that incestuous scenarios on pornography websites are surprisingly popular (for both sexes) and laboratory-based experiments, particularly those incorporating subliminal messages, have demonstrated that priming Oedipal sensitivities (attachment to mother or hostility to father) can have an impact on a range of mood and performance indices consistent with Freudian theory. Psychoanalysts argue that the most convincing evidence for the Oedipus complex is clinical. The complex is routinely uncovered during treatments and its resolution is associated with positive therapeutic outcomes.

The Oedipus complex is at least partially supported by evolutionary, social, experimental and clinical evidence; however, it is a single construct that demands two narratives – one for boys and one for girls – and the female narrative is, without doubt, altogether weaker and less persuasive than the male narrative. Freud was aware that his phallic-Oedipal account of female sexual maturation was problematic. In 1926 he wrote 'We know less about the sexual life of little girls than of boys', and he described the sex life of women as 'a dark continent' for psychology. A concept like 'penis envy' implies deficiency and inferiority – and his suggestion that a clitoral orgasm is somehow less mature than a vaginal orgasm supposes that a woman can only be truly satisfied by penetrative sex. The work of maturation isn't complete, Freud explains, until the clitoris has passed on its excitement to adjacent female parts, 'just as a piece of kindling can be used to light the harder logs'. Freud, usually brilliant at generating just analogies, seems to lose his

flair. Harder logs? Our confidence in him is eroded further when
he declares that the Oedipus complex resolves less successfully
in women, leaving them prone to moral weakness.

In his defence, Freud was a man of his time, and it would
have been extraordinary if his thinking reflected modern feminist values. Even so, the female Oedipal complex remains a
ramshackle construct that sags and creaks under a weight of
questionable assumptions and baseless inferences. The best that
can be said for Freud in this context is that he was willing to fully
engage with female sexuality, whereas many of his colleagues
were content to view women as innocent, naive and sexually
'anaesthetic'. Indeed, the female Oedipus complex, irrespective
of its shortcomings, can be understood as a misguided attempt
to bring male and female sexuality into alignment, to establish
gender parity and identify commonalities.

The starting point of Freud's sexual theory was his self-
analysis, but Freud the man was also Freud the citizen of
Vienna. In a very real sense, sex was all around him. His patients
confessed their forbidden wishes, many of his colleagues were
sexologists, and sex featured significantly in the work of Vienna's
most celebrated writers and artists. When Freud stopped at
coffee houses, he would have seen pornographic postcards and
magazines changing hands under tables; and when he visited
urinals, he would have been surrounded by walls covered with
obscenities and sexually explicit drawings. Sex workers cruised
the streets in such large numbers they were impossible to miss.
In his autobiography, Stefan Zweig recalled that their services
were 'for sale at every hour and at every price, and it cost a man
as little time and trouble to purchase a woman for a quarter of
an hour, an hour, or a night, as it did to buy a package of cigarettes or a newspaper'. In 1906, Felix Salten – now famous as
the author of *Bambi* – wrote a scandalous bestseller titled *Josefine
Mutzenbacher: The Story of a Viennese Whore, as Told by Herself.*

Brandstaetter Images/Getty Images

Even Vienna's green spaces were eroticised. The Belvedere Gardens, where affluent families strolled on Sunday afternoons, was (and still is) a safari-park of busty stone sphinxes. When Freud stood next to these exotic creatures, his identification with Oedipus must have felt particularly intense.

What do we know of Freud's sexuality?

Freud was introduced to sex by his nanny. Today, such behaviour would be regarded as abusive, but in Freud's time, attitudes were somewhat different. Acceptable and unacceptable conduct were less clearly defined. Nannies, for example, calmed children by stroking their genitals. Domestic employees were frequently expected to act as sex instructors. When the sons of bourgeois families reached puberty, attractive maids were hired to school them in the art of seduction.

At the age of three, Freud may have engaged in some sexualised play with his nephew John and his niece Pauline. Thirteen years later, at the age of sixteen, Freud fell in love, rather inconsequentially, with Gisella Flüss (a friend of the Freud family who was his junior by a year) – and the next person he fell in love with was his wife.

During his long engagement to Martha Bernays, it is possible that Freud visited brothels. If he did, this would have been entirely unremarkable. Around 75 per cent of medical students lost their virginity with a sex worker. It has been alleged that Freud told Marie Bonaparte that he was not a virgin when he married. Viennese young men were always visiting brothels or plying shop girls with gifts for sexual favours. Freud's preferred method of releasing sexual tension prior to marriage was masturbation – although it made him feel extremely guilty. He seems to have internalised an opinion expressed by several contemporary medical experts, that masturbation was morally and physically dangerous. His guilt persisted, which is odd, because his attitude to sexual practices, even the most perverse, was generally permissive. Ernest Jones believed that Freud's uneasiness about masturbation was connected with an underlying neurosis.

Freud's marriage was fecund, but sexually uneven. He suggested that ardour cools in marriage after two years, which some have supposed reveals something of his own experience. His relationship with Martha became less physical relatively early and he suffered from episodes of sexual dysfunction. In a letter he wrote to Fliess in 1896 (the year after Anna Freud was born) he complained of loss of sexual desire and 'impotence'. This diminution of sexual interest in Martha might explain – if the allegations are true – why he became intimate with his sister-in-law. Tiredness was also a problem. Freud aged prematurely, or at least he felt older than his actual age. Fatigue was probably attributable to long working hours and his insistence on writing into the night. Martha matched his industry in her own way. She was a conscientious and dutiful *hausfrau*, even after she had given birth to six children in quick succession.

Another factor that might explain Freud's dwindling sexual

interest was his bisexuality. Up until his middle years he was in the habit of forming very close friendships with men, and many of these friendships had – by his own admission – strong homo-erotic undercurrents. As far as we know, Freud never had any homosexual experiences. But perhaps the homosexual aspect of his sexuality was more developed than even he was prepared to acknowledge.

Around the age of forty, Freud seems to have resigned himself to a sexless marriage. The man whose name came to be associated with sex more than any other (with the exception, perhaps, of Casanova), the man whose name dominated debates about sex throughout the twentieth century, the man reputed to be the world's greatest love specialist, was – ironically – sexually active for less than a decade.

Freud's renunciation of sex suggests priesthood, retirement from the world to pursue arcane knowledge – the redirection of libido in order to serve a higher purpose. Once again, Freud seems to be yielding to the influence of mythic narrative. We are reminded of ancient prophets, whose physical blindness accentuates the heightened acuity of their supernatural vision. By giving up sight, they see more. Freud renounced sex to probe deeper into its mysteries. When he was writing his *Three Essays on the Theory of Sexuality*, he was very likely celibate; however, his sex life wasn't quite finished. A phantom sex life lingered in his unconscious. Freud continued to have erotic dreams, which he analysed with great pleasure. And there must have been occasional, if rare, moments of intimacy. In July 1915 Freud had a dream about taking out a pencil to write something in a notebook for his wife. He supposed the dream was related to 'successful coitus Wednesday morning'. He was fifty-nine.

Relatively late in life, several women became extremely important to Freud. He acquired a 'harem' of devotees with whom he formed meaningful, close relationships. This is partly explained by the increasing number of women with an interest in psychoanalysis who entered his circle from the 1920s onwards; but not all his female friends were aspirant psycho-analysts. He was very fond, for example, of Yvette Guilbert, a theatrical performer who delivered monologues in a manner between speech and song. Her appearance on stage was demure but her original lyrics were often risqué. She was a favourite subject of Toulouse-Lautrec. Freud saw Yvette perform in Paris and Vienna and found her company life-affirming. In one of his final letters, written in exile in 1938, he described missing the rejuvenating effect – the 'magic spell' – of just one hour in her company.

Lou Andreas-Salomé was a member of the German aristocracy. She became a well-known novelist, essayist and psy-choanalyst. She was also a dazzling beauty with a penchant for furs, boas and capes. Devotion to one man was, for her, spiritual bondage, and she had many distinguished lovers, among them the poet Rainer Maria Rilke. Nietzsche wanted to marry her – 'I have never known a more gifted and understanding creature'. Freud insisted, rather defensively, that Lou's beauty was incon-sequential as far as he was concerned. However, he frequently escorted her back to her hotel after psychoanalytic meetings, which suggests a degree of 'romantic' enchantment.

Princess Marie Bonaparte, Freud's junior by over twenty years, was the grandniece of Napoleon and heiress to an immense fortune. Her mother had died shortly after Marie was born and she was raised by her father and grandmother. Her father was a distant figure and once, while considering her mar-ital prospects, callously commented: 'If I saw you in a brothel, you are certainly not the one I would pick.' In 1907 she was introduced to Prince George of Greece and Denmark, and by the end of the year they were married. Her virginity was taken 'in a short, brutal gesture' and the Prince – a homosexual – only had intercourse with her because he was duty-bound to produce children. In due course she sought sexual satisfaction elsewhere and enjoyed the company of many distinguished lovers, including a French prime minister and a German winner of the Nobel Peace Prize; however, she was sexually 'unresponsive' and her mental health suffered as a consequence. She was close to suicide when Freud accepted her as a patient. Psychoanalysis proved to be enabling, but her 'frigidity' persisted. In a desperate attempt to overcome her sexual problem, she opted for a surgical procedure that involved moving her clitoris nearer to her vagina. A second operation was as ineffective as the first. Despite pain and discomfort, she continued having affairs and she was always open-minded about sex. According to Freud, she had 'no prudishness whatsoever'. Perhaps she was too open-minded. Her son, after undergoing psychoanalysis, proposed that they sleep together for one night to see if it would cure him. She considered undertaking the experiment and raised the possibility with Freud. He thought it was a very bad idea. Freud and Marie could talk about anything. Indeed, he used Marie's therapy sessions to ventilate his own feelings. On one occasion he confessed to feeling let down by everyone. He added, glumly, 'You may disappoint me too.' Marie was lying on the 'couch', and she reached back so that Freud could take her hand. 'My dear friend,' she said, 'no, I will not disappoint you.' Never has a promise been so faithfully honoured. Marie championed psychoanalysis, translated Freud's works, gave Freud financial assistance, and was instrumental in getting Freud and his family out of Austria after the Nazis arrived in 1938. He affectionately referred to her as 'Princess', and she loved him in return as a surrogate father.

Freud's theory of sexual development is a curious amalgam of insight, empathy and absurd speculation. Yet it is arguably one of the most influential theoretical formulations in the history of science. We can detect its seismic after-effects in disciplines

as disparate as evolutionary biology, personality theory and
Shakespeare studies (Oedipal conflict is frequently used by
directors to explain Hamlet's indecisiveness). The *Three Essays
on the Theory of Sexuality* changed the way people talk about
sex. Victorian sexologists frequently protected their readers
from explicit descriptions of sexual behaviour by slipping into
Latin. Entire paragraphs suddenly became opaque and impen-
etrable. The lay reader was immediately distanced from the
subject matter, and by implication, his or her body. Sex was
medical, not personal; anatomical, not sensual. Freud's use of
Latin was sparing, and his German was remarkably direct and
accessible. In effect, he made it easier for ordinary people to
have conversations about sexual predilections and preferences. It
seems unlikely that, without Freud's liberating social influence,
someone like John Lennon, for example, would have been able
to admit having once touched his sleeping mother's breast and
been tempted to go further. Freud democratised sex. Every vote
counts. We are all born perverts so no one in a civilised society
should be marginalised or pathologised simply because they are
attracted to same-sex partners or find the feeling of silk underwear exciting. By inviting everyone to join the conversation,
Freud catalysed attitude change and ultimately expedited the
transition of modern democracies from places characterised
by narrow-minded prejudice to nation states in which sexual
freedoms are respected and legally protected. After Freud, sex
could no longer be described as degenerate or sinful.

Chapter 10

Secession

In 1898, Gustav Klimt designed a poster for an art exhibition. It showed a naked Theseus slaying the Minotaur. His contemporaries would have understood the symbolism. This was the old guard being vanquished by the new. Before the poster could be displayed in public, it had to be approved. The relevant official ruled that the poster could only be used if Klimt agreed to cover Theseus's genitals. Consequently, he was obliged to introduce a tree into his design that provided the necessary concealment.

A few years later Klimt exhibited a faculty painting, *Philosophy*. Thirty-four thousand people came to see it in only two months. The university professors were not impressed by Klimt's emaciated figures. They didn't want to see his nightmarish cyclone of limbs and nether parts installed in their hallowed aula, and they protested with a petition. In Freud's Vienna, pompous professors, supercilious high officials, generals and bishops, the mayor and the Emperor, all supported by bureaucratic institutions, were a constant reminder of tradition, orthodoxy and suffocating patriarchy. A restless younger generation were becoming increasingly frustrated.

Licences were required to produce books or sell newspapers;

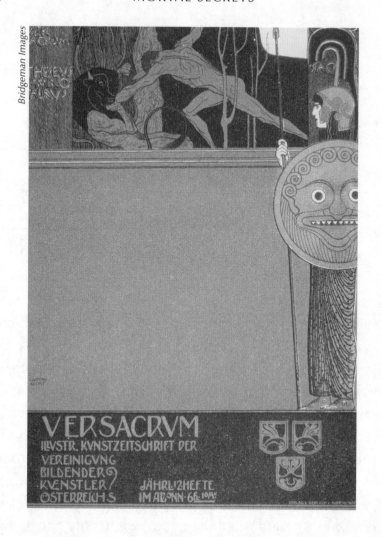

contentious articles were frequently suppressed by the state censor; police officers interfered with publishing activities. Everything was scrutinised and regulated. Few projects could proceed without the necessary signing of forms, rubber-stamps and permits. Twenty-seven officials were needed to process a single tax payment. Pedantic civil servants strangled innovation with red tape. Sometimes, the pettiness of the Habsburg behemoth resembled despotism. In 1906, an Italian worker was imprisoned because he insisted on calling the Emperor 'King'.

Inevitably, patriarchal rule, emphasised by portraits of the ageing, grizzled monarch in every public area, inspired a general Oedipal revolt. The cultural dynamics of Vienna in the early years of the twentieth century were Freudian: repression, followed by a build-up of tension, leading to a discharge of displaced, sublimated energies.

The Oedipal character of Viennese insurgency is evident in the eagerness with which various dissatisfied groups self-identified as being youthful or young. In the late 1870s, Die Jungen (The Young) emerged as a new left in the Constitutional Party. A literary movement interested in exploring psychological truth and sexuality known as Jung Wien (Young Vienna) appeared in the 1890s. When Art Nouveau reached Vienna in the mid-1890s, it was rebranded Jugendstil (Youth Style).

In 1905, Klimt and his colleagues resigned from the pre-eminent artists association (the Vienna Künstlerhaus) and declared themselves independent. Originally they were known as Die Jungen, although they became better known as 'The Vienna Secession'. The secessionists created their own gallery designed by the architect Joseph Maria Olbrich, a simple white building, minimal in appearance, but finished with a striking dome of gilded laurels. Passing conservatives could read their militant rallying cry – *To the age its art, to art its freedom* – prominently displayed over the entrance.

The origins of psychoanalysis were also Oedipal. Freud viewed the medical establishment as monolithic, resistant to change, and patronising. He wrote grudgingly, and sometimes untruthfully, about old professors. He stressed that his early followers were not just 'doctors', but 'young doctors'. Stirring up Oedipal angst had predictable consequences. The young men in his coterie soon started to see Freud as a stubborn, over-controlling patriarch. Within three years of forming the Vienna Psychoanalytic Society, Freud was beset by the first of several secessions. In 1911, Alfred Adler resigned in order to found the

Society for Free Psychoanalysis. Freud alleged that Adler had said to him: 'Do you think it gives me such great pleasure to stand in your shadow my whole life long?' The most significant Oedipal revolt against Freud, however, was the secession of a man whose very name – Jung – was foreshadowed by epithets such as Die Jungen, Jung Wien and Jugendstil. Unlike Adler, when Carl Jung seceded to create his own school, Analytical Psychology, Freud lost not only a colleague but his intellectual son and heir. The experience was extremely traumatic – for both of them.

Freud and Jung began writing to each other in 1906. Jung sent a copy of his book, *Diagnostic Association Studies*, his latest paper and a covering letter (which no longer exists) to Freud, and on 11 April, Freud responded with a graceful but brief acknowledgement. Although its collegiate tone is spoiled, perhaps, by a boast: 'everything I have said about the hitherto unexplored fields of our discipline is true'. Jung was a psychiatrist at the famous Burghölzli Psychiatric Hospital near Zurich. He had joined the staff in 1900 and his first academic assignment had been to read and evaluate *The Interpretation of Dreams*. From around 1901, another Burghölzli psychiatrist, Franz Riklin (who eventually married one of Jung's relatives), began treating patients using Breuer and Freud's cathartic method. In 1904, Jung attempted

History/Getty Images

to treat a young Russian woman, Sabina Spielrein, using psychoanalysis.

It wasn't until the publication of *The Freud/Jung Letters* in 1974 that Spielrein's clinical history came to light. Jung mentions her to Freud early on in their correspondence: 'Difficult case, a twenty-year-old Russian girl student, ill for six years'. Before 1974, Spielrein was known only as one of the first female psychoanalysts – not as a patient. In 1977, a 'carton' of her personal papers was discovered in the basement of the Palais Wilson in Geneva. She had lectured there when it housed a teaching centre. More of her personal papers were subsequently discovered in the archives of two Swiss neurologists. The revelations contained in her letters and journals were so sensational that they have since formed the basis of a popular book by John Kerr (*A Most Dangerous Method*), two stage-plays – by Snoo Wilson (*Sabina*) and Christopher Hampton (*The Talking Cure*) – and a 2011 film directed by David Cronenberg (*A Dangerous Method*).

When Spielrein was eighteen, she was admitted into the Burghölzli Hospital. She fluctuated between extremes of depression and laughter, could not make eye contact, screamed, and when touched poked her tongue out. Eventually her delirium subsided, and Jung was able to begin treatment. Jung's version of psychoanalysis was necessarily improvised. Spielrein didn't lie on a 'couch', for example. She sat in a chair with Jung sitting behind her. Sessions lasted for up to two hours and took place every other day.

As a child, Spielrein had been spanked by her father. This punishment (and seeing her brother's naked buttocks being spanked) produced thoughts about having defecated on her father's hand, and in due course a desire to soil her own feet. Between the ages of four and seven she would sit with a heel pressed against her anus, while attempting to simultaneously defecate and also prevent defecation. From puberty, imagining her father's hands made Spielrein sexually excited. Chastisements or reprimands of any kind, real or imagined, were equally arousing. When sexually excited, she would masturbate (even in the presence of others). She was aroused by masochistic fantasies involving her father but also disgusted. Jung treated Spielrein successfully in under two months. She was able to enrol as a medical student at the University of Zurich and thereafter she continued to see Jung as an outpatient.

Unfortunately, Jung was unable to maintain his clinical distance. Doctor and patient became friends, close friends, then lovers. They imagined that they could read each other's minds, and Spielrein became convinced that she was destined to bear Jung a son. Jung was completely carried away by their overheated talk of dreams, visions, Wagner, *Das Rheingold*, 'Siegfried' and 'love-gods'. They met at several locations: Jung's office, in the countryside and, less prudently, in Spielrein's apartment. By 1909, Jung was having doubts about the wisdom of conducting a reckless affair with a former patient. He was a respectable bourgeois doctor married to a wealthy heiress who was pregnant with their third child. A scandal could prove catastrophic. He decided to bring his association with Spielrein to an end, a consequence of which was that she turned up at his office brandishing a knife. It is unclear what actually happened, but afterwards, when concerned onlookers found her crying on a trolley outside Jung's room, they saw blood on her hand and arm.

In May 1909, Spielrein wrote to Freud, and Jung had to explain himself. He claimed, disingenuously, that he had devoted 'a large measure of friendship' to Spielrein in order to prevent her from relapsing. She had wanted to seduce him and now she wanted revenge. Lately, she had been spreading rumours. Freud's response was sympathetic. The practice of psychoanalysis was a perilous business. He too had only narrowly escaped seduction.

The following month, Jung confessed everything, although he stopped short of admitting that he and Spielrein had engaged in sexual intercourse. Freud continued to be non-judgemental, managed the situation calmly, and a scandal was avoided.

Freud had supported Jung during a crisis, but Jung was proud, and being indebted to Freud made him feel uneasy, particularly so given that – if Jung is to be believed – Freud was unaware of his reciprocal indebtedness to Jung. When, two years earlier, Jung had visited Freud for the very first time, Minna – Freud's sister-in-law – had confessed that Freud was in love with her and that they were having an affair. Jung hadn't mentioned this to anyone – even Freud. And in the years that followed, Spielrein's subsequent allegiance to Freud must have caused Jung a certain amount of Oedipal irritation. In 1914, as Jung was seceding, Spielrein wrote to Freud: 'Everyone knows that I declare myself an adherent to the Freudian Society and J. cannot forgive me for this.' (Although it should be noted that Spielrein's relationship with Freud had its own tensions and difficulties.)

Psychoanalytic mythmakers invite us to imagine the first meeting of Freud and Jung as an epic encounter, a coming together of the mighty dead. Yet, the truth is considerably less Homeric. There were moments of unintentional comedy, awkwardness, embarrassment and farce. Jung (accompanied by his wife and his pupil, Ludwig Binswanger) arrived at Berggasse 19 to have lunch with Freud and his family on Saturday 2 March 1907. Martin Freud recalled Jung's commanding presence: tall, broad-shouldered, with blue eyes and closely cropped hair – more like a soldier than a doctor. From the moment Jung entered the apartment, he talked continuously, addressing Freud while ignoring everyone else. It was only after lunch, in the seclusion of Freud's study, that Freud managed to interrupt Jung's monologue. The ensuing conversation lasted until two o'clock the following morning. Jung was so impressed by

Freud that he struggled to find adequate superlatives. 'Freud was the first man of real importance I had encountered; in my experience up to that time, no one else could compare with him. There was nothing the least trivial in his attitude. I found him extremely intelligent, shrewd, and altogether remarkable.' Spielrein informs us that Jung found Freud's face 'enormously likeable, particularly around the ears'.

On Monday 4 March, Jung and Binswanger returned to Berggasse 19 and Freud asked his visitors to recount their dreams. He then offered them some impromptu interpretations. According to Freud, Binswanger wanted to marry Freud's daughter and Jung wanted to dethrone Freud and take his place. Even after a single conference, Freud and Jung were in explicit, Oedipal competition. Two days later, Jung and Binswanger attended a meeting of the Psychological Wednesday Society. A patient obsessed with the numbers three, seven and forty-nine was being discussed. Freud sagely suggested that the number three might represent the Christian penis, seven the small penis, and forty-nine 'the large Jewish penis'. Jung and Binswanger, being the only gentiles present, must have made heroic efforts to hide their discomfort.

Although Jung was in awe of Freud, he thought that Freud's followers lacked substance. Privately, Freud had similar concerns. After the Wednesday night gathering, Freud took Binswanger aside and said, 'Well, now you have seen the gang.' He realised that they were unconvincing torchbearers. Jung, on the other hand, was the perfect ambassador: vigorous, charismatic, brilliant, and above all a Teuton. Jung's advocacy of psychoanalysis would confound critics who asserted that Freud's new science was an exclusively Jewish phenomenon. Jung would be Freud's 'Crown Prince'. He would spread the gospel of psychoanalysis beyond Vienna and Zurich. He would make it credible and convert the world.

After Jung's first meeting with Freud in Vienna, the two men exchanged photographs. Jung had his image of Freud enlarged and he was delighted with the result. 'It looks marvellous.' Jung even admitted to having developed a 'crush' on Freud – a crush with an undeniable 'erotic undertone'. Freud's letter to Jung written on 3 May 1908 is saturated with romantic sentiment: 'I am quite certain that after having moved a few steps away from me you will find your way back, and then go far with me. I can't give you any reason for this certainty; it probably springs from a feeling I have when I look at you. But I am satisfied to feel at one with you and no longer fear that we might be torn apart.' Their father–son relationship, with its attendant Oedipal encumbrances, was also complicated by feelings of homosexual longing. This explains, perhaps, why Spielrein acquired symbolic significance in their subsequent power struggles. She is easily cast as the third party in a notional 'love triangle'. In Christopher Hampton's play *The Talking Cure*, for example, Freud addresses Spielrein possessively: 'If you still love him, it's because you haven't yet understood the hatred he deserves.'

Freud and Jung's friendship became stressed along several fault lines. When Jung visited Freud for the second time in March 1909, he found himself irritated by Freud's dismissal of the paranormal. He experienced a build-up of heat in his chest and then a bookcase emitted a loud 'report' that made both men start. Jung claimed that they had just witnessed a 'catalytic exteriorisation phenomenon'. Freud said that this was 'sheer bosh'. Jung predicted another detonation which, when it happened, left Freud aghast. After Jung's departure, Freud examined his furniture and concluded that the noises had been caused by two heavy Egyptian antiques on shelves in an adjacent room. In a subsequent letter, a less bullish Jung admitted to 'spookery'; however, in the same letter, Jung goes on to airily declare that he is feeling less oppressed by Freud's paternal authority having had a 'great dream'. He doesn't mention that in this 'great dream' Freud had appeared in the person of an old and disgruntled imperial customs official. For Jung, parapsychology offered tantalising glimpses of the numinous, and Freud's pedantry ruled out exciting possibilities.

In 1909, Freud and Jung were invited by Stanley Hall (a significant although somewhat eccentric psychologist) to deliver a series of lectures at Clark University in America. This was a great opportunity for the two analysts to further their cause and enhance their reputations. They were to be accompanied by the Hungarian psychoanalyst Sándor Ferenczi, who immediately became obsessed, not with the prospect of storming a continent with new ideas but with what clothes he should bring.

The party assembled in Bremen on 20 August. At dinner, Jung spoke at length about some recently discovered peat-bog mummies. Freud wanted to change the subject, but Jung continued until Freud fainted. Freud would respond to contradiction in precisely the same way three years later in Munich. After regaining consciousness, Freud said that he thought Jung's talk of corpses showed that he wanted him dead. This was not an auspicious way to begin a joint enterprise.

The following day, the three analysts set sail for America on board the *George Washington*. This was a luxurious transatlantic liner with interconnected decks, a two-storey smoking room, a reading room, murals and a vast white and gold dining room (extending across the entire width of the ship) where passengers could sit in comfortable red Morocco chairs beneath a domed ceiling. Freud, Jung and Ferenczi spent much of the eight-day crossing analysing each other's dreams. Once again, Freud found further evidence that Jung wanted him dead when Jung reported a dream featuring two skulls on the floor of a cave. Jung probed Freud's private life, hoping to learn more about Freud's relationship with his sister-in-law. Freud, however, became suspicious, refused to cooperate, and exclaimed: 'But I cannot risk my authority!' Jung identified this moment as the beginning of the end.

Freud developed health problems. He was urinating every thirty minutes and suffering from intestinal symptoms. Jung thought that Freud was being neurotic and attention-seeking. Later in the trip, in New York, Freud actually wet himself. Jung, displaying little sympathy, told Freud that he needed to be in psychoanalysis. On the evening of 29 August, the *George Washington* floated past the Statue of Liberty and proceeded towards Hoboken, New Jersey. The decks would have been crowded, the atmosphere exhilarating. Yet Jung and Freud chose to ruin the occasion by engaging in a petty argument about ambition.

Freud, Jung and Ferenczi were met by A. A. Brill (the first analyst to practise in America) and escorted to the Manhattan Hotel at the corner of 42nd Street and Madison Avenue. The next five days were hectic. They visited the Metropolitan Museum of Art, Tiffany's (where Freud purchased a Chinese bowl), the Museum of Natural History, the Psychiatry Department of Columbia University, Coney Island Amusement Park, Chinatown and Harlem. Freud and Ferenczi saw moving images for the first time in a cinema. They dined at Hammerstein's Roof Garden, although Freud detested American food and he refused to drink iced water. He claimed that American food had ruined his digestive system and on returning to Vienna would often refer to his 'American colitis'.

On 4 September, the tourists travelled by overnight steamer to Fall River before taking two trains, to Boston and finally to Worcester. They were received by Stanley Hall and his wife, whom Jung described as 'plump, jolly, good natured and extremely ugly'. Mrs Hall, overwhelmed by heat, fanned herself by an open window, while Stanley warmed himself next to an open fire. The Europeans were astonished by American affluence: black servants dressed in white gloves and dinner jackets, carpets, thousands of books, and cigar boxes in the lavatories!

Freud's first lecture was scheduled for 7 September. Given the importance of the event, it is remarkable that – as was his custom – he prepared minimally. Indeed, the majority of his preparation seems to have taken place in the thirty minutes preceding his entry into Jonas Clark Hall. He went for a short walk with Ferenczi during which he discussed the broad areas he might cover. He then entered the building and improvised an absorbing and well-structured lecture without consulting a single note. He free-associated four more lectures on as many consecutive days. In the audience were the Nobel Prize-winning physicists Albert Michelson and Ernest Rutherford, as well as the 'founding father' of American psychology, William James. The anarchist Emma Goldman also attended; however, she had to leave the second lecture because of disruptive behaviour. Freud was unflappable and used the disturbance to construct a helpful analogy. In fact, Goldman was a great admirer of Freud. She had attended lectures given by him in Vienna in 1896 (when she was studying to be a midwife) and in her autobiography she remembered Freud at Worcester, 'among an array of professors', standing out 'like a giant among pygmies'.

In spite of their Oedipal issues and bickering, when it mattered, Freud and Jung could work together as an excellent double act. They were happy to turn in performances as old-world savants. When a medium was produced, as a kind of test, Freud and Jung passed easily, exposing her as a fraud and extracting a confession. On 10 September, they were awarded honorary doctorates at a grand ceremony. National and local newspapers gave them glowing reviews. They were treated like celebrities.

From Worcester the analysts travelled to Niagara Falls and then to the Adirondacks, where their host was the neurologist

James Putnam. In the evenings, Jung sang songs and Freud and Ferenczi learned how to play a board game. Freud had jokingly suggested that his main reason for visiting America was to see a wild porcupine. Unfortunately, the only one that he came across was dead. Putnam compensated Freud with a porcupine paperweight, and Freud was so touched by the gesture that he kept the gift on his desk for the rest of his life.

After their sojourn in the Adirondacks, the analysts returned to New York. They boarded the *Kaiser Wilhelm der Grosse* and set sail for Bremen on 21 September. The crossing was rough, and Jung went home directly. Freud and Ferenczi stayed on in Berlin, where they investigated a psychic. Freud was far more willing to accept paranormal phenomena in Jung's absence and he concluded that the psychic might indeed possess telepathic powers.

Freud arrived in Vienna on 2 October. After all the excitement of America, he was tired and a little irritable. Reunion with his disciples reminded him of their mediocrity. By contrast, William James – the pre-eminent American psychologist – had travelled to Worcester just to meet him. In the early 1920s, Freud remembered James with great affection. He told his student Abram Kardiner that James was the only American genius he had ever known. 'Furthermore,' Freud added, 'he had one attribute for which I have unstinted admiration; he spoke German better than I did.'

Kardiner was curious. 'Well, Professor, what did he think of you?'

Freud responded, 'Oh, he thought I was crazy.'

Perhaps Freud wasn't joking. In a letter to his friend the eminent Swiss psychologist Théodore Flournoy, James said of Freud: 'I confess that he made on me personally the impression of a man obsessed with fixed ideas. I can make nothing in my own case with his dream theories, and obviously "symbolism" is a most dangerous method.' Nevertheless, James still conceded – to Ernest Jones – that Freud would 'throw light' on human nature and that the future of psychology most likely belonged to Freud and his disciples.

Freud had been feted in America. Lionised. His American doctorate would, in fact, be the only university distinction he would ever receive. America had extended its arms and welcomed him with a warm embrace. Americans had been generous and respectful. The Boston *Transcript* had hailed him as 'a man of great refinement'.

America's appreciation of Freud was never reciprocated. What began with 'American colitis' became a generalised antipathy, an irrational wariness of an entire country, its values and its inhabitants. According to Freud, America was an unsuccessful experiment, brash and lacking in sophistication. It flirted with barbarism. He shared with Jones his view that America was 'a gigantic mistake'. Tobacco was the only excuse for 'Columbus's misdeed'. Americans were superficial, lacking in judgement, and probably didn't understand his ideas at all. By the 1930s, he was censuring Americans for not talking clearly – a sure sign of their lax social attitudes.

After conquering the New World, Freud and Jung resumed their correspondence, but Freud's remark about not wanting to risk his authority had shaken Jung's confidence in both Freud and psychoanalysis. Three years later he reminded Freud of the incident in a letter, and in 1925 he claimed that Freud's remark was the most 'important factor' in his subsequent relations with Freud. Jung was still writing about the incident in 1961: 'Freud was placing personal authority above truth.'

The reason why Jung seceded from the psychoanalytic movement – the reason that he gave and the reason that has since been repeated in countless histories – is that he found Freud's description of mental life too narrow. Freud placed too much emphasis on sex. Jung advocated a broader psychology that

accommodated spiritual aspects of experience. It is certainly
true that Freud and Jung had differences of opinion. But there
were still significant areas of overlap: repression, dream interpretation, symbols, levels of consciousness – hinterlands of
anthropology, archaeology, art, myth and legend. Jung always
accepted that sex was a primary drive (particularly in youth and
early adulthood) and Freud had an enduring interest in spirituality, albeit as an 'oceanic' feeling, the product of sublimations,
or as a psychological defence. Both men believed that ancestral
memories might be preserved in the deepest reaches of the
unconscious. In many respects, Jung seceded not because his
understanding of the mind was radically different from Freud's,
but because it was so similar. They both wanted to dominate
what was essentially the same field, depth psychology, and
their competitive relationship was aggravated by Oedipal and
homoerotic sensitivities. Inevitably, affection – possibly even
love – transmuted into contempt.

By 1912, Jung and Freud's letters had become a bruising
exchange of insults and accusations. Freud accused Jung of
making fun of him; Jung accused Freud of 'playing the father'
and being oblivious of his own faults. They accused each other
of being neurotic. In January 1913, Freud had had enough: 'I
propose that we abandon our personal relations entirely.' Freud
shared his disappointment with Sabina Spielrein: 'My personal
relationship with your Germanic hero has definitely been shat-
tered. His behaviour was too bad.' Nine months later, Freud and
Jung were in the same room together for the last time. They
were both attending the Fourth International Psychoanalytic
Congress. There was no reconciliation. They had nothing to
say to each other.

The lives of Freud, Jung and Spielrein continued to be
discreetly entangled for many years. Spielrein became a
committed Freudian. But she also corresponded with Jung

until around 1920. She practised as a psychoanalyst in Berlin, Geneva and Moscow, married, and had two daughters. In 1942, she was living in her hometown of Rostov-on-Don, which at that time had been occupied by Nazi forces. She was murdered with her daughters by a death squad, and it is believed that her tragic end was hastened because she censured a Nazi officer in German.

Although she published a great deal, after her death her reputation was almost exclusively defined by one of Freud's footnotes. On the basis of this single footnote (appended to Freud's 1920 essay *Beyond the Pleasure Principle*), Spielrein has been routinely and incorrectly credited with having anticipated Freud's thinking on the death instinct. In fact, her writing was concerned principally with destructive aspects of the sex drive. The impact of her intellectual legacy is more readily discerned in the work of child psychologists such as Jean Piaget and Melanie Klein.

After his secession, Jung suffered a 'mental breakdown' which, by his own admission, had pronounced psychotic features. He experienced apocalyptic visions, painted strange canvases, and played with stones like a child. He also encountered imaginary beings. Two such visitors were a bearded patriarch, Elijah, and his beautiful young companion, Salome. Although Jung under-stood that Elijah represented wisdom and Salome the erotic, he never admitted that his unconscious was clearly struggling to accept the loss of Freud and Spielrein. Notwithstanding his hallucinatory episodes, Jung's 'illness' was remarkably pro-ductive – a period of creative self-exploration and discovery. He emerged from his illness revitalised, went on to develop analytical psychology, and became the most significant depth psychologist, second only to Freud.

But what of Freud himself?

Freud never forgave Jung for seceding. Much of his 1914

History of the Psychoanalytic Movement is dedicated to an extended attack on Jung which ends with an emphatic if somewhat florid good riddance: 'Psychoanalysis will survive this loss and gain new adherents in place of these. In conclusion, I can only express a wish that fortune may grant an agreeable upward journey to those who have found their stay in the underworld of psychoanalysis too uncomfortable for their taste.' But Jung wasn't merely a discomfited, temporary 'adherent', an ungrateful son. He was also a competitor. A brilliant, charismatic competitor. Freud may have wished him a dyspeptic *bon voyage*, but there was a very real chance that Jung's example would inspire others. Psychoanalysis (according to Freud and Freud alone) had to be protected.

Ernest Jones had already sprung to Freud's assistance before Jung's departure. He was, perhaps, too much a man of action, a figure-skating physician who had been accused of exposing himself to two 'mentally defective' girls on one occasion, and on another, talking inappropriately about sex to a ten-year-old 'hysteric'. A magistrate dismissed the first case, but Jones was asked to resign from his job after the second. In 1911, Jones tried to silence another 'hysteric' – this time a woman who claimed that he had seduced her – by giving her $500. She was eventually sent to a sanatorium, and Jones, once again, survived a scandal. In 1917, he married Morfydd Owen, a gifted musician. The following year, she died after surgery for an abscessed appendix. The emergency operation was performed in Jones's family home in Craig-y-môr, even though Swansea Hospital was only four miles away. Jones was devastated after Morfydd's death, but his wife's friends were uneasy and suspicious. The marriage had been troubled. Had Jones been dilatory? Why had he hesitated until Morfydd's condition was critical? Had Jones administered the general anaesthetic himself? And why had it taken so long to have the death certified? Loe Kann, a former mistress of Jones, wrote a letter to Freud (some months after Morfydd's death) in which she suggested that both she and her husband were in possession of incriminating information: 'how much have you guessed (psycho-analytically) about Jones's marriage and the consequent death of his wife. We'll tell you about it someday.' It isn't known whether this conversation ever took place.

Jones proposed the creation of a secret committee, a small group of Freudian loyalists who would, like Charlemagne's paladins, guard the kingdom and policy of their master. Freud loved the idea: 'I know there is a boyish and perhaps romantic element too in this conception, but perhaps it could be adapted to meet the necessities of reality.' Freud's note of caution doesn't quite conceal his excitement and he was soon ready to appoint his secret guardians: Jones, Ferenczi, Karl Abraham, Otto Rank and Hanns Sachs. They met for the first time in Vienna on 25 May 1913. Like members of a magical fraternity, each member was given a special signet ring.

Although the secret committee was ostensibly another cabal, similar to the Psychological Wednesday Society, it operated like a politburo. It existed to provide leadership, promote a unitary doctrine, and to keep the psychoanalytic community under surveillance. When Jones was writing his celebrated biography of Freud in the 1950s, he recollected the secret committee with great fondness. It had functioned 'perfectly' for at least ten years, and he described its members as 'a happy band of brothers'. The reality was quite different. The principal business of the secret committee was political. There were disputes, feuds and Machiavellian manipulations. In due course, Jones was rumoured to have called Rank a 'swindling Jew', and Rank tried to get Jones expelled. Soon after, Freud stopped attending. To make matters worse, young Rank started to develop ideas of his own and quickly transitioned from secret guardian to blacklisted heretic.

According to Freud, that which is repressed returns, and
Oedipal revolts are biologically and psychologically preordained. The secret committee was doomed from the start
because it failed to recognise that its aims would be frustrated
by the very ideas it had sworn to defend. Innovations in art and
science can never be suppressed. The young will always seek to
overthrow the old. And Freud, as he hurried past the new white
and gold temple of the Vienna secession, must have felt the penetrating chill of its symbolism deep in his bones.

Chapter 11

Games of Love and Death

On 13 October 1899 a shoemaker's assistant and his daughter were searching for mushrooms in the Vienna woods. The child strayed and discovered the body of a fashionably outfitted woman. The dead woman was dressed in a dove grey suit, a black jacket, black stockings and yellow shoes. A yellow hat with a dark blue ribbon and veil lay on the ground beside her, and next to this was a revolver. Her face was covered in blood. A short distance from the woman was the body of a six-year-old girl in a red dress, brown stockings and, like the woman, yellow shoes. Her face was hidden by a hat made of white lace, but her earrings were visible. They were gold with blue stones, arranged to resemble flowers. Beside the six-year-old was a discarded blue jacket and a bloody handkerchief. The dead woman had a bullet wound in her right temple; the six-year-old, in her left. When the police arrived, they searched the dead woman's pockets and found a gold watch on a chain, a key, and a black leather purse. In her blue silk reticule they found a pair of yellow deerskin gloves, the child's gloves, some sugar, a ham sandwich, a box of bullets, and the photograph of a man. On the back of the photograph the woman had written 'I have loved you till my unhappy end'. It was dated two days earlier.

Detectives were able to establish the woman's identity and reconstruct her past. Her name was Hedwig Keplinger and she had travelled to Vienna at the age of seventeen from Styria, a mountainous southern state. Unaccustomed to life in the big city, Hedwig was easy prey. She was seduced and then abandoned with a child, but a wealthy man (the man in the photograph) took her as his mistress and she was able to live in relative luxury. The man's gifts and favours were enough to persuade Hedwig that she was in love, but her love wasn't returned and her wealthy patron tired of Hedwig's charms. He decided to end their association. Feeling guilty, perhaps, he attempted to make Hedwig's future more secure by introducing her to a prospective husband, an engineer who was just about to leave Vienna to work in Bulgaria. Hedwig corresponded with the engineer and in due course they considered themselves engaged. Unfortunately, when the engineer returned to Vienna and learned that Hedwig had an illegitimate daughter, he refused to go ahead with the planned marriage. At which point Hedwig could see only one way out of her predicament. Abused, heartbroken and desperate, she went to the woods where she shot her daughter, then herself.

The story of 'the corpses in the woods' attracted a great deal of public interest. A leading newspaper featured the story under the heading 'Murder and Suicide'. These words were resonant for the Viennese in 1899. Two years earlier, the bodies of Crown Prince Rudolf, the only son of the Emperor and Empress, and his seventeen-year-old lover Baroness Mary Vetsera, had been found in the bedroom of a hunting lodge at Mayerling (also in the woods outside Vienna). Doctors concluded that the prince had pulled the trigger both times: murder and suicide.

Around 1900, Vienna had the highest suicide rate compared with any other European city. Disappointed lovers, jilted lovers, dishonoured lovers. Paradoxically, when Vienna was at its most romantic, it was also at its most deadly.

The casual attitude to suicide exhibited by the Viennese, especially in matters of love, betrays the powerful and lasting influence of German Romanticism. The entire Romantic movement was launched by Goethe's 1774 novel *The Sorrows of Young Werther*, which ends with its eponymous hero shooting himself in the head because of unrequited love. Thereafter, German Romantic poetry repeated the formula with such frequency, many judged suicide to be the fitting solution to the problem of lovesickness. Moreover, Wagner had knotted together love and death so tightly in the Germanic soul by means of the 'Liebestod' of *Tristan und Isolde* that the two concepts became effectively inseparable.

The ease with which the Viennese killed themselves was linked not only with Romanticism but also with several aspects of local culture. Viennese writers were obsessed with the ephemeral, and fleeting experiences were celebrated in the feuilleton, their preferred (and most popular) literary form. The acceptance of ephemerality became so characteristic of Viennese psychology that it led to a loosening of the collective grip on existence. The Viennese were extraordinarily willing to let go of life.

Decadence, as a late Romantic 'attitude', was another factor that raised suicide numbers. Although the decadent movement was primarily a French phenomenon, its transgressive values were adopted by artists and writers across Europe, and then disaffected members of the social mainstream. The Viennese were particularly adept at exhausting the senses, after which they tended to sink into a state of cynical, world-weary detachment. Heavy meals, pastries, dancing, cigars, brandy, immersion in music and theatre, thrilling rides in the amusement park, cocaine, morphine, brothels providing 'special' services and shop girls in hotel rooms – for middle-class professionals, Vienna was a pleasure garden. Yet, excessive indulgence always seemed to leave the Viennese sensualist feeling empty. Death was often viewed as a welcome escape from a carousel of sexual compulsion, disillusion and sour comedy.

The Viennese were gleefully morbid. They had a talent for turning death into spectacle. The Abbey of Melk, only a short distance from Vienna, housed (and still does) a collection of bejewelled skeletons. After the death of her husband, Empress Maria Theresa spent the remaining fifteen years of her life in a suite of rooms draped with black silk. The Viennese were renowned for their bravura funerals. Pall bearers wore elaborate outfits and hearses were pulled by liveried horses. There were wreaths, sashes, torches and flags. In 1910, close to a million people attended the funeral of Mayor Karl Lueger. The peculiarity of the Viennese attitude to death is exemplified by the once common expression *schöne Leich* – 'beautiful corpse'. To be a beautiful corpse was something to aspire to. Clearly, the citizens of Vienna wanted to carry their dark glamour to the grave – like the macabre bling of the Melk skeletons.

Theatricality and deadly insouciance collided on the field of honour, where heedless duellists played the quintessential game of love and death. By 1900, with the exception of Austria and Germany, duelling was rare in most European countries. A duelling culture survived in France, but it was mostly high spirits and posturing. There were few fatalities. Germanic duels, however, frequently ended with one or other participant being taken to a mortuary. It wasn't until 1917 that the practice was finally outlawed in Austria.

Before pistol duels, the Viennese resolved arguments with swords and sabres. The duelling scar – usually found on the left cheek because most opponents were right-handed – became a desirable fashion accessory. It signalled virility and breeding and acted as a potent aphrodisiac. When the writer Arthur Schnitzler was a medical student, the possibility of acquiring a duelling scar was used as an inducement by a colleague who wanted him to join a fraternity. It was suggested to Schnitzler that a scar would look good on him. As in every domain of Viennese life, sartorial standards had to be upheld, even when a gentleman was in mortal danger. Duellists often wore shirts with detachable sleeves to avoid the unspeakable vulgarity of bleeding out with one's sleeves rolled up.

Some very unlikely people fought duels. Arthur Schnitzler's friend Felix Salten fought a sabre duel in 1896. Schnitzler thought such behaviour was 'stupid and bestial'. Four years earlier, after the Austrian Princess Pauline von Metternich had argued with a Russian-born countess over a flower arrangement intended for a Viennese exhibition, the two women agreed to settle the matter honourably. They travelled to Liechtenstein to fight a duel. Before engaging for three rounds with rapiers, the rivals stripped to the waist as a 'safety precaution'. Inevitably, a story about topless noblewomen in bloody combat received international coverage. On 23 August 1892, subscribers of the *Pall Mall Magazine* in London learned that after inflicting wounds on each other (a slashed arm and a cut nose) the two ladies renewed their friendship with an embrace and kisses. Whether or not they troubled to repair the insufficiency of their wardrobe prior to the embrace was left to the reader's imagination.

The longevity of duelling in Vienna is explained by several factors: the prevalence of duelling fraternities, the cult of honour (which was strongly associated with class), and later, familiarity with firearms because of national service. Although they were fought for many reasons, the majority of serious duels – that is, duels ending with a death – were fought to defend the honour of a woman. The reputation of a seduced daughter or wife accused of infidelity could be swiftly restored with a steady hand and a well-aimed bullet. Duelling drew Wagner's knot of love and death even tighter.

A form of duel that amalgamated the idea of playing a game of chance with murderous intent and suicide was the so-called American duel. It was designated American not because it had originated in America, but because the word 'American' was being used pejoratively. Lots were drawn and the loser killed himself within an agreed period of time. This hybrid of Russian roulette and suicide pact, the outcome of which depended on neither mettle nor skill, suggested transatlantic gimmickry to well-bred 'Germans'.

Between the mid-nineteenth century and the start of the Second World War, a quite extraordinary number of Viennese intellectuals decided to end their own lives. Among the names on this grim roster are several acquaintances of Freud, the great physicist Ludwig Boltzmann and the composer Hugo Wolf. There were also significant losses by suicide to literature and art, for example Freud's friend the writer Stefan Zweig (who overdosed on barbiturates with his wife in 1942) and the pioneer expressionist painter Richard Gerstl.

Gerstl's story combines the key elements of Viennese tragedy: sex, death, genius and nerves. Artistically, he was a lone voice, and for many years his work was almost forgotten. Even today he is often overlooked. Gustav Klimt, Egon Schiele and Oskar Kokoschka occupy so much of the cultural foreground it is difficult to catch sight of Gerstl. Yet he is as psychologically sophisticated as his contemporaries, perhaps even more so. Gerstl's 1907 self-portrait shows the head of a young man laughing, but there is nothing merry or uplifting about this penetrating study. The laughter is manic, nightmarish, diabolical. Gerstl exposes the existential horror beneath the wry comedy and wistful melancholy of languid decadents and coffee-house wits. His last painting, dated 12 September 1908, is a disturbing full-length nude self-portrait, admired and imitated by significant post-Second World War artists (including Freud's grandson

Lucien Freud). Genitals dominate the composition – a clear indication that sex featured in the narrative that brought the young artist to this strange, abstract space, illuminated by a blue, eldritch light. We are in oblivion's antechamber. The whiteness of his skin will make him a beautiful corpse.

Gerstl was only twenty-two years old when the composer Arnold Schoenberg welcomed him into his circle. He found himself standing at the epicentre of a musical revolution and painted all the participants. Schoenberg's wife Mathilde (a small, demure mother of two children) was the most unlikely object of desire. Although, beneath her matronly exterior, Mathilde may have been a wild, passionate romantic. She was described by Alma Mahler (the wife of Gustav) as being 'man mad'. In 1908, Gerstl joined the Schoenbergs and their friends for the summer at the spa resort of Gmunden. Gerstl and Mathilde were 'discovered' together, possibly in Gerstl's rented farmhouse, and they subsequently ran away; however, they eventually returned to Vienna, and Mathilde resolved to end the affair for the sake of her children.

On 4 November 1908, just around the corner from Freud's apartment, Gerstl stabbed and then hanged himself in front of a mirror. He was only twenty-five. A few days after his suicide, Schoenberg wrote a letter to Gerstl's brother, Alois: 'I am afraid, that, if one discovers the reason for your poor brother's death, the newspapers, in view of my position in society, will give vent to their lust for sensations, and in a more or less obvious way, will turn me, the innocent party, into a laughing stock.' Alois Gerstl agreed to say nothing and Richard's paintings were packed and transported to a storage warehouse where they remained, unseen, for twenty-three years. The reason why Gerstl had taken his own life remained a secret until the 1950s.

A final point needs to be made concerning the Viennese propensity for suicide. Perhaps Viennese intellectuals found it relatively easy to let go of life because many of them supposed that they had already been sentenced to death. As they played their games of love and death, they must have been acutely aware of the greater game that was being played by kings, politicians and revolutionaries. A game in which love of country would replace love of person and mortar shells would replace bullets and rapiers. The prospect of having to fight a suicidal war must have had a profound effect on how they chose to live – and die.

When war broke out in 1914, Freud was uncharacteristically optimistic. He supported the triple alliance and was confident of victory. He felt a sudden surge of patriotism and expressed his willingness to give the empire 'another chance'. He was delighted to hear news of 'German' advances. His belligerence was tempered only by being cut off from Ernest Jones – 'It has generally been decided not to regard you as an enemy!' – and his affection for England. In August that year he wrote to his Berlin-based disciple Karl Abraham and expressed the sentiment, with evident regret, that it was difficult for him to support the war with 'all my heart' knowing that 'England is on the wrong side'. Freud's patriotic zeal is puzzling to us now. A man who was so well acquainted with the darker aspects of human nature should have been more fearful.

But Freud's flag-waving was symptomatic of the militaristic euphoria that had swept across the whole of Europe. The writer and historian Frederic Morton has suggested that the outbreak of war was universally celebrated because, at least initially, it satisfied a deep emotional need for unity, a need that had been hitherto frustrated by post-industrial social fragmentation. 'Until now they had been mutually separated. Competition had driven them against each other. Or poverty had marooned them. Or they had been isolated in their cocoon of envy and alienation. Now it was all marvelously different. Now the worn-down unemployed, the trodden-under scullion, the unfulfilled genius, the bored coupon clipper, the jaded boulavadier [*sic*] – they could all link arms and walk forward together in the same electrifying adventure, against the enemy. Now they were Germans together, Frenchmen together, Englishmen together, Russians together and – most astounding – ethnically motley Habsburg subjects together.' Writers such as Rainer Maria Rilke,

Thomas Mann and Hermann Hesse were equally excited by the prospect of upheaval and change. Mann viewed war as 'a purification, a liberation, an enormous hope'.

Freud's jingoism did not last long. Within months the grim realities of war had started to depress him. In a letter to Lou Andreas-Salomé, written in November 1914, he asserted that the world would never be happy again. 'It is too hideous. And the saddest thing about it is that it is exactly the way we should have expected people to behave from our knowledge of psychoanalysis.' Finally, he was connecting his theories with corpses on battlefields. Every day he worried about the safety of his three enlisted sons – and his practice dwindled to nothing.

There were intermittent moments of light relief. He was, for example, cheered by news of his faithful disciple Ferenczi who, while serving as a doctor in the Hungarian army, had conducted the first analysis on horseback: 'Hippic psychoanalysis'. Humorous asides, however, were not enough to sustain Freud's spirits through the coming years of loss and hardship. The year 1917 was dismal and testing. Freud's nephew, Hermann Graf, was killed on the Italian front aged only twenty. Winter came, and it was so cold Freud could barely write with his numb fingers. Food was scarce. A few patients trickled back, only three, and the meagre income generated by his tiny practice wasn't enough to match the rising cost of living. He was solvent, but only just. By 1918 Freud had lost all his savings and he was no longer feeling any affection for the empire: 'The Habsburgs have left nothing but a pile of crap.' Defeat was followed by ruin.

After being detained in an Italian prisoner-of-war camp, Martin Freud returned to a much-changed city, but he did not receive a hero's welcome. He had to hide his officer's gold stars beneath a scarf to avoid being assaulted. There were mobs roaming the streets and 'hooligans' chanting. Passengers stripped the loose fittings from train carriages. A ham sandwich cost the equivalent of a year's rental of a luxury apartment. Money put aside for a suit in the morning might not be enough to buy a waistcoat by the afternoon.

With the collapse of empire, memories of Old Vienna – with its waltzing, carousing and duelling – faded. On the streets, hussars accoutred in plumed caps and embroidered capes were replaced by widows, dressed in black. The war had changed everything. It had even weakened the theoretical foundations of psychoanalysis.

Freud had rejected trauma as the primary cause of neurotic illness when he abandoned his seduction theory. But thousands of shell-shocked soldiers had returned from active service exhibiting 'neurotic' symptoms that were clearly connected with traumatic experiences. At first, it seemed that the war might provide psychoanalysis with opportunities for expansion. The question of why some soldiers and not others developed war neuroses was one that Freud could answer. Vulnerability might be explained in terms of underlying sexual conflicts. And psychoanalysis was a more palatable alternative to widely used treatments such as the administration of electric shocks. But it soon became evident that psychoanalytic theory was discrepant with clinical findings. The nightmares of battle-scarred veterans did not conceal sexual wishes. No matter how deeply nightmares were excavated, there was nothing erotic to be discovered beneath the nocturnal replays of exploding ordnance and decapitated comrades. In addition, successful therapeutic outcomes seemed to rely on the release of strangulated emotion, consistent with Breuer's cathartic method rather than psychoanalysis. Freud's fundamental understanding of the human animal was also in need of revision. His emphasis on the primitive was largely sexual. Mankind's capacity to orchestrate violence on a global scale strongly suggested that equal importance should be given to the destructive as well as the procreative drive.

While the war was still raging, another calamity began to unfold. A deadly flu virus, originating in China, mutated in America and then spread through France, Europe, and thereafter engulfed continents. It killed between twenty and fifty million people in four successive waves between 1918 and 1920. An early casualty of the so-called 'Spanish flu' pandemic was Freud's twenty-six-year-old daughter, Sophie. She was living in Hamburg with her husband and two children when she fell ill and died, suddenly. Freud was unable to attend her funeral because the railway system wasn't operating. Sophie was regarded as the family beauty, the 'Sunday child'. Freud was devastated, but his extraordinary ability to accept adversity – a characteristic that he would display again and again, particularly in his final years – comes into sharp focus for the first time. 'It is a brutal, absurd act of fate that has taken our Sophie from us, something in the face of which we can neither accuse nor ruminate, but only bow our heads under the blow, we poor humans without recourse, playthings of the higher powers.' Ferenczi was deeply concerned about the effect of this tragic loss on Freud, but Freud responded by sending his solicitous disciple a gentle rebuke: 'Do not be concerned about me. I am just the same but for a little more tiredness.' Of course, Freud wasn't the same – and never would be. For the rest of his life he carried Sophie's image in a locket attached to his watch chain.

Only three years later, Freud discovered a cancerous growth in his mouth. Recalling the event in his autobiography, Martin Freud wrote that this disease would eventually cause his father's death sixteen years later. This isn't strictly true. Cancer didn't kill Freud. What really killed Freud was an overdose of morphine administered by a physician at Freud's request. In making such a request, Freud appended his name to the long roll call of Viennese intellectuals (and duellists) for whom games of love and death were simply a part of life.

The Viennese penchant for suicide can be construed, perhaps, as another dimension of their 'modernity'. Today, global suicide rates have never been higher. The more the modern world has to offer us, the more eager we are to leave it.

Chapter 12

The Rat Man

He is twenty-nine years old, knock-kneed, and a little shorter than his doctor. He has black hair, dark brown eyes, a sharp nose and an oval chin. Lying on Freud's 'couch', the young man talks, at first, about a friend who calms his nerves when he gets anxious. A memory surfaces of an acquaintance who betrayed his trust when he was an adolescent and he declares that the betrayal was a great shock. The young man is aware that his doctor, sitting out of view, has a special interest in sexual development. Like many educated people in Vienna, he has glanced through *The Psychopathology of Everyday Life*. Perhaps it is this prior acquaintance with Freud's ideas that makes the young man change the subject. Without preamble, he starts to talk about an event that happened when he was four years old. 'We had a pretty governess called Fräulein Rudolf. One evening she was lying on the sofa, reading – and she had very little on. I was lying beside her, and I begged her to let me crawl under her petticoats. She said that I could, providing I didn't tell anyone about it. She wasn't wearing much underneath, and I fingered her genitals and touched her belly – which struck me as odd.'

There is no scratching, no movement of a pen nib across

paper. Freud isn't taking notes because that would be distracting. He prefers to give his patients his full attention, otherwise something important might be missed.

The young man continues: 'After this, I was left with a burning curiosity to see the female body. At that time, I was still allowed to go to the baths with the governess and my sisters and I can remember the suspense, the intense excitement, as I waited for the governess to take off her clothes and get into the water. I can remember more from the age of five. We had another governess, who was also young and good-looking. She had abscesses on her buttocks which she used to squeeze every night. I would wait, furtively, for that moment, so I could satisfy my curiosity.'

More memories. He is seven years old. Fräulein Paula is twenty-three – not very intelligent, unmarried and with a child of her own. 'She allowed me to take liberties with her. In her bedroom, I'd remove the covers and touch her – and she never objected.' He explains that, as a child, he used to get erections. He complained about them to his mother. Sex became mired in morbidity. 'I had an urgent desire to see the girls I liked naked. These wishes were accompanied by an uncanny feeling, a sense that something bad would happen if I allowed myself to think like this. I felt as though I had to take preventative measures.'

Freud stirs. 'Can you give me an example of what you thought would happen? What you feared?'

The young man takes a deep breath. 'Yes. For example, that my father would die.'

He admits that he still thinks about his father dying. He is deeply troubled by the possibility that his thoughts will, in some magical way, cause his father harm.

The session continues, and suddenly Freud is perplexed. He leans forward. Did he mishear? Did the young man make a verbal slip? No. Neither. Freud is astonished. The young man's father died several years earlier. He is worried about harming someone who is no longer alive.

Who was he, this serious, articulate young man?

Freud referred to him only as 'my patient' or 'our patient'; however, his name was Ernst Lanzer and his identity wasn't made public until 1986. Ernst's first consultation with Freud was on 1 October 1907. Earlier that year, on 17 July, he had received his doctor juris and he was qualified to practise law. He was also a reserve officer in the Austrian army and from 11 August to 7 September had participated in military exercises in Galicia. Ernst's case was presented by Freud to his colleagues at the inaugural International Psychoanalytic Congress on Sunday 26 April 1908, in a conference room at the Bristol Hotel in Salzburg. Freud sat at the head of a long table and delivered his address in a low, conversational register. He began at eight o'clock in the morning and spoke until eleven, at which point he suggested a break. His audience was rapt and demanded that he continue. He acquiesced and continued until one o'clock. It was a virtuoso per-formance, and none of the attendees – among them Jung, Adler, Ferenczi and Jones – had heard anything quite like it before. The following year, Ernst's history was published as *Notes Upon a Case of Obsessional Neurosis* – a title somewhat eclipsed by a more dramatic alternative preferred by psychoanalysts: *The Rat Man*.

In addition to worrying about causing harm to his dead father, Ernst suffered – or had suffered – from several supplementary problems: worry about causing harm to his cousin Gisela Adler, suicidal urges, concern that his thoughts could be read by others, counting compulsions, obsessive fears, and senseless, self-imposed prohibitions. Ernst's case is unique, because it is regarded by many as the single instance of successful psycho-therapy both undertaken and written up by Freud. His other successful case study, *Analysis of a Phobia in a Five-year-old Boy*, details a treatment that Freud only supervised.

Ernst was born on 22 January 1878 into a well-off Jewish family, although his parents were not (by any measure other than solvency) typical representatives of the Viennese bourgeoisie. Heinrich Lanzer (Ernst's father) had married his wealthy and much younger cousin Rosa. Although he was reputed to be kindly, generous and tolerant – indeed, Ernst claimed that he and his father had been best friends – he could also be cloddish and reckless. As a non-commissioned officer he had gambled away a significant sum of money that belonged to his unit. It was an impulsive act that might have got him into very serious trouble with his superiors. His blunt, barrack-room manner sometimes shaded into vulgarity. He mixed up the meanings of words, tested his wife's patience with excessive flatulence, and overused scatological expletives. He also beat his children. On one occasion, while beating the infant Ernst, he was stunned by his son's reaction. Ernst was too young to have learned conventional derogations, so he employed some ready substitutes: 'You lamp, you towel, you plate.' Heinrich made a prophecy: 'This boy will either be a great man one day, or a great criminal!' In spite of Heinrich's many shortcomings, Freud, rather surprisingly, chose to describe him as 'a most excellent man'.

Little is known about Rosa, Ernst's mother. Her immediate family were poor, but she was adopted and raised by rich relatives. When she married, the union was very much to Heinrich's advantage – a fact that she never allowed him to forget. Although Rosa was irritated by her husband's flatulence, a shared proclivity for fouling the atmosphere made them a curiously compatible couple. Rosa didn't like baths and emitted unpleasant genital odours due to an illness. Ernst responded to these various domestic assaults on his nose by growing up exceedingly clean.

Ernst was the fourth of seven children and the Lanzer household was animated and generally happy; however, when Ernst was only three years old, his sister Camilla died. He was already thinking 'magically' and feared that he had caused her death by masturbating. Ernst's four surviving sisters do not feature in the published case study, but we know – from Freud's notes – that Ernst was sexually attracted to Olga, his junior by two years, and that when they kissed they did so in such a way as to arouse suspicions of incest among the servants. Ernst once dreamed of having sexual intercourse with Olga, and when she got married, Olga's husband became jealous. 'If Olga has a baby in nine months' time,' Ernst assured his brother-in-law, 'you needn't think I am its father; I am innocent.' It is doubtful that this ill-judged remark proved very helpful.

There was only one brother, Robert, who was younger, stronger, more handsome and 'better loved'. Before they were school age, Ernst encouraged Robert to look down the barrel of a toy gun because he would 'see something interesting'. He then pulled the trigger. Over twenty years later he remembered the event and asked Freud, 'How could I possibly have done that?' In spite of this early infraction, Ernst was a protective 'big' brother. He casually mentioned to Freud that he was thinking about murdering the woman Robert wished to marry. He wanted to save Robert from an act of 'folly'. Freud didn't take the remark very seriously.

When he was twenty, Ernst's family employed an emotionally needy dressmaker. She asked Ernst if he could love her and his response was evasive. A few days later he learned that she had died after throwing herself out of a window. This sad event inflated his sense of personal influence. Around this time he fell in love with his cousin Gisela; however, his feelings for her were mixed. Periods of intense desire alternated with indifference. During their chequered courtship she would reject two proposals of marriage and inflame an attack of jealousy. When Gisela's uncle Richard started showing her 'numerous little attentions',

Ernst's thoughts, once again, turned to murder. Although, in actuality, all he did was go on a strict diet.

Heinrich disapproved of Gisela as a prospective wife for Ernst because she was sickly and poor. Consequently, Ernst viewed his father as an insuperable obstacle to their future happiness. There was, however, a solution to their predicament. If Heinrich were to die, his death would not only put an end to his meddling, it would also release Ernst's inheritance. Brooding on such possibilities soon made Ernst feel very guilty. Heinrich died in the summer of 1899 and for a long time Ernst was unable to adjust. When he heard a good joke, he would think: 'I must tell father that.' A knock on the door would prompt the thought 'That will be my father'. Even when he was finally able to accept his bereavement, he still expected his father's ghost to appear. It was as though, for Ernst, the boundary separating the living and the dead had become porous.

Ernst stopped masturbating in his adolescence, but the urge returned after his father's death. Bizarrely, his lapses were not abetted by sexual stimuli. He masturbated after hearing the horn of a mail coach on a 'lovely summer's afternoon' or when he chanced upon an uplifting passage in Goethe's autobiography, *Poetry and Truth*. Beautiful moments and elevated literature were his preferred erotica. Eventually, he worked out that masturbating while thinking about Gisela was a more natural and satisfying alternative.

When he was studying law, at the age of twenty-three, Ernst developed an extraordinary ritual. Between midnight and one o'clock in the morning – 'the witching hour' – he would interrupt his work, open the front door of his apartment, and expect to see his father waiting outside. Then he would drop his trousers and examine his penis in the hall mirror. Sometimes he would insert an additional mirror between his legs to get a better view.

In 1906, Ernst went to Munich for hydrotherapy, where he had regular sex with a waitress, an experience that he enjoyed, but mostly because it awakened thoughts of patricide. 'This is a glorious feeling! One might do anything for this – murder one's own father, for instance.'

The following year (the year in which he consulted Freud), Ernst was obliged to take part in military exercises in Galicia. Although his private thoughts and behaviour were distinctly odd, he was still able to function in the field. He is described in his military dossier as a very competent soldier, decisive, intelligent, reliable and skilled, companionable with his equals and a good influence on his subordinates. During an afternoon halt, Ernst sat down between two officers. One of them was a captain called Nemeczek, a man Ernst feared because he was known to have a cruel streak. Nemeczek had been keen to introduce whipping as a punishment and once, in the officers' mess, Ernst had opposed him. After some general conversation, Nemeczek started to talk about an oriental torture.

Ernst tried to narrate what Captain Nemeczek had described in his second session with Freud, but he was suddenly overwhelmed by anxiety. He stopped talking, jumped off the couch and pleaded with Freud to be excused from continuing his story. Freud cannot resist exploiting the drama in his case study. He abandons his measured, professorial tone and creates a sense of urgency by switching to the present tense: 'At this point he breaks off, stands up and asks to be dispensed from any account of the details. I assure him that I have no liking for cruelty myself and certainly have no desire to torment him.' Ernst was so distressed, when he spoke again he mistakenly called Freud 'Captain'.

Freud made a suggestion. Perhaps Ernst could be excused from providing explicit and distressing details. Perhaps they could proceed if Ernst was willing to provide a few hints from which Freud could make extrapolations? Ernst was coaxed back on to the couch and a kind of psychoanalytic parlour game based on oblique questioning followed.

'Do you mean . . . impaling?'

'No, not that. But the condemned man was tied up.'

'Tied up? How was he tied up?'

Ernst mumbled an answer.

'I don't understand. How was he tied up? In what position?'

'A pot was turned upside down on his buttocks . . . some rats were put into it . . . and they . . .' Ernst jumped off the couch again. His face was contorted with horror, and he could barely speak. 'Bored their way in . . .' He couldn't go on.

Freud finished his sentence for him: 'Into his anus.'

Ernst looked horror-struck, but there was something about his expression that merited interpretation: complexity, layers of sub-text – meaning. Freud judged that Ernst was horrified not only because the torture was horrific, but because he was also experiencing unconscious pleasure: *'horror at the pleasure he does not even know he feels'*.

With enormous difficulty, Ernst continued: 'An idea flashed through my mind. It occurred to me that this might happen to a person very dear to me.'

'You imagined yourself carrying out the torture?'

'No . . . not really. I thought about the torture being carried out in an impersonal way.'

In order to establish the identity of the victim, another guessing game ensued. At its conclusion, Freud was convinced that Ernst had imagined Gisela being tortured.

Ernst explained to Freud that the idea of harming others was completely alien to him. When such thoughts occurred, he was compelled to perform parrying measures to prevent the bad things he imagined from happening. 'As Nemeczek was describing this awful torture, I used my usual preventative formulas. I say *but*, and wave my hand in a dismissive way. And then I add *Whatever are you thinking of?* I did this to ward off the torture for both of them.'

Freud was taken aback. 'Both of them? You've only mentioned the lady.'

'A second idea came into my head – simultaneously. I thought of my father being tortured too.'

The oriental torture is the shocking, central image of Freud's case study. Once encountered, it's hard to forget – rats, frustrated by their confinement, attempting to escape through a human body by the only available route, gnawing through flesh and viscera. It is reminiscent of Edgar Allan Poe. In fact, the source of the torture *was* fictional: it appears in an 1899 decadent novel, *The Torture Garden*, by the French author Octave Mirbeau. In Mirbeau's story, a character describes a single rat agitated by a red-hot rod inserted through a hole in the pot: 'he panics, jumps, writhes and wriggles, turning around, climbing up the sides of the pot, and running over the buttocks of the man who he first tickles and tears with his claws and bites with his sharp teeth as he seeks for an issue through the torn and bleeding flesh'. Curiously, *The Torture Garden* wasn't identified as the source of Captain Nemeczek's cruel yarn until the 1960s.

In the same session that Ernst discussed the oriental torture he described another incident, but in such a convoluted way that Freud had to hear the story repeated three times before he could understand it. Essentially, it concerned a modest sum of money that Ernst believed he had to repay in a particular way, otherwise rats would – once again – anally penetrate Gisela and his deceased father.

From childhood, Ernst had feared that bad things would happen to those he loved, not only in this world but the next world, and for all eternity. As an adult he was not religious and adopted the attitude of a 'free-thinker', but logic was an ineffectual weapon against his anxiety and easily subverted. How can anybody, he reasoned, know anything about the afterlife? He might as well perform his protective rituals, just in case. What did he have to lose?

Freud's understanding of Ernst's extreme sensitivity was typically counterintuitive. He believed that Ernst's fears and protective rituals were really a kind of overcompensation for hostility that he, Ernst, harboured primarily towards his father and that ultimately dated back to infancy. Ernst had repressed these feelings and they had been stored in his unconscious for decades. Freud explained to his patient his model of how the mind works by means of his favourite metaphor. He drew Ernst's attention to the antiquities in his consulting room and observed that buried artefacts are usually well preserved. Ernst's infantile hostility was still raw and easily diverted towards others. Heinrich's disapproval of Gisela had stirred up patricidal hatred and Ernst's guilty denial of his father's death had been defensive. Ernst could not accept that he was the kind of person who relished the idea of rats feasting on his father's innards.

Ernst had never been able to repress his sadistic inclinations completely. There was the incident with his brother and the toy gun when he was a child, and as an adult he indulged in elaborate revenge fantasies in which Gisela threw herself at his feet and begged him for mercy. On one occasion, he sexually assaulted a servant girl with kisses. His sadism also bled into his relationship with Freud, and he admitted to having had dreams and daydreams in which Freud and his family were abused and humiliated. He imagined, for example, Freud's wife performing anilingus. His most surreal fantasy involved a herring being stretched between Freud's mother's anus and Freud's wife's anus. When Ernst made these disclosures, he was usually distraught: 'Most honoured professor, how can you allow yourself to be insulted in this way by filthy scum like me? You ought to throw me out; I don't deserve any better.' Disturbed by his own depravity, Ernst would leap off the couch and pace around the room. Freud asked him why he did this, and Ernst explained that he thought it extremely disrespectful to dispense insults while lying down. Eventually he was more candid. In fact, he was putting himself beyond Freud's reach. The infant Ernst (surviving in the adult Ernst's unconscious) was anxious to escape another 'paternal' beating.

Freud augmented his fundamental understanding of Ernst's bedevilments with various speculations in which anal eroticism, Oedipal conflicts and the symbolic meaning of rats are all afforded explanatory value. Even Ernst's ostensibly innocent pince-nez could, Freud argued, be viewed as representing the gonads. Freud was evidently aware that his interpretative latitude was imperilling his credibility, because, in the middle of a passage in which he asserted that a rat can sometimes represent a penis, he introduced a footnote, solely to fortify the confidence of his readers: 'Let me remind anyone who is inclined to shake his head over such leaps of the neurotic imagination of similar capriccios with which the artist sometimes indulges his imagination.' He supplies an example: the *Diableries érotiques*, a series of admittedly very odd lithographs by the nineteenth-century French painter Le Poitevin. But Freud's argument is weak. Clearly, the ingenuity of the artistic imagination does not, in any way, legitimise his assertion that Captain Nemeczek's rat torture was, among other things, a metaphor for anal sex.

Freud's attempt to describe the workings of Ernst's mind feels somewhat haphazard, but he is struggling to describe the indescribable, and the subsequent sense of confusion experienced by some readers reflects (at least in part) the difficulty, or even impossibility, of the task. A more forgiving appreciation of these fanciful passages – especially those dealing with anal eroticism and rat symbolism – might acknowledge Freud's willingness to grapple with mental complexity. Indeed, this can be viewed as a defining feature of Freud's modernity: his total engagement with compound meanings and contradictions; his continuous excavation of mental life, all the way down to its primal substances. We do not think logically like characters in a novel. The mind is messy and loose chains of association unravel in unexpected directions. In the figure of Ernst, Freud presents us with a modern 'Everyman'. To be human is to be perplexed and driven by primitive urges; prone to imagining the middle-aged wife of one's doctor on her knees, licking one's anus. Ernst's mental chaos is our mental chaos.

Ernst is frequently likened to literary protagonists in stories by Dostoevsky, Schnitzler and Zweig. His infantile sexual investigations, aided by complicit governesses, were pitifully comic, but he was also a deeply troubled, sensitive soul who was destined, like many of his contemporaries, to meet a tragic end. He was also very agreeable. On 28 December 1907, Freud wrote a cryptic short sentence in his notes: 'He was hungry and was fed.' It appears that Freud invited Ernst to join him for dinner. Even in 1907, this would have been judged extremely irregular behaviour for a psychoanalyst.

Freud destroyed the case notes of every patient he later wrote up as a case study, with one exception. Ernst's notes were found among Freud's posthumous papers and in 1955 they were abridged and published in James Strachey's *Standard Edition* of Freud's complete works. Nineteen years later, the unabridged case notes were published in a bilingual French-German edition. For several decades, psychoanalysts were inclined to gloss over discrepancies between Freud's day-to-day clinical notes and *Notes Upon a Case of Obsessional Neurosis*; however, after the 1986 publication of Patrick J. Mahony's *Freud and the Rat Man* – a scholarly and forensic comparative study – it became clear that these discrepancies were more than just 'a handful of interesting

deviations'. The two texts are significantly different. Freud
omits key incidents in the published case study; his fickle editing
is clearly intended to produce a more compelling narrative; he
puts his own words into Ernst's mouth. And sometimes, he just
lies. For example, he claims that the treatment took a year when
in fact it took about three months. The discrepancies between
the posthumous case notes and the published case study demonstrate that Freud's *Notes Upon a Case of Obsessional Neurosis*, his
psychoanalytic showpiece, is uncomfortably close to being a
work of fiction, a 'novelization' of a psychoanalytic treatment
rather than a rigorous, scientific paper. And for many – not only
Freud's critics – this degree of invention is entirely unacceptable.

But Freud tells us precisely what he is doing on the very first
page. He states quite clearly that we are not going to get the
truth, the whole truth and nothing but the truth: 'I cannot provide a complete treatment history because this would require
too detailed an account of my patient's circumstances.' He
laments the fact that the reader is being offered 'distortions'. A
few pages later, he declares that his case study is 'imperfect and
incomplete'. He is supplying only 'fragments of understanding'. Although these qualifications might not exonerate Freud
completely, they do cast accusations of fraud in a softer light. In
Freud's mind, the case of the Rat Man was a kind of compromise – a knowing half-truth – to be used as a 'starting point'
by 'other investigators'. It is of some note that Freud's nemesis,
Patrick J. Mahony, favours a balanced assessment. *Notes Upon a
Case of Obsessional Neurosis* undoubtedly contains 'exaggerated
claims', but it also contains 'momentous insights'. He praises
Freud's 'graphic imagination, his magisterial analytic powers,
and his imposing awareness of temporal convolutions and the
intricacies of antecedents and consequences in intrapsychic life.'

Freud claimed that Ernst's treatment was a great success,
and from what is known of Ernst's professional and personal

life we can be reasonably confident that Freud's claim was justified. Ernst found employment in several offices, including his brother-in-law's, which suggests, perhaps, that family relationships were no longer strained. After twelve years of unsatisfactory courtship, Gisela finally accepted Ernst's proposal of marriage and the ceremony took place in the Templegasse synagogue in 1910. It seems likely that Ernst's analysis with Freud provided the necessary impetus. At the age of thirty-four, Ernst was formally recognised as an 'attorney' and his career prospects were good. A young Viennese lawyer could expect to live well. Unfortunately, fate intervened with tragic consequences. As a reserve officer, Ernst was activated in the military after the outbreak of the First World War in August 1914. He was taken prisoner by the Russians on 21 November and four days later he was dead. His death was not officially confirmed until 9 September 1919.

In 1923, Freud added a footnote to *Notes Upon a Case of Obsessional Neurosis*. 'The patient's mental health was restored to him by the analysis which I have reported upon in these pages. Like so many other young men of value and promise, he perished in the Great War.' The fact that Freud was minded to compose this footnote, to memorialise Ernst's service to his country and subsequent death, is a measure of Freud's attachment to Ernst. During his analysis, Ernst saw Freud as a father figure, but it is equally true that Freud reciprocated and saw Ernst as a son. Freud's third son, also a soldier in the First World War, was called Ernst and could easily have met a similar, violent end. The idea of joining the Freud family was so appealing to Ernst that he fantasised about marrying Freud's daughter. It was a fantasy that he thought Freud shared. Freud fed Ernst when he was hungry, showed him his antiques, asked to see a photograph of Gisela, and even sent Ernst a postcard. Freud didn't exhibit the traditional cool reserve of a seasoned psychoanalyst.

Notwithstanding its many problems, *Notes Upon a Case of Obsessional Neurosis* remains a key work in the modernist canon. Indeed, it can be argued that its problematic nature, its curious blend of authenticity and distortion and its uncertain status as a scientific document are the very things that make it modern. Like much of Freud's work, it defies categorisation, breaks rules and straddles 'genres'. Furthermore, Freud's portrait of Ernst anticipates the late twentieth-century conception of the anti-hero. He gives us a complicated character assembled from contradictions: a courteous gentleman whose sensitivity disguises violence; an honourable soldier who is simultaneously ridiculous and absurd. The Ernst who faced the Russian army is also the same Ernst who inspected his penis from different angles after being summoned to the door by his father's ghost. Ernst oscillates between tragedy and farce.

Over the course of our lives, we can all expect to experience moments of valour and distinction. But there will also be times when we stand figuratively with Ernst in a hallway and tilt a mirror between our legs. This is a very Freudian view of humanity, a view that was resisted almost universally for millennia in works of art and literature. Indeed, it is only after Freud that depictions of human absurdity have become commonplace.

As a character, Ernst anticipates the theatre of the absurd. His ridiculousness is amusing, but it also exposes a bedrock of metaphysical terror. Where does masturbating to the sound of a mail coach horn fit into God's divine plan? What purpose, in the grand scheme of things, is served by a child crawling under the petticoats of a governess? We can easily reposition Ernst on Samuel Beckett's country road with tree in *Waiting for Godot*, a play that combines the stuff of nightmares with vaudevillian repartee. Beckett, who suffered from debilitating anxiety and depression, was treated at the Tavistock Clinic by the psychoanalyst Wilfred Bion. He was familiar with the psychiatric literature. In the final scene of *Waiting for Godot*, Estragon's trousers drop. Pierre Latour, the actor who played Estragon in the first production of the play in 1953, resisted this direction. Beckett was insistent. Not only was it necessary for Estragon's trousers to drop, but they must drop completely to the ankles. When the Lord Chamberlain demanded that there should be no dropping of trousers in the first London production of the play, Beckett was very reluctant to make this cut, even though he had agreed to many other changes. The image of Ernst, with dropped trousers, mirror in hand, is potent beyond comedy. It is, in its own way, essential. An honest and humbling recalibration. A necessary challenge to outmoded, narcissistic delusions of grandeur. Yet, even standing as a vaporous entity between Estragon and Vladimir, Ernst's presence is quietly reassuring. He is absurd, but he is also likeable. So likeable that Freud invited him to dinner.

Whatever we do behind closed doors, however strange we appear when we are caught in the spotlight of reason – with dropped trousers pooled around our ankles – there is always the possibility of acceptance and friendly conversation. Freud has prepared a place for us at his table. We are still invited – we are still human.

Chapter 13

The Architecture of the Mind

Every human skull contains three pounds of gelatinous tissue and a continuous consciousness that is interrupted by dreamless sleep. We tend to think of the consciousness as a person's mind and the gelatinous tissue as a part of their body. This duality is of course an illusion. As far as we know, the brain is the physical organ that produces the mind. The brain and mind are not really two things, but rather two ways of describing the same thing.

During the Enlightenment, the rational brain was likened to the precision mechanism of a clock. The great twentieth-century neurophysiologist Charles Sherrington famously compared the brain to a telephone exchange, and after Alan Turing's pioneering papers on computational science, the brain was judged to function like a computer.

Technological metaphors – and there have been many of them – are essentially attempts to make it easier to think about the brain and 'picture' the mind. They allow us to envisage a construct that would otherwise be invisible.

We instinctively try to 'picture' things when we struggle to understand them. This shouldn't be surprising because vision is our dominant sense. Unfortunately, images created to summarise hidden complexities are frequently very misleading. Think, for example, of the so-called 'March of Progress'. This usually shows a line of apes and proto-humans marching from left to right, getting taller and less stooped as natural selection perfects the straight-backed, spear-carrying hunter gatherer. But evolution is accidental. It does not 'progress' towards a goal. And there wasn't one line of hominid ancestry, but many. Creating a useful, accurate picture of something complex and abstract is very difficult. And there is nothing more complex and abstract than the human mind.

The human mind perceives, forms concepts, learns, makes judgements, feels emotions, uses language, remembers, invents, dreams, desires. How can so much complexity be captured in a single image? Clearly, some aspects of mental life must be prioritised at the expense of others. But which ones? And after those choices have been made, does the 'picture' that emerges serve its purpose? Do we recognise ourselves? Does it correspond with what we know of human motivation and behaviour? Is it consistent with larger patterns of human behaviour: social organisation, culture, history?

Identifying the mind's essential features and understanding how they relate to each other was a lifelong preoccupation for Freud. It took him thirty years and three attempts to work out what the mind looks like. His solution is deceptively simple; and if absorption into the cultural mainstream and widespread influence are measures of an idea's success, then Freud's model of the mind is unquestionably pre-eminent. It has travelled between disciplines and crossed continents. It has become a universal reference point.

Throughout most of 1895, Freud was labouring over what is now known as *Project for a Scientific Psychology*. His intention was to produce a description of the mind rooted in neurology and he recorded his thoughts in two notebooks that he sent to Wilhelm

Fliess for criticism. Although he had been working obsessively on his 'psychology for neurologists', sometimes to the point of exhaustion, he didn't request the return of his notebooks and the project was never mentioned in any of his subsequent publications. Many years after Freud's death, when the notebooks were found and published, it was his English translator who chose the title *Project for a Scientific Psychology*.

Like many details in Freud's life, his 'abandonment' of *Project for a Scientific Psychology* has been mythologised somewhat. It has been portrayed as a turning point, the impasse at which he was obliged to throw off the shackles of neurology and ascend to a higher intellectual plane where he would be free to imagine the mind in whatever way he wished. Freud never deserted neurology. His 'psychology' was always mindful of the body. Nor was *Project for a Scientific Psychology* a dead end. He was, in fact, still developing his ideas in a third notebook which was unfortunately lost. It is wrong to think of Freud's notebooks as abortive or stillborn – the 'false start' of psychoanalytic folklore. They were, in fact, the conceptual seedbed of psychoanalysis. Pathological defences, the investment of psychic energy, regression and wish fulfilment in dreams were all discussed.

Two ideas that Freud introduced in *Project for a Scientific Psychology* survived as fundamental features of his final model of the mind: 'primary' and 'secondary' processes. These are 'modes' of mental functioning and thinking. The primary process is operational before the secondary process and it is associated with basic biological drives, the unconscious, and the need for instant gratification. When a baby is hungry and screaming to be fed, we are witnessing primary process behaviour. The baby is responding instinctively to bodily sensations, and it is unable to tolerate frustration.

The primary process is said to be governed by the 'pleasure principle', although the word 'pleasure' isn't quite right in this context. A baby seeks the breast because physical contact and feeding are pleasurable, but it also seeks the breast to relieve hunger pangs. Freud understood that we are motivated equally by pleasure and the avoidance of 'unpleasure' – a term that he used for pain, discomfort and tension. The 'pleasure-unpleasure principle' would be a more accurate designation – and it was one that he often employed.

As a child matures, primitive urges must be controlled, and gratifications delayed. The 'secondary process', associated with conscious thinking, orients the mind and body towards external reality and it is governed by the 'reality principle'. Primitive urges are 'censored' and inhibited so that the child can function in social environments. If a child is teased, for example, it must learn to resist the urge to retaliate with violence. The pleasure principle and the reality principle continue to govern the primary and secondary processes throughout an individual's life. An adult, for example, cannot punch his or her boss because of unfair treatment in the workplace, but he or she might retaliate in a less self-defeating manner by scheming to inconvenience his or her boss at a future time.

Project for a Scientific Psychology was Freud's first attempt at describing the mind; however, his first 'official' model of the mind didn't appear until five years later. It is now known as 'The Topographic Model' because it uses hypothetical 'regions' to represent levels of consciousness (topography is a branch of geography concerned with the arrangement of real and artificial features). The model was introduced in chapter seven of *The Interpretation of Dreams*, although only incidental to an ongoing exploration of the psychology of dream processes. Freud suggested that the impulse for dream formation arises in the unconscious and that the thoughts and images that coalesce around the initial impulse pass into the 'preconscious' – a kind of mental antechamber where dream content is censored – before finally being admitted into consciousness. This description is not only relevant to dream formation, but mental functioning in the broadest possible sense. Unconscious content is continuously rising from 'below' and subject to censorship in the preconscious with varying degrees of success. Thus, the mind is a dynamic system divisible into three regions: unconscious, preconscious and conscious. The unconscious region operates according to the primary process and the conscious region according to the secondary process.

Various analogies have been employed to help us picture this model, the most famous being 'Freud's iceberg analogy'. The conscious mind is like the small tip of an iceberg, and below the waterline (which represents the threshold of awareness) are, firstly, a large preconscious area and, secondly, an even larger unconscious area. Parts of the preconscious area will rise above the waterline as the iceberg bobs up and down. It's a perfectly serviceable analogy, but it doesn't appear anywhere in Freud's writings, so to call it 'Freud's iceberg analogy' is something of a misnomer.

Another helpful analogy, popularised by the psychiatrist David Stafford-Clark in the late 1960s, is the 'searchlight'. Imagine a searchlight sweeping over a landscape. Everything illuminated by the beam corresponds with conscious content and everything within range but unilluminated is preconscious. When the beam moves across the landscape it brings preconscious material into consciousness. Everything beyond the range of the searchlight is dark and corresponds with unconscious content.

Over the years, Freud became dissatisfied with his model because it admitted certain ambiguities surrounding how defences operate. He recognised that although everything that is repressed is unconscious, it isn't the case that everything unconscious is repressed. He ruminated about these technical conundrums and produced some rather arcane theoretical papers while he circled the problem. Then, rather late in life, he produced a revised model that was not only his final, truly major contribution to psychoanalysis, but also probably his greatest. A remarkable accomplishment given Freud's circumstances.

One evening in April 1923, Freud asked his doctor, Felix Deutsch, to examine his mouth. He warned Deutsch to be prepared. He was about to see something 'unpleasant', something he wouldn't like. Deutsch instantly recognised advanced cancer. A grim conversation followed in which Freud raised the subject of his own euthanasia. Arrangements were quickly made for Freud to receive surgery. After the operation – and rather bizarrely – the eminent Professor Freud was left to recover on a cot in a tiny room with a man described by Deutsch (using the accepted medical terminology of the time) as 'an imbecile dwarf'. Yet this 'imbecile' probably saved Freud's life. Freud was bleeding profusely, and it was only because the 'imbecile' alerted a nurse that a doctor was called. Had the 'imbecile' not done so, Freud – out of sight – would have silently bled to death.

Freud's cancer couldn't have come at a worse time. The First World War and the death of his daughter Sophie were still recent, raw memories. His nephew Hermann Graf (his favourite sister's only son) had been killed. And as if these bereavements weren't enough, fate was about to deliver a further devastating blow. Freud had become exceedingly fond of Sophie's youngest son, Heinz Rudolf, but the boy fell seriously ill in May 1923 and died the following month. Freud described the days after Heinz Rudolf's death as 'the blackest' in his life. It was the first time that Freud had been seen crying in front of others – and many years would pass before he cried openly again. He told Ernest Jones that although previous losses had caused him pain, the loss of Heinz Rudolf had killed something inside of him, for good.

Freud was getting old. He should have been weak, tired and broken. He should have been ready to give up. But instead he was as intellectually engaged as he ever was, perhaps even more so. While his followers were reeling from the shock of his diagnosis, Freud was anxious to forge ahead. He still wanted to solve outstanding theoretical problems and expand the scope of psychoanalysis. Even though he admitted in a letter that his cancer diagnosis was clearly 'the beginning of the end', much of his most compelling work – some of his most ambitious essays, in fact – were yet to be written. At a juncture when most would have been disabled by despondency, Freud unveiled a new model of the mind and launched into a final phase of exceptional productivity.

Freud's new model – 'The Structural Model' – was described for the first time in *The Ego and the Id*, an extended essay published in the third week of April 1923. Freud had been thinking about a new model of mind since the previous July. He had even presented a short paper in September 1922 which previewed the gist of his thinking. The term 'structural' is used because Freud pictured the mind as being composed of three 'psychic' structures – that is, permanent features of the mind that can be meaningfully considered in a relational framework. What goes on in one structure can influence what goes on in another. As such, it is more accurate to think of them as 'agencies'. The structural model wasn't a complete departure from the existing topographic model, but rather a substantial revision.

The three structures that Freud identified are the id, the ego and the super-ego. They are frequently referenced in both arts and science articles and almost every educated person in the anglophone world will have some idea, even if just an inkling, of their origin and meaning. However, id, ego and super-ego were not Freud's terms; they are James Strachey's Latinised translations of Freud's *Es*, *Ich* and *Über-Ich*. The literal translations of *Es* and *Ich* are 'It' and 'I'; *Über-Ich* is more accurately rendered as 'Above-I', 'Over-I', or 'Upper-I'.

Since Bruno Bettelheim questioned the propriety of Strachey's 'neologisms' in *Freud and Man's Soul* in the 1980s, some have favoured the use of literal rather than Latinised translations. There are good reasons for doing this. For example, the term 'Upper-I' has clear connotations. Upper houses have authority over lower houses; 'upper' suggests a higher location, eminence and superiority. The position of the 'Upper-I' relative to the other two structures in Freud's model is immediately apparent. 'Super-ego' is more ambiguous. It could be a term used to describe a flamboyant, arrogant narcissist. Even so, the case for abandoning Strachey's terms is far from straightforward. Factors other than fidelity must be considered. Language is not static, it evolves, and Strachey's terms have been evolving for a century now, acquiring nuances, finding their way into different discourses, occupying niches. They have a life of their own and they can't just be 'cancelled'. Furthermore, 'It', 'I' and 'Upper-I', employed as technical terms in English sentences, sound awkward and can be confusing – for example, 'the unconscious mechanisms in his I kept his forbidden desires locked in his It'. Strachey is frequently accused of distorting Freud because he wanted psychoanalytic terms to sound emotionally neutral and more scientific, which is probably true, but he also chose id, ego and super-ego for pragmatic reasons.

In 1923, Georg Groddeck, a Baden-Baden physician and correspondent of Freud, published a work titled *Das Buch vom Es* (The Book of the Id). When Groddeck read Freud's *The Ego and the Id*, which was published shortly after Groddeck's book, he was furious. He believed that Freud had plagiarised his work and had advanced psychoanalytic theory in 'a very sneaky way'. Groddeck's indignation was unwarranted because Freud *had* acknowledged Groddeck's priority in *The Ego and the Id*. In fact, the basic concept of the id can be traced back to Nietzsche and several nineteenth-century 'Romantic' philosophers, so neither Groddeck nor Freud were being wholly original.

In *New Introductory Lectures on Psychoanalysis*, published in 1932, Freud provided a very colourful description of the id: 'We approach the id with analogies: we call it chaos, a cauldron full of seething excitations . . . It is filled with energy reaching it from the instincts, but it has no organization, produces no collective will, but only a striving to bring about the satisfaction of instinctual needs subject to the observance of the pleasure-principle.' If we were able to descend into the id, we would find ourselves in a dreamworld. 'The logical laws of thought do not apply in the id, and this is true above all of the law of contradiction. Contrary impulses exist side by side, without cancelling each other out or diminishing each other.' Freud continues: 'There is nothing in the id that could be compared with negation . . . There is nothing in the id that corresponds to the idea of time.' Desire and rage can co-exist simultaneously, nothing is postponed, and the passage of time is inconsequential. 'Wishful impulses which have never passed beyond the id, but impressions, too, which have been sunk into the id by repression, are virtually immortal.' Everything that is repressed is 'pushed' beneath a notional barrier of 'resistance' into the id.

The wishful impulses that arise in the id are assumed to have a genetic, evolutionary basis. Thus, they are related to Darwinian objectives. For example, self-preservation, defence of territory, overcoming rivals, and sexual reproduction.

When a baby is born, it is all id. The perceptual system registers the world, but 'experience' cannot be interpreted. Eventually, sensory stimulation – the world impressing itself on the brain – will become a kind of proto-consciousness, but until then the mind is almost synonymous with the body. There is no self, no identity; just unconscious instinctual need. The perceptual system is associated with awareness of whatever is being perceived, and perceived experience will leave memory traces that accumulate and organise over time. In due course, internally generated sensations will define the embodied self as something distinct from its environment. The body is the bedrock of personal identity. A boundary beyond which everything else is 'other'.

A part of the id becomes more organised and increasingly differentiated until it separates. This is the ego. In Freud's structural model, it corresponds with the colloquial 'self', although it is perhaps more accurate to think of the ego as a set of functions. The ego has (largely but not exclusively) a managerial role and it is obliged to respect the reality principle. It monitors thoughts, exercises restraint, assesses opportunities and initiates actions judged appropriate in a given context. Freud wrote: 'the ego stands for reason and good sense while the id stands for the untamed passions'. Unlike the id, which is completely unconscious, the ego has conscious, preconscious and unconscious regions.

Later in infancy, a further stage of organisation and separation occurs. Just as a part of the id became the ego, so it is that a part of the ego becomes the super-ego – an agency that functions in a similar manner to 'conscience'. What is understood to be right and wrong will be informed first by parental authority, and in the fullness of time by exposure to social authority (for example, the institutions of law and order). Like the ego, the super-ego has conscious, preconscious and unconscious regions.

The super-ego is arguably the most original feature of Freud's structural model and he felt obliged to specify the precise factors and conditions that lead to its evolution. His starting point was the observation that children don't develop a sense of morality until they are about five or six years old. These ages coincide with the end of the 'infant sexuality' phase of his theory of sexual development, and Freud suspected that there was some connection.

The marriage of the structural theory of mind and the theory of sexual development is yet another example of Freud's commitment to synthesis; however, the result isn't altogether successful. The theory of sexual development, already a problematic formulation and vulnerable to criticism, contaminated the structural theory of mind with pre-existing theoretical weaknesses.

As boys mature, Oedipal conflicts intensify anxiety, and a massive amount of repression is required to maintain mental equilibrium. A special agency – the super-ego – comes into existence to prohibit disturbing Oedipal wishes. The super-ego can be likened to an internalised same-sex parent – that is, the threatening rival in the domestic Oedipal drama. For young boys, the most feared threat is real or imagined castration. The super-ego demands self-control and the maintenance of standards and ideals. Under normal circumstances, the ego will accept the super-ego's moral strictures. Occasionally, however, the ego may respond to an excessively harsh and critical super-ego by muting it with repression. This frequently results in unconscious guilt, which can engender neurotic symptoms.

Unfortunately, Freud's thinking becomes less persuasive, as it often does, when applied to women. Girls do not have to worry about castration for obvious reasons. Therefore, Oedipal wishes produce less anxiety and there is a reduced need to maintain mental equilibrium by means of massive repression. A super-ego develops, but it is weaker than the male super-ego. Thus, women are less moral than men, and when they transgress, they experience less guilt than men. There is, of course, no evidence to support this supposition; quite the contrary, in fact. Moral development is a complex process, influenced by many more obviously germane factors than the Oedipus complex – for example, aptitude, emotional sensitivity, and the ability to generate theories about the minds of others. Common sense was an early casualty as Freud strained to carry off his grand integrative coup.

Freud entangled sex and structure to explain the super-ego's nativity; however, he also believed that human beings are predisposed to develop a super-ego because they inherit a kind of biogenetic 'template' – a residue of ancestral memories. This highly speculative idea is a further example of Freud's preoccupation with connecting mental phenomena with an 'archaeological' stratum of the unconscious. He had previously proposed that dreams could be analysed to the depth of 'archaic inheritance'. This aspect of his thinking remains contentious, even among psychoanalysts.

According to Freud, the ego must transact with the real world, but it must do so while balancing the needs of two opposing task masters. The id is constantly attempting to influence behaviour so that libidinous and primitive urges are instantly gratified, whereas the super-ego is constantly seeking to censor behaviour that might violate socially sanctioned codes of conduct. Before permitting an action to take place, the ego must consider three factors: the situation, fundamental needs, and morality. It is not appropriate for a man to strip naked in a public place or importune a non-consenting woman. Nor is it satisfactory for a man to eschew sex altogether because of excessive scrupulosity. Sex is a basic need (and an evolutionary necessity). Clearly, the optimal solution is a compromise that allows sex to occur without causing offence or harm. The man can strip naked in a private space and enjoy consensual sex. Then, both task masters – the id and super-ego – are (to a greater or lesser extent) satisfied.

The relationship between Freud's new structures and consciousness can be clarified by extending the searchlight analogy. The range of the searchlight beam determines what is conscious and what can become conscious. The ego operates the searchlight, but the mechanism that allows the beam to be aimed in different directions doesn't move freely. Both the id and super-ego introduce biases that usually work in opposition to each other. Thus, what eventually enters consciousness is, like behaviour, a compromise.

Freud's structural model has a famous classical precedent: Plato's account of the soul in *Phaedrus*. The soul is like a chariot being pulled by two horses with contrasting dispositions, one noble, the other base and impulsive. Therefore the charioteer must be sensitive to their conflicting natures if he is to steer the chariot successfully.

The human animal is sexually motivated and aggressive. But it is also a social animal and early humans could only survive in the ancestral environment by working together in groups. Without exercising restraint – without compromise – group members would be constantly fighting each other for food and access to sexual partners. The group would soon tear itself apart, and then none of its members would survive. Little has changed over the past twelve thousand years, which is how long humans have been living in settlements and regulating social behaviour. We are still sexually motivated, aggressive animals, and we still make compromises to benefit from living in large cooperative groups – except today, groups are the size of countries. Even in a modern city landscape of glass towers and technological devices, seemingly quite different from the ancestral savanna, for most people life is primarily about finding satisfactory accommodations between higher and lower selves. For example, the id discharges its potentially explosive sexual energies through the safe conduits of romance and marriage, and the 'collective' super-ego approves the compromise in a church, temple or registry. The principal milestones of autobiography in a modern life remain stubbornly Darwinian: mate selection, pair-bonding and procreation. Moreover, a certain amount of aggression (but not too much) facilitates the accomplishment of these milestones because we still discover our position in the social hierarchy by competing for limited resources. Freud's structural model unifies the person, society and civilisation.

The *Ego and the Id* contains a diagram of the structural model, although by the time Freud was preparing his *New Introductory Lectures on Psychoanalysis* he had altered it slightly. This modified diagram, which Freud described as an 'unassuming sketch', is his final 'picture' of the mind. It is a vertical oval with a rounded protuberance on top which represents the perceptual system and consciousness. Within the oval and in descending order are the super-ego, ego and id. There is a gap at the bottom of the oval, suggesting that the mind is 'open' to the body. Various perforated and continuous lines partition levels of consciousness and show 'repression'.

We judge good science according to its economy. A simple

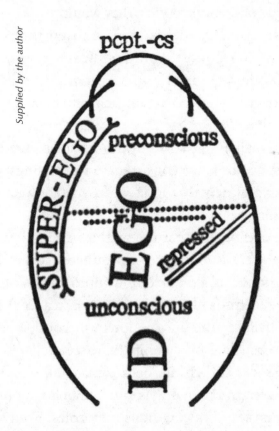

Supplied by the author

equation, with only a few letters and symbols, can encapsulate something as grand and all-encompassing as 'the arrow of time'. Freud's model employs a minimal framework to explain a great deal. It also has enormous intuitive appeal. It 'feels' right. Which probably accounts for its popularity. After 1923, the structural model was accepted by psychoanalysts, then psychiatrists, then academics in allied disciplines, then psychoanalytically informed anthropologists, sociologists and historians, then artists and critics, and finally – to a lesser but still significant extent – the public. Its fortunes have waxed and waned, but it has never slipped beneath the cultural horizon in a hundred years. In 2012, the Nobel Prize-winning neurophysiologist Eric Kandel described Freud's 'theory of mind' as 'a monumental contribution to modern thought' and 'perhaps the most influential and coherent view of mental activity that we have'.

Freud's structural model is predicated on three key ideas. Firstly, mental life is mostly unconscious. Secondly, primitive urges are constantly vying for gratification. Thirdly, primitive urges must be inhibited so that rational and cooperative behaviours can evolve.

The topographic and structural features of Freud's model of the mind are broadly consistent with findings from neuroscience, experimental cognitive psychology and clinical neuropsychology.

Although the precise nature of the unconscious is still a subject of debate, the existence of the unconscious – or at least, processing that occurs outside of awareness – is now universally accepted. This is of considerable significance, because not so long ago belief in the unconscious was considered by many academics to be something comparable to a belief in ghosts. In retrospect, this is surprising, because it is blindingly obvious that at any given moment only a small bubble of consciousness floats on a vast sea of unconscious memories. Even something as simple as standing on two feet requires an extraordinary number of automatic, involuntary adjustments of weight distribution to avoid toppling. Contemporary neuroscientists, whose conclusions have been informed principally by brain-scanning investigations, assume that most activity in the brain makes little or no demand on consciousness. Of course, acknowledging that 'processing' occurs outside awareness is not the same as accepting the Freudian unconscious (with its dreamscapes, nefarious intent and echoes of nineteenth-century Romantic philosophy). Nevertheless, the general notion of the unconscious is no longer considered controversial.

The idea that information is analysed unconsciously before passing through a 'preconscious' stage of processing prior to entry into awareness is doctrinal. It has been repeatedly demonstrated using numerous paradigms in laboratory settings. Censorship – as a feature of the processing system – is now widely accepted, albeit in the more general sense of 'filtering'. Only a fraction of what is registered by the brain is admitted into consciousness, otherwise we would experience information overload and be unable to function. More specifically, there is abundant psychophysiological and neuropsychological evidence to suggest that censorship – understood more narrowly as inhibition of instinctual impulses – is a task carried out continuously by the frontal lobes of the brain.

When the inhibitory centres of the brain are damaged, patients tend to use inappropriate sexual and crude language, show emotional volatility, and demonstrate hypersexuality and aggression. It is as though the reality principle is no longer being applied and the person's behaviour is being guided by the pleasure principle. The lid has been taken off the id. Patients suffering from frontal-lobe damage behave as though they are in a Freudian dream, a dream in which everyday situations, like entering a doctor's office, can be made surreal by inappropriate behaviour, such as masturbating. It has been suggested that the inhibitory functions of the super-ego are sourced in the ventral frontal cortex.

There are several brain systems that have been proposed as the neurological substrate of the ego. For example, the dorso-frontal and posterior sensory cortices. The most recent candidate is the default mode network, a large system composed mainly of the medial prefrontal cortex, the posterior cingulate cortex, the inferior parietal lobule, the lateral and inferior temporal cortex, and the medial temporal lobes.

As neuroscience has advanced into the twenty-first century, the scientific community has been increasingly willing to connect cutting-edge research with Freud's model of the mind. The current brain model favoured by contemporary neuroscientists is the 'predictive brain'. The brain is constantly making predictions about the world. Predictions that match 'reality' are used to refine internal representations and expectations (for future reference) while mismatches – or prediction errors – are suppressed. The predictive brain has much in common with Freud's general understanding of how the mind functions. Predictions are comparable to desires (or wishes), and desires encounter limitations imposed by reality. Behaviour is a compromise, a middle way negotiated between internal drives and the environment. These compromises are, in effect, revised 'predictions' that influence how we negotiate similar situations (so that they can be managed optimally) when they are encountered again in the future.

A compelling example of the new accord between Freud and cutting-edge neuroscience can be found in several review papers that explore the psychoanalytic ramifications of Karl Friston's 'free energy principle'. Friston, a brain-imaging pioneer based at University College, London, is the world's most influential neuroscientist. His free energy principle is a 'natural law' from which it is possible to derive many features of biological evolution. It combines concepts from a broad range of disciplines and anchors contemporary models of brain functioning in statistical mathematics and physics. Since Friston published his initial paper on the free energy principle in 2006, it has been lauded as a major theoretical breakthrough – albeit one that even neuroscientists find difficult to fully comprehend. The free energy principle has acquired a 'fan-base' of scientifically informed individuals who provide regular internet bulletins of their ongoing efforts to appreciate the finer points of Friston's 'mathematical philosophy'.

According to Friston, living organisms must maintain a body boundary and resist entropy, which would otherwise lead to the disintegration of their internal states. Cohesion is accomplished by minimising free energy, where free energy is total energy minus the amount of energy already employed (or average energy minus entropy). This quantification of energy can be understood from various perspectives, most notably information theory. At the level of behaviour, the minimisation of free energy can be understood as the minimisation of surprise. Organisms strive to minimise 'surprise' because surprises can represent a threat to survival. For example, a human being does not wish to be 'surprised' by total and prolonged immersion in water. This would ultimately lead to a breakdown of the body boundary and the disintegration of internal states. Free energy can be minimised by neural computation, as the brain anticipates and responds to sensory information.

In essence, Friston's principle explains how living systems defy (at least temporarily) the second law of thermodynamics and achieve homeostatic stability. Broadly speaking, the free energy principle is consistent with Freud's principle of constancy, which asserts that the nervous system conserves energy and tends towards stability.

The free energy principle is so fundamental it can be used as a foundation for understanding the evolution of all forms of biological organisation, and more specifically neurological and mental organisation. Remarkably, when the implications of the free energy principle are worked through, the end point seems to be a model of mind that has much in common with Freud's.

Robin Carhart-Harris and colleagues have argued that the Freudian primary process is characterised by high levels of entropy. The primal, infant brain state is disorganised; however, as the infant matures, organisation is the inevitable by-product of a system in which free energy is minimised. The ensuing (low entropy) 'structure' that emerges equates with the Freudian ego (and provides the machinery of secondary process thinking). In 2010, Carhart-Harris and Friston published an intellectually exhilarating paper in the journal *Brain* titled 'The default mode, ego functions and free-energy: a neurobiological account of Freudian ideas'. In this paper, the authors explore the relationship between Freudian constructs and the predictive brain, and identify formal similarities between free energy minimisation and the treatment of energy in Freudian formulations.

Freud supposed that primary process brain activity is associated with the 'free' exchange of neuronal energy. Secondary process activity can be conceptualised as the conversion of 'free energy' into what Freud called 'bound energy'. Thus, the architecture of the mind and optimisation of sensory 'representations' (essential for the survival of sophisticated organisms) are both outcomes of free energy minimisation.

Carhart-Harris and Friston also suggest, albeit speculatively, that Freudian repression is commensurate with specific measures of spontaneous neural activity in the default mode network.

Current speculation about the biological substrates of psychoanalytic constructs is reminiscent of Freud's 'psychology for neurologists' – the project that he was unable to complete in the late nineteenth century. Neuroscience wasn't sufficiently advanced in Freud's time to supply the foundations for what he called the 'psychical apparatus'; however, today, abstractions like the ego and repression are more readily 'located' in the brain. A new discipline, neuropsychoanalysis, emerged in the 1990s. It continues to develop and, in a way, exists to complete Freud's *Project for a Scientific Psychology*.

Freud's structural theory has also inspired advances in the field of artificial intelligence. Marvin Minsky, one of the most significant AI theorists of the late twentieth and early twenty-first centuries, once declared: 'Freud has the best theories so far, next to mine, of what it takes to make a mind.' Minsky argued that artificial intelligence can be best accomplished by independent and parallel processing systems (comparable to Freud's trio of agencies) rather than a single monolithic system.

Freud's division of the mind into the id, ego and super-ego was an inspired choice. The mind has so many faculties, so many dimensions, he could have chosen any number of alternative constructs and combinations. For example, he might have decided that the mind was divisible into the 'will', memory and imagination. But would we recognise ourselves so readily when presented with this 'picture' of the mind? Would we see it reflected in our cultural landmarks? Could it explain the abduction of Helen, the Trojan war, the rage of Achilles or Agamemnon's brutality? Freud's three agencies are just right. Their functions and dynamic relationships produce behaviour that makes sense to us. Timeless sense.

Freud's personal interest in archaeology and ancient civilisations explains, perhaps, why the structural model resonates so strongly with the tropes of classical literature; however, the structural model has such wide appeal, MGM Studios thought it fit for the twenty-third century. The iconic science fiction

film *Forbidden Planet* was released in 1956. It is loosely based on Shakespeare's *The Tempest*, but its subtext is pure Freud. The crew of a spacecraft, led by dashing Commander Adams, arrive on Altair IV, where they find the survivors of an interplanetary expedition: a scientist, Dr Morbius, and his scantily dressed daughter Altaira. Adams suggests that he and his men could take Altaira back to Earth, at which point an advanced alien technology allows Morbius's id to manifest as a vengeful monster that attacks the crew.

The fact that Freud's structural model of the mind provides psychological fuel for narratives as different as *The Iliad* and *Forbidden Planet* strongly suggests that it captures essences, core dispositions, deep truths. And it continues to be relevant in an ever-changing, modern context. For example, in *Group Psychology and the Analysis of the Ego*, published in 1921, Freud, expanding on the work of Gustave Le Bon, suggested that when human beings gather in crowds, the voice of conscience is attenuated by diffusion of personal responsibility and primitive urges are vented more easily. Crowds have an inherent tendency to degenerate into baying mobs. The internet has created a global crowd, inhibitions have been lifted, and the collective id – unfettered – roars for instant gratification. Which is why the internet is awash with pornographic and violent imagery. Threats of sexual violence and hate-speech are commonplace. Primary process thinking does not discriminate. Groups – Freud says – 'have never thirsted after truth'. The id does not care about facts or evidence. The id's favourite literature is 'fake news'.

Many models of the mind have come and gone. The clock, the telephone exchange, the computer – the quantum hologram. None of these models have succeeding in shining a very bright light on the human condition, and none of these models have left particularly deep cultural impressions. Freud's structural model of the mind stands alone, a conspicuous Olympus surrounded by foothills.

By clarifying what the mind looks like, Freud also clarified the cardinal purpose of psychoanalysis, and ultimately the primary objective of all forms of personal development. The intention of psychoanalysis is 'to strengthen the ego, to make it more independent of the super-ego, to widen its field of perception and enlarge its organization, so that it can appropriate fresh portions of the id'. Freud concludes Lecture 31 of *New Introductory Lectures on Psychoanalysis* with a famous phrase that is frequently quoted. It sounds like a commandment issuing from the mouth of an Old Testament prophet: 'Where id was, there ego shall be.'

We must reclaim as much of ourselves as we can. We must discover a personal morality shaped by experience rather than 'tribal' prohibitions. We must wrestle our minds free of prehistory so that we can make better, rational choices. We must lose the stooped apes who tread closely on our heels in the 'March of Progress' and stand tall, spear in hand – the emblem of our intelligence – in readiness to conquer the future.

In 1923, after having just been given what was effectively a death sentence, that is precisely what Freud did.

Chapter 14

Coffee and Conversation

Nothing evokes Freud's Vienna more than a coffee house. The writer Stefan Zweig claimed that the Viennese coffee house was a unique institution, 'a sort of democratic club', where, for the price of a cup of coffee, patrons could sit undisturbed for hours, reading an unlimited number of German-language newspapers as well as publications from further afield – France, Italy, England and America. In addition to providing reading material and a table at which to think and write, the coffee house also offered a collegiate environment in which it was possible to socialise, pursue professional interests and participate in discussions and debates. A head waiter, familiar with his patrons, would direct newcomers to specific tables according to their need. One could also find a chess partner, join a card game, or play billiards. In every conceivable way, the Viennese coffee house transcended mere functionality, its ostensible purpose of providing beverages and sustenance. Regular customers used the coffee house like an office. It was where they had their mail sent and staff took telephone messages. For a man like Peter Altenberg, the coffee house was a sanctuary, a safe retreat: 'You have troubles of one sort or another – to the COFFEEHOUSE!

She can't come to you for some reason no matter how plausible – to the COFFEEHOUSE! You have holes in your shoes – the COFFEEHOUSE!' He even proposed the coffee house as a solution to suicidal despair. The novelist Joseph Roth wrote: 'Sometimes the coffee house resembled a winter encampment of nomads, sometimes a bourgeois dining room, sometimes a great anteroom in a palace, and sometimes a warm heaven for the frozen.' The Viennese coffee house was a university, a theatre, a casino, a pleasure garden, or simply somewhere to keep warm.

Photographs taken in the 1890s show a predominantly male clientele, although women certainly enjoyed coffee and cake in the afternoon – a Viennese three o'clock ritual. From 1910, women start to appear more frequently in coffee-house images. For example, in a Gustav Kalhammer lithograph of Café Heinrichhof, dated 1912, men and women are present in equal numbers.

The coffee house is embedded so deep in the Viennese soul that it has its own origin myth. After the 1683 siege of Vienna and the decisive repulsion of Ottoman forces, a Habsburg spy, Georg Franz Kolschitsky, was offered a reward for his services. He chose the coffee beans that the Ottomans had left behind and opened the first Viennese coffee house near St Stephen's Square. Thus, the coffee house, stocked with plunder, was linked with the defeat of Islam, and Vienna was reinvented as the guardian of Europe. It is a myth that resonates with the historic Greek victory over the Persian Empire in 449 BC. In fact, the first coffee houses in Vienna were opened by two Armenians. Friedrich Torberg, a twentieth-century chronicler of Viennese life, described Vienna as 'the city of functioning legends', and the coffee house was, in his estimation, 'by far the most complicated of these legends'. Some would suggest that the 'idea' of the Viennese coffee house is as confected as *punschkrapfen* – a bright pink Viennese sponge cake with its own hazy origin myths.

Around 1900, coffee houses could be found in most European cities, and many of them, for example those in Paris and Berlin, were very similar to their Viennese counterparts; however, there are several factors that may have made the Viennese coffee house a more sociologically diverse, creative and inspirational environment.

A shortage of accommodation in Vienna obliged impecunious artists and intellectuals to spend a great deal of time (and almost all the winter) ensconced in coffee houses. Exchanging ideas became their principal form of recreation. The Viennese coffee house was also remarkably egalitarian. Class and disciplinary boundaries were unusually porous. A political theorist, for example, could seek the opinion of a factory worker. Another distinctive feature of the Viennese coffee house was its high level of Jewish patronage. According to the literary historian Harold B. Segel, Jews enlivened and enriched the milieu because they were typically gregarious, intellectually curious and argumentative. This isn't glib racial typecasting. Viennese Jews were necessarily gregarious as a bulwark against antisemitism, intellectually curious because knowledge cannot be confiscated by persecutors, and argumentative because Judaism is a faith that encourages debate. Finally, and perhaps most importantly, the Viennese coffee house was not only a setting, but also a subject. Unlike French and German writers, Viennese authors and journalists chose to describe coffee-house life – almost obsessively – and they created a form of literature that was exquisitely attuned to the atmosphere of its birthplace. The Viennese coffee house became something close to a philosophical school, an attitude, or even a state of mind.

The first great literary coffee house was Café Griensteidl. It was the home of 'Young Vienna', the literary movement that included writers such as Arthur Schnitzler, Felix Dörmann, Peter Altenberg, Hermann Bahr, Richard Beer-Hoffmann, Felix Salten and Hugo von Hofmannsthal. The interior of Café Griensteidl was austere: no marble, no velvet. Only the gold mirrors suggested grandeur. A photograph taken in 1897 shows a large, crowded space beneath an arched ceiling, with table surfaces covered with newspapers. Another photograph taken the same year shows the billiard room, with its gigantic table, surrounded by well-dressed spectators. A stylish patron wearing a shiny top hat leans forward, cue balanced, in readiness to take a shot.

One of the founding members of the Griensteidl circle was Schnitzler's friend Theodor Herzl, a journalist and playwright who is now almost exclusively remembered (not entirely

accurately) as the father of Zionism. Schnitzler and Herzl had known each other as students; however, they were very different personalities. In 1895, Herzl visited Schnitzler to discuss the 'Jewish Question'. Schnitzler wasn't much enthused by Herzl's idea of establishing a Jewish homeland. Schnitzler liked posing in wide-brimmed Rembrandt hats and showy cravats. He was cosmopolitan, and the prospect of resettlement in Palestine, or indeed moving anywhere that didn't have good coffee houses and easy access to billiard tables, had no appeal whatsoever.

The writers of Young Vienna began to get noticed when they reached their late twenties or early thirties. By today's standards, none of them would attract the appellation *wunderkind*, with the notable exception of Hugo von Hofmannsthal, whose prodigious talent was freakish and at times disturbing. It was Hermann Bahr who received a sublime essay submission for his magazine, sent by the hitherto unknown 'Loris'. Bahr assumed that the essay had been written by a venerable genius who had been perfecting his craft in isolation for decades. Irrespective of the man's assumed age, Bahr arranged to meet Loris in Café Griensteidl, where a boy in short trousers arrived and declared in a piping voice: 'Hofmannsthal! I am Loris.'

Schnitzler had a similarly disconcerting experience. The pubescent Hofmannsthal asked Schnitzler to judge the quality of a recently completed verse play. Schnitzler invited the boy to a literary gathering in his rooms, albeit with low expectations. Hofmannsthal arrived, still in short trousers, and began to read with evident nervousness. Recounting the occasion to Stefan Zweig, Schnitzler recalled that the effect was so uncanny that his associates looked at each other with fear in their eyes. 'We had never heard verses of such perfection, such faultless plasticity, such musical feeling, from any living being, nor had we thought them possible since Goethe.' Although Hofmannsthal exerted a massive influence over Zweig's generation, he was not – as many believed – a new Goethe or Shakespeare. His popularity waned as the twentieth century progressed. Even so, international audiences are still frequently exposed to his writing in the opera house. In later life he wrote librettos for Richard Strauss.

In 1897, Café Griensteidl was demolished, and its circle of writers migrated to Café Central – a more ostentatious establishment situated in what was once a stock market building. Its principal spaces were the 'pillar hall', a room dense with columns beneath an impressive, vaulted ceiling, and a spectacular glass-roofed 'courtyard' surrounded by pilastered windows, an arcade, striking architectural features and ornamental trees. Café Central immediately became the new home of Viennese literary excellence. So much so that even its waiters were reputed to be discerning littérateurs. It retained its dominant position for at least two decades. Alfred Polgar – a master of 'small forms' – wrote an essay titled *Theory of the Café Central*, the opening lines of which declare that the Café Central is 'unlike any other coffee house. It is a world view.'

Young Vienna ceased to be a cohesive movement, and Arthur Schnitzler, who had always been regarded as a figurehead, emerged as the most significant free-standing talent. His writing captures the very essence of Vienna's golden age, and unlike his peers, Schnitzler produced a body of work that is completely accessible to modern readers. He invented the term 'sweet girl' to describe the barmaids, shopgirls and dressmakers of Vienna who willingly participated in 'games' of seduction and doomed infatuation with educated, wealthy young men – like Schnitzler – whose cynicism was typically modulated by wistful melancholy. He is also famous for keeping a diary in which he recorded his sexual conquests, and occasionally the number of orgasms he experienced. During one non-monogamous affair that lasted for eleven months, he had intercourse with 'Jeanette' 326 times.

His major works include *Reigen*, a 'scandalous' play about sexual couplings that found new relevance in the early years of the AIDS epidemic; *Fräulein Else*, an experimental 'stream of consciousness' short story that also includes passages of musical notation; and *Dream Story*, a distinctly Freudian novella that blurs the boundary between reality and unconscious mental life (filmed by Stanley Kubrick as the 1999 conjugal mystery *Eyes Wide Shut*). Schnitzler's least-known work, his autobiography – *My Youth in Vienna* – is in many ways his most interesting. Firstly, because it is full of exotic period details (for example, he describes seeing 'wild women', prostitutes on horseback, riding around a dimly lit area of the Prater when he was fifteen years old). And secondly, because the reader will inevitably wonder how such a sex-crazed idler ever managed to qualify as a doctor and achieve literary immortality.

Coffee houses feature extensively in *My Youth in Vienna*. Although Schnitzler claimed to like medicine, he didn't really like studying it. Nor did he like the company of medical students. When he did mix with them, he preferred to do so on what he called 'neutral ground' – 'usually some coffee-house, in those days the Central, where I would spend hours reading the papers, playing billiards and dominoes, and, more rarely, chess, with a grey-bearded polish Jew called Tambour'.

Later, he describes a dalliance with Theresa, 'the much-courted cashier of my favourite café, where I played billiards in the morning, cards in the afternoon, billiards and cards in the evening and cards and billiards at night'. Schnitzler was supervised by an eminent doctor and music lover who used to entertain Wagner when the great composer visited Vienna. The proximity of such an august person had little effect on Schnitzler's attitude and behaviour. With customary breezy indifference, Schnitzler writes: 'After I had participated with a greater or lesser degree of attentiveness in the morning round of bedside visits, and had charted and completed as many case histories as was required of me, off I went, usually to the coffee-house, to read the papers or play a game of skittle-pool on the billiard table with some acquaintance or other, in those days more often than not with an elderly gentleman called Wolf . . .' As an afterthought he adds: 'Around noon I would put in an appearance at the polyclinic . . .'

Some of Schnitzler's coffee-house reminiscences are extremely colourful: a night of carousing in the notorious Café Laferl with his friend Eugene, 'fat Baron Flotow', 'blond Dr. Billinger' and a troupe of 'musical clowns'; a chance encounter in Café Central with an associate, drunk on absinthe, staring into a mirror and attempting to induce visions of sexual excesses. Anyone who has read *The Interpretation of Dreams* will recognise the territory. Schnitzler's coffee houses are not only located in Vienna; they are also located in the unconscious.

In 1906, Freud wrote to Schnitzler: 'I have often asked myself in astonishment how you came by this or that piece of secret knowledge which I had acquired by a painstaking investigation of the subject, and I finally came to the point of envying the author whom hitherto I had admired.' On 14 May 1922, Freud wrote to Schnitzler again and confessed, in strict confidence, that he had been avoiding him all his life because he feared that Schnitzler was his double. (When Hitler started burning 'Jewish filth' in 1933, Schnitzler's works were tossed into the flames along with those written by his 'psychic twin', Sigmund Freud.) It has been said that Freud succeeded in evading Schnitzler until the author died nine years later – finally ensuring that they would never meet. In fact, on 8 June 1922, Freud invited Schnitzler to dinner. He explained to his prospective guest in the letter that only his wife and daughter would be present, 'besides my person'. He stressed the intimacy of the occasion: 'There will be no one else with us.' The dinner was a great success and Freud didn't want the evening to end. Even though it was late, he accompanied Schnitzler back to his apartment. Over dinner, they had talked genially about the Viennese medical world. But walking through the streets at night their conversation turned towards more substantial subjects. They discussed ageing and dying.

Freud and Schnitzler shared a critic – another Viennese Jew, Karl Kraus. Kraus frequented Café Griensteidl in the 1890s, moved to Café Central along with all the other writers in 1897, and then – intolerant of noise – relocated to the more genteel Café Imperial. He is best known today for founding *Die Fackel* (The Torch), a publication full of caustic journalism that became the accepted model for all subsequent satirical magazines. It was the *Mad*, *Charlie Hebdo* or *Private Eye* of its day. Kraus exposed corruption, denounced sloppy journalism, and attacked hypocrisy. The first edition appeared in April 1899 and the last edition was published in February 1936.

In *The Demolished Literature*, published in 1896, Kraus accused the Café Griensteidl circle of writers of dilettantism and he gleefully anticipated the café's destruction. All of their 'literary implements' would have to be 'gathered up': 'lack of talent, premature mellowness, poses, megalomania, sweet young girls, neckties, affectation, false datives, monocles, and rarified nerves'. His references to sweet girls, neckties and affectation clearly identify Schnitzler as being especially deserving of contempt. Although Kraus was never personally disrespectful to Freud, he was certainly disrespectful of psychoanalysis. Indeed, he armed all future critics with a line so razor sharp that it never fails to draw at least a few drops of blood: 'Psychoanalysis is the mental illness for which it claims to be a cure.' After the assassination of Crown Prince Franz Ferdinand, Kraus wrote a eulogy in which he describes Austria as a 'laboratory of the apocalypse'. It is a quote that appears in almost every book on Vienna and the collapse of the Habsburg Empire.

Freud – who read *Die Fackel* – occasionally visited Kraus's haunt, Café Imperial, but he never visited Café Central. That would have risked an encounter with either Schnitzler, his doppelganger, or his former disciple Alfred Adler, whom he had grown to despise. One of Adler's chess partners at Café Central was a political firebrand from Russia, a dapper man who wore pince-nez and looked vaguely aristocratic. His name was Leon Trotsky. Their wives became very good friends.

Trotsky lived in Vienna from 1907 to 1914. He would have preferred to spend his exile in Berlin, but the Berlin police were less laissez-faire than the Viennese police. Although Trotsky was a revolutionary, he loved the courtly mannerisms that he observed in the coffee house: the bowing, the clicking of heels, the kissing of hands. When, eventually, the Bolsheviks came to power, he would write a booklet in which he offered the proletariat some improving guidance: 'Civility and politeness and cultured speech are a necessary lubricant in daily relationships.' He also honed his oratory skills in Café Central.

Trotsky had a lot in common with Adler. Socialism, for example. But he also had a lot in common with Freud. Trotsky relaxed by reading books in French, in the same way that Freud relaxed by reading in English. And around 1913, Trotsky, like Freud, was the leader of a 'sect' troubled by dissenting voices.

Freud's favourite coffee house was Café Landtmann – a very respectable establishment only a short walk from Berggasse 19. Its patrons were mostly politicians from the Town Hall and actors from the Court Theatre. The interior was clean and well upholstered, the reading matter conservative. It was a venue that appealed to the upper stratum of the bourgeoisie. Clearly, Freud liked Café Landtmann's restrained atmosphere. But it would be a mistake to confuse his preference for restraint with self-denial.

In 1912, Moses Allen Starr, an American psychiatrist, recollected time spent undertaking neurological research in the Austrian capital: 'Vienna is not a particularly moral city, and working side by side with Freud ... I learned that he enjoyed Viennese life thoroughly. Freud is not a man who lives on a particularly high plane. He is not self-repressed. He is not an ascetic. I think his scientific theory is largely the result of his environment and the peculiar life he leads.' Starr's observation is a calculated slur, but it should not be dismissed. Paradoxically, the Viennese coffee house, which we now associate with refined intellectualism, was a place of primal, oral gratifications – warmth, coffee, cake and cigars. We don't think of Freud as a sensualist – quite the contrary, in fact – but he was Viennese, and therefore exceedingly fond of indulgences.

Martin Freud's memories of Freud family dinners are mouth-watering. Every day was a feast. Viennese boiled beef was unimaginably different from British beef – 'so juicy and tasty' – and served with at least seven different sauces. The sweet 'was always a work of supreme culinary art'. These claims are supported by contemporary accounts of Viennese dining. On Monday 26 November 1900, Alma Mahler (then Schindler) wrote that she ate 'Oysters, lobster, suckling-pig, artichokes, duck, chocolate with whipped cream, ice-cream, cheese, fruit-basket, black coffee, liqueurs, pineapple punch'. She happily concludes: 'It was a terrific blow-out.' The Viennese loved eating: stews, dumplings, noodles, layer cakes, iced fancies, chocolate wafer biscuits, crispy mountains of pancake batter and rivers of plum compote. One of Martha Freud's specialities was *gugelhupf* – a ring cake, the shape of which resembled Vienna's infamous eighteenth-century lunatic asylum, the Fool's Tower. 'He belongs in the *gugelhupf*' was a local insult. In Freud's Vienna, even cakes couldn't escape the ubiquity of nerves.

The Viennese coffee house is the victim of its own success. It has detached itself from reality and exists as a Platonic ideal – the fulfilment of an unconscious wish; a perfect, egalitarian meeting place where the sensual and the cerebral, play and work, art and science, are represented in equal measure. The Viennese coffee house, or at least the Viennese coffee house as it exists in our imagination, resembles a model society. Sceptics suspect something too good to be true: a false memory of Old Vienna, a sentimental journey, *punschkrapfen* for tourists – in short, an illusion. Which is ironic, because almost all the significant figures who frequented Vienna's coffee houses before the First World War were searching for truth. Trotsky, a Ukrainian Jew whose real name was Lev Bronstein, was always seeking benefactors among the Café Central clientele to help fund his monthly magazine, *Pravda*. *Pravda* means 'truth'. Moreover, the truths articulated in Vienna's coffee houses were often challenging and provocative. They were adamantine truths. 'The truth', Freud wrote in a letter to Sándor Ferenczi in 1910, 'is for me the absolute aim of science.' For Karl Kraus, the very purpose of language was to expose truth, to show the 'difference between an urn and a chamber pot'.

The Viennese coffee house is steeped in its own legend, and many of its patrons were dreamers. But these patrons dreamed the modern world and their dreams 'came true'. Today, to a very large extent, we live in their dreams.

Chapter 15

Excavating the Soul

The American writer Hilda Doolittle was once an admired member of the literary elite. She published her novels and poems not as Hilda Doolittle, but as 'H.D.' – an idea suggested to her by Ezra Pound (to whom she was engaged for a period). Pound had recognised her burgeoning talent when Doolittle showed him examples of her work in the British Museum tea-room. This was a particularly fitting venue because Doolittle's writing is steeped in classical references. She had studied Greek literature at college. Photographs of Doolittle show a striking, somewhat androgynous woman with a severe fringe and intense, luminous eyes. She was one of the first 'imagists' (a movement that bridged French symbolism and modernism) and in her forties she appeared alongside the singer and actor Paul Robeson in a ground-breaking silent movie. Doolittle died in 1961. She was briefly hailed as a genius and then forgotten.

A decade passed and Doolittle was rediscovered by second-wave feminists. Her best narrative poetry interrogates the inner lives of ancient heroines and explores gender and identity. New editions of her work began to appear, but scholarly interest was not enough to restore Doolittle's mainstream literary reputation and again she slipped into obscurity. She deserves better. She speaks more directly to the twenty-first century than many of her much-lauded 'modernist' male contemporaries and she is the godmother of present-day women writers who have reached a wide readership retelling classical stories from a feminist perspective.

Throughout the course of her life, Doolittle's mental state was fragile. She experienced several breakdowns, unease about her bisexuality, and even suffered from hallucinations. She consulted several psychoanalysts and was eventually referred to Freud, whom she consulted five times a week for four months in 1933, and then for six weeks in October 1934. She was forty-seven and Freud was seventy-seven. Doolittle kept a therapy journal – later published as *Advent* – and ten years later she wrote a therapy memoir titled *Tribute to Freud*. It is one of the most candid and intimate portraits of Freud that we have. We find him fretting over his age, petting his dog, and sitting quietly like 'an old owl in a tree'.

When Doolittle stepped into Freud's consulting room for the first time, she was completely overwhelmed by what she saw: shelves crowded with figurines, fragments of wall paintings, vases, reliefs, reliquaries, funerary linen, and a large picture of the rock temple of Abu Simbel hanging above Freud's famous couch – 'treasures', 'pricelessly lovely objects'. As she stood there, dumbstruck, Freud observed: 'You are the only person who has ever come into this room and looked at the things in the room before looking at me.'

Freud and Doolittle's love of antiquity added warmth to their relationship. They talked informally about Egypt, excavations and mythology. Freud gave Doolittle guided tours of his collection, and he even took her into his inner sanctum – his study – where he showed her the special figures on his desk. '*This* is my favourite,' he said, selecting a bronze of the goddess

Athena. 'She is perfect. *Only she has lost her spear.*' Although Doolittle wrote that she could never tell whether Freud's tours were an innocent diversion or a pretext for some deeper purpose, it is difficult to resist interpreting the Athena incident. Athena sprang, fully developed and adult, from her father's head. Was Freud anointing Doolittle as a spiritual daughter? Was she going to be reborn from Freud's head with the magic of psychoanalysis?

Doolittle's account of being in analysis with Freud is vivid and immediate. The couch was slippery, the head rest at the back was hard. She could feel chilly, even though Freud provided a rug, which she would stroke to remove the folds. If she had been a little taller, her toes would have touched the porcelain stove in the corner. And Freud certainly didn't follow his own best practice guidelines. On one occasion, he thumped his fist on the head rest. Doolittle turned to face him, and he said: 'The trouble is – I am an old man – *you do not think it worth your while to love me.*' Doolittle was surprised. Surely he was too wise, too famous, to act like a 'child hammering a porridge-spoon on the table'.

Doolittle wasn't 'cured' by Freud. Nevertheless, she did experience some improvement and when she was in her seventies she was able to look back with some satisfaction on a successful literary career, happy relationships, and to take pleasure in her four grandchildren. The active ingredient of change was probably the great man's charisma rather than the resolution of her complexes. There are passages in Doolittle's *Tribute* that resemble ecstatic hagiography: 'I knew the things in his room were symbols of Eternity and contained him then, as Eternity contains him now.' Or: 'He is midwife to the soul.' After 1934, Doolittle and Freud corresponded – as friends – and Freud's letters were exceedingly tender: 'Life at my age is not easy, but spring is beautiful and so is love.'

In *Advent*, Doolittle wrote: 'Sigmund Freud is like the curator of a museum, surrounded by his priceless collection of Greek, Egyptian, and Chinese treasures.' It seems extraordinary that a 'humble', middle-class doctor could finance his own private museum. However, in Freud's Vienna it was possible to obtain antiquities at bargain prices. Conservative homes favoured Baroque and Biedermeier décor, not dusty relics. Only a few decades before Freud started collecting, three hundred Trojan antiquities and prehistoric remains (together with ninety-one painted Greek vases) were sold at Sotheby's in London for £8 10s. Eight pounds and ten shillings was a significant amount of money in the 1870s, but clearly nothing like the sum required to purchase an equivalent treasure trove today. In the 1920s and early 1930s, Freud's antiques dealer was Robert Lustig. Lustig sold Freud a figure of Isis suckling the infant Horus – a Twenty-seventh Dynasty Egyptian bronze dating from 664 BC. He had acquired the piece in a second-hand shop, where it had been weighed and sold for the value of its metal.

Isis suckling the infant Horus is one of the finest pieces in Freud's collection. It was probably cast as a domestic cult figure and prefigures the Christian Madonna and child. Freud was deeply attached to his figurines. Fondling them aroused 'strange secret yearnings'. When he acquired a new sphinx, falcon god or terra-cotta horse, he couldn't leave it alone. He would bring the new figure to the dinner table and admire it as he ate his boiled beef. When he fled from the Nazis in 1938, he asked Marie Bonaparte to smuggle two treasured items out of Austria. One was a small jade screen depicting the Chinese character for 'long life', and the other was his bronze Athena – the 'favourite' he had shown Doolittle. He was obliged to leave the rest of his collection in Vienna, and separation from his precious objects caused him considerable distress. He didn't feel that he was truly free from Nazi persecution until his antiquities had followed him across Europe to London. At the time of his death he had acquired well over two thousand artefacts, including (he was a sexologist, after all) around twenty phalluses.

Freud's fascination with antiquity was so central to his character that almost every aspect of psychoanalysis was influenced by classical literature and archaeology. The structural model of the mind was presaged by Plato, the Oedipus complex owes a debt to Sophocles, and Freud frequently compared psychoanalysis with excavation. In a letter to Stefan Zweig, he claimed to have read more archaeology than psychology: 'despite my much vaunted frugality I have sacrificed a great deal for my collection of Greek, Roman and Egyptian antiquities, [and] have actually read more archaeology than psychology ... ' This can't be true, but it tells us a great deal about how Freud wanted others to see him. Long before Freud had coined the term 'psychoanalysis', he was making connections between antiquity and mental states. As a young man, when he was studying under Charcot in Paris, he visited the Louvre and wrote to his fiancée: 'There were Assyrian Kings – tall as trees and holding lions for lap dogs in their arms, winged human animals with beautifully dressed hair, cuneiform inscriptions as clear as if they had been done yesterday, and then Egyptian bas-reliefs decorated in fiery colours, veritable colossi of kings, real sphinxes, a dreamlike world.'

Freud was taught Latin and Greek at school, introduced to classical literature around the age of nine, and his earliest heroes were the military giants Alexander the Great and Hannibal. During his adolescence, archaeologist adventurers such as Heinrich Schliemann were household names. The idea of journeying to exotic places and hunting for buried treasure would have been particularly appealing to Freud, who once claimed to be temperamentally more an 'adventurer' than a 'man of science'. Schliemann, who made many discoveries, is most famous for excavating Homer's Troy. Freud was only seventeen when Schliemann's 1873 excavations became headline news. There is a famous 1874 photograph of Schliemann's beautiful Greek wife wearing the 'Jewels of Helen'. She looks as glamorous as a Klimt society portrait. In the 1890s, when Freud could finally afford a few luxuries, he treated himself to some expensive editions of Schliemann's archaeological reports. They remained among his most cherished possessions. Once, when on board a boat travelling from Brindisi to Greece, Freud recognised one of Schliemann's associates. He was so awestruck he was unable to introduce himself. Freud psychoanalysed Schliemann by studying an autobiographical account of his childhood. He concluded that Schliemann was made profoundly happy by his discovery of Priam's treasure, because he had fulfilled a childhood wish. In *Ilios*, Schliemann wrote that he had resolved to find and

© akg-images

excavate Troy when he was only seven. Freud's reflections on Schliemann's happiness were undoubtedly tinged with personal regret. He admitted to Ferenczi that the 'strange yearnings' he felt as he fondled his little figures were 'for a life of quite another kind'. He would have been happier if he'd been an archaeologist. Perhaps this explains why he transformed psychology into a form of archaeology – 'depth' psychology.

On 4 July 1901, Freud ended a letter to Wilhelm Fliess in a state of excitement: 'Have you read that the English have excavated an old palace in Crete (Knossos) which they declare to be the original labyrinth of Minos?' He was so exhilarated that a heady flight of ideas spilled from his pen: 'Zeus seems originally to have been a bull. The god of our own fathers, before the sublimation instigated by the Persians took place, was worshipped as a bull. That provides food for all sorts of thoughts which it is not yet time to set down on paper . . . ' The English archaeologist Arthur Evans and his excavation of Knossos came up in one of Freud's conversations with Hilda Doolittle. She asked Freud, casually, if he had a Cretan serpent goddess in his collection and offered to procure one for him by using her connections. Freud responded, somewhat tartly: 'I doubt if even *you* could do that.'

Evans believed that the serpent goddess figurines he had unearthed at Knossos were evidence of a matriarchal earth-goddess cult. His thinking was greatly influenced by the Swiss antiquary Johann Bachofen, who forty years earlier had proposed that prehistoric human societies were matriarchal before patriarchy became the dominant form of social organi-sation. Freud, like Evans, was also familiar with Bachofen, and equally susceptible to his influence. For boys, the resolution of the Oedipus complex involves replacing a mother fixation with a paternal identification. Ultimately, boys must imitate their fathers and find an age-appropriate partner of their own. It seemed to Freud that the psyche of the individual resonates with ancestral echoes.

Minoan Crete was the earliest Aegean civilisation and preceded by waves of Anatolian settlement from 6000 BC. The legend most strongly associated with Knossos is that of Theseus and the Minotaur, and it is arguably the oldest surviving European story. The version of the narrative that we are familiar with was handed down to us from Greek and Roman sources. Every seven years, the city of Athens was obliged to send seven of its finest youths to Knossos, where they were forced to enter a labyrinth inhabited by the Minotaur – a monster with a bull's head and a man's body. Theseus contrived to enter the labyrinth as a sacrificial victim, but only after attaching the end of a ball of thread (given to him by the King of Crete's daughter, Ariadne) to the entrance. After battling and slaying the Minotaur, Theseus led the Athenian youths out of the labyrinth and to safety by following the thread he had previously allowed to unravel on the inward journey.

The legend of Theseus and the Minotaur is full of imagery and incident that lends itself to psychoanalytic interpretation:

the minotaur – half man, half animal – embodies the essential conflict between ego and id; the labyrinth, which coincidentally resembles the sulci of the cortex, suggests the complexities of the mind. In 1927, Freud told an interviewer that psychoanalysis 'supplies the thread that leads a man out of the labyrinth of his own unconscious'. Once again he had cast himself as a hero, a twentieth-century Theseus who had offered humanity a clue that could be followed out of the darkness and into the light of Athenian rationality: 'Where id was, there ego shall be.'

Freud longed to visit ancient cities. He visited Rome in his dreams long before he became, in his words, 'a constant pilgrim'. He dreamed that he was in a railway carriage looking out at the Tiber and the Sant'Angelo bridge; that he was surveying the mist-shrouded capital from the top of a hill; that he was standing on a Roman street looking at walls covered with German posters. He had so many dreams about Rome, they are referred to as the 'Rome series'. Freud was desperate to visit the city, but his plans were always scuppered by a curious phobic prohibition. 'My longing for Rome is deeply neurotic,' he admitted to Fliess. Once, he got as far as Lake Trasimeno, only fifty miles away, and turned back.

The idea of Rome as the Eternal City inspired one of Freud's most memorable metaphors. In *Civilization and Its Discontents*, Freud imagines a fantastical Rome 'in which nothing that ever took shape has passed away, and in which all previous phases of development exist beside the most recent'. In this truly eternal city, every building would exist in a superposition, and 'the observer would perhaps need only to shift his gaze' to reveal one structure rather than an another. A blink might replace the Colosseum with the vanished Domus Aurea; the Palazzo Caffarelli with the temple of Jupiter Capitolinus. Freud suggested that this vision of Rome is like the mind. Everything that we ever were co-exists with what we are. But Freud's fantastical

Rome is also *his* Vienna. The ring road, which he walked around every day, is a mix of Classical, Renaissance and Gothic architecture. Vienna, too, is timeless.

Psychoanalysis excavates personal history. But Freud's passion for archaeology made him dig ever deeper into the mind. He excavated childhood memories, speculated about birth trauma, and continued digging, going deeper, and therefore further back in time, beyond the limits of personal history to collective history. In the symptoms of neurotics, the behaviour of children and the symbolic language of dreams he found archaic vestiges. In myths and legends he found prototypes of complexes. The notion of the collective unconscious, a reservoir of inherited, transpersonal memories, is now strongly associated with Jung. But in a letter to Fliess dated 12 December 1897, Freud refers to 'endo-psychic myths', which many years later he described as 'the wishful phantasies of whole nations – the age-long dreams of young humanity'.

Collective memory underpins four interlinked essays published together for the first time in 1913 as *Totem and Taboo*. Freud thought that this volume contained his best writing, a judgement shared by the Nobel Prize-winning novelist Thomas Mann, who declared it a 'literary masterpiece'. Another fine writer, Lawrence Durrell, said that it should always be in reach when travelling the Greek islands. Inspired by Charles Darwin, James Frazer (the author of *The Golden Bough*) and the anthropologist James Jasper Atkinson, Freud speculated about the prehistoric origins of an inherited Oedipal disposition. He acknowledged that aspects of his thinking were 'impossible to prove', and that his hypothesis appeared 'fantastic', but the prospect of another grand synthesis – 'creating an unsuspected unity' – proved irresistible.

Humanity once lived in primal hordes dominated by a patriarch who had exclusive access to females. The sons of the tribe – a band of brothers – rebelled, murdered the patriarch and ate his body (an act dimly recalled in cannibalistic religious rituals such as the Eucharist). Subsequent competition for females resulted in social disintegration and it became necessary to restore social stability by introducing laws. The brothers renounced their claims on women from their own tribe – thus making exogamy obligatory – and they assuaged their guilt by instituting a taboo against killing a substitute father (or totem).

According to Freud, primal patricide left indelible and heritable traces in the 'mass' unconscious – in effect, a proto-narrative, the elements of which are conveniently consistent with his 'discoveries' concerning sexual development: forbidden desires, a prohibitive father figure, murderous intent, remorse, latency, the redirection of sexual interest, and finally, the resolution of conflict. Viewed more broadly, Freud's speculative primal crime germinates civilisation by creating the earliest expressions of religion and law.

Although Freud's cross-stitching between disciplines is deft and his resulting synthesis is imaginative, it remains an inescapable fact that all of Freud's arguments, examples and ingenuity amount to – as one critic correctly observed – nothing more than 'a just so story'. Curiously, Freud was inclined to agree. In 1921, when the subject of primal patricide was raised by his student Abram Kardiner, he responded: 'Oh, don't take that too seriously. That's something I dreamed up on a rainy Sunday afternoon.'

Totem and Taboo is a deeply problematic work. Although it can be enjoyed as a literary experiment – a Darwinian parable or psychoanalytic origin myth – its suppositions are untestable and Freud the scientist is entirely eclipsed by Freud the fabulist. Why did he write it? Perhaps armchair anthropology was the nearest Freud could get to 'a life of quite another kind'. The cultural historian Élisabeth Roudinesco has written: 'Reading this book leaves one with the impression of seeing Freud strolling about in the heart of a wilderness populated by the adventure stories he had so loved in his childhood.' *Totem and Taboo* documents a personal expedition into deep time, an idiosyncratic search for the source of a psychological Nile. Freud once described the answer to the problem of hysteria as 'a source of the Nile'. Perhaps, like his idol Schliemann, Freud was seeking happiness by fulfilling, as far as he could, a childhood wish.

The idea of inherited memory has mystical connotations. It is conceptually close to the idea of reincarnation. Some researchers claim that memories of past lives can be recovered under hypnosis. In *The Ego and the Id*, Freud suggests that the unconscious can be thought of as a repository of past lives. 'The heritable id accordingly harbours within it remnants of countless numbers of previous egos ...' Individual experience leaves traces that, under the cumulative weight of successive generations, become compressed in the deepest layers of the mind. Later in the same work he suggests that the id is 'a reincarnation of previous ego forms'. Our primitive urges belong to our ancestors as much as ourselves. Freud strongly disapproved of Jung's mysticism, which appears unreasonable considering his endorsement of endo-psychic myths and archaic vestiges; however, there are significant differences between Freud's 'mass psyche' and Jung's collective unconscious. Jung believed, for example, that the collective unconscious was situated mostly outside the brain. Freud, on the other hand, espoused a 'mass psyche' that was relatively consistent with the science of his day.

In the early nineteenth century, Jean-Baptiste Lamarck had proposed that characteristics acquired during the lifetime of an organism can be passed down to offspring. Thus, giraffes have long necks because their ancestors repeatedly stretched to feed on higher and higher leaves. Lamarck's theory was eventually superseded by Darwin's theory of evolution. Long necks are in fact the cumulative result of morphological variation (caused by genetic mutation) and differential survival rates. Freud accepted Lamarck's mechanism and believed that experiences leave impressions in the human mind. These impressions are then passed down to offspring like the stretched necks of giraffes. Freud's acceptance of Lamarck was not unusual. Almost all contemporary biologists were, to a greater or lesser extent, Lamarckian. Even Darwin accepted Lamarck's mechanism as a supplement to his own.

Darwin used the term 'survivals' to describe the persistence of primeval traits. The wings of earthbound birds such as the penguin are 'survivals', but they can also be thought of as morphic memories of flight. The general idea that bodies 'remember' is associated with Ernst Haeckel. Haeckel was a major figure who dominated German evolutionary biology for the second half of the nineteenth century. He expressed views on human evolution before Darwin, and Darwin acknowledged his priority. Haeckel is famous for his biogenetic law: ontogeny recapitulates phylogeny. Ontogeny is the history of the individual, phylogeny the history of the species. He was (and still is) a controversial thinker whose key speculations remain contentious.

Haeckel's law can be seen operating in the womb. For example, pigs, cows, rabbits and humans all seem to recapitulate their common ancestry before birth. In the early stages of embryonic development, mammals are almost indistinguishable. They approximate the form of a common ancestor. Moreover, embryos are atavistic. The human embryo 'remembers' its evolutionary history when 'gill-slits' and a short 'tail' make fleeting appearances. If bodies 'remember' the entire history of the species – and brains are part of the body – then by extension, minds could (at least theoretically) contain ancestral memories. Haeckel exerted an enormous influence on Freud. He even anticipated Freud's thinking about the survival of archaic vestiges in the mind by suggesting that there was a need for a 'phylogenetic psychology'.

There is no direct evidence for a collective unconscious, neither Freudian nor Jungian, but it is an intriguing concept that has considerable intuitive appeal. Countless commonalities link the myths, symbols and ceremonies of very disparate cultures and it is tempting to imagine the same archaic material bubbling up from the depths of a shared memory pool. Like embryonic mammals, cultures at earlier stages of development show greater similarities. The oldest cave paintings were made forty-five thousand years ago. With the single exception of Antarctica, early cave paintings have been found on every continent. Even though they are distributed across the globe and separated by oceans, they are uncannily similar. Stencilled hands, dots, cross-hatched lines, animals, 'humanoids' and human-animal hybrids are almost universal. Perhaps the most famous of these hybrid figures is the amusingly Freudian 'birdman' of Lascaux, a stickman with a bird's head and a conspicuous erection. Myths from around the world share plots. Monsters are slain, women are abducted, and heroes embark on perilous quests. None of these universals necessitate the existence of a transpersonal unconscious. They can be more parsimoniously explained by evolutionary convergences: identical nervous systems, identical emotions, identical priorities. Naturally, these correspondences will harmonise different story-telling traditions. Even eerily uniform non-figurative cave art has a simple explanation. Substances like psilocybin produce abstract and geometric hallucinations like the dot patterns and hatched lines found on cave walls. Ancestral humans most probably descended into a shamanic underworld, where they ingested psychedelics and performed rituals, just as Freud descended into his own unconscious to discover the secret of dreams.

Critics have dismissed Freud's collective unconscious because it is Lamarckian. Lamarck's credibility gradually ebbed away when the principles of Mendelian inheritance became more widely known in the early twentieth century. However, having been consigned to history for over a century, Lamarckianism is enjoying something of a revival.

In 1984, Lars Bygren, a nutrition researcher, began to study the population of a remote rural region of Sweden. He discovered that experiences, such as living through seasons of sufficiency as opposed to seasons of famine, had transgenerational effects. For example, women with paternal grandmothers born during or just after famines demonstrated an elevated risk of dying from heart disease. It had long been understood that the health of a mother during pregnancy can affect foetal development. Bygren's research suggested that grandchildren, and perhaps even great grandchildren, might also be affected. In the early 2000s, similar transgenerational effects were produced in laboratories where animals were exposed to toxic substances.

In a 2014 paper published in *Nature Neuroscience*, Brian Dias and Kerry Ressler reported the results of a laboratory experiment using mice, showing that a specific trauma experienced by one generation can result in specific changes of behaviour in two subsequent generations. If a cherry-like odour, acetophenone, is paired with an electric shock, then this will condition fear in mice. The 'children' and 'grandchildren' of fear-conditioned mice exhibited 'behavioural sensitivity' to acetophenone, even though they had no experience of traumatic acetophenone conditioning. These results look very much like Lamarckian inheritance, the translation of experience into heritable memories. This is not a unique study. On the subject of 'transgenerational inheritance of environmental information', the authors write: 'Although our understanding of such non-Mendelian modes of inheritance is continually being revised in terms of the epigenetic inheritance of traits, empirical data to support transgenerational epigenetic inheritance of behavioral traits in mammals are beginning to accumulate at the level of morphological, behavioral and metabolic traits.' Clearly, an acrobatic leap is required to get us from inherited behavioural sensitivity in mice to the collective unconscious in humans; however, this developing literature hints at exciting possibilities. The study of transgenerational trauma in the descendants of holocaust survivors is another growing area of research that reflects the increasing willingness of scientific communities to entertain the possibility of non-Mendelian inheritance. One is reminded, albeit tangentially, of a staple of Greek drama: the 'transgenerational curse'. In Aeschylus's *Seven Against Thebes*, we learn of a curse on the race, the *genos* of the Palace of Thebes and the house of Oedipus.

In 1936, Freud published an open letter to the French novelist Romain Rolland titled 'A disturbance of memory on the Acropolis' in which he described visiting the Acropolis thirty-two years earlier with his brother, Alexander. The two travellers arrived in Athens on 3 September at noon. The following morning, Freud prepared for his ascent by putting on his best shirt. Visiting the Acropolis was as close as Freud would ever get to an epiphany. It was one of the high points of his life. Yet, while he was surveying the Parthenon and its surroundings, he had a very odd thought: *So this all really does exist, just as we learned in school!* Freud analysed this thought and concluded that he must never have truly believed in the existence of the Acropolis in his unconscious, otherwise he wouldn't have been so astonished by its evident reality. It is an observation that can be linked, perhaps, with another of Freud's insights: that none of us really believe in our own demise. Some things are so vast or overwhelming that we effectively pretend they aren't there until reality forcefully obtrudes and our defences crumble. Freud finally settled on an Oedipal explanation for his 'feeling of estrangement'. A man from his modest background wouldn't ordinarily be found admiring the Acropolis. He had exceeded expectations, and in doing so he had also fulfilled a forbidden childhood wish to better his father's achievements. The Parthenon was metaphorically splashed with Jacob Freud's blood. Belief in the former was linked with discomfort associated with the latter.

Freud's meditation on his visit to the Acropolis underscores the degree to which classicism, archaeology and psychoanalysis are entangled. Freud could have developed a system of psychology untouched by his knowledge of myths, legends and ancient history, but it would not have been psychoanalysis. The figurines on his desk were not merely objects. They were tools. When he fondled and caressed them, he was invoking a kind of sympathetic magic that allowed him to explore his own prehistory and the history of humanity.

The extraordinary paradox of psychoanalysis is that it looks backwards to move forward. The modern mind has very deep foundations. They are older than Rome, the Acropolis and the oldest cave paintings, and they are constructed not from stone, but amino acids. Freud's excavations ultimately return us to the twenty-first century via Watson and Crick's discovery of DNA in 1953. At its deepest level, psychoanalysis is a *biology* of the mind. A psychology of primal instincts and atavisms; a psychology that can connect Photoshopped selfies with chromosomes, and video games with 'nature, red in tooth and claw'. Freud shouldn't have been envious of archaeologists. He dug deeper than *all* of them. He explored the brain of *Homo sapiens*, a labyrinth that is roughly three hundred thousand years old.

When Hilda Doolittle was being analysed by Freud in 1933, his pet chow would sit at his feet. Freud used to describe his dog as a lioness. This description prompted Doolittle to imagine the three of them as an archetypal group, 'an ancient cycle or circle, wise-man, woman, lioness'. They were like figures on a fragment of ancient pottery. Freud chose to die in his study sur-rounded by his books and artefacts. After he had been cremated, his ashes were placed in a Greek vase. To paraphrase Doolittle: a symbol of Eternity, containing him for Eternity.

Chapter 16

False Gods

On his first trip to Rome in 1901, Freud visited St Peter in Chains to see Michelangelo's *Moses*, a statue commissioned in 1505 for the tomb of Pope Julius II. The exterior is inauspicious. Steps rise to five identical arches, above which a line of small windows perforate an unadorned wall. It could easily be mistaken for a municipal building of middling importance. Yet the basilica contains extraordinary treasures: the chains that shackled St Peter, and Michelangelo's statue – a seated giant with strong, muscular arms, massive veined hands, cascading beard and horns (the horns should be beams of light and owe their existence to a translation error). This imposing figure looks less like a prophet and more like a character from a science fiction or fantasy film. Freud was deeply affected by Michelangelo's masterpiece. In fact, no statue had ever moved him in quite the same way. Whenever Freud returned to Rome, he felt compelled to go back to St Peter in Chains. In 1912, for example, he stood in front of Michelangelo's *Moses* every day for 'three lonely weeks'. His recollections of these solitary excursions possess a distinctly Gothic flavour: 'How often have I mounted the steep steps from the unlovely Corso Cavour to the lonely piazza where the

deserted church stands ...' It is a description reminiscent of an M. R. James ghost story, many of which feature antiquarians irresistibly drawn to desolate places where slumbering supernatural powers might be inadvertently disturbed.

In 1914, a curious essay appeared in the psychoanalytic and cultural magazine *Imago*. Its subject was Michelangelo's *Moses*, and it was written by an anonymous author 'personally known' to the editors. He was a man who moved in 'psychoanalytic circles' and whose 'mode of thought' resembled 'the methodology of psychoanalysis'. The anonymous contributor was Sigmund Freud, and the essay, titled *The Moses of Michelangelo*, treated the statue like a psychoanalytic patient, a conscious entity with a discoverable inner life.

Michelangelo's *Moses* appears to show the prophet at a precise moment in time. He has descended from Mount Sinai, carrying the ten commandments on two engraved tablets, and he has just caught sight of the children of Israel, dancing and worshipping the golden calf. He is about to leap to his feet in anger and the tablets will either drop to the ground or be cast aside and shatter. Freud saw a different Moses. He studied every aspect of the statue and his close attention to detail reminds the reader of Sherlock Holmes: 'the lines of the face reflect the feelings which have won the ascendancy; the middle of the figure shows the traces of suppressed movement; and the foot still retains the attitude of the projected action'. Moses is not about to leap up. He is a man who has overcome his anger 'and he will now remain seated and still, in his frozen wrath and in his pain mingled with contempt'. Freud was aware that, for some, replacing the revered scriptural Moses with a psychoanalytic alternative was tantamount to blasphemy. Nevertheless, he was unapologetic, and he remained so for the rest of his life. The last of Freud's works to be published during his lifetime was *Moses and Monotheism*, in which he argued that Moses wasn't a Jew but an Egyptian and that monotheism was an Egyptian innovation. He begins: 'To deprive a people of the man who they take pride in as the greatest of their sons is not a thing to be gladly or carelessly undertaken.' Nevertheless, that is precisely what he goes on to do, regardless of the offence he might cause to his co-religionists. Freud's sense of being Jewish ran deep, but his hostility to religion ran deeper.

Much has been written about Freud's ambivalent feelings

concerning Judaism. He enjoyed the company of Jews, attended a Jewish lodge and collected Jewish jokes. Yet he also banned Jewish observances at home, expressed concern that psychoanalysis might appeal only to Jews, and occasionally used antisemitic slurs. He once described someone he knew as 'a typical little Jew with sly features'. In fact, there was nothing ambivalent about Freud's attitude to Judaism. He was an implacable enemy of *all* religion, including Judaism. Even so, being Jewish was central to his sense of self. He explained his position very clearly in an interview conducted in 1926. He had always considered himself 'German', until the growth of antisemitism forced him to identify more strongly as a Jew. Freud was haunted by an incident recounted to him by his father when he was a child. An antisemite had once knocked a new cap off Jacob's head. It had flown through the air and landed in filth. 'And what did you do?' Freud asked. His father replied: 'I stepped into the road and picked up my cap.' In a letter to the Swiss pastor and psychoanalyst Oskar Pfister, written in 1918, Freud described himself as a 'godless Jew', and throughout his life he made efforts to compensate for his father's lack of heroism by standing up to antisemites – even when they started wearing swastika armbands and saluting Adolf Hitler.

Martin Freud recalled an unpleasant incident that occurred when the Freud family were on holiday in Thumsee in the summer of 1901. While Martin was fishing with his brother Oliver, a group of men baited them, called them 'Israelites' and accused them – quite unjustly – of stealing fish. The boys returned from their expedition prematurely and told their father what had happened. Freud's response was to explain that they were likely to encounter this sort of thing again and that they should be prepared for it.

Later, Freud had to go to Reichenhall, and the boys rowed him across the lake to shorten his walk. As they approached the shore, they saw the men who had called them Israelites standing in the road beyond the landing place. There were about ten of them, and some women had joined the gathering. As Martin moored the boat, the men, encouraged by the women, started shouting abuse. They were armed with sticks and umbrellas and clearly meant to block the road. Freud jumped out of the boat and marched directly towards the hostile crowd. Martin followed and Freud commanded him to stay back with uncharacteristic vehemence. Prior to that moment, Martin had never heard his father address him in anything other than 'kindly tones'. Freud charged forward, swinging his cane, and the crowd dispersed. The experience affected Martin deeply. After more than fifty years he could still remember 'the faces of these crusaders in racial hatred'. Freud, on the other hand, seems to have regarded the ugly confrontation as just another tedious instance of antisemitism that he was obliged to deal with. Martin wrote: 'He never recalled the incident at home, and I am not aware that he ever mentioned it in any of his letters to our family or friends.'

Although Freud rejected religion, he was extremely interested in its origins, its development and its effects on social organisation; however, his first thoughts about religion were informed by clinical practice. He began by identifying certain parallels between religious ceremonies and psychopathology. In 1907 he published a paper titled *Obsessive Actions and Religious Practices*. Obsessional symptoms often take the form of prohibitions and the performance of rigid, ritualistic routines that have a protective purpose. For example, they might be executed (albeit superstitiously) to ward off malign influences or misfortune. Obsessional problems are also strongly associated with guilt, the emotion most likely to arise after a sin has been committed. Freud described obsessional neurosis as a form of 'private religion'. Conversely, religion can be viewed as 'a universal obsessional neurosis'.

The superstitious thinking associated with obsessional neurosis resembles the magical thinking found in children and primitive societies. Both the child and the shaman accept cause-and-effect relationships that defy the laws of physics; merely thinking about something can make it happen. Freud supposed that human belief systems typically progress through three phases. The first is dominated by magical thinking; the second by religious thinking (which coincides with the emergence of a male deity who fulfils needs associated with a universal 'father complex'); and the third by scientific thinking. Advanced cultures and the psychoanalytic patient both outgrow the primitive, resolve complexes, and thereafter become more rational.

Freud's most significant work on religion was *The Future of an Illusion*, published in 1927. It is the intellectual precursor of numerous 'new atheist' polemics, such as *The God Delusion* by Richard Dawkins, widely read during the first decade of the twenty-first century. New atheists share with Freud a gleeful and sometimes combative disdain of irrationality. Freud argued that the human condition is precarious and social organisation evolved primarily as a defence against the destructive power of nature. Such defences are always imperfect and human beings are inevitably subject to cruel exigencies. Cooperative communities, however advanced, cannot stop accidents, disease and untimely death. The reality of human helplessness is almost unbearable and religion provides a ready balm; it reduces the terror of nature, reconciles humanity to fate, and offers every individual the comforting prospect of eternal life. Religion also promotes codes of behaviour that enhance social cohesion. Freud concluded that religions are the fulfilment of humanity's oldest wishes – wishes for a just world and happy endings; for good behaviour to be rewarded, for evil acts to be punished, and for suffering to be expunged by the bountiful love of an eternal father.

Religion is comforting and serves several purposes, but in the end it is nothing more than vaporous hopes, airy fantasies and self-deception. An anodyne illusion. Why, then, are human beings so willing to embrace false gods and pipe dreams?

Freud's answer to this question is 'narcissism'. From earliest times, human beings have watched the sun, moon, planets and stars cross the sky. For most of history it was assumed that these apparent celestial revolutions were indicative of humanity's centrality and therefore importance. With the arrival of the gods, and eventually monotheism, this perceived importance was used to justify the separation of humanity from the biological world. Theologians concluded that a creature ennobled by divine love must be closer to an angel than a gorilla. In 1917, Freud contended that human exceptionalism was built on crumbling foundations: 'In the course of centuries the naïve self-love of men has had to submit to two major blows at the hands of science.' Firstly, Copernicus demonstrated that human beings are not pivotal. In fact, humanity exists on 'a tiny fragment of a cosmic system of scarcely imaginable vastness'. Secondly, Darwin 'destroyed man's supposedly privileged place in creation and proved his descent from the animal kingdom and his ineradicable animal nature'. Freud immodestly placed himself in the company of these two Titans of science by asserting that psychoanalysis had delivered the third and 'most wounding blow': the ego is 'not even master in its own house, but must content itself with scanty information of what is going on unconsciously in its mind'. We blunder through life, lacking self-knowledge. We cannot account for our own actions. Our thoughts float like flotsam on a sea of darkness.

Believing in God makes us feel special and safe. But faith is regressive, a return to the nursery, and there are psychological risks associated with infantile megalomania and the loosening of ties with reality. Freud entreats humanity to grow up, to accept responsibility, to reflect, and to consider consequences. It is a message that has acquired new relevance on a world that spins ever closer to innumerable iterations of ruin.

Ernest Jones once told Freud of a surgeon who imagined that if he ever reached the eternal throne he would produce a cancerous bone and ask the Almighty 'what he had to say about it'. Freud replied: 'If I were to find myself in a similar situation, my chief reproach to the Almighty would be that he had not given me a better brain.' Jones writes: 'It was the remark of a man not easily satisfied.' Freud's statement is clearly yet another example of the false modesty he habitually displayed in the company of his most gullible disciple. Nevertheless, it is quite revealing. It suggests that, unlike Jones's surgeon, Freud didn't feel that the problem of human suffering was of paramount importance. What was most important to Freud was mental capacity and the pursuit of knowledge. In his final decades, Freud became less and less interested in psychotherapy as an answer to human suffering, and increasingly enthusiastic about abstract philosophical issues, anthropology, archaeology and culture. Psychoanalysis was no longer just a practice method but rather an outlook – a general mode of intellectual engagement. He compared psychoanalysis to electricity, which can be used in medical settings, for example to power radiological equipment, but is not *categorically* medical. Electricity can be harnessed for other purposes, and it is more correctly understood as a universal physical phenomenon. Psychoanalysis began as a treatment for mental illness, but psychoanalytic thinking, Freud argued, is relevant beyond the clinic. 'Psychoanalysis is a part of psychology; not of medical psychology in the old sense, nor of the psychology of morbid processes, but simply of psychology.'

Despite Freud's assertion that psychoanalysis should be understood as a general rather than a specific discipline, he declared (in the early 1930s) that psychoanalysis should *not* be conceptualised as a *Weltanschauung*, or world view. 'It is a part of science and can adhere to the scientific *Weltanschauung*.' As is often the case with Freud, it is unwise to accept what he says at face value, because the tone and scope of his late publications clearly reveal that he considered psychoanalysis to be not merely a part of science but a *new* science, a new attitude, a new lens through which to study the mind – and more importantly, the mind in its broadest possible context. In other words, a *world view*.

Ironically, Freud, the sworn enemy of religion, synthesised a world view that often feels like a substitute for the religious world view. Indeed, it is possible to think of psychoanalysis as a kind of secular religion. Erich Fromm, for example, described psychoanalysis as a response to 'Western man's' spiritual crisis; a pragmatic answer to the alienation, anxiety, despair and existential angst associated with modern living. Psychoanalysis, with its emphasis on realism, self-discovery and sexuality, is a 'good fit' for the modern mind set. Bruno Bettelheim has pointed out that the 'spiritual' nuances of Freud's writing are missed by English readers 'because nearly all his many references to the soul, and to matters pertaining to the soul, have been excised in translation'. Freud's quest for the unconscious is also a search for the soul – the absolute essence of being. The soul 'is what makes us human', writes Bettelheim; 'in fact, it is what is so essentially human about us that no other term could equally convey what Freud had in mind'.

Perhaps, as Freud stood in St Peter in Chains, he was coveting Moses' pedestal. The toppling of an old prophet would certainly make space for a new prophet. In the 1970s, Freud did get his own pedestal. Oscar Nemon's impressive bronze statue of Freud, seated like Moses, is now positioned in front of the Tavistock Clinic in London. When Freud delivered his 'third blow', he was aware that the collapse of western religion would leave a vacuum; a vacuum that psychoanalysis might fill.

Camera Press London

Psychoanalysis begins with an embattled leader, a coterie of devotees, and ritualistic meetings behind closed doors. It is a familiar story. Disciples convert others to the cause. Heretics threaten the integrity of the congregation and must be excommunicated. When the leader dies, his followers continue his work – guided by a sacred text – and establish shrines, places of pilgrimage, where holy relics (such as the 'couch') can be hallowed.

The similarities between psychoanalysis and religion have been enumerated on countless occasions, mostly by critics eager to discredit Freud: psychoanalysis masquerades as a science, but it is more like a doctrinal faith; Freud aligns himself with Copernicus and Darwin, but he has much more in common with nineteenth-century Romantic philosophers. Psychoanalysis was not built on replicable proofs, but rather received wisdom, accounts of miraculous cures and esoteric practices such as interpreting dreams.

If we accept that psychoanalysis can be construed (at least in part) as a response to 'Western man's' spiritual crisis, then we must ask: What characteristics does psychoanalysis share with religion? Are there some faiths that it resembles more than others? To what degree do they overlap? And does psychoanalysis possess anything like a credo or set of cardinal values?

Naturally, there has been a tendency among academics to look for spiritual commonalities that link Judaism and psychoanalysis. It is certainly the case that ideas found in the Jewish mystical tradition also correspond with psychoanalytic formulations. Sexual 'energy', dream interpretation, close attention to language, and symbolism – all feature in psychoanalysis and Kabbalah. By the end of the first millennium Islamic physicians had developed psychological treatments for mental illnesses, although their interventions were not associated with a model of the mind linked with Koranic teachings. Medieval Islamic doctors practised according to Hippocratic principles. The Christian notion of conscience and the super-ego are roughly equivalent concepts, but beyond this, Christianity and psychoanalysis do not have a great deal in common. There are, however, many meaningful correspondences between psychoanalysis and Buddhism – correspondences that were largely unexplored until the late twentieth century, presumably because there was little dialogue between psychoanalysts and Buddhists before counter-culture emissaries set off for India in the 1960s and widened channels of communication.

More than any other spiritual belief system, Buddhism is associated with the study of the mind. Buddhism has its own distinct, detailed and complex 'psychology' which was refined over centuries by monks practising a rigorous discipline of self-observation. Minute examination of mental phenomena was also Freud's investigative tool when he undertook his own psychoanalysis. The early Buddhist concept of mind, like Freud's, is rooted in the body. It can be affected by 'latent tendencies' – that is, trains of unconscious thought – and it is motivated by desires that arise from 'physical' dispositions. Thus, human beings pursue 'sense gratifications' according to the Buddhist equivalent of Freud's 'pleasure principle'. Wants and wishes are a significant feature of mental life. Buddhism also recognises destructive urges that ultimately derive from 'cravings' for self-annihilation – a source of motivation comparable to Freud's death instinct. In *Beyond the Pleasure Principle*, Freud acknowledges this correspondence explicitly by borrowing the term 'nirvana principle' from Barbara Low.

A central tenet of Buddhism is that the self is illusory. We are more than our conscious minds and we are wrong to think of our autobiographical self as a 'true self'. Freud's 'ego' is also illusory, insofar as it generates a misleadingly comprehensive sense of selfhood, whereas in reality it is only a small part of a much larger, opaque totality. Ego and id have approximate Buddhist equivalents, and something akin to the super-ego can be inferred from aspects of the 'eightfold path' (such as right action, right speech and right livelihood). Injunctions of this kind clearly assume the operation of a moral faculty.

The Freudian and Buddhist concepts of the unconscious are comparable at all levels. K. N. Jayatilleke, a renowned authority on Buddhist philosophy, asserted that a human being is 'a conscious mind as well as an unconscious in which is stored the residue of emotionally charged memories going back to child-hood as well as into past lives'. For Freud, the unconscious and emotionally charged memories of childhood are self-evidently significant and formative; however, his system also permits the less obvious influence of unconscious ancestral memo-ries. In *The Ego and the Id*, for example, he proposed that the id might contain residual imprints of 'previous ego forms', and in *Moses and Monotheism* he suggested: 'the archaic heritage of human beings comprises not only dispositions but also subject-matter – memory traces of the experience of earlier generations'. Memories of 'past lives' are buried deep in the Buddhist soul *and* the Freudian mind. The idea of karma (cause and effect oper-ating across cycles of rebirth, driven by ignorance, desire and hatred) bears interesting comparison with the transgenerational 'working through' of Freud's primal crime in *Totem and Taboo*.

Commonalities shared by Buddhism and psychoanalysis account for convergent formulations with respect to the human condition. The first noble truth of Buddhism states that life is suf-fering. Freud described the default lot of humanity as 'common unhappiness'. According to both the Buddha and Freud, an embodied mind, endlessly driven by desires, is unlikely to find easy contentment. In fact, neurosis is almost unavoidable. A well-known Buddhist axiom declares 'All worldlings are deranged'. Freudian defences, which warp reality, correspond closely with Buddhism's 'distorted perceptions'. Mechanisms in the mind inhibit our full and profitable engagement with real-ity. Consequently, we are ill equipped to successfully negotiate pathways out of suffering.

Buddhism lays special emphasis on attachment as a cause of unhappiness. We must learn to let go of things because nothing is permanent. Many of Freud's psychoanalytic prescriptions are predicated on the abandonment of very specific forms of attachment. Complexes that cause neuroses are essentially attachments that have outlived their utility. An unresolved Oedipus complex is an infantile maternal attachment that has survived, detrimentally, into adulthood. Similarly, narcissism is an attachment to the self (that ultimately makes loving others impossible).

Given that there are so many commonalities linking psycho-analytic and Buddhist thinking, it is not surprising that both frameworks recommend similar answers to the problems of living. Compromises must be made between the agencies of the Freudian mind, which, in Buddhist terms, translates as a recommendation that we should attempt, whenever possible, to find the middle way. Our desires must be tempered, and our perceptions corrected. We must liberate ourselves from the past and be more alert to present-moment experience.

Freud's 'three blows' suggest three *acceptances* that stand in readily for 'noble truths': acceptance of cosmic insignificance, acceptance of animal ancestry, and acceptance of limited self-understanding. And there is, perhaps, the implicit and supplementary acceptance of embodiment and all that follows from embodiment – indignity, disease, dotage and, ultimately, dissolution. Psychoanalysis has its principal *virtues*: humility to combat narcissism, restraint to ensure social cohesion, rational-ity to enhance engagement with truth. Erich Fromm suggested that, in a way, Freud was never offering a treatment method, but rather a form of salvation. This is probably overstating the case. But Freud was certainly bequeathing *more* than a treatment method. His intellectual legacy can function as an alternative form of 'spirituality' and it speaks directly to modern people living in the modern world.

There is a curious moment of autobiography recorded in *The Moses of Michelangelo*. Freud, remembering his many visits to the poorly lit church of St Peter in Chains, describes how he would sometimes creep 'out of the half-gloom', approach the great statue and feel the 'angry scorn' of Moses' gaze. Freud experienced an uncanny sense of being one of the 'mob', one of the idolatrous Jews who had danced around the golden calf. He was, of course, an extraordinarily idolatrous Jew. He had filled his rooms with idols. His cautious approach suggests trepidation, a sudden reversion to magical thinking – fear of the marble cracking and splintering, the Lawgiver rising, the commandments exploding on the floor, the massive stone head aiming its horns in Freud's direction, and an accusatory finger penetrating a cloud of expanding dust.

God (as Nietzsche famously declared) is dead. But in the unconscious, God is eternal.

Chapter 17

The Wolfman

Early in 1973 a young journalist entered an apartment building in central Vienna and climbed the stairs to the fifth floor. Her name was Karin Obholzer and she was looking for an exclusive story that would enhance her reputation and further her career. She had just read a new book, recently translated into German, that contained a collection of writings about Freud's most famous patient: the Wolfman. This arresting clinical alias, with its tantalising but misleading suggestion of lycanthropy, alludes to a dream of wolves that the patient had reported to Freud some sixty years earlier. Included in the book, among several articles and commentaries, was the Wolfman's autobiography. He was a 'Russian' aristocrat who had lost his fortune. Obholzer would later describe him as an 'Art Nouveau personality'. She resolved to trace him and request an interview. It would be quite a scoop.

The fifth-floor apartment did not have a name plate. On a previous visit, a neighbour had explained that the Russian was rarely at home and a late riser. This time, however, Obholzer rang the doorbell and the door was opened by a slight old man with white combed-back hair. His manner combined reproach and friendliness. He asked Obholzer how she had managed to discover his address and said: 'I don't give interviews.' But he invited the young woman into his apartment and their conversation was cordial and polite. He was surprised that she wanted to write about him. 'In Vienna, hardly anyone is interested in psychoanalysis.' He agreed to see Obholzer again and promised to show her some of his paintings. It was a pastime that he enjoyed.

In due course, Obholzer published an article based on her meetings with the Wolfman. It was well received, praised in some quarters, but ultimately inconsequential. She wrote: 'but I had expected more'. Eighteen months later, a publisher encouraged Obholzer to re-establish contact with the Wolfman. She was still the only journalist who knew where to find him. Perhaps her article could be expanded into a book? The Wolfman consulted members of the psychoanalytic community – Kurt Eissler, Wilhelm Solms-Rödelheim and Muriel Gardiner – who urged him not to cooperate. Nevertheless, Obholzer continued to meet him from time to time and he was always pleased to see her.

One day, the Wolfman declared: 'It seems that I want you to write something after all. But it must not be published until after my death.' From September 1974 to January 1976, Obholzer and the Wolfman met every two to three weeks. Their meetings were less frequent thereafter, but they continued to talk, even when the Wolfman was admitted into a hospital. As agreed, none of the material was published until after the Wolfman's death. A German edition of Obholzer's book was published in 1980 and this was followed by an English translation in 1982: *The Wolf-Man: Sixty Years Later*. It consists mostly of transcriptions of taped conversations, set out like a play.

There is something unnerving about these dialogues. They read a little like Anne Rice's Gothic novel *Interview with the Vampire*. The Apollo moon landings had already come to an end and space stations were orbiting the Earth. Yet, we find the

Wolfman sitting in late twentieth-century Vienna, dressed elegantly in a pin-striped suit, remembering peasants with shoes made of rags, an uncle who lived like King Ludwig II of Bavaria, and travelling to a seaside resort in a horse-drawn carriage. He is like a temporal anomaly, a voice displaced from an impossibly distant past.

The Wolfman, whose real name was Sergei Konstantinovitch Pankejeff, was born in 1886 in Ukraine. He was raised on two vast estates and a villa in Odessa that had grounds abutting the shore of the Black Sea. His grandfather was one of the richest landowners in southern Russia. The landscapes of Pankejeff's childhood were magical and populated by fairy-tale characters. One of his earliest memories was peering through a gap in a garden fence and seeing horses, gypsies and 'other strange people' arguing around a campfire in winter. He hunted wolves in primeval forests and attended celebrations at which juvenile peasants performed 'native' dances.

Pankejeff attended a gymnasium, contracted gonorrhoea at the age of eighteen, and became depressed. A year later he suffered a relapse after his sister, Anna, a gifted polymath, poisoned herself. As she was dying, she regretted her decision, but by the time she sought medical help it was too late. A well-known neurologist diagnosed Pankejeff's condition as neurasthenia. Pankejeff then visited several German sanatoria, including one located in Neuwittelsbach, near Munich. There he attended a fancy dress ball, where he became fascinated by a beautiful woman: 'Her blue-black hair was parted in the middle, and her features were of such regularity and delicacy that they might have been chiselled by a sculptor.' Her name was Terese Keller. She was a nurse, a divorcee, and the mother of a child. A fraught romance followed that ended somewhat melodramatically when both parties agreed 'Never to meet again'. Pankejeff travelled and diverted himself with cabarets and one-night stands.

In 1908, Pankejeff's father was found dead in a Moscow hotel room. He was forty-nine years old and had probably overdosed on Veronal (a barbiturate). Pankejeff returned to Munich to resume his treatment, although this was merely a pretext for seeing Terese again. The relationship was rekindled but it was still volatile. After an explosive argument in Berlin and a letter of farewell, Pankejeff returned to Russia, confused and deeply despondent.

At this juncture, Pankejeff became acquainted with the extraordinary figure of Dr Leonid Drosnés. He was outwardly conservative. Early thirties, black morning coat, white tie, gold-rimmed spectacles, and a square reddish beard. But he was somewhat dissolute and partial to baccarat and casinos. He was also the only person in Odessa who had heard of Sigmund Freud. With typical impulsive haste, Drosnés began to psycho-analyse Pankejeff, heedless of the fact that he had no experience of practising as a psychoanalyst and only a rudimentary grasp of psychoanalytic concepts. He quickly recognised that these were significant handicaps, and he recommended a trip to Geneva to consult the renowned neuropathologist Paul Dubois. As Vienna was on the way to Geneva, he suggested that they might also consult Freud. Furthermore, Drosnés proposed that they should bring a medical student, whose principal duty, it transpired, was to play the third hand in card games.

When Pankejeff met Freud in January 1910, he promptly abandoned the idea of proceeding to Geneva. It was inconceivable that Dubois would prove to be Freud's equal. 'Up to now,' Freud opined, 'you have been looking for the cause of your illness in your chamber pot.' This was literally as well as metaphorically true insofar as, in addition to baths, massages and other physical treatments, Pankejeff had also been prescribed regular enemas.

The Russians settled into a pension run by an American woman, and Pankejeff consulted Freud every day for one hour.

This left Pankejeff and his medical team with plenty of time to fill with leisure activities. They walked around the Prater, visited coffee houses, went to see Jewish comedians and played cards until two or three in the morning. Drosnés took to womanising in low-life taverns. On one occasion he had to ward off 'weird male figures' with a revolver to ensure his safe exit.

Freud claimed that, at this time, Pankejeff was completely dependent on others and 'incapable of autonomous existence'. It is difficult to reconcile this description with Pankejeff's eager pursuit of diversions and pleasure. Moreover, after Drosnés and the medical student returned to Russia, Pankejeff was perfectly capable of keeping himself amused. For example, he took fencing lessons from a former Italian officer. A photograph of Pankejeff taken in 1910 shows a fabulously suave character who looks like a cross between an early screen idol and Marcel Proust: dark eyes, slightly upturned moustache, glossy hair, the sleeves of an exquisitely cut jacket pulled back just far enough to reveal his stylish cufflinks.

Pankejeff's psychoanalysis lasted for four years, and publication of his case study – *From the History of an Infantile Neurosis* – was delayed for another four years because of the First World War. From the late 1920s onwards, psychoanalysts referred to this work more plainly as 'The Wolf-Man'. James Strachey described it as the most elaborate and important of Freud's case histories. For Ernest Jones it was 'assuredly the best of the series', a classic, delivered by a 'confident master', 'at the very height of his powers', worthy of 'every reader's admiration'.

From the outset, Freud's tone is commanding. We are immediately informed that psychoanalysis was a success – inhibitions have been dissolved, symptoms eliminated – and we are promised 'details' that are curious and incredible. Freud raises expectations with a little help from Shakespeare: 'I could not do otherwise than recall those wise words that tell us there are more things in heaven and earth than are dreamt of in our philosophy.' When Pankejeff began his analysis, his stormy relationship with Terese was uppermost in his mind; however, *From the History of an Infantile Neurosis* is concerned primarily with problems that Pankejeff experienced before his adolescence. Consistent with his general approach, Freud looked for the origins of Pankejeff's current problems in his past.

Pankejeff had been a very gentle and obedient child, until, quite suddenly, he underwent a rapid personality change. He became morose, irritable, quick to take offence and prone to rages during which he would yell 'like a savage'. At the age of five, his sister showed him a picture in a book of a wolf standing on its hind legs, which frightened him so much he would scream. He then became fearful of other animals and insects, such as horses, beetles and caterpillars. Around the same time he derived sadistic pleasure from beating horses (and torturing insects). Between the ages of five and possibly eight or ten, Pankejeff exhibited signs of obsessional piety. He felt compelled to cross himself, pray and kiss holy pictures. When he experienced blasphemous thoughts, he would 'neutralize' them by modifying his breathing. Towards the end of his childhood, Pankejeff stopped feeling attached to his father and began to fear him instead.

Pankejeff's sexual development was unremarkable. At the age of three, he was 'seduced' by his sister. They examined each other's buttocks in a toilet. On a later occasion, during a game, she played with his penis. When Pankejeff was ten (or perhaps a little older) he pressed his body against his sister while they were looking at pictures of nude women, but she rejected his advances. Pankejeff turned to a servant girl for sexual favours, a formative experience which probably 'imprinted' a lifelong preference for women below his class.

The most significant sections of Freud's case study relate to a dream that Pankejeff had the night before his fourth birthday. A sketch (given to Freud by Pankejeff during his treatment) shows the dream's central image: white wolves sitting on the bare branches of a tree. This image has become so iconic it is still being reproduced on mugs, pillows, bedcovers and greetings cards. 'I dreamed that it is night,' Pankejeff recalled, 'and I am lying in my bed (the foot of my bed was under the window, and outside the window there was a row of old walnut trees. I know that it was winter in my dream, and night-time.) Suddenly the window opens of its own accord and terrified, I see there are a number of white wolves sitting in the big walnut tree outside the window. There were six or seven of them. The wolves were white all over and looked more like foxes or sheepdogs because they had big tails like foxes and their ears were pricked up like dogs watching something. Obviously fearful that the wolves were going to gobble me up I screamed and woke up.'

Pankejeff's nurse rushed into the room to see what was wrong. He was so distressed it took him some time to accept that he had been dreaming. Apart from the spooky opening window, the dream was entirely static. The wolves had been unnaturally still. 'It looked as if they had turned their full attention on me.'

The dream was described early in Pankejeff's analysis and Freud was immediately convinced that it concealed the cause of his patient's infantile neurosis; however, it took him years to discover its meaning. Indeed, Freud didn't arrive at a full understanding of the dream until the last months of Pankejeff's treatment. He concluded that Pankejeff's dream was a symbolic transformation of something Pankejeff had witnessed when he was only eighteen months old: his mother and father having sex. Freud called this the 'primal scene'. The dream had occurred – so Freud asserted – the night before Christmas, which is why the wolves are arranged in the walnut tree like presents in a fir tree. As a child, Pankejeff had heard fairy stories like *Little Red Riding Hood* and *The Wolf and the Seven Little Kids*. Wolves were a prominent feature of his fantasy landscape and readily available for use as symbolic substitutes. Whiteness – displaced from his parent's bedlinen and underclothes – determined the wolves' blanched appearance. The dream contains several defensive reversals, things transformed into their opposites (to reduce anxiety). In the real world, Pankejeff had stared at his parents, but in the dreamworld, the wolves stare at him. His copulating parents were moving, but the wolves are motionless. Six or seven wolves are perched in the tree (rather than two) to dilute the disturbing reality of his parents' 'coupling'. The uncharacteristically benign appearance of the wolves, like foxes or sheepdogs, was also defensive, to reduce fear associated with the threat of violence (rooted in castration anxiety).

Freud shows extraordinary confidence in his powers of deduction by giving precise details relating to the circumstances of the primal scene. The eighteen-month-old Pankejeff was suffering from malaria. He was asleep in a cot, in his parents' bedroom, when he was awakened by a mounting fever. It was late afternoon, perhaps five o'clock, on a hot summer's day, and his parents had retired for a siesta (only half dressed). They were relatively young and had only been married for a few years. Naturally, they took the opportunity to make love. On waking, Pankejeff witnessed his parents engaged in 'coitus a tergo' – intercourse from behind – which was repeated three times. Pankejeff's father, standing behind his mother, was rutting like an animal. In fact, he resembled a wolf in a picture book standing on its hind legs.

Freud informs us that, as an adult, Pankejeff found buttocks particularly exciting and intercourse from behind was the only position that gave him sexual pleasure. We are on familiar Oedipal territory: an explicit, unconscious memory of his

mother – so it seems – was the prototype for his sexual preferences. However, Freud then overwhelms the reader with a
plethora of additional hypotheses and explanations. He dives
deep into Pankejeff's psyche and surfaces with evidence of anal
eroticism and homosexuality; he discusses the symbolic equiv-
alence of money and faeces, faeces and babies, religious themes
and sublimated sadism. Finally, he arrives at a startling conclusion. Pankejeff's animal phobias were an instance of displaced
anxiety, anxiety that originally surrounded a masochistic desire
to be sexually satisfied (as his mother was) by his father. 'It is not
fear of the *father* that comes to consciousness, but fear of the *wolf*.'
Pankejeff's initial screaming fits, Freud reveals, were an attempt
to attract his father's attention – a form of infantile seduction.

Freud seems to be aware that his assertions are becoming
increasingly wild, and he intermittently interrupts the flow of
his writing to defend himself – often quite colourfully. 'The
whale and the polar bear, it has been said, cannot wage war on
each other, for since each is confined to his own element they
cannot meet.' In other words, critics have no right to question
his authority because they have no experience of psychoanalysis. The absence of any common terms of reference precludes
meaningful debate.

Freud had good reason to be defensive, because 'The Wolf-
Man' – his most elaborate and important case history – is based
on the flimsiest of foundations: a childhood dream, remembered
after twenty years, freely interpreted, and subsequently accepted
as evidence for an event that probably never happened. Modern
memory research suggests that our earliest memories date from
the age of two and a half years. Pankejeff was only eighteen
months old when he supposedly witnessed the primal scene.
Even if we entertain the possibility that Pankejeff was exceptional, and that a memory of the primal scene did register in his
unconscious, Freud's deductions remain incredible. Intercourse

from behind? Three times? At five o'clock in the afternoon? Today, only the most devout Freudians are convinced by his reasoning. Freud established the exact time that the infant-Pankejeff observed his parents having sex from the cyclicity of the adult-Pankejeff's mood disturbance. Pankejeff's depression intensified around five o'clock. Clearly, correspondences of this kind are somewhat arbitrary. Later in the case study, Freud suggests that the primal scene might have been a fantasy, but he clearly wants us to believe it was an actual event: 'The seduction of my patient by his older sister was an indisputable reality; why not the observation of his parents' coitus, too?'

Freud accelerated Pankejeff's 'recovery' by imposing a ter-mination date on his treatment. Critics have compared this manoeuvre to emotional blackmail. It is plausible that Freud applied pressure in this way, because at that time he needed a model case study to use as ammunition against renegades such as Adler and Jung.

Irrespective of these shortcomings, Pankejeff's case study was hailed as an invaluable contribution to the Freudian canon, the clinical equivalent of works such as *The Interpretation of Dreams* and *Three Essays on the Theory of Sexuality*. Like Strachey and Jones, many applauded its brilliance.

There is a curious disconnect between the subject matter of *From the History of an Infantile Neurosis* and what was on Pankejeff's mind when he started his analysis. Childhood fears and childhood piety were not a pressing concern in 1910. He was much more preoccupied with his failed romance. For Freud, however, Terese was a distraction. In fact, Freud advised Pankejeff to postpone further meetings until some progress had been made in therapy. Freud's prohibition seems to have been counter-productive, because Pankejeff continued to mention Terese in every session – which Freud found exasperating. It wasn't until early in 1911 that Freud permitted a reunion. By this time, Pankejeff had no idea where to find Terese and he had to hire a private detective agency to discover her whereabouts.

Terese had given up nursing and now owned a small pension in Munich, where she lived with her daughter, Else. When Pankejeff visited her, he was deeply disturbed by her appearance. She was obviously miserable and horribly emaciated – 'scarcely more than a skeleton'. Pankejeff felt guilty, blamed himself for Terese's suffering, and vowed 'never again to leave this woman'. They started seeing each other again, and Terese became pregnant. Allegedly, Freud 'demanded' that Terese should have a termination – a procedure that resulted in infection and sterility. When Freud was introduced to Terese, he praised her serious-mindedness, declared that she looked like a czarina, and fully approved of Pankejeff's plan to marry her.

In the final weeks of Pankejeff's analysis, Freud did something extremely unprofessional. He suggested to Pankejeff that at the end of treatment, a gift given by a patient to his or her therapist might reduce burdensome feelings of gratitude and 'consequent dependence'. Pankejeff responded by purchasing a figure of an Egyptian princess of comparable quality to those exhibited in museums. Sixty years later, Karin Obholzer commented: 'That must have cost a fortune.' Pankejeff replied, 'I can't remember. Probably. Considering my situation at the time, it was of no consequence.' He was a very rich man.

On 28 June 1914, after going for a walk on the Prater, Pankejeff returned to his apartment, where his maid handed him a newspaper. Archduke Franz Ferdinand had been assassinated in Serbia. The following day, Pankejeff visited Freud for his last appointment. They spoke about the assassination, but neither of them appreciated its true significance. When the Archduke and his wife's remains were returned to Vienna, Pankejeff watched the hearses being driven down Mariahilfer Strasse at night, lit by torches flickering in the rain.

Pankejeff and Terese were married in Odessa. Terese travelled back to Germany in 1918 when Else, who was then living with relatives, became seriously ill. Pankejeff and Terese were not reunited again until the following year.

On his way to Germany, Pankejeff stopped in Vienna to visit Freud. He didn't think he required more help, but Freud recommended a short 'reanalysis' to treat Pankejeff's constipation – which was assumed to have a psychological cause. Freud's finances were in a parlous state after the war and Pankejeff was indifferent to Freud's astronomical fee of forty crowns an hour.

Shortly after Pankejeff's arrival in Germany, Else died. Pankejeff buried Else and returned to Vienna. Meanwhile, the political situation in Russia was becoming increasingly hostile to his interests. Freud's reanalysis took longer than expected and Pankejeff thought it prudent to go home and settle his 'financial affairs'. Freud told him to stay. The analysis dragged on. The Red Army marched into Odessa, and Pankejeff's property was seized by the Bolsheviks. In the 1970s, Pankejeff would reflect: 'It was stupid of me that I listened to Freud and stayed in Vienna.' Moreover, after his reanalysis, he was still constipated.

Suddenly, Pankejeff was an indigent exile. Freud must have felt some responsibility. He waived his fee and gave Pankejeff some financial assistance – enough to help him pay his rent. Freud was also reputed to have organised annual collections for Pankejeff, but this was probably a fiction invented by Freud's disciples. With Martin Freud's assistance, Pankejeff managed to get a position at an insurance company, where he remained an employee for the next thirty years.

In 1926, Pankejeff consulted Freud again, because he had developed a new set of symptoms. Freud, by then diagnosed with cancer, referred him to Ruth Mack Brunswick (one of Freud's students and collaborators), who saw Pankejeff for five months. Her account of his treatment, *A Supplement to Freud's*

'*History of an Infantile Neurosis*', was published in the *International Journal of Psycho-Analysis* in 1928. Pankejeff's principal problem was distress connected with 'unsightly' nasal injuries, allegedly caused by electrolysis for obstructed sebaceous glands. On inspecting Pankejeff's 'small, snub, typically Russian nose', Mack Brunswick could detect 'nothing whatsoever'. Pankejeff also reported general health concerns and complained bitterly about doctors and dentists. His sexual relationship with his wife had become less satisfying, and in the years preceding his sessions with Mack Brunswick, Pankejeff had resumed his former habit of visiting prostitutes, who would masturbate him while he studied 'obscene' pictures.

Pankejeff's mental state worsened considerably. 'During the analytic hours he talked wildly in terms of fantasies, completely cut off from reality.' After reading in a newspaper that one of his doctors had died, he 'sprang from the couch, clenching his fists and raising his arms'. In desperation he cried: 'My God, now I can't kill him any more!' Soon after, he threatened to shoot Freud, as well as Mack Brunswick herself. Mack Brunswick concluded that Pankejeff had developed persecution mania, which she glibly connected with his famous wolf dream. The wolf is a substitute father, doctors are father figures, and the 'wolves' were trying to destroy him. Pankejeff believed that since his youth he had suffered misuse and abuse from the medical profession. Indeed, his suffering had been so great, he compared himself to Jesus Christ.

Given that Pankejeff was so disturbed, it is surprising that his 'recovery' was relatively swift. Improvement coincided with the occurrence of two dreams. The first was of his mother breaking holy pictures, and the second – a rural idyll – was judged by Mack Brunswick to be a benign version of the wolf dream. Pankejeff had dreamed of looking out of a window at a sunlit meadow and trees, one of which possessed pleasingly entwined branches. According to Mack Brunswick, the second dream showed that Pankejeff had overcome his primal fear of castration, and that he could finally 'admire what others find beautiful – a love scene between a man and woman'.

Mack Brunswick confessed that she had done little to restore Pankejeff's mental equilibrium. Her role had been 'negligible'. She supposed that Pankejeff had simply 'worked his way through the unconscious material behind his delusions of persecution'. Nevertheless, she believed that she had identified the cause of Pankejeff's breakdown. According to Mack Brunswick, Pankejeff had relapsed because he had been unable to free himself of his father fixation during his treatment with Freud. Her general arguments tend to rely on contentious assertions. Concerning symbolism in psychosis, for example, she confidently informs us that 'The nose is, of course, the genital.' Pankejeff's recovery turned out to be provisional. In 1930 he consulted Mack Brunswick again to discuss whether he should leave his wife for a younger woman.

An unprecedented period of calm and contentment followed. Pankejeff enjoyed Sunday outings with Terese, month-long holidays in the mountains, landscape painting, and trips to the theatre and cinema. It seemed to Pankejeff that his life would continue in this way for ever. With some poignancy, he recalled in his autobiography: 'I had not the slightest foreboding of the cruel game that fate was playing with me, or that very soon everything would end in tragedy.'

On 12 March 1938, German troops occupied Vienna. Artillery appeared on the streets, planes circled overhead, and antisemitic rioting began. Three weeks later, Pankejeff returned home and discovered Terese slumped over the kitchen table next to a gas jet, surrounded by suicide notes. 'The sight was so terrible that I simply cannot describe it.' She had been dead for several hours. Pankejeff was utterly devastated. He confessed that his mental torment would have been unendurable 'had not a lucky chance come to my help'. This 'lucky chance' was an accidental meeting with Muriel Gardiner.

Muriel Gardiner was a wealthy American who had travelled to Vienna to be analysed by Ruth Mack Brunswick in 1926. Eager to become an analyst herself, Gardiner settled in Vienna, became acquainted with members of Freud's circle, and in 1932 enrolled to study medicine at the university. In the late 1920s, she had wanted to learn Russian. Mack Brunswick had arranged for Gardiner to meet Pankejeff, who taught Gardiner 'for a year or two' and continued visiting her occasionally to renew her insurance policies. When Gardiner met Pankejeff on a busy street in the spring of 1938, he was in an extremely distressed state. Gardiner invited him back to her apartment where he repeatedly asked: 'Why did this have to happen to me? Why did my wife kill herself?' After several such meetings they both agreed that he would benefit from more psychoanalysis. Psychoanalysis had been banned by the Nazis and it could only be practised at great personal risk. Gardiner managed to overcome extraordinary logistical problems and arranged for Pankejeff to travel to Paris and London for further sessions with Ruth Mack Brunswick. Freud and his family had been forced to leave Vienna and were now living in London. Pankejeff took the opportunity to pay Freud a visit. He returned on two further occasions. They talked for a very long time and – according to Freud's maid – after Pankejeff's departure, Freud was 'terribly weary'. When Pankejeff returned to Vienna, Gardiner made sure that a friend of hers was available to offer Pankejeff continued support on a fortnightly basis.

It is extraordinary that Gardiner found time to help Pankejeff because, immediately after the Anschluss, she was very busy flushing illegal literature down lavatories, attaching false passports to her body with adhesive tape and synchronising her

watch to the second. She had joined the Austrian underground –
code name 'Mary' – and was active in the field. Her principal
objective was to provide Jews with the means of escaping from
the Nazis. If she had been discovered, she would have been interrogated and executed by the Gestapo. Gardiner never publicised
her heroism.

That is, not until after 1973, which was when the writer Lillian
Hellman published a book titled *Pentimento*. Gardiner's friends
immediately alerted her to the content. The pertinent section
of Hellman's book was subsequently made into a film. *Julia*,
released theatrically in 1977, was nominated for eleven Academy
Awards and won three. Gardiner had never met Hellman
and realised that the author had most probably learned about
her underground activities through a mutual acquaintance.
Hellman almost certainly modelled Julia on Gardiner because
Gardiner was the *only* American woman who had worked with
the Austrian anti-fascists. To set the record straight, the exceptionally modest Gardiner published an autobiography in 1983:
*Code Name Mary: Memoirs of an American Woman in the Austrian
Resistance*. In addition to detailing her dangerous missions, she
also reminisces about: an affair with the poet Stephen Spender
('I've never been in love with a woman before'); an encounter
with the young Kim Philby (later to become a notorious double
agent); afternoon tea with the Freud family (she found Freud
charming); and – taking up less than two pages – assisting
Pankejeff.

After the war, Gardiner – then back in America – sent
Pankejeff clothes and food packages. They maintained a regular
correspondence, but Pankejeff was still suffering from depression, which worsened after his retirement in May 1950.

In 1951, Pankejeff mistakenly entered the Russian zone of
Vienna. He was apprehended by soldiers, interrogated, and
released after four days. He was terrified of being arrested again

and for a short period he seems to have suffered from symptoms of post-traumatic stress. His whole body shook, and he couldn't stop crying.

Gardiner paid for Pankejeff to receive yet more psychoanalysis. She couldn't have been confident about its benefits, because she started sending him Dexamyl (an anti-depressant). In a letter to Gardiner dated 27 October 1960, Pankejeff thanked her profusely: 'My only consolation, dear Frau Docktor, currently lies in your pills, which are the only thing able to improve my mood.' In addition to maintaining a correspondence, Gardiner also visited Pankejeff eight times between 1960 and 1970.

In 1971, most of the extant literature on Pankejeff was published in a book titled *The Wolf-Man by the Wolf-Man: The double story of Freud's most famous case*. It contained Pankejeff's autobiography, Freud's original case study, Ruth Mack Brunswick's supplementary case study, and Muriel Gardiner's recollections of the Wolfman. The tone of the general commentary is positive. In her introduction, Gardiner claims: 'Thanks to his analysis, the Wolf-Man was able to survive shock after shock and stress after stress – with suffering, it is true, but with more strength and resilience than one might expect.' At the end of the book, she concludes: 'There can be no doubt that Freud's analysis saved the Wolf-Man from a crippled existence, and Dr. Brunswick's reanalysis overcame a serious acute crisis, both enabling the Wolf-Man to lead a long and tolerably healthy life.'

This, then, was the official verdict – the intended last word.

Pankejeff was in his eighties when Karin Obholzer conducted her recorded interviews. His responses to her questions are repetitive, digressive and sometimes self-contradictory; however, what emerges is a strong sense of the person. And the person we meet was certainly not, as Muriel Gardiner asserts, 'saved' from a 'crippled existence' by psychoanalysis. Quite the contrary. He strikes us as vulnerable, needy and indecisive. Moreover, he is still very much enmeshed in the world of psychoanalysis, to the extent that his identity has become completely subsumed by his clinical alias. Obholzer recounts picking up the telephone and hearing him say: 'This is the Wolf-Man.' Over-identification of this kind is disquieting – a good premise for a horror novel. However, it was encouraged by the psychoanalytic community. Pankejeff sold his paintings to Muriel Gardiner, her students and her colleagues, including several paintings of his wolf dream. Every member of the International Psychoanalytic Association wanted one. Pankejeff also wrote articles on diverse subjects inspired by psychoanalysis.

It has been said that the psychoanalytic community took Pankejeff under its wing, but critics maintain that a cabal of analysts closed ranks around Pankejeff to protect Freud's repu-tation. Whatever the truth, Pankejeff ultimately resented their

Freud Museum, London

involvement: 'the disciples of psychoanalysis should not have laid hold of me after Freud … I would have acted more independently. This outside interference has not had a good effect.'

Pankejeff was torn between loyalty and suspicion. Concerning Gardiner and *The Wolf-Man*, Pankejeff declared: 'they made a showpiece of me. The book is really intended to prove that psychoanalysts can cure such a serious case.' Immediately, he felt a pang of guilt and added: 'Well, it certainly helped me.' Contradictions of this kind are frequent: 'If you look at everything critically, there isn't much in psychoanalysis that will stand up. Yet it helped me.' Pankejeff disputed official accounts of his 'symptoms'. Freud was wrong to suggest that he, Pankejeff, could only enjoy intercourse from behind. This was categorically untrue. Mack Brunswick had reported that Pankejeff only masturbated on 'big holidays'. 'What she wrote there is stupid.' On the subject of Ernest Jones's pronouncements, Pankejeff is almost lost for words: 'is that fellow crazy or what, writing such nonsense'.

The many instances of misreporting that Pankejeff enumerates are trifling when set against his damning judgement of the wolf dream: 'Freud traces everything back to the primal scene which he derives from the dream. But that scene does not occur in the dream. When he interprets the white wolves as nightshirts or something like that, for example, linen sheets or clothes, that's somehow farfetched I think … It's terribly farfetched.' Moreover: 'The whole thing is improbable because in Russia, children sleep in the nanny's bedroom, not in their parents'. It's possible, of course, that there was an exception, how do I know? But I have never been able to remember anything of that sort.'

Freud declared Pankejeff cured in 1918. His inhibitions had been dissolved and his symptoms eliminated. Ruth Mack Brunswick declared Pankejeff cured in 1928. At that time, he had been 'well' for eighteen months. Notwithstanding having seen him again for even more therapy in 1938, Mack Brunswick optimistically described her results (around 1940) as 'excellent'. And in 1971, Gardiner, reflecting on Pankejeff's sixty-year clinical history, assured readers that he had been 'saved'.

In fact, Pankejeff was symptomatic for most of his life. He suffered from obsessions and depression, and from the early 1950s he became locked into a long-term dysfunctional relationship that drove him to contemplate suicide. Although he dutifully repeated that he had been helped by psychoanalysis, he eventually made a chilling admission to Obholzer: 'I am in the same state as when I first came to Freud.' Following a heart attack in 1977, Pankejeff was admitted into a psychiatric hospital, where Obholzer continued to visit him. Like an addict, Pankejeff craved more therapy. When the journalist left his bedside, he would call out after her: 'Give me some advice!' Pankejeff died in the arms of a private nurse – paid for by Gardiner – at the age of ninety-two, on 7 May 1979. The psychoanalytic community, who had always been wary of Obholzer, reneged on a promise and did not invite her to the funeral.

The accuracy of Pankejeff's late testimony *can* be questioned. When he spoke to Obholzer, he was an old man with a long history of mental illness, prone to rambling and contradicting himself – even in consecutive sentences. We can also query the accuracy of Obholzer's 'transcriptions'. Some are reconstructed from memory, and all of them, even those that were tape-recorded, are edited. Obholzer admits in her introductory chapter that editing was necessary, because 'taped protocols do not yield a readable book'. But this still leaves psychoanalytic stalwarts who insist that *From the History of an Infantile Neurosis* is a towering accomplishment, with significant problems. The beneficial effects of psychoanalysis were short-lived, and the importance of the iconic centrepiece of the case study – the wolf dream – rests entirely on immoderate and improbable speculation.

Muriel Gardiner concluded her introduction to *The Wolf-Man* with the following statement: 'The Wolf-Man himself is convinced that without psychoanalysis he would have been condemned to lifelong misery.' Of course, it is possible that without psychoanalysis Pankejeff would have led an even more wretched and miserable life. He was a tragic figure and deeply traumatised. A complete psychoanalytic cure would have been close to miraculous. However, if psychoanalysis did Pankejeff any good, it also did him a great deal of harm. He lost himself in his clinical alias and psychoanalysis became an inescapable dependency. He could not disengage. The psychoanalytic community treated him like a precious heirloom that required tightly controlled atmospheric conditions to prevent its dissolution. His personhood, his very *being*, became secondary to his pre-eminence as a Freudian relic – a cynosure in an imaginary museum of dreams.

Obholzer's description of Pankejeff on his hospital bed is harrowing: 'It is as if the obsessional neurosis itself were lying on its deathbed. In this ineluctable process of decay, he clutches at some obsessional thought. Everything was for nothing, pointless, false, I would like to start life all over, do everything differently. And only this pathological circling of his thoughts seems to keep him alive.'

Obholzer's image is nightmarish. A human being – memories, feelings, thoughts – reduced to nothing but a residue of torment and regret. It is hard to envisage how Pankejeff's life could have been very much worse if he had never travelled to Vienna to consult Sigmund Freud.

Chapter 18

Stranger Things

Nineteenth-century Romanticism inspired its own school of German Romantic philosophy. Thinkers such as Friedrich Wilhelm von Schelling, Gotthilf Heinrich von Schubert and Carl Gustav Carus were preoccupied by mysterious Nature, universal symbols and the unconscious. Anything shadowy, liminal or strange excited the Romantic imagination: atypical mental states, such as dreams, daydreams, madness and creative genius; paranormal phenomena, such as telepathy, ghosts, demons and doppelgangers. The Romantics were even fascinated by the 'otherness' of animals. Cats and dogs often behave as though they can see or hear things that can't be perceived by humans. Freud shared these Romantic preoccupations, and they surface repeatedly in his writings. In many respects, psychoanalysis can be viewed as a late offshoot of German Romantic philosophy.

The phenomena that interested Romantic philosophers might appear somewhat arbitrary. Mental illness, ghosts, animal behaviour? But anomalous and exceptional phenomena can be thought of as a point of weakness between the perceived material world and something greater beyond. Ultimately, German Romantic philosophy was a spiritual endeavour. According to

Heritage Images/Getty Images

von Schelling, 'Nature is visible Spirit, Spirit is invisible Nature.' Behind the world is the 'world soul'. Caspar David Friedrich's 1818 painting *Wanderer Above the Sea of Fog* is the quintessential Romantic image: a lone figure stands on an elevated rocky outcrop and stares over an expanse of mist at distant peaks. By exposing himself to the overwhelming majesty of Nature, the Romantic enters an altered state of consciousness that facilitates connection with the deeper truth behind appearances. Freud's heart was Romantic. He loved walking in natural landscapes. Whenever the opportunity arose, he cast himself as the Wanderer and marched off into the mountains. It was almost as if he needed to connect with the world soul, to dissolve his

personal identity in oceanic Nature – to imbibe unadulter-
ated truth.

Although Freud was profoundly influenced by German
Romantic philosophy, he was also a scientist, a man who espoused
Enlightenment values. The light of Freud's enlightenment, however, is always a little eldritch, and never quite powerful enough
to chase away the shadows. When he was writing his academic
articles, he was surrounded by gods and funerary relics. Any fictional physician with arcane knowledge – Bram Stoker's Abraham
Van Helsing or Sheridan Le Fanu's Martin Hesselius – can be
imagined comfortably seated behind Freud's desk.

Freud characteristically qualifies his probing of Romantic subject matter with disclaimers. 'Unfortunately I must confess that
I am one of those unworthy individuals before whom ghosts
desist from their haunting, and the supernatural eludes me, so I
have never been in a position to experience anything that might
persuade me to believe in signs and wonders.' However, there
was one paranormal phenomenon that he approached with an
open mind. With the help of Sándor Ferenczi, Freud and his
daughter Anna conducted a series of telepathy experiments,
the results of which persuaded Freud that, under the right
conditions, the contents of one mind could be transferred to
another. Father and daughter were very close. Disconcertingly
close. Indeed, their entire relationship can be viewed as a special
instance of the uncanny.

Anna was a difficult child. She was moody, probably suffered
from an eating disorder, and was jealous of her sister Sophie.
When she reached adolescence, her parents sent her to country
retreats, hoping that a change of environment would have a
beneficial effect on her health. Freud's letters to Anna are warm
and frank: 'You know, of course, that you are a bit odd.' As Anna
matured, Freud became protective, even proprietorial. When,
at the age of eighteen, Anna took her first holiday in England,

Ernest Jones was waiting for her on the landing stage with a bouquet of flowers. The same day, Freud wrote a rather panicky letter to Anna, informing her that he had reason to believe that Jones was intent on wooing her: 'try not to find yourself alone with him'. He immediately repeated himself: 'Postpone your visits to London until you have company and do not allow yourself to be picked up by him alone.' Freud then composed a letter to Jones intended to dampen the Welshman's ardour. He, Freud, had reached an 'understanding' with his 'little daughter' and 'marriage or the preliminaries' were not to be considered for another two or three years. Jones responded with good humour, but he also observed: 'She is of course tremendously bound to you.' A year later, Anna added a rather disquieting postscript to one of her letters to Freud: 'Recently I dreamed that you were a king and I was a princess, and that someone wanted to separate us through political intrigues.' She was happy with her situation: a princess – an unattainable object of desire – in her father's court.

At the age of twenty-two, Anna began the first of two psychoanalyses. Her analyst was her father. The practice of analysing friends and relatives was not unusual at that time. Carl Gustav Jung, Karl Abraham, Ernst Kris and Melanie Klein all analysed their offspring. Nevertheless, when it was rumoured that Freud was analysing his daughter, even his students became a little uneasy. Anna was 'quite an attractive girl'. Why wasn't she married? Had Freud become her unsurpassable ideal? A benchmark of 'manhood' that no suitor could ever rival? Aspiring analysts gossiped about Anna like fishwives.

As a child, Anna had fantasised about being beaten. These fantasies became a stimulus for masturbation, and eventually a masturbation substitute. Her dreams – what she called her 'nightlife' – were violent and disturbing. In a letter dated 5 August 1919, Anna offered Freud a typical example: 'I murdered somebody or something like that. As punishment I was put into

a large room where there were many people who could do with
me what they pleased. The people wanted to tear me to bits and
throw me out of the window ... It seems that most of my dreams
have something terrible in them, killing, shooting, or dying.'
Demonstrating the oddity that Freud had noted when she was
younger, Anna signs off with airy abandon: 'Write me a long
letter soon. Margaretl sends her regards. With a kiss, Your Anna.'
Freud's 1919 paper *A Child is Being Beaten*, subtitled *Contribution to
the understanding of the origin of sexual perversions*, collects several
cases with common features. One of them is Anna.

Anna became a member of the Vienna Psychoanalytic Society
in 1922 and specialised in the treatment of children. She was
intelligent, insightful and articulate, and quickly earned the
respect of Freud's colleagues.

In 1925, after separating from her husband, Dorothy
Burlingham (the heiress of Tiffany & Co.) brought her children
to Vienna to be analysed by Anna. The two women became
inseparable. They drove around the city in Dorothy's Model T
Ford (with Freud in the back) and dressed in identical clothes.
Freud, already party to Anna's inner life, became equally knowl-
edgeable about Dorothy's when he accepted her as a patient in
1927. Dorothy and her children moved into Berggasse 19 in 1929.
She installed a telephone line between her bedroom and Anna's
so that they could talk into the night.

Freud described the living arrangements of the Freud
and Burlingham families as symbiotic. Their 'community',
composed of individuals whose inner worlds had been made
mutually available to each other though psychoanalysis, resembled a hive mind. In his 1932 lecture *Dreams and Occultism*, Freud
refers to an article written by Dorothy Burlingham in which she
gives examples of telepathy that occurred when both a mother
and a child (in fact herself and her son) were simultaneously in
analysis. Freud was convinced that such observations had the

potential 'to put an end to remaining doubts on the reality of thought transference'. He supposed that telepathy was a form of 'archaic' communication that had been replaced by language and that certain phenomena, for example excitable mobs acting with a 'common purpose', could be explained by telepathy.

The symbiotic relationships of the Freud household were not exclusively human. Animal symbionts were also assimilated. Anna acquired a German shepherd, Wolf, and Dorothy Burlingham gave Freud a chow which he named – according to various sources – Lin Yug, Lün Yug, Lün Yu, or simply Lun. Freud referred to these dogs as 'additions to the family'. This wasn't hyperbole, because Wolf, Lun and the pets that followed (two more chows, Jofi and another Lun) were loved as much as children or grandchildren. In his correspondence, Freud imparted news of humans and dogs as though they were equals. His language was extremely anthropomorphic, and he would refer to a dog as having a 'first husband' or a 'baby'. Freud's favourite dog was Jofi. She would sit with him while he analysed his patients. He didn't have to look at his watch, because at exactly the right time, Jofi would signal the end of sessions by standing up and yawning. Freud claimed that she was never wrong by more than a minute – and always at the patient's expense. Jofi was also considered an excellent judge of character. If she sniffed visitors 'haughtily' and then walked off, the whole Freud family – as well as the maid – would view them with suspicion. On Freud's birthday, he would receive a poem ostensibly composed by his pets (but really written by Anna and Martin Freud). The poems were delivered 'personally' by the dogs, attached to their necks by red ribbon. In 1930, because Freud was away in Tegel, Jofi's birthday poem was delivered by a tortoise, which Freud considered a poor substitute. In this poem, Jofi promised to be better behaved in future, and signs off: 'So speaks Jo Fie sad at heart / sorry that we are apart'.

Marie Bonaparte, the disciple with whom Freud was most open and intimate, shared his anthropomorphic love of dogs. In 1936, she sent him the manuscript of her book *Topsy: The Story of a Golden-Haired Chow*. It is ostensibly an account of her pet's illness and treatment, but it can also be read as a book about mortality and a metaphor for a sickening Europe. Freud enjoyed the manuscript immensely and with Anna's help translated the book into German. He asked Marie in a letter: 'Does Topsy realize she is being translated?'

The neurologist and psychoanalyst Ernst Simmel recalled once warning Freud not to approach a chained police dog that he thought would be vicious. Freud simply unchained the dog and offered the animal his face to lick. 'If you had been chained up all your life,' said Freud, 'you'd be vicious too.'

Freud's final pet was Jumbo, a small Pekingese purchased for him as a temporary replacement for Lun number two (who had to be placed in quarantine when the Freud family emigrated to England in 1938). Unfortunately, Freud never formed a deep attachment to Jumbo because he felt that this would be disloyal to Lun. For Freud, canine fidelity was something that should be reciprocated. There is very little film of Freud. All that we have are a small number of home movies shot at the very end of his life. What is striking about these movies is the amount of time Freud shares the screen with dogs.

Freud's relationship with cats was less straightforward. He didn't warm to cats because they lacked the characteristic of unwavering devotion. Although in 1913 he told Lou Andreas-Salomé that, once, he did become very friendly with a cat that entered his office through an open window. The cat would settle on his 'couch' or inspect the antiques that he had left on the floor. Apparently, Freud's heart melted, and he ordered it milk. He became fascinated by the cat's self-satisfied purr and indifferent manner. She clearly didn't consider Freud an equal.

The following year, in his essay *On Narcissism*, he attributed the charm of cats to their inaccessibility – their lack of concern for others. With humorous intent he observed that certain women possessed cat-like qualities. Commenting on the wife of one of his colleagues, he wrote: 'She certainly has her share of the charm and grace of a cat, but it's no longer an adorable young kitten.'

Animals were interesting to Freud because, like any advocate of the theory of evolution, he found it instructive to identify continuities between animals and humans; however, he also viewed animals through the lens of Romanticism. They are part of the symbolic language of the unconscious; they appear in dreams and speak in fairy tales. Freud found monkeys extremely unnerving because they are both like us, and not like us. The prevalence of monkeys, either as mangy Victorian toys or demonic tormentors, in horror writing – Le Fanu's *Green Tea*, for example – indicates that Freud's discomfort is widely shared. Ambiguity was central to Freud's understanding of all things eerie and disturbing. It was something that he wrote about extensively in his definitive exploration of the strange, *The Uncanny*, published in 1919.

The Uncanny had an uncanny prelude. Because of a calculation made by Wilhelm Fliess (based on his mathematical biology), Freud believed that he was going to die at the age of fifty-one. Fliess's calculation was evidently wrong. Nevertheless, Freud continued to worry. For no obvious reason he became convinced that he was going to die at the age of sixty-one or sixty-two. Moreover, he imagined that this 'presentiment' was being repeatedly confirmed by chance encounters with these numbers. His sixty-first birthday arrived, then his sixty-second, and finally his sixty-third. He had escaped the mausoleum that his unconscious had been carefully preparing for him. In a sense, he was now both dead and alive – a thing of uncertain status. This was the point at which he started working on *The Uncanny*.

The Uncanny is a peculiar piece of writing that proves its central thesis by unsettling the reader with its own uncertain status. Like *The Interpretation of Dreams*, *The Uncanny* resists categorisation. Freud seems to be working out what he's writing about as he writes. It has been poetically described as 'a strange theoretical novel'. Unfortunately, most newcomers never get to enjoy its twists and surprises because, having had their expectations raised by a sensational title, they are immediately disappointed by a lacklustre introduction that reads less like a novel and more like a dictionary. It is a book that is easily and prematurely thrown aside.

The German word for uncanny is *unheimlich*, which is the opposite of *heimlich*, meaning 'homely'. Freud suggests that we are easily unsettled when something familiar (or homely) suddenly appears unfamiliar (or unhomely). Reversals of this kind supply pivotal moments of drama in genre fiction and film. A husband, wife or, more commonly, a child says or does something strange and we are no longer sure who or even what they are. Freud supports his argument by analysing a classic of uncanny literature: E. T. A. Hoffmann's 1817 short story *The Sandman*. Hoffmann was the most significant Romantic author to incorporate Gothic and fantastic elements in his work. The key figures in Hoffmann's short story are the student Nathaniel, who as a child was disturbed by an old woman's description of the Sandman (a supernatural being who removes the eyes of children), and Olympia, a girl Nathaniel falls in love with (but who turns out to be an automaton).

Freud suggests that fear of having one's eyes pulled from their sockets is common among children, and he connects this fear with his sexual theory. Enucleation, he claims, is a symbolic substitute for castration. Thus, the effect of the Sandman's threat of violence is ultimately rooted in the Oedipus complex. Freud's account of why we find automata disturbing is less encumbered by psychoanalytic dogma. Like monkeys, automata have uncertain status. They are like us, and not like us. The same is true of dolls, mannequins, ventriloquist's dummies and waxwork figures (which also appear frequently in horror and weird fiction). They switch from being familiar to unfamiliar. Homely to unhomely. The bedrock of this unease is possibly confusion about whether something is dead or alive. Freud attributes this insight to the German psychiatrist Ernst Jentsch. A doll is a dead thing, but it might look like a baby. Madness can produce uncanny effects for similar reasons. For example, jerky movements suggest broken machinery. Are we looking at a human in distress or something inanimate that is merely 'behaving' like a human in distress?

Freud continues his inquiry into the uncanny by examining another eerie phenomenon that features in Hoffmann's writing: the doppelganger – a double of a living person. The doppelganger is strongly associated with German folklore, but the general concept can be traced back to Ancient Egypt. In the early nineteenth century, the idea of the double fascinated German Romantics. One of Franz Schubert's most performed songs (composed in 1828) is a setting of Heinrich Heine's poem *Der Doppelgänger.* In German folklore, the appearance of one's doppelganger often presages death. Ernest Jones tells us that Freud met his double on the way to Naples in August 1902. He consequently wondered whether (as the well-known saying augurs) he would see Naples and die. However, Freud's doppelganger proved to be as fatal as the numbers fifty-one, sixty-one and sixty-two.

For Freud, the double represents unacceptable parts of the self that have been separated from the person and projected on to a duplicate. There is of course an element of ambiguity inherent in this formulation. Is it me, or isn't it? The double is a bespoke

Mr Hyde, composed of primitive, unattractive aspects of the self that the individual attempts, usually with only partial success, to expel. These unwanted characteristics can also be understood as those parts of the self that the individual has been unable to accept and integrate into his or her totality. The double, therefore, is also – in a sense – our 'unfinished business'.

Doppelgangers are ultimately the product of a fundamental mechanism that Freud supposed could explain the discomfort associated with all uncanny phenomena: the return of the repressed. This explanatory principle is generally regarded (particularly by literary theorists) as one of Freud's major intellectual contributions. The idea was foreshadowed by von Schelling, who suggested that the term uncanny 'applies to everything that was intended to remain secret, hidden away, and has come into the open'. Freud adds an extra dimension to von Schelling's secrets coming into the open by defining them as a form of transition from homely to unhomely. Thus, uncanny phenomena are 'nothing new or strange, but something that was long familiar to the psyche and was estranged from it only through being repressed'. Freud's explanatory mechanism is very versatile. Ghosts, like doubles, can also be understood as aspects of the self that we find difficult to accept. When we are haunted, we are in fact being haunted by ourselves, our unresolved infantile complexes, primitive desires and forbidden wishes – traumatic experiences that we cannot process. We repress, and what we repress returns. In Henry James's 1898 novella *The Turn of the Screw* (widely recognised as the pre-eminent psychological ghost story) a chaste governess is haunted by ghosts who represent her own frustrated sexual longings.

The versatility of Freud's mechanism is demonstrated by another staple of weird fiction, entrapment in a repeated experience. A similar phenomenon features in the 1993 film *Groundhog Day*, the title of which has entered the English language as a convenient blanket term for all variations of what Freud termed 'repetition of the same thing'. Freud gives a personal example. He was once strolling around a small Italian town when he accidentally wandered into the red-light district. Embarrassed, he hurried away, but his escape route brought him back to where he had started. He departed again by a different road and the experience was repeated. Freud was immediately seized by a sense of the uncanny. He had wanted to avoid temptation, but desire had unconsciously returned him to the place where his forbidden wishes could be fulfilled. The repressed had returned – albeit in a circuitous manner.

The influence of Freud's *The Interpretation of Dreams* on the surrealist movement is well documented. But *The Uncanny* was equally influential. Many surrealists were intrigued by the idea of discovering strangeness in the ordinary, the unhomely in the homely. Salvador Dalí's 1936 surrealist object *Lobster Telephone*

Isabel Infantes/AFP via Getty Images

is illustrative. There is nothing particularly disconcerting about lobsters or telephones, but Dalí's juxtaposition immediately transforms the ordinary into the extraordinary. A household object – a Bakelite telephone – is suddenly bizarre and vaguely menacing. *The Uncanny* has continued to provide an intellectual rationale for many contemporary art works. For example, the highly disturbing mutant mannequins of children created by Jake and Dinos Chapman explore aspects of the return of the repressed.

Freud points out that psychoanalysis is itself uncanny. It seeks to uncover demons in the unconscious. When Freud was studying with Charcot in Paris, he would frequently visit the Cathedral of Notre Dame and climb up to its famous gallery of chimeras. Among these horrors, many of them demonic, is the figure of an alchemist (wearing a Phrygian cap and lab coat) whose direction of gaze is reputed to indicate the location of the fabled Philosopher's Stone. Freud was a modern alchemist who reformulated medieval demons as complexes and Darwinian imperatives. He translated all things devilish – lust, violence, cruelty – into terms that were compatible with twentieth-century thinking.

Perhaps the most explicit example of Freud's fascination with the demonic is his 1923 publication *A Seventeenth Century Demonological Neurosis*, which begins, like so many tales of the supernatural, with the author telling his readers about the recent discovery of an old manuscript in a library – a 'demonological case history'. Christoph Haizmann was a seventeenth-century painter who signed several 'bonds' with the devil, not in exchange for power or sex but rather, Freud deduced, to be freed from a debilitating depression that had stifled his creativity after his father's death. Freud supposed that Haizmann's illness was functional. The devil (who had first appeared in the guise of an 'honest' old man) was a father substitute. Over a decade earlier,

Freud had written: '*The delusional formation, which we take to be the pathological product, is in reality an attempt at recovery, a process of reconstruction.*' The idea that madness is a therapeutic journey, a process of repair and regeneration with its own internal logic, is now principally associated with R. D. Laing and the radical psychiatry movement of the 1960s. Freud was seeding the concept as early as 1911.

Freud's curiosity concerning demonic power is tangentially related to his interest in Leonardo da Vinci. In his 1910 essay *Leonardo da Vinci and a Memory of his Childhood*, Freud reminds his readers that Leonardo was dubbed the 'Italian Faust'. A man with such prodigious gifts is easily suspected of being in league with the devil. From the perspective of German Romantic philosophy, Leonardo's condition – that of a supreme genius – can be viewed as a kind of altered or abnormal state. Freud's purpose was to explore the processes underlying Leonardo's extraordinary talent and to understand the 'uncanny, enigmatic character' of the *Mona Lisa*'s smile. Freud quotes the German art historian Richard Muther, who felt 'demonic magic' emanating from those curved lips. Rather predictably, Freud's solution to the enigma is Oedipal. The *Mona Lisa*'s smile belongs to Leonardo's mother. And the uncanniness of the smile is attributable to its ambiguity, its suspension between 'boundless tenderness' and 'sinister menace'.

The memory of childhood referred to in the title of Freud's paper is a strange, early reminiscence, recorded in one of Leonardo's notebooks. Leonardo could remember being in a cradle and a vulture descending and striking his lips with its tail. Freud believed that this was a 'screen memory' and he offers an analysis predicated on Ancient Egyptian symbolism. In Egyptian mythology, the mother goddess was represented by a vulture's head and Freud supposed that Leonardo's screen memory concealed a true memory of being suckled at his

mother's breast. Unfortunately, all of Freud's reference works were poorly translated. The bird of prey named in Leonardo's original notebook was in fact a kite, not a vulture, so Freud's argument is based on a false premise.

Leonardo's extraordinary imaginative gifts represent the pinnacle of human creativity; however, creativity, even on a modest scale, is still a mysterious phenomenon. Naturally, Freud thought that the mystery could be solved using psychoanalysis. On 6 December 1907, he delivered a talk – *Creative Writers and Day-Dreaming* – at the literary salon of the book dealer, art dealer and publisher Hugo Heller. The talk was published the following year. Freud concludes: 'A strong experience in the present awakens in the creative writer a memory of an earlier experience (usually belonging to his childhood) from which there now proceeds a wish which finds its fulfilment in the creative work.' This is essentially a restatement of his dream theory. Experiences activate childhood memories; infantile wishes are aroused and symbolically fulfilled. The imaginative writer is a 'dreamer in broad daylight'. It is a theory of creative writing conveniently confirmed by Marcel Proust, whose madeleine, once tasted, activated deep longings (some Oedipal) for a lost personal history, which he then recovered and reconstructed in a book: *À la Recherche du Temps Perdu*. Of course Freud's explanation isn't the only explanation of the creative process, but it is one that many writers recognise.

Freud was an avid reader of fiction. Dickens, Thackeray, George Eliot, Goethe, Zola, Anatole France, Wilhelm Jensen, Schnitzler, Zweig – and Disraeli. Later in life he regarded Dostoevsky's *The Brothers Karamazov* to be the greatest novel ever written. He adored Mark Twain's *Sketches* and Kipling's *The Jungle Book*. He also enjoyed British crime writing: Sir Arthur Conan Doyle, Agatha Christie and Dorothy L. Sayers. Freud claimed to be amazed by novelists. In *Creative Writers*

and Day-Dreaming, he states that laypeople – himself included –
are 'intensely curious' concerning how that 'strange being, the
creative writer' performs his miracles. But Freud, judged as a
writer, was a far stranger phenomenon than any of the contemporary authors he praised and admired. He was in a class
of his own. He crafted case studies that read like short stories
and some of his books can be appreciated as ground-breaking
literary experiments. His greatest works are uncannily
ambiguous.

Freud's forays into the shadowlands of German Romantic
philosophy, like his preoccupation with archaeology and the
ancient world, can feel backward-looking. Yet, his treatment
of subjects that even his disciples considered 'regressive' – the
paranormal, demons, ghosts – have been a source of inspiration for generations of modern artists. Perhaps the most
compelling and unexpected example of Freud's backward-
looking psychology finding vanguard relevance is in the
field of robotics. The Japanese roboticist Hiroshi Ishiguro is
renowned for building 'Geminoids' – highly sophisticated
life-like robots capable of facial expression. Ishiguro has
made 'doppelgangers' of himself and his daughter. The most
common emotional reaction reported by humans when they
encounter a Geminoid is fear. This is probably because of their
uncertain status. As robots look increasingly human, they
elicit positive feelings; however, at a certain point, 'rapport'
is replaced by unease, suspicion and anxiety. Positive feelings
return if progressive refinements make robots look even
more human. When this pattern of relationships is plotted
on a graph, the sudden loss and recovery of positive feelings
describes the shape of a valley. Roboticists term this 'dip' the
'uncanny valley'. The familiar has suddenly become unfamiliar, and the observer cannot determine whether what they are
looking at is dead or alive.

Freud's interest in strange phenomena has provided much ammunition for his critics. They assert that he should be consigned to history along with a supporting cast of outmoded Romantics with occult sympathies. His fascination with telepathy, doppelgangers and omens – so they say – reflects very badly on him as a scientist. But Freud's interest in the strange was no less 'scientific' than his interest in infantile sexuality, bowel movements or slips of the tongue. Any feature of the human condition that his peers overlooked or dismissed was, as far as Freud was concerned, an ideal subject for psychoanalytic study. Joke telling is ostensibly trivial. However, it is a universal human activity, so why not study it? Strange experiences are also universal, so why not study them too? Obviously, ghosts are not dead people. But they *do* exist. They have been 'observed' throughout history on every populated continent. They merit an explanation beyond bland statements about 'chemical imbalances' in the brain. What do ghosts mean? What are the psychological mechanisms associated with ghostly visitations? Why do ghosts frighten us? These were the sort of questions that Freud was interested in answering. He might not have provided definitive answers, but he did provide thought-provoking answers that have stimulated debate and inspired artists in every creative sphere. He should be commended for venturing into uncharted territory, not ridiculed.

The argument that Freud's interest in the uncanny undermines his scientific credibility has become less convincing over time. Physics has advanced to the point where it is constantly generating uncanny hypotheses. Consider 'Boltzmann Brains'. Given eternity, it is possible that long after the extinction of the stars, a spontaneous reduction of entropy might produce configurations of particles structurally identical to a human brain. The number of these configurations will increase with the protraction of time, to the extent that the population of disembodied brains at the 'end of the universe' will eventually outnumber the sum of historical human brains. One of these configurations might be an exact copy of your brain, which allows the possibility that – right now – you are not a physical being reading a book, but a collection of particles suspended in a void – an entirely 'hallucinated' entity composed of false memories. Physicists do not regard Boltzmann Brains as ludicrous or outlandish. According to Brian Greene, the director of Columbia University's Center for Theoretical Physics, 'What makes this more than the beginnings of a B-grade sci-fi plot is that as we look to the far future, the conditions appear ripe for these bizarre-sounding processes to actually happen.'

Contemporary physicists challenge our complacency with strange phenomena: cats that are neither dead nor alive, 'spooky action at a distance', particles that can bilocate like a Catholic saint. In a sense, the awe and wonder that we feel when we encounter 'mind-blowing' physics is identical to the awe and wonder excited by German Romantic philosophy. We stand with Caspar David Friedrich's Wanderer on his rocky promontory above a sea of fog and marvel. The world is an uncanny place. Our home, when scrutinised, can easily become unhomely.

The insights that Freud gained by looking backwards find increasing and paradoxical relevance in a society with fast-forward momentum. Technological advances have accelerated the rate at which the denizens of western liberal democracies have had to adjust to change. The familiar is constantly becoming unfamiliar; thus, the modern human lives in an environment that is, to a greater or lesser extent, perpetually uncanny.

The Uncanny is not the 'dying fall' of German Romantic philosophy. And Freud was not the last Romantic. The more we scrutinise his Romanticism, the more likely it is that its familiarity – its Gothic tropes and Hoffmannesque charm – will start to appear unfamiliar. What we are looking at, in fact, is modern thinking about modern minds in a modern age. As always with Freud, you must watch his hands very carefully. He is perfectly capable of turning base metal into gold while you are still denouncing him as a fraud.

Chapter 19

The Case of Gustav M

At 8.30 a.m. on Monday 9 December 1907 around two hundred well-wishers assembled on the platform of a train station in Vienna to bid farewell to Gustav Mahler and his wife, Alma. The morning air was cold, the sky overcast. Among those gathered were many individuals connected with the musical life of the city. The composers Arnold Schoenberg, Alexander Zemlinsky and Alban Berg; Alfred Roller, the stage designer at the opera house. Gustav Klimt had also come to say goodbye. He was a close friend of the Mahlers. Although, 'friend' doesn't quite capture the nature of his relationship with Alma. When Alma was nineteen, he had attempted to seduce her. He was the first man she had ever kissed and she recorded the event in her diary: 'It's indescribable: to be kissed for the first time in my life, and that by the only person in the whole world that I love.' A few years later she kissed Zemlinsky: 'I took his head in my hands, and we kissed each other on the mouth, so hard that our teeth ached . . . ' Alban Berg – who Alma hadn't kissed – presented his fiancée, Helene, to Mahler. Mahler dropped one of his gloves, and when Helene picked it up for him, the softening of his expression affected her deeply. The well-wishers, many of them tearful, had brought so many flowers it was possible to decorate Gustav and Alma's train compartment from floor to ceiling.

Mahler was ready to leave Vienna. He had been tested by its antisemitism, its hostile journalists, its vainglorious divas and recalcitrant orchestral players. The city had exhausted him, and he expected life to be a great deal easier in New York.

A whistle sounded; wheels turned. Inside the train compartment, there were no backwards glances. On the platform, however, the crowd stared at the receding carriages until they rattled out of view. Klimt succinctly summarised the significance of the occasion with a leaden, valedictory judgement: 'It's over.' Mahler's departure seemed to presage the end of everything that turn-of-the-century Vienna had come to represent – profligate invention, limitless creativity, visionary brilliance. Of course, Klimt was quite mistaken. He was still in his 'golden period'. Schoenberg was about to completely revolutionise music by liberating discord. Egon Schiele was yet to have his first exhibition. Schnitzler's *Dream Story* wouldn't be published until 1926. Freud's last great work, *Civilization and Its Discontents*, wouldn't be published until 1930. Vienna would continue to animate western culture for decades. Nevertheless, when the train carrying Gustav and Alma Mahler disappeared, it seemed to Klimt and those around him that they had just witnessed the soul leaving the body.

From 1897, Mahler had been the director of Vienna's opera house. This was the most exalted musical post in the Habsburg Empire. He was ultimately answerable to the Emperor, although his dealings with the palace were mediated by a steely, grudge-bearing aristocrat. Mahler was recognised by almost everyone. Breathless housemaids would exclaim, 'Mahler is here!' People in coffee houses would leave their tables and crowd around windows just to get a better look at him. And when he married

Heritage Images/Getty Images

Alma Schindler, the most beautiful woman in Vienna, public curiosity made him even more famous.

Alma's legendary 'beauty' is largely euphemistic. Photographs of the young Alma show an attractive woman with thick hair and arresting eyes; however, she is not preternaturally beautiful. What her many admirers meant when they referred to her beauty was her sexual allure. We know from her diaries that sex was frequently on her mind: 'Why am I so boundlessly licentious? I *long* for *rape*! – Whoever it might be.' The secret of Alma's teenage sex appeal might have been, at least to some extent, rather mundane. She was a little deaf and consequently stood very close to men during conversations. Proximity may have been misinterpreted as a sexual provocation.

For much of the twentieth century, Klimt's 'It's over' seemed unmerited and melodramatic. Mahler's bright star dimmed after his death in 1911. He was never – as myth makers have claimed – totally neglected, but for at least fifty years he was a rather peripheral figure in the classical music world. Today his music is immensely popular, and his symphonies are universally acknowledged as masterpieces. Identifying the reasons for Mahler's extraordinary return to the musical mainstream has become a scholarly parlour game. Was it because Leonard Bernstein championed Mahler's music in the 1960s and 1970s? Was it because the slow movement of the 5th Symphony was used by Luchino Visconti in his 1971 film *Death in Venice*? Or was it because of Ken Russell's *Mahler*, a controversial biographical film released in 1974? Factors such as these probably played some part, but the simplest explanation for Mahler's delayed success is that it took half a century for audiences to catch up with him.

Bernstein underscored this point in an impassioned appreciation: 'It is only after fifty, sixty, seventy years of world holocausts ... the smoking ovens of Auschwitz, the frantically bombed jungles of Vietnam ... only after all this can we finally listen to Mahler's music and understand that it foretold all. And that in the foretelling it showered a rain of beauty on this world that has not been equalled since.' Mahler, like Freud, was a prophet. He saw the consequences of equipping the id with advanced military technology. And he saw what must inevitably follow: the suffering, loss, pity and sorrow. By the time audiences were receptive to Mahler's warnings, the worst had already happened.

Mahler did not stay in America. He commuted between continents and spent the next three summers composing at a villa in the Austrian Tyrol, just outside Toblach. In June 1910, Alma was admitted into a sanatorium in Tobelbad (near Graz). She was suffering from depression. The summer before Gustav and Alma had left Vienna for New York, their eldest daughter had died from scarlet fever. The couple never really recovered from the trauma. 'She lay choking,' Alma later recalled, 'with her large eyes wide open.' When the end came, Mahler's grief was so terrible it threatened his sanity. 'It was more than he could bear.' Arthur Schnitzler – a doctor as well as a writer – wondered whether Mahler had lost the will to live. Mahler accompanied Alma to the sanatorium, and then went to Vienna to organise rehearsals for his 8th Symphony – which was to receive its premiere in Munich in September.

Immediately after arriving at the sanatorium Alma met Walter Gropius, a promising architect and the future founder of the Bauhaus school. Alma was thirty, Gropius was twenty-seven. They talked, danced, went for moonlit walks, and became lovers. For about a month they saw each other every day and their lovemaking was, apparently, spectacular. There is some evidence to suggest that Alma believed her depression was partly due to sexual frustration. Mahler, almost twenty years older than Alma, had been suffering from decreased libido and very probably impotence. He had told her to stop demanding 'symphonies' when he was sometimes capable of only 'suites'. Given Alma's beliefs about sex and mental health, it was perhaps inevitable that she would seize the opportunity to supplement her sanatorium diet of lettuce and buttermilk with an alternative therapy of her own devising.

Alma, much refreshed by her 'treatment', resumed her life with Mahler in Toblach. While Mahler was working on his 10th Symphony, Alma maintained an intimate correspondence with Gropius. She had instructed him to send letters by general delivery, which meant that she could arrange secret collections – and Mahler would have no reason to suspect that she had a lover. However, Gropius, if he can be believed, made a quite astonishing Freudian slip. He wrote a letter to Alma and 'accidentally' addressed it to Mahler at their Toblach villa.

Mahler was sitting at the piano opening his mail when he

asked Alma: 'What's this?' We know that Gropius's letter –
which no longer exists – contained explicit sexual references.
Mercifully, Mahler never reached those passages: he handed the
letter to his wife before he had finished reading it. The letter had
been placed on the piano by Alma herself. Why she had failed to
recognise the Tobelbad postmark or Gropius's handwriting is a
mystery, although her oversight can be understood as another
Freudian slip. Perhaps, deep down, she *wanted* to hurt Mahler.
Her response to being found out certainly suggests this: 'Now –
at last – I was able to tell him all.'

Alma had accumulated many grievances. She accused her
husband of being self-obsessed. She felt unloved, 'overlooked'.
He had unreasonably insisted that she make enormous personal
sacrifices. Prior to their marriage, Mahler had asked Alma to
give up composing and to surrender herself 'unconditionally' to
his every need. In fact, Alma had never stopped composing and
Mahler was an unusually devoted husband. His letters are consistently tender and affectionate: 'I kiss you a thousand times,
my dearest, and take good care of yourself, so I can hold you
in my arms very soon.' Instead of refuting Alma's accusations,
Mahler accepted that he had been a negligent husband and he
tried to make amends. He was terrified of losing her. He kissed
her slippers and left the door open at night so that he could hear
her breathing. He wrote her notes and love poems. Alma would
wake in darkness to find him standing by her bedside, staring at
her. In his composer's shack she would discover him not composing, but lying on the ground, weeping. Mahler addressed her
like a goddess – 'wondrous being' – or with infantile diminu-
tives: 'Almschilitzilitzilitzi!'

Gropius had been told by Alma to stay away from Toblach;
however, as she was riding through the village one day, she saw
the young architect standing under a bridge. Alma informed
Mahler, who – bizarrely – went to get him. Night had fallen

and Mahler ventured out with a lamp. When he found Gropius, he issued a laconic invitation: 'Come.' Gropius followed at a respectful distance. Alma talked with Gropius only briefly. After which, Mahler escorted Gropius to the edge of the property, where it seems they shook hands before parting.

Mahler's mental health was not good. Richard Nepallek, a medically qualified cousin of Alma, arranged for Mahler to consult Sigmund Freud – although the initial impetus for the referral probably came from Mahler's protégé Bruno Walter (Walter had consulted Freud in 1906 because of arm cramps that might have had a psychological cause). Mahler cancelled the first two appointments but accepted a third – which turned out to be most irregular. Freud never saw patients when he was on holiday, but he made an exception for Mahler. The Freud family were staying at a seaside resort in Holland, and he suggested to Mahler that they meet in Leiden (an hour's journey from the coast by steam trolley). On 26 August 1910, Gustav Mahler and Sigmund Freud – the two most emblematic figures of turn-of-the-century Vienna – met at the Golden Turk Café. They then embarked on a four-hour walk, during which Mahler told Freud about his life and problems.

Ostensibly they were an ill-suited pair. Mahler was sceptical about psychoanalysis and music was his universe. Conversely, Freud's universe was psychoanalysis and he was, by his own admission, musically ignorant. But Mahler, like all Viennese intellectuals, was fascinated by the mind. Sleep states and symbolism are recurring ideas in his compositions. Moreover, the prevailing view of Freud as a man who actively disliked music is quite wrong. Freud never attended concerts, but he did go to the opera. Indeed, he had favourite operas – *Don Giovanni* and *The Magic Flute* – and occasionally he would break into song, although his Mozart arias were invariably painful and tuneless. Caricaturing Mahler and Freud as an odd couple is misleading.

They had an enormous amount in common. In fact, they were very nearly psychological twins.

Freud and Mahler were born in the same geographical area (now in the Czech Republic). They adored their mothers and felt ambivalent about their fathers. Both experienced the death of a sibling or siblings when very young, and both viewed themselves as outsiders. Mahler said: 'I am three times without a Heimat, as a Bohemian in Austria, an Austrian among Germans and a Jew throughout the world – always an intruder, never welcomed.' Freud said: 'My language is German. My culture, my attainments are German. I considered myself German

intellectually, until I noticed the growth of antisemitic prejudice in Germany and German Austria. Since that time, I prefer to call myself a Jew.' Both men were voracious readers and they loved walking in natural settings. When in Vienna, they followed rigid routines. Mahler attended morning rehearsals, walked home for lunch, had a quick sleep, went for a stroll, dealt with paperwork, and finally conducted an evening performance at the opera house. Both men had distinctly neurotic tendencies, experienced episodes of impotence, suffered from various psychosomatic symptoms, and feared that their deaths were presaged by numerical omens. Mahler postponed writing his 9th Symphony because few great symphonists ever survived long enough to write a tenth. He once had a dream in which Death, disguised as an elegant, urbane party guest, seized his arm and said: 'You must come with me.'

Mahler's music and Freud's psychoanalysis merit comparison at many levels. They both offer 'world views'. Mahler famously told Jean Sibelius: 'the symphony is like the world, it must encompass everything'. Freud, too, created a psychology of everything, a massive theoretical architecture that can 'explain' the totality of human behaviour. Love and death are the cornerstones of Mahler's music, in much the same way as the life instinct and the death instinct are fundamental to Freud's work. Mahler's love music is transcendent. He wrote 'love songs' not only to his wife, but also to the entire cosmos. However, for Mahler, love is always overshadowed by death. It is ever-present, from the *Funeral March and Polka* he wrote at the age of five to the last movement of his final symphony. The urbane party guest was always looking over his shoulder as he composed, even when he was a child. Freud and Mahler were broad-canvas thinkers, but neither of them dismissed the minutiae of existence. They were willing to acknowledge the 'small' things that others might overlook. Humour, for example. They were both ironists, acutely aware that human beings often say one thing but mean another. A single event – musical or psychological – can have several meanings. Mahler and Freud share the distinctly modern attribute of being comfortable with ambiguity. Swift oscillations between happiness and sadness – the homely and the unhomely. Mahler once said, 'What is best in music is not to be found in the notes.' This cryptic pronouncement is consistent with the psychoanalytic principle that what people say isn't as important as what people don't say. It is possible to prolong this comparative exercise – enumerating biographical and abstract similarities – almost indefinitely. Freud avoided meeting Schnitzler because he didn't want to encounter his doppelganger. He should have been avoiding Mahler.

Freud and Mahler met in the Golden Turk at 4.30. They were about the same age – Freud presenting a stouter figure than his wiry companion – and they walked and talked until sunset. The details of their route are unrecorded, so all we can do is imagine them strolling down cobbled streets, stopping on a bridge to admire a canal, Freud taking the opportunity to light a cigar. However, we do know what they talked about – albeit from fragmented and sketchy sources. Mahler is referred to twice in the 1911 minutes of the Vienna Psychoanalytic Society, Freud discussed Mahler with his disciple Marie Bonaparte in 1925, and he also wrote an informative paragraph about Mahler in a 1935 letter to his student Theodor Reik. Alma is a less trusted source, largely because she casts Freud as her champion. We are expected to believe that Freud scolded Mahler: 'How dare a man in your state ask a young woman to be tied to him?' It seems unlikely that Freud would have concluded, so decisively, that Alma was the wronged party, and then elected to express his outrage using this kind of language.

What did Freud discover?

Freud believed that Mahler's attraction to Alma was

fundamentally Oedipal, and he shocked the composer by guessing his mother's name: 'Your mother's name was Marie?' Mahler
was dumbstruck: 'But how do you know?' Freud then wondered
aloud how it was that Mahler hadn't married a woman called
Marie. Mahler was even more astonished. In fact he *had* married a woman called Marie: Alma-Marie Schindler. According
to Alma, Mahler had wanted to address her as Marie at the
beginning of their relationship, even though he had difficulty
pronouncing the letter 'r'. The name Marie was also unconsciously associated with a Marian ideal that Freud later termed
Mahler's 'Holy Mary complex'. Energies generated by the complex fuelled Mahler's worship of Alma. Freud then suggested
that if Mahler was attracted to Alma because of a mother fixation, it was also likely that Alma was attracted to Mahler because
of a father fixation. Alma's father was a painter – *ein Maler* in
German. She had chosen to marry a man whose surname was
also the word for her father's profession. Gropius was a young
competitor. But Mahler shouldn't be threatened by Gropius's
youth. In fact, Mahler's age was an advantage. Alma agreed
with this interpretation. In *Gustav Mahler: Memories and Letters*,
she affirmed that she had always looked for 'a small, slight man'
who had 'wisdom and spiritual superiority', as these were the
characteristics she had 'known and loved' in her father. Gustav
and Alma had complementary complexes that neatly slotted
together. Consequently, Freud supposed that the unconscious
bond between Gustav and Alma must be very strong. This was
immensely reassuring, and Mahler was greatly relieved. On the
train home, he wrote a poem for Alma which contains the following cheerful couplet: 'The nightmare's dispelled by force of
persuasion, / Dispersed are the torments of self-contemplation'.

Freud's 'walking cure' was clearly helpful, insofar as Mahler
felt happier and much calmer after their conversation. But
Freud's analysis – if it deserves to be distinguished with the

term – was meretricious. Do all men with mother complexes marry women with their mothers' names? Was Alma's attraction to a man whose name also meant her father's profession really any security against marital breakdown? Freud recognised that he wasn't going to excavate Mahler's unconscious in four hours. What progress he made he later likened to digging a 'single shaft through a mysterious building'. But really, his shaft was neither deep nor illuminating. Mahler's immediate improvement owed much more to Freud's stagecraft than his perspicacity. Guessing the name of Mahler's mother was shamanistic, a 'trick' to enhance his authority. He dispelled a 'nightmare' with the 'force of persuasion'. Meanwhile, Alma was still writing to Gropius, eagerly anticipating more sexual adventures: 'There is not one spot on your body that I would not like to caress with my tongue.'

Mahler must have realised that his situation was essentially unchanged. He did his best to propitiate Alma. He praised her songs and used his influence to get them published. He dedicated his 8th Symphony to her. He tried to amuse her (perhaps unwisely) with light verse: 'My love sits beside me – it fills me with pride, / To be riding to town with my wife at my side!' On 4 September, Mahler wrote to Alma from the Grand Hotel Continental in Munich: 'Freud is quite right: this utter dependence on you has always been latent in me, you have always been my light and the centre of my universe.' His naive, romantic optimism is pitiful. 'But just as love always engenders love, fidelity always wins through to fidelity, and as long as Eros remains the master of men and gods, I too shall succeed in winning back what was once mine, in regaining the heart that once beat for me and can indeed be united only with mine on its journey towards God and serenity.'

Laying bare his soul had no effect on Alma. She arranged secret assignations with Gropius in Vienna and Munich, and when Mahler conducted the premiere of his 8th Symphony, Gropius was sitting in the audience. Eight months later, Mahler was dead. He died on Walter Gropius's birthday.

Alma claimed that the death of her husband precipitated 'a long period of mental and spiritual agony'. It is difficult to ascertain what she was feeling. She continued to correspond with Gropius, but had several affairs with other men, starting with Joseph Fraenkel, Mahler's doctor. She then moved on to Franz Schreker, a composer, the biologist Paul Kammerer and the artist Oskar Kokoschka. Finally, she married Walter Gropius in 1915. Within a few years she was embroiled in another affair with the poet and novelist Franz Werfel, her junior by eleven years. After divorcing Gropius, Werfel became her third outstandingly gifted husband. Kokoschka had to make do with a life-size replica of Alma that he ordered from a renowned Munich doll-maker (after providing very detailed specifications). The result was a nightmarish 'surrogate woman', with massive thighs, shagpile 'skin' and prominent breasts. The Alma doll served as Kokoschka's muse until, dissatisfied, he beheaded it and doused it with wine – presumably to create the effect of a bloody murder scene.

Alma and Franz Werfel fled from the Nazis and arrived in America in 1940. There they became part of a distinguished émigré community living in Beverly Hills. In her seventies – a widow once again – Alma moved into an apartment in New York on East 73rd Street. By this time she had become a rather thick-set woman. Even so, she remained acutely aware of appearances. Photographs taken in the early sixties show a blonde matron, dressed in black, draped with pearls, still sufficiently motivated to apply lipstick and pluck her eyebrows. She died in 1964, aged eighty-six.

Like Dora and the Wolfman, Alma's longevity bridged completely different worlds. Mahler had told her about discussing the future of music with Brahms, yet she almost outlived Beatlemania. When the popular satirist Tom Lehrer discovered her obituary, he composed a comic song – 'Alma' – that brought her to the attention of hip, young, educated audiences. 'Alma, tell us! All modern women are jealous, / You should have a statue in bronze, / For bagging Gustav and Walter and Franz.' Alma is as much a modernist as her 'modernist' lovers and husbands. Her audacious behaviour is like the work of a conceptual artist: a lived exploration of new ways of being a woman. She is the antithesis of all the sexually frustrated women seen by Charcot, Breuer and Freud: women who, in the absence of any viable alternative, were forced to rail against sexual double standards and sexual inequality by becoming 'hysterics'. She is without doubt a morally ambiguous character, but she does deserve a measure of sympathetic understanding.

Mahler and Freud's meeting in Leiden has transcended reality. It is surrounded by a mythic aura: two prophets in conversation before the fall. In retrospect, Klimt's words – 'It's over' – have acquired deeper layers of meaning. Mahler had abandoned the imperial capital. His relationship with Alma was doomed, but so too was the Habsburg Empire. Mahler and Freud's meeting fascinates. It has been dramatised in a play by Ronald Harwood – *Mahler's Conversion* – and a film directed by Percy Adlon, *Mahler on the Couch*. Musicologists and psychoanalysts still pore over the scant documentation. Yet, despite its fascination, narrative charm, symbolism and valedictory resonances, this unique and now legendary meeting of great minds was curiously inconsequential. Mahler was given a false sense of security based on some relatively superficial observations, and Freud – a man ordinarily excited by genius – never went on to speculate about the psychodynamics of Mahler's creativity, even after the composer's death had mitigated concerns about patient confidentiality. This is rather odd, because during their conversation it became apparent that one of Mahler's most distinctive musical traits (the proximity of emotional depth and cliché) could be linked to a traumatic childhood memory. Freud could have written about this, and much more no doubt, but he chose not to. Nevertheless, it is possible, perhaps, that the Leiden meeting left a shallow but detectable impression in Freud's oeuvre.

In 1912, Freud published *On the Universal Tendency to Debasement in the Sphere of Love*, his principal contribution to the study of impotence. He suggested that impotence arises when men fail to overcome mother or sister fixations. In addition to being very fond of his mother, Mahler was extraordinarily close to his sister, Justine. They lived together for many years, and although there is no reason to suspect that their relationship was ever incestuous, she performed many 'wifely' duties for him. Freud described the core problem of men with impotence in the following way: 'Where they love they do not desire and where they desire they cannot love.' Was Freud thinking about Mahler's 'Holy Mary complex' when he wrote these words? Alma's slippers could be kissed like religious relics, but her elevation, to the level of a 'wondrous being', raised her to an Empyrean beyond the senses. In Mahler's mind, love – pure, sublime love – and animalistic passion were perhaps incompatible. They could not be combined.

In the early 1930s, the writer Elias Canetti visited Alma Werfel. In a display case he saw the unfinished score of Mahler's 10th Symphony, opened to show the page on which a despairing Mahler had written 'To live for you! To die for you! Almschi!' Alma was standing close by. Canetti recalled: 'From all who looked at this showpiece she expected the look of admiration due to her for this dying man's homage, and she was so sure of the effect of his writing in the score that the vapid smile on her face expanded into a grin.'

Canetti was horrified.

Chapter 20

Thanatos

In the weeks before Christmas 1909, a young man who had come to Vienna desperate to study art had descended into destitution. He was hungry, dirty, his feet were sore, and his threadbare blue check suit was crawling with lice. At a doss house he shared a dormitory with tramps and alcoholics. During the day he frequented public warming rooms and queued at a convent for charitable bowls of soup. He tried to earn money shovelling snow, but he didn't own a coat and the cold was intolerable. He loitered in a train station offering to carry baggage, but his bedraggled appearance put off potential customers.

Many years later, Adolf Hitler returned to Vienna. He was chauffeured through the city in a cavalcade of limousines, and he received a rapturous welcome. In *Last Waltz in Vienna*, published some forty years after the event, George Clare recollected levels of excitement comparable to 'erotic' delirium: 'The whole city behaved like an aroused woman, vibrating, writhing, moaning and sighing lustfully for orgasm and release. This is not purple writing. It is an exact description of what Vienna was and felt like on Monday 14 March 1938, as Hitler entered her.'

Church bells rang out and adoring crowds lined the streets and cheered. When Hitler arrived at the Imperial Hotel, a massive banner, emblazoned with a swastika, had been unfurled down the façade. He was escorted to the royal suite. The mob outside were shouting, 'We want to see our Führer! We want to see our Führer!' Repeatedly, Hitler had to satisfy them by standing on the balcony.

Not far away, Sigmund Freud was sitting in Berggasse 19, considering the implications of Hitler's triumph. As far as the Nazis were concerned, Freud was the Jewish founder of a Jewish science. His system of thought was degrading and dishonourable and psychoanalysis was a practice that could not be tolerated. Freud had been slow to acknowledge the perilous nature of his situation. When his books were burned in 1933, along with works written by Einstein, Thomas Mann, Erich Maria Remarque and Stefan Zweig, he joked: 'At least I burn in the best of company.' For a long time he didn't think Hitler's ascendancy posed a direct, personal threat; however, after Hitler's unopposed invasion of Austria, it soon became clear to Freud and the rest of his family that they were *all* in great danger.

On 15 March, the day after Hitler's arrival at the Imperial, he addressed a quarter of a million Viennese supporters in the Hero's Square. On the same day, a gang of armed thugs forced their way into Freud's independent publishing business. This relatively small concern had been established with support from benefactors to promote psychoanalysis. Martin Freud was in the office when the gang arrived. He had gone there to destroy documents that the Nazis might use to incriminate his father. After the Nazi invasion, many legal activities suddenly became illegal – investing in foreign currencies, for example. The gang were not party ideologues but 'shabbily dressed' antisemites, emboldened by the Nazi invasion. They threatened to shoot Martin and stole some money.

Shortly after, another band of 'Nazis' – some, perhaps, from the same gang that had forced their way into the publishing business – arrived at Berggasse 19. Freud's wife Martha opened the door, politely asked them to leave their rifles in the umbrella stand and invited them to sit down. They started to ransack the apartment. Martha collected all the cash she could find, placed it on the dining room table and said: 'Won't the gentlemen help themselves?' Freud's daughter, Anna, realising that the gang were not going to be pleased so easily, escorted them to the safe, which contained 6,000 Austrian schillings. The gang were acting without jurisdiction, and they belatedly paused to discuss how to avoid getting into trouble with the authorities. At this juncture, Freud appeared. 'He had a way of frowning,' wrote Ernest Jones, 'with blazing eyes that any Old Testament prophet might have envied, and the effect produced by his lowering mien completed the visitors' discomfiture. Saying they would call another day, they hastily took their departure.'

'Well,' Freud asked, 'how much have they taken?'

Martha told him.

'Hmm,' Freud responded. 'I never got so much for a single house call.'

Ernest Jones was present during both incidents, at the publishing house and Berggasse 19. He had travelled to Vienna to persuade Freud to leave. A few days after Jones arrived, Princess Marie Bonaparte appeared. She too had come to offer Freud help and support. She also assumed the role of a rather glamorous guard dog. Draped in a black mink coat and giving off a heady perfume, she sat on the stairs outside Freud's apartment, ready to browbeat brownshirts with her crocodile-skin handbag.

One week later, the Gestapo arrived. They searched Berggasse 19, and when they left, they took Anna Freud with them. She was oddly composed for a woman being abducted by four heavily armed members of the SS. Anna was taken to

Gestapo headquarters, the Hotel Metropole on Morzinplatz, and deposited in a corridor where she was at risk of being assigned for deportation – and shot. Fortunately, some friends used their influence, and she was transferred to a room where she sat and awaited interrogation. Anna was carrying a lethal dose of Veronal that she could swallow if it looked like she was going to be tortured. Both Anna and Martin had asked Freud's physician, Max Schur, to supply them with the drug; however, Freud was never informed of their request or Schur's acquiescence. Anna was asked questions about psychoanalysis and her father's 'activities'. The Gestapo seemed to think that the Freud family were political subversives, perhaps even terrorists. Back at Berggasse 19, Freud paced, smoked and said nothing. At seven o'clock in the evening, after hours of agonising uncertainty, the door opened, and Anna entered. This was the second and final time in Freud's life that he was ever seen crying. Anna had been released after she had persuaded the Gestapo that the aims of the Psychoanalytic Society were non-political and purely scientific. But her success was merely a stay of execution. If they didn't get out of Vienna soon, they would all be dead.

Shortly after Hitler's invasion of Austria, one of Freud's disciples, Theodor Reik, visited his master for the last time. Reik found Freud much changed. He was withered – skin and bones – yet his eyes were still 'lively and kindly'. They talked about the future of psychoanalysis, and of course the cruelty of the Nazi regime. Freud wasn't surprised by Nazi brutality, but he struggled to comprehend how the majority of Germans – an intelligent people with a great cultural tradition – had been seduced by a pernicious ideology. Freud smiled and said: 'Look how poverty-stricken the poet's imagination really is. Shakespeare, in The Mid-summer Night's Dream, has a woman fall in love with a donkey. The audience wonders at that. And now, think of it, that a nation of sixty-five millions have . . . ' He was lost for words – it was all too much – and he could only complete his sentence with a wave of his hand.

Hitler adored Germanic myth: the twilight of the gods, funeral pyres, Valhalla burning, the glorious conflagration of Wagnerian tragedy. Devotion to Hitler's ideals among the SS brotherhood was rewarded with a death's head ring. National Socialism was a kind of death cult, and in the end – as is often the case with death cults – the Messianic leader killed himself. The Nazis epitomised destructive and ultimately self-destructive impulses. This 'attitude' was not alien to the Viennese. They were key participants in the broad, 'German' engagement with morbid Romanticism. The Viennese wrote about death (Hugo von Hofmannsthal's

Bridgeman Images

Thor and Death), sang songs about death (Mahler's *Songs on the Death of Children*) and painted death (Klimt's *Death and Life*). The black heart of Vienna was, and still is, the crypt of the Capuchin church where the Habsburg dead have decomposed in elaborate bronze sarcophagi since the seventeenth century.

As previously discussed, the Viennese were fond of games of love and death. Matters of honour were settled by duel-ling and heartbroken lovers often sought solace in oblivion. Today, ending one's life because of a romantic disappointment seems disproportionate, but the Viennese were minded to kill themselves in response to even the mildest provocations. The dramatist Ferdinand Raimund set an early precedent when he shot himself after being bitten by a dog. Eduard van der Nüll, who with August Sicard von Sicardsburg designed Vienna's glorious opera house, hanged himself when he learned that the Emperor thought the building looked rather low. One success-ful novelist chose to end his life at least partly because he was horrified by the direction and style of new writing.

Several individuals in Freud's social ambit committed suicide. The neurologist Nathan Weiss hanged himself in a public bath in 1883, creating a vacant position for Freud to fill at the medical faculty. In 1919, the brilliant psychoanalyst Viktor Tausk wrote a farewell note to Freud before he simultaneously hanged and shot himself. The psychoanalyst Herbert Silberer – a friend of Wilhelm Stekel – hanged himself in 1923. Stekel would kill him-self in 1940. Freud's niece, Martha Gertrud, who later became known as an author and illustrator of children's books, killed herself in 1930 by taking an overdose of sleeping pills. Margaret Wittgenstein, who consulted Freud, came from a family whose members were particularly prone to suicide. She had five brothers (the most famous being the philosopher Ludwig): two killed themselves and a third was a very probable suicide. Kurt Wittgenstein shot himself at the end of the First World

War when soldiers under his command refused to obey his orders. Rudolf Wittgenstein strolled into a Berlin bar, ordered some drinks, asked the pianist to play his favourite song, and then ingested a lethal quantity of cyanide. Hans Wittgenstein, a musical prodigy, disappeared from a boat in Chesapeake Bay. Presumably he drowned. In his autobiography, Freud's patient Sergei Pankejeff described a 'wave' of Jewish suicides after the Nazi occupation of Vienna. The intellectual and polymath Egon Friedell jumped out of his apartment window while storm troopers were being delayed by his housekeeper.

Freud, being Viennese, had been thinking about death long before the Nazis arrived. In *The Interpretation of Dreams*, he recollected being introduced by his mother – at the age of six – to the Biblical axiom that all are dust and to dust must return. Young Sigmund wasn't convinced. His mother rubbed her hands together and produced 'dusky' flakes of skin, thus furnishing her sceptical son with evidence of the 'dust of which we are made'. This vivid demonstration left Freud with a diffuse feeling of discomfort that he was later able to connect with an expression: 'You owe nature a death'. For Freud, death wasn't merely mechanical dissolution, a neutral unravelling. It was a latent potential, something we carry around within us, a debt that must be paid. In effect, something that motivates.

Death surfaces frequently in Freud's writings. Bodies and funeral rites appear in the dreams he described, and patricide is the goal of Oedipal rage. Freud approaches death from several perspectives – anthropological, religious and psychological; however, it was only towards the end of his life that his wide-ranging and disjointed thoughts about death became more cohesive and his various considerations of melancholy, suicide, self-destructive behaviour, compulsive repetition and war coalesced and informed his last major modification of psycho-analytic theory: the death instinct.

The minutes of the Vienna Psychoanalytic Society in 1911 record Freud's contributions to a group discussion in which he suggested that extinction can be hastened by a psychical influence. This discussion took place shortly after Gustav Mahler's death, and Freud believed that the composer's demise was partly attributable to an unconscious death wish.

In 1915, when war was raging, Freud published an extended essay titled *Timely Reflections on War and Death*. He repeats his already familiar assertion that primitive, destructive urges are a fundamental feature of human nature. The global calamity of the First World War might have looked (to his contemporaries) like an anomalous, regressive slide into chaos, but Freud supposed that this was an illusion. Humanity routinely overestimates its sophistication. According to Freud, the uncivilised, brutal behaviour unleashed by war showed that human beings 'have not fallen as far as we feared, because they had not risen nearly so far as we imagined'. War is inevitable. It is human nature to prosecute wars. Freud's summation is chilling: 'If you want to endure life, prepare yourself for death.' As a species, we are illogical, and the destructiveness of human beings frequently escalates to the point at which mutual self-destruction is assured.

Around this time, Freud was also thinking about destructiveness at the level of the individual. In *Mourning and Melancholia*, written in 1915 and published in 1917, Freud links melancholy (or what we would now call depression) with aggression – but aggression turned inwards. Self-criticism, for example, can be construed as a form of violence against the self. The precise mechanisms underlying 'melancholia' that Freud describes (implicating grief, anger and identification with lost objects) are somewhat convoluted, but the general principle that he espouses explains why severe depression frequently results in suicidal behaviour. Deeper levels of depression are associated with greater amounts of aggression that can potentially 'rebound' and annihilate the person.

After reflecting on death wishes, illogical violence and self-destruction for many years, Freud finally introduced the idea of the death instinct, a construct that others would later dub Thanatos (after the Greek god of death). A preliminary account of the death instinct appears in *Beyond the Pleasure Principle*, a major theoretical work that he completed in 1920. Freud had never been entirely satisfied with his single drive theory of human behaviour. Eros – the sex drive – was well established as the 'life force' of psychoanalysis; however, Freud's clinical observations and theoretical formulations emphasise compromise and conflict. It seemed to Freud that at its most basic level, psychoanalytic theory lacked an opposite force with which Eros could clash and contend. Moreover, it was self-evident after the war that human beings are not motivated by the pleasure principle alone. He had previously suggested that deviations from the pursuit of pleasure could be explained by the moderating effects of the reality principle. Thus, a form of discomfort (for example, hunger) might be self-inflicted because it is a *realistic* way of achieving the satisfying aim of an ideal weight (and physical attractiveness). Freud wanted to get beyond the pleasure principle, to explain *all* behaviour (even perversely self-destructive behaviour) with reference to an ultimate, perhaps even quasi-mystical duality.

Curiously, Freud began his theoretical revision by discussing the clinical phenomenon of the compulsion to repeat. Patients frequently feel compelled to reproduce patterns of behaviour, many of them self-defeating. Identical arguments recur in relationships, the same dilemmas arise – the same mistakes are made. Again and again, situations associated with the past are re-enacted. Behaviours that are compulsively repeated have (what Freud described later as) a 'daemonic' quality. It is as if something deep and instinctual has risen from the unconscious and taken possession of the person's conscious mind. Freud then makes a gigantic (and highly controversial) conceptual leap: 'At this point we cannot help thinking that we have managed to identify a universal attribute of drives – and perhaps of *all* organic life – that has not hitherto been clearly recognised, or at any rate not explicitly emphasised. A drive might accordingly be seen as *a powerful tendency inherent in every living organism to restore a prior state . . .*' Repetition is equated with a general principle that approaches the status of a natural law. It is a principle that can be applied to drives, but it can also be applied to the substances which combine to form organisms in which drives arise. Life evolves from inorganic matter; however, all living systems eventually revert to their prior inorganic state. Therefore, 'the goal of all life is death'.

This principle is readily apparent in the lifecycle of certain species. Salmon, for example, are 'compelled' to return to the location where they were conceived and when they reach their destination they spawn and die. Migrating birds exhibit similar patterns of behaviour. Organisms are not compelled towards indiscriminate, haphazard deaths. Thanatos guides organisms towards deaths that are congruent with their repetition needs. Obviously, a salmon will have a very different set of repetition needs from a human being. It is also the case that Thanatos – like Eros – can be expressed in a variety of ways (particularly in a higher organism). When the death instinct is channelled outwards, the result might be aggressive behaviour; however, when directed inwards, the result might be masochistic behaviour. The introduction of the death instinct made psychoanalytic drive theory pleasingly symmetrical. It also provided a fundamental cause of self-defeating behaviour, suicide, stasis, masochism, hostility, aggression and war.

Usually, Freud's theoretical revisions were instantly accepted by his devotees. Additions and refinements were automatically applauded and judged to be further confirmation of his incomparable genius. The death instinct met with a mixed reception. Many psychoanalysts were bewildered. The new formulation solved some problems but created others. *Beyond the Pleasure Principle* is full of logical snares from which Freud struggles to extricate himself with the aid of dubious arguments. The death instinct was largely incompatible with existing biological knowledge. Even Ernest Jones (who rarely criticised Freud) was sceptical. The conceptual leap that enabled Freud to get from repetition compulsions to the restoration of prior states was, according to Jones, 'a step' in Freud's reasoning 'not easy to follow and which has given rise to much misgiving'. Since its introduction into psychoanalysis, almost every consideration of the death instinct has been routinely prefaced by caveats and qualifications. In 1936, the renowned English psychologist William McDougall declared that Freud's death instinct was 'the most bizarre monster of all his gallery of monsters'.

A minority of psychoanalysts embraced the death instinct with enthusiasm, some warmed to the idea over time, but the majority remained perplexed. A consensus emerged that the death instinct was a lapse in judgement attributable to Freud's personal foibles, his preoccupation with his own mortality, his self-destructive cigar addiction – and so on. It is also likely that the idea of the death instinct enjoyed ideal conditions for incubation as Freud was immersed in a death-obsessed social milieu. However, Thanatos is not an aberration or intellectual misstep that can be conveniently sidelined. Although Freud introduced the death instinct as a tentative speculation, he found it increasingly indispensable. In 1932, he wrote: 'And now the instincts that we believe in divide themselves into two groups – the erotic instincts, which seek to combine more and more living substance into ever greater unities, and the death instincts, which oppose this effort and lead what is living back into an inorganic state. From the concurrent and opposing action of these two proceed the phenomena of life which are brought to an end by death.'

Much of Freud's attachment to the idea of the death instinct can be explained by his love of grand theories and epic narrative. He offers us a vision of the mind as a battlefield, where two warring gods, Eros and Thanatos, are locked in eternal combat. The death instinct also widens the scope of psychoanalysis to the extent that it can compete with any of the great transcendental systems of thought, most of which recognise fundamental antithetical dualities, such as the Manichaean struggle between good and evil – light and darkness. Freud had a penchant for embedding the personal in expansive contexts. Sexual desires in infancy, for example, can be linked with Greek mythology (the Oedipus legend) and Darwinian anthropology (the tribal patricide discussed in *Totem and Taboo*). The death instinct is perhaps the most extreme example of Freud's holistic, integrative thinking. It allows Freud to unite the relatively mundane – for example, masochism – with a cosmic duality. In the same way that the human body is made from elements forged in stars, so it is that the human mind obeys principles that determine the creation and destruction of everything in the biosphere. Freud cross-stitches every mind into the dynamic fabric of the universe.

Thanatos was never fully accepted by the psychoanalytic community, but it seems to find increasing relevance in the modern world. Suicide rates and the number of individuals developing life-threatening addictions are at an all-time high. Modern living seems to provide ideal conditions for the conversion of common unhappiness into self-destruction. Climate change will probably deliver an apocalyptic outcome in one form or another in a matter of decades. Even so, the prospect of wildfires, dying oceans, famine, unbreathable air, plagues, a global refugee crisis, drowned cities and economic collapse doesn't appear to be providing ruling elites with the necessary incentive to take comprehensive preventative action. Some climatologists believe that it is already too late to save the planet. Since 'atomic bombs' were dropped on Hiroshima and Nagasaki in 1945, a third world war has been utterly unthinkable for the simple reason that no one would survive it. Yet, within weeks of the Russian invasion of Ukraine in 2022, President Vladimir Putin promised that any western interference would lead to an immediate 'response' – 'consequences that you have never encountered in your history'. The possibility of a third world war was being discussed by politicians with remarkable complacency. Human beings might not be motivated by Freud's death instinct, but they certainly behave as if they are.

The death instinct is undoubtedly a flawed concept, but it is powerfully descriptive. Freud had an uncanny ability to identify important aspects of human behaviour, and right now, humanity's collective death-wish is arguably more important (and consequential) than any other. Thanatos did not strengthen Freud's reputation as a scientist, but his percipient recognition of the importance of self-destructive tendencies demonstrates once again that he was a very impressive prophet. Both *Beyond the Pleasure Principle* and *Timely Reflections on War and Death* can be read as urgent warnings.

The relevance of the death instinct isn't restricted to behaviour that is manifestly self-destructive. The death instinct is also expressed across a spectrum of mental states characterised by passivity and inertia. These states can be construed as small resistances and oppositions to vitality, and they seem particularly prevalent in the modern world: tiredness, fatigue, apathy, lassitude – and boredom. The influence of Thanatos is reflected in colloquial English, which has needed an increasingly large lexicon to describe those who are habitually indolent – 'slob', 'slacker', 'couch-potato'. Perhaps Thanatos also achieves small victories when internet users suspend productive existence and engage in protracted periods of hypnotic 'doom scrolling'. Sitting still for long periods of time is a significant cardio-vascular health risk.

States of torpor and resignation are so typical of modern exist-ence that they have become one of the most distinctive features of twentieth-century portraiture. Edward Hopper produced countless studies of men and women staring into nothingness with blank expressions. In *Morning Sun*, a woman sits on a bed, her arms around her legs, her single visible eye disconcertingly black and dead. Similarly, *A Woman in the Sun* shows a cadaver-ous nude, smoking. The emotional neutrality of her expression presages the vacancy of oblivion, a link that is stressed by the coffin-shaped rectangle of light in which she stands. David Hockney's *Mr and Mrs Clark and Percy* shows a relaxed but detached couple with their cat. Mr Clark lounges in a chair, a cig-arette between the fingers of his limp left hand, and Mrs Clark, although standing with hands on hips, looks as though she is about to release a weary sigh. It is a marriage that will not last. A dying marriage. Perhaps the most compelling artistic explo-ration of contemporary exhaustion is Tracey Emin's infamous creation *My Bed*, first exhibited in 1999. The installation records in its chaotic debris and stained sheets the accumulated evidence of four days of self-starvation, excessive alcohol consumption, depression and sexual intercourse. Energies have been spent and the bed has become a staging-post on the way to the grave.

In Freud's time, the most significant citizen of Vienna to choose death, instead of life, was Ludwig Boltzmann. He is remembered today for his statistical description of the second law of thermodynamics and for defining entropy. The second law of thermodynamics states that everything in the universe progresses from an ordered state to a disordered state (as energy is converted into less and less usable forms). The second law of thermodynamics also provides a rationale for temporal directionality – what the poet Rainer Maria Rilke called 'the eternal current'. Time flows in one direction only, from the past to the future, and, unlike almost everything else in physics, time appears to be irreversible. Boltzmann performed the ultimate irreversible act when, in 1906, while he was on holiday with his wife and daughter in Trieste, he hanged himself. It is now widely recognised that the second law of thermodynamics is owed several deaths: the death of heat, the death of humanity, and the death of the universe. As Bertrand Russell once lamented, 'the whole temple of Man's achievement must inevitably be buried beneath the debris of a universe in ruins'.

Evolution by natural selection appears to resist entropy. Chaos can be postponed by the 'life force'. The trend towards dissipation and dispersal is delayed when disorganised inorganic matter is organised into highly complex structures like fruit flies, porcupines and psychoanalysts. In the end, however, the second law of thermodynamics always applies. Local decreases in entropy are exceeded by more than compensatory general increases in entropy – a phenomenon that the physicist Brian Greene has dubbed 'The Entropic Two-Step'. Evolution can battle with entropy, but the expected net increase in entropy will ultimately be consistent with predictions based on the second law of thermodynamics. This account of the struggle between life and death has clear Freudian parallels.

The death instinct underscores the self-destructive aspect of human nature and posits a 'natural law' that ultimately brings all life to an end. Naturally, most students of psychoanalysis find Thanatos a deeply depressing construct. However, Freud was a Stoic. He accepted self-destructiveness (in much the same way as he accepted 'perversity' or the embarrassing consequences of embodiment) with equanimity, and he was, if anything, uplifted by the idea of a 'universe in ruins'. In his essay *On Transience*, written in 1915, he described embarking on a summer walk in the Dolomites. One of his companions was a young poet. Although supporting evidence is weak, it is now generally accepted that this was Rilke, whose eternal current of time 'Draws all the ages with it'. Rilke could feel no joy in the beauty that surrounded him because it was ephemeral. Everything passes. All that he loved and admired 'seemed to him to be shorn of its worth by the transience which was its doom'. Freud proposed an alternative view. The transience of beauty, he asserted, increases its value. 'Transience value is scarcity value over time.' The brevity of human life makes every fleeting moment unimaginably precious. This was not Freud playing the part of the sage, fulfilling expectations by dispensing 'wise words' to the young. Freud was articulating what he really believed. The prospect of death, or even a universe in ruins, wasn't enough to stop Freud from fully engaging in life. When the Nazis arrived in Vienna, there was a real risk that he would be transported to a death camp. This was the tragic fate of four of his sisters. Yet, he continued writing, taking pleasure in his antiques, reading, corresponding and making plans. Naturally there were dark moments. But overall, he practised what he preached. It would take considerably more than entropy to convince Freud that life is futile.

Freud claimed that he found Vienna oppressive. He once described the steeple of St Stephen's Cathedral as 'detestable'. For Freud, Vienna had many negative associations: early hardship, academic resistance to his ideas, a lengthy struggle for recognition, and antisemitism. But Vienna was also Freud's home, and Freud was typically Viennese. He was a *Stammgast*, a regular, at Café Landtmann and he enjoyed a slice of *Gugelhupf* with his coffee. He was sociable, fond of Mozart arias, and liked telling jokes. It is almost impossible to disentangle the man from his urban context. Vienna shaped Freud's thinking – and, conversely, Freud's thinking became emblematic of Vienna's golden age.

When Ernest Jones pointed out that the time had come for Freud to leave Vienna, Freud didn't want to go. He protested. If he abandoned his 'native land', it would be like a soldier deserting his post. Jones suggested a superior analogy. The second officer of the *Titanic* declared that he had never left his ship, but rather, the ship had left him. This won Freud over and he agreed to relocate to London.

Jones returned to London on 22 March 1938 to expedite British permissions for the Freud family to emigrate. Princess Marie Bonaparte also played an important role, negotiating bureaucratic obstacles and providing financial assistance. Payments had to be made to the Nazi authorities to avoid confiscation of property (such as Freud's antiques collection); assets had to be managed with enormous care to avoid punishments for 'illegality'; and the famous 'couch', on which so many patients had reclined and disclosed their innermost secrets, had to be stored in readiness for shipping.

Jones and Bonaparte's efforts to assist Freud were augmented by those of several others, most notably William Bullitt, the American ambassador to France. In addition to being a diplomat (he had negotiated with Lenin in 1919), Bullitt had also worked as a script editor for the Paramount Famous Lasky Corporation (which later became Paramount Pictures), and his novel *It's Not Done* sold more copies than its now greatly admired contemporary *The Great Gatsby*. Freud had treated Bullitt for depression in 1925. The two men became friends, and eventually collaborated on a somewhat peevish psychoanalytic biography of Woodrow Wilson (although this wasn't published until 1967). Freud granted Bullitt a rare privilege. Along with *only* H. G. Wells and

Yvette Guilbert, he permitted his American friend to call him 'Freud' instead of 'Professor'.

The least likely individual to get involved in making Freud's wish 'to die in freedom' a reality was Anton Sauerwald – a Nazi bureaucrat. Sauerwald was not a sympathetic figure; he used terms of abuse such as 'Jewish pigs', and he could easily have made sure that Freud was trapped in Vienna. Yet, incredibly, Sauerwald developed an interest in Freud's writing and chose to withhold 'incriminating' documents from his superiors until Freud was safely beyond Nazi jurisdiction. His motivation remains obscure.

Prior to Freud's departure, he was obliged to sign a document stating that he had been treated respectfully by the Gestapo and that he had no reason for complaint. Freud is supposed to have complied, but with the addition of an ironic postscript: 'I can heartily recommend the Gestapo to anyone.' When Freud's release papers were traced, researchers found no evidence of this amusing but provocative farewell. The incident was reported by Jones in his biography of Freud, and it is sometimes dismissed by Freud's critics as a self-serving lie. Although it is true that Freud didn't amend the statement, he *did* take a comparable risk. Paula Fichtl, Freud's maid, heard him ask the supervising Nazi official if he could add one more sentence – the hearty recommendation reported by Jones. Miraculously, the official only glowered at Freud. The document was signed and the official left. The consequences of such an ill-judged remark at that late juncture could have been catastrophic.

The Freud household – Sigmund, Martha, Anna, Paula the maid and Lun the dog – occupied two compartments on the *Orient Express* and they arrived in Paris on 5 June 1938. Marie Bonaparte, William Bullitt and Freud's son Ernst (already living in London) were waiting for them. A cluster of journalists and photographers had also assembled on the platform. Bonaparte promptly led the family to two cars, a Bentley and a Rolls-Royce, and all were driven to her villa in St Cloud. Later, Bonaparte presented Freud with some new 'Greek terracotta figures' for his collection, as well as his favourite statue of Athena, and presumably his jade screen – the two 'treasures' which she had smuggled out of Austria. The much-loved statue was given with a note: 'Athena – Peace! Reason! Greets those who have fled from the mad inferno!' After a day of rest, the family resumed their journey and crossed the English Channel on a night boat. Train carriages were loaded straight on to the ferry, so Freud was able to stay in his compartment undisturbed. They arrived at Victoria station on the morning of 6 June, where they were welcomed by Freud's son (Martin) and daughter (Mathilde), and the ever-faithful Jones (with his wife Katherine). Finally, the Freuds were driven by Jones to their destination, 39 Elsworthy Road in Primrose Hill, with some of the well-wishers following behind in taxis. As they passed London's famous sights – Buckingham Palace, the Houses of Parliament, Piccadilly Circus – Freud pointed them out to Martha.

Freud entered his new home and went into the garden. He raised his arms and cried: 'Heil Hitler!' It set a precedent. Whenever he felt appreciative of his novel situation, he would repeat a Nazi slogan: 'We thank our Führer.'

That evening Freud wrote to the psychoanalyst Max Eitingon. It was his first letter from London. Not surprisingly, he begins by admitting 'Everything is still unreal, as in a dream.' He informs Eitingon that members of the Freud family left Vienna at different times and that they arrived in England separately over a period of a month. The more serious newspapers, Freud reports, have printed 'friendly lines of welcome' and he admits to expecting 'All kinds of fuss'. Then, quite suddenly, he is homesick. 'The feeling of triumph on being liberated is too strongly mixed with sorrow, for in spite of everything I still loved the prison from which I have been released.' He is no longer 'in a dream'. It is as though, at that moment, he experienced a dreadful awakening. Never again would he enjoy coffee and cake in Café Landtmann. Never again would he see the magical, fairy-tale Town Hall, the sphinxes in the Belvedere Gardens, or Athena standing proudly before the Parliament building. To paraphrase Klimt: it was well and truly over. Even though Freud is exhausted and a little disorientated he is still disposed to wonder: 'How long will a fatigued heart be able to accomplish work?' He isn't finished. He has more to say. His spirit rallies: 'We have become popular in London overnight.' Strangers recognise him – they even know where he lives – and he has been inundated with flowers. The letter ends with a warm adieu: 'Affectionate regards to you and Mirra. Yours, Freud.'

He had escaped one death, but now he was facing another.

Freud was accustomed to living on a single floor. Now he had to adjust to what he called 'living vertically'. Staircases were not ideal for a man in his infirm state, and he had to be carried to his bedroom. As rent-paying tenants, the Freuds occupied Elsworthy Road for several months. They then moved into a hotel in Maida Vale while a permanent home was being readied. This was 20 Maresfield Gardens, in Hampstead – now the London Freud Museum – where a lift had to be installed. When Freud finally moved into Maresfield Gardens, his couch, antiques and desk had been safely delivered, and Anna and the maid had reconstructed Freud's study, just as it was in Vienna.

From the moment Freud arrived in London, his presence aroused considerable interest. Many significant figures wanted to meet him. His first visitor was an Elsworthy Road neighbour, the Jewish Biblical scholar Abraham Shalom Yahuda. Yahuda welcomed Freud to England, but he also pleaded with him to abandon his iconoclastic book on Moses and monotheism – a somewhat insensitive project to be working on at a time when Jews and Judaism were already under attack. The first two of Freud's three Moses essays had already been published in 1937 in the psychoanalytic journal *Imago*. Freud continued writing the third essay regardless.

Freud's most famous visitor (again at Elsworthy Road) was the artist Salvador Dalí. Dalí had tried to meet Freud in Vienna on three occasions without success. Unable to tolerate disappointment, he seems to have hallucinated a substitute Freud, with whom he conducted extended imaginary conversations; 'he even came home with me once', Dalí confessed in his autobiography, 'and stayed all night clinging to the curtains of my room in the Hotel Sacher'. A few years later, Dalí claimed to have experienced a moment of profound illumination during which the 'secret' of Freud's physiology was revealed. 'Freud's cranium', Dalí declared, 'is a snail!' It was an insight that later informed a sketch of Freud that Dalí surreptitiously produced during his visit to Elsworthy Road. The sketch was the prototype of a pen and ink drawing, but neither the sketch nor the drawing was shown to Freud, because they were thought to be too upsetting. They were clearly portraits of a man close to death.

Dalí did not visit Elsworthy Road alone. He was accompanied by Stefan Zweig – who, like Freud, was also living as an exile in England – and Edward James (a poet and patron of surrealist art). Dalí was only thirty-four; however, he had already collaborated with Luis Buñuel on the film *Un Chien Andalou*, painted the melting clocks of *The Persistence of Memory*, and constructed his *Lobster Telephone*. He was internationally renowned and notoriously eccentric. Dalí's theatricality didn't disconcert Freud, but Freud's composure certainly disconcerted Dalí. The artist attempted to impress Freud by assuming the air of 'a kind of dandy of "universal intellectualism"'. Freud responded mostly with silence, and he failed to show much enthusiasm when he was shown Dalí's *Metamorphosis of Narcissus*. Dalí – somewhat desperate – begged Freud to read an article he had written about paranoia. He produced a magazine, insisted that he had written a serious scientific article, repeated the title, and pointed at the text. Freud stared at Dalí before he exclaimed, addressing Zweig: 'I have never seen a more complete example of a Spaniard. What a fanatic!' The meeting was a disaster. Nevertheless, Freud wrote to Zweig the following day, expressing gratitude and suggesting that the 'young Spaniard' had made him 'reconsider' his opinion of surrealism.

Other visitors included the writer and journalist Arthur Koestler, the anthropologist Bronisław Malinowski, the historian Charles Singer and the visionary author H. G. Wells. Freud's British publishers, Leonard and Virginia Woolf, were also granted an audience. Leonard believed that he was in the presence of true greatness and described Freud using magisterial language; he was – according to Leonard – like 'a half extinct volcano'. Virginia was less complimentary. Although Freud was charming and presented her with a flower, she remembered him as a shrivelled, shrunken, inarticulate old man who was nevertheless 'alert' with a 'monkey's light eyes'.

The names of the three visitors Freud was probably most happy to receive are now unfamiliar: Sir Albert Seward, Professor A. V. Hill and J. D. Griffith Davies. They were secretaries of the Royal Society, and on 23 June they journeyed to Elsworthy Road to ask Freud to sign their Charter Book. Previous signatories included Charles Darwin and Sir Isaac Newton. On one previous occasion only had the Charter Book been carried to a signatory, and this was when the King was made an honorary member. An exception was made for Freud because of his infirmity. All his life, Freud had fantasised about greatness. Now, his greatness was indisputable. The peasant woman who had accosted Amalia Freud in that Moravian pastry shop over eighty years earlier had been right. Amalia *had* brought a great man into the world; a man who had risen from humble origins to become a scientist with a global reputation. Freud's accomplishment was quite extraordinary, but quietly reflecting on his recognition by the Royal Society was a pleasure he would enjoy only briefly.

Freud had been diagnosed with oral cancer in 1923. For fifteen years he had endured recurrent leucoplakias, excisions (around thirty surgical procedures) and electrocoagulation. Pain was variable, but at times it could be excruciating. He tended to take nothing stronger than aspirin to manage his pain, because he didn't want to use any drugs that would impair his ability to think. Part of his right upper jaw and the roof of his mouth had been removed and he was obliged to wear a prosthesis to make eating possible. The prosthesis – Freud called it 'the monster' – had to be regularly removed, cleaned and reinserted, a complicated procedure that sometimes lasted half an hour. Occasionally, shrinkage made reinsertion impossible, and the prosthesis had to be modified. Freud's Eustachian tubes had been damaged, so he could only hear properly through his left ear. Smoking was an irritant, but he refused to give up.

In September 1938, Freud had yet another surgical procedure.

What is quite remarkable about Freud in his final year is his resilience. He was always courteous, never irritable, rarely complained, and he was fully engaged intellectually. He still wanted to discuss what was happening in psychoanalytic circles and maintained a lively correspondence with friends and colleagues. He was even seeing a limited number of patients. Shortly after arriving in London, Freud had started work on *An Outline of Psychoanalysis* – a technical overview of psychoanalysis. Although he was old, exhausted and dying, the writing is muscular and the content forward-looking. 'New light is thrown on whatever he touches,' Albert Dickson (one of James Strachey's editorial successors) later observed with wonder.

'There are even occasional hints of entirely new developments . . . ' In the sixth chapter, Freud speculates about a future in which psychoanalysis will be made redundant by advances in psychopharmacology. It is as though he had foreseen the discovery of 'neuroleptics' and 'tricyclics' – novel drugs destined to revolutionise the practice of psychiatry in the 1950s.

In November, the BBC requested a recording of Freud's voice for their archive. The following month the recording was made in his study. His English is characteristically accented, and his delivery is slow and deliberate. 'I started my professional activity as a neurologist, trying to bring relief to my neurotic patients. Under the influence of an older friend and by my own efforts I discovered some important new facts about the unconscious in psychic life, the role of instinctual urges and so on. Out of these findings grew a new science, psychoanalysis, a part of psychology and a new method of treatment of the neuroses. I had to pay heavily for this bit of good luck. People did not believe in my facts and thought my theories unsavoury. Resistance was strong and unrelenting. In the end I succeeded in acquiring pupils and building up an International Psychoanalytic Association. But the struggle is not yet over.' He lapses into German for a few seconds and then adds, 'My name is Sigmund Freud.'

But the struggle is not yet over. Even in December 1938, even after he had signed the Royal Society Charter Book, there were still battles to be fought and won.

A biopsy was performed on 28 February 1939, and the results were positive for a malignant epithelioma. The position of the lesion made further surgery dangerous and unfeasible. Radiotherapy was started immediately, but daily travel and X-ray sessions were extremely taxing. Freud's mouth bled, he experienced severe headaches, he had episodes of dizziness and, over time, he lost the hair that made up the right side of his beard.

The sixth of May 1939 was Freud's eighty-third birthday. He spent some time in the garden celebrating with his relatives and friends, but he had to retire early because he found socialising too demanding. He secreted himself in his study where he could rest and recover. Freud's physician, Max Schur, was in America from April to July. When he returned he found Freud unusually apathetic, and on examination he discovered a new 'carcinomatous ulceration'. Freud had also started to emit a 'fetid odour'. The stench became so bad that Freud's dog wouldn't go near him. It would sit on the other side of the room. Freud had written to Marie Bonaparte in June and he had described his existence as 'a small island of pain'.

Schur's account of Freud's subsequent deterioration is harrowing. 'During August everything went downhill rapidly. There could be no doubt about an extended recurrence with ulceration. The discolouration of the cheek became more and more marked, indicating the development of skin necrosis. The fetor became more and more unbearable, and could not be controlled with any kind of mouth hygiene. It was apparent that the odor was coming from the necrosis of the bone.' There were no antibiotics available at that time. Freud was beyond help.

War was declared in September, and air-raid sirens sounded. Freud listened to them wailing while reclining in his garden. He was unperturbed and quietly pleased. Hitler would be defeated. He was confident that this would be the ultimate outcome.

Freud could no longer use the lift, so a special invalid's couch was placed in his study. He could still read. As his mouth rotted away, he diverted himself with a novel by Balzac – *Le Peau de Chagrin* – in the original French, about a man called Raphael who acquires a magical talisman made from ass's skin. Every time one of Raphael's wishes is fulfilled, the talisman shrinks – along with his life. Freud quipped to Schur that it was the 'proper book' for him to be reading. It is a dark tale that begins with a protagonist intent on suicide and the introductory sections are full of Gothic images: a skeleton, a sarcophagus, ghostly shadows. Only a few pages into the story and there are lines such as 'Every suicide is a sublime poem of melancholy' and 'Night, the hour of death, had suddenly arrived'. It is remarkable, given Freud's circumstances, that he didn't find the content and tone unbearably depressing. Freud's fetor, like the putrid miasma around a corpse, was now attracting flies, and it was necessary for him to lie underneath a mosquito net.

On 19 September, Ernest Jones came to say goodbye to his master. Freud was dozing, but he opened his eyes, recognised Jones, and summoned enough strength to briefly raise his hand. Jones was deeply moved by this simple gesture which seemed to communicate a wealth of meaning – greetings, farewell, resignation. No words were exchanged. On 21 September, Freud reminded Schur of a conversation they had once had and what they had agreed. 'Now it's nothing but torture,' Freud said, 'and makes no sense any more.' He then instructed Schur to tell Anna about their 'arrangement'. After consulting Anna, Schur injected his patient with two centigrams of morphine. The dose was repeated twelve hours later. Freud drifted from sleep into a coma. At three o'clock in the morning on Saturday 23 September 1939, Thanatos prevailed. That, at least, was Schur's recollection of events. Subsequent research suggests that Freud didn't die until after he had received a third dose of morphine administered by Josefine Stross (a physician who had accompanied Freud on his journey to London). It is also possible that Freud's time of death was misreported and that he died not at three o'clock in the morning, but around midnight on 23 September. In 1939, 23 September was a significant date in the Jewish calendar. It marked the end of the holiest day of the year: Yom Kippur, the Day of Atonement.

Freud died surrounded by books, miniature gods and his

famous couch. He was cremated at Golders Green cemetery on 26 September in the presence of a large number of mourners. His remains – some calcium phosphate, traces of potassium and sodium, and a little carbonate – were placed in his favourite 2,300-year-old Grecian urn. The temporary organisation of the inorganic had yielded, as it always must, to the second law of thermodynamics. And the world descended into chaos.

Chapter 21

Magus

Freud was slow to realise the magnitude of the Nazi threat. However, when the Nazi Party became the second most important political force in German politics, after the Social Democratic Party, he added a sentence to his already completed essay *Civilization and its Discontents*. He had previously concluded the work with a paragraph in which he states that human destiny will be settled, at least provisionally, by the battle between Eros and Thanatos. Before Hitler's electoral success, Freud's conclusion was mildly optimistic. Civilisation may have equipped human beings with technologies that ensure self-destruction – 'down to the last man' – but he trusted that this imbalance, in Thanatos's favour, would be corrected by a natural homeostatic mechanism: 'And now it is to be expected that the other of the two "heavenly powers", immortal Eros, will try to assert himself in the struggle with his equally immortal adversary.' After the Nazi electoral success on 13 September 1930, he wasn't so sure. In 1931, Freud added a final, uneasy equivocation: 'But who can foresee the outcome?'

The Nazis displaced the Social Democratic Party, seized power, precipitated global carnage – and were ultimately defeated. 'Immortal Eros' reasserted himself 'in the struggle with his equally immortal adversary'. Nevertheless, the Second World War ended with the detonation of two atomic bombs, and the subsequent nuclear stalemate between East and West guaranteed that Freud's anxious question would remain highly relevant. Who can foresee the outcome? Events such as the Cuban missile crisis in 1962 and the Russian invasion of Ukraine in 2022 have been uncomfortable reminders that the future of humanity is far from certain.

Civilization and its Discontents is a wide-ranging work which briefly alights on many subjects including religion, sociology and politics, but it is essentially a penetrating account of why human beings – and particularly human beings living in the modern world – are chronically dissatisfied and unhappy. For many psychoanalysts, *Civilization and its Discontents* represents Freud's last landmark publication; however, its central thesis, concerning the conflict arising between personal and collective interests, was implicit in Freud's earliest case studies. To enjoy the comforts of civilised living many of his female patients were obliged to repress their sexual needs. Their unhappiness was linked to self-denial. This observation is reiterated in the 1908 essay *'Civilized' Sexual Morality and Modern Nervous Illness* – which is almost a first draft of *Civilization and its Discontents*. In this paper, Freud suggests that evolved, moralistic societies prohibit sexual freedom and that the repression of primal desires results in elevated levels of neurotic illness. Twenty-two years later, in *Civilization and Its Discontents*, Freud developed this argument more broadly. Our freedoms are necessarily restricted by moral indoctrination, religious dogma and laws. As Freud puts it: 'The replacement of the power of the individual by that of the community is the decisive step towards civilization.' Consequently, 'Much of mankind's struggle is taken up with the task of finding a suitable, that is to say a happy accommodation, between the claims of the individual and the mass claims of civilization.' We balance our personal needs with our need to live with others; however, such 'balances' are usually delicate. Indeed, it is possible that desire and prohibition are fundamentally irreconcilable. The degree of self-sacrifice required to achieve social cohesion might be impossible to sustain. Marriage, for example, is a civilised 'accommodation'. Sexual needs are satisfied within a single relationship and the 'family' is the basic unit of stable societies. Yet, adultery is a common cause of divorce. The institution of marriage, particularly in western liberal democracies, is constantly weakened by a proclivity for opportunistic sex.

Civilization and Its Discontents was not Freud's title. It is James Strachey's very loose and somewhat ambiguous translation of Freud's original. Freud preferred 'malaise' or 'discomfort' to 'discontent'. In fact, Freud's German title – *Das Unbehagen in der Kultur* – is more accurately rendered in English as *The Uneasiness Inherent in Culture*. Significantly, Freud's title does not include the word 'and' – a connective that encourages the reader to make a distinction between civilisation and a subset of individuals who can be described as 'discontents'. As Bruno Bettelheim has pointed out, Freud's German makes 'uneasiness' and 'culture' inseparable. Everyone who lives in the modern, industrialised world will experience at least some level of malaise or discomfort.

The idea that living in the modern world makes us unhappy, or even ill, is not a new one. In 1869, the American physician George Beard introduced the idea of neurasthenia, a condition characterised by exhaustion and mood disturbance caused by 'fast' urban living. In *'Civilized' Sexual Morality and Modern Nervous Illness*, Freud discusses this idea at length and (in an extended quotation taken from a work by the neurologist Wilhelm Erb) lists many potential sources of stress. For example, the effect of expanding telecommunications networks on trade and commerce; night travel disturbing the body-clock; financial

crises; intemperate political argument; over-stimulation; sen-
sationalism; noise; reduced sleep; insufficient rest; and 'highly
spiced' leisure activities that deplete energy. It is a list that can
easily be translated into modern equivalents: the internet;
doom-scrolling; political extremism; light pollution; insomnia;
loud construction projects; and ease of access to pornography.
Modern city-dwellers reliably complain: 'I'm tired all the time.'
The complaint is so common that health workers routinely use
the acronym TATT to describe a general fatigue syndrome.
Freud accepts that modern life can have a deleterious effect on
the nervous system, but he doesn't find enervated nerves a very
satisfying explanation for the uneasiness inherent in culture. For
Freud, the root problem is conflict, the inner tensions generated
by being the only animal on the planet that dresses for dinner,
eats in restaurants and observes table manners.

Freud's position is entirely consistent with evolutionary
psychology. Human beings are social animals. A lone human
could not have survived in the ancestral environment. Ancestral
humans compensated for their physical weakness and the unique
vulnerability of their young by forming large cooperative groups
and many 'accommodations' were necessary for these groups to
function effectively. An ancestral human incapable of making
compromises would be expelled from the group – and would
die. Evolution has tied a knot in desire. Our survival strategy –
cooperation – 'bakes in' dissatisfaction. The more cooperative
and civilised we become, the more we are obliged to inhibit.

The increasing demands of civilisation are relevant to what
biologists call evolutionary time lags. Evolution progresses
slowly in response to pressures produced by gradual environmental changes. Because civilisation is effectively a form of
accelerated environmental change, the brain does not have time
to make suitable adaptations. Consequently, we must negotiate the modern world with a Stone Age brain. This mismatch

admits many possibilities for frustration, maladaptive coping (some of which is self-destructive) and dissatisfaction.

Freud's principal thesis in *Civilization and Its Discontents* is preceded by an interesting and insightful discussion concerning the nature of pleasure. Human beings obey the pleasure principle and pursue pleasure to be happy. Usually, primitive impulses (for example, the sexual impulse) are associated with more intense and rewarding pay-offs (for example, orgasms). However, our capacity to experience pleasure is self-limiting. It is an 'episodic phenomenon', and if we try to prolong pleasure beyond its natural limits we will experience diminishing returns. The pleasure will be attenuated. 'We are', as Freud pointed out, 'restricted by our constitution.'

Once again, this observation is consistent with evolutionary psychology. If satisfaction after sexual intercourse was enduring, this would result in reduced procreative activity and an elevated risk of extinction. Natural selection does not want us to be continuously happy, because in the ancestral environment, too much happiness could have been fatal. A satisfied animal might stew in its own contentment, whereas a dissatisfied animal would be more impelled to improve its lot, to find safer habitats, more food – and healthier mates.

In *Civilization and Its Discontents*, Freud circles back to his beginnings, the famous concluding remarks of *Studies in Hysteria*, where he discusses psychotherapy turning 'hysterical misery into common unhappiness'. *Civilization and Its Discontents* is a mature deconstruction of 'common unhappiness'. It provides a compelling explanation for why we are frequently unhappy, and why the modern world deepens our unhappiness. Of course, Freud understood that there are many things that make us unhappy – narcissism, for example, because it negates our capacity to love. But the task he set himself in *Civilization and its Discontents* was to uncover the deepest and most fundamental causes of unhappiness. Unlike many visionaries who were writing between the wars, writers and political theorists who were predicting the arrival of socialist or technological utopias, Freud foresaw a future of uneasiness, restlessness, malaise and dissatisfaction. Mental health statistics have vindicated Freud's pessimism. Today, someone, somewhere, chooses to end their own life every forty seconds. More lives are claimed by suicide than wars. Prescriptions for anti-depressant and anxiolytic medication are on a steep upward trend. The global economic cost of mental illness is now calculated in trillions of dollars.

Freud's analysis has implications for how we think about ourselves and how we live in the modern world. It recommends the adoption of a specific set of attitudes and values – rationality, realism, acceptance, modest expectations and qualified, cautious hope. A psychoanalytic 'world view'.

By the time Freud was writing *Civilization and Its Discontents*, he had for over a decade been thinking of psychoanalysis as a discipline with a much broader range of application than medical psychology. In 1921, when Abram Kardiner (then Freud's student) asked him what he thought of himself as an analyst, Freud replied: 'I'm glad you ask, because, frankly, I have no great interest in therapeutic problems.' In Freud's opinion, the great Sigmund Freud wasn't a 'great analyst'. He had become too impatient to be a good clinician and he laboured under the weight of his own stature. He had other things on his mind. 'I am much too much occupied with theoretical problems.' The treatment of neurotic illness was interesting, but not as interesting as anthropology, the origins of religion, elucidating how unconscious mechanisms really work, genius, mythology, sculpture, supernatural phenomena, archaeology, politics and literature. Freud had recognised that the boundary of psychoanalysis was infinitely elastic. It could be expanded and encircle the entire universe of human behaviour. In the 1935 postscript of *An Autobiographical Study*, Freud declares: 'My interest, after making a lifelong *détour* through the natural sciences, medicine and psychotherapy, returned to the cultural problems which had fascinated me long before, when I was a youth scarcely old enough for thinking.'

Civilization and Its Discontents can still be read as a wake-up call. In one of his footnotes, Freud talks of human beings being 'born between urine and faeces'. We are embodied creatures, and our minds are in closer relation to our bowels and genitals than we care to acknowledge. We are propelled by primitive impulses, and throughout history we have only just managed to stay ahead of our self-destructive tendencies. Climate change and nuclear weapons have diminished our lead considerably. Indeed, it is possible that the gap has already been closed. Freud begs us to consider the evidence of history: the incursion of the Huns, the Mongol horde, the conquest of Jerusalem by pious crusaders, and the horrors of the Great War. He cites a Latin proverb: *Homo homini lupus* – Man is wolf to man. 'Who, after all that he has learnt from life and history, would be so bold as to dispute this proposition?' He finds religious platitudes such as 'love thine enemies' absurd, and political solutions illogical. Freud points out that for communists, property is the ultimate cause of violent aggression. But 'Aggression was not created by property' – 'It already manifests itself in the nursery, where property has hardly given up its original anal form.' Our Stone Age brains make us dangerously tribal. We exist in a state of common unhappiness and the way we live makes us even unhappier. And yet, instead of facing these realities, and working tirelessly to find solutions to our existential problems, we prefer to neutralise our anxieties with anodyne, infantile fantasies. The important challenges that we face are what 'nurse maids seek to mitigate with their lullaby about heavens'. Fairy stories, angels, illusions. And more recently, social media, celebrity gossip and shopping. *Wake up!* Freud is saying. One is reminded again of the younger Freud, who was intent on disturbing 'the sleep of the world'. He is shaking us violently and reminding us that we cannot afford to be complacent. 'But who can foresee the outcome?' The stakes are too high.

On 19 June 1940, Freud's disciple Theodor Reik was living in an apartment in New York. It was two o'clock in the morning and the last news summary had reported the terms that Hitler and Mussolini intended to offer vanquished France. Reik could hear the cars on 6th Avenue and the voices of people returning from parties. He became absorbed in a famous portrait of Freud seated at his desk. In a moment of uncanny derealisation, Freud appeared to stand up in readiness to step out of the frame. 'For the space of a few quickened heart-beats,' Reik wrote, 'I thought: he is alive.' The impression passed, and he experienced a wave of grief. Yet the vision left him hopeful. 'The lamp that burns in the night over the scientist's desk gives more powerful light than artillery fire. Freud shall live long after Hitler and Mussolini are dust.'

Authenticated News/Getty Images

In an article first published in 2009, the distinguished cognitive psychologist John Kihlstrom declared: 'More than Einstein or Watson and Crick, more than Hitler or Lenin, Roosevelt, or Kennedy, more than Picasso, Eliot, or Stravinsky, more than the Beatles or Bob Dylan, Freud's influence on modern culture has been profound and long lasting.' Surprisingly, this eulogy appears in an article that argues Freud's model of the mind and psychoanalysis are dead. Even if we disagree with Freud, it is impossible to deny his influence.

For over a century, legions of critics have denounced Freud. Yet he remains an inescapable feature in our cultural and intellectual landscape. The simplest explanation for his durability is that we still need him. We still need his hand on our shoulder. We still need him to shake us into wakefulness. Despite his flaws – of which there are many – he remains the nearest thing we have to a modern magus. There are no comparable figures who could realistically replace him, no pretenders or credible claimants, no competitors who have been as widely influential. He is unique, and as such, he is indispensable.

The thread may be broken in places, but we still need the pearls.

References

Preface

Indeed, there are weighty critical works . . . character assassination See, for example, Frederick Crews (2017), *Freud: The Making of an Illusion*, Profile.

By the 1930s . . . Aryan science and Jewish science David Lindorf (2004/2009), *Pauli and Jung: The Meeting of Two Great Minds*, Quest Books: Wheaton, Illinois, 49.

We don't reject Copernicus . . . believed in astrology Andreas Sommer (2021), 'Forbidden Histories', interview published in *The Psychologist*, September 2021, 76.

an electrified metal brush thrust down the throat Hannah S. Decker (1991/1992), *Freud, Dora, and Vienna 1900*, The Free Press: A Division of Macmillan Inc. New York, 11.

and 'big data' analysts See, for example, Seth Stephens-Davidowitz (2017), *Everybody Lies: What the internet can tell us about who we really are*, Bloomsbury: London.

Robert Trivers . . . re-evaluated from an evolutionary perspective See Robert Wright (1994/1996), 'Chapter 15: Darwinian (and Freudian) Cynicism', in *The Moral Animal: Why we are the way we are*, Abacus: London; Randolph M. Nesse (2019), 'Chapter 10: Know Thyself – Not!', in *Good Reasons for Bad Feelings: Insights from the Frontier of Evolutionary Psychiatry*, Allen Lane, an imprint of Penguin Books: Penguin Random House, UK.

in the 'distant future', psychology would be based on a 'new foundation' Charles Darwin (1859/1985), *The Origin of Species: By means of natural selection or the preservation of favoured races in the struggle for life*, edited with an introduction by J. W. Burrow, Penguin Books: Harmondsworth, 458.

The International Neuropsychoanalysis Society . . . Antonio Damasio Mark Solms (2021), *The Hidden Spring: A Journey to the Source of Consciousness*, Profile Books: London, 45–6.

'one of the most interesting neuroscientists of our time' Oliver Sacks (1998/2005), foreword in *Phantoms of the Brain*, Sandra Blakeslee and V. S. Ramachandran, Harper Perennial: London, vii.

Freudian defence mechanisms have neural correlates Ibid, 156.

the most forward-looking models . . . neurobiological substrates See R. Carhart-Harris and K. Friston (2010), 'The default-mode, ego-functions and free-energy: a neurobiological account of Freudian ideas', *Brain*, 133: 1265–83.

'Time for a new deal between neurology and psychoanalysis' Diego Centonze and Mario Stampanoni Bassi (2021), 'Time for a new deal between neurology and psychoanalysis', *Brain*, 144: 2228–2230.

The great physician . . . on a very thin thread Havelock Ellis (1910) 'Review of: A Psycho-Analytic Study of Leonardo da Vinci by Sigmund Freud', *Journal of Mental Science*, 523.

Chapter 1: Destiny's Child

We begin in a pastry shop Ernest Jones (1953–7/1977), *The Life and Work of Sigmund Freud*, edited and abridged by Lionel Trilling and Steven Marcus, Penguin, 34.

He was born with a translucent hood Ibid, 33.

an entertainer in a restaurant Ibid, 34.

'Thus the hero's garb . . . ' Ibid 34.

'sleep of the world' Sigmund Freud (1914/1993), *Sigmund Freud. 15. Historical and Expository Works on Psychoanalysis. On the History of the Psychoanalytic Movement*, the Penguin Freud Library, vol. 15, Penguin, 79. NB: Freud is quoting the dramatist Christian Friedrich Hebbel. The original German is also translated as 'the sleep of mankind'.

full head of black hair Ernest Jones (1953–7/1977), *The Life and Work of Sigmund Freud*, edited and abridged by Lionel Trilling and Steven Marcus, Penguin, 33.

'entered the Jewish covenant' Peter Gay (1988), *Freud: A Life for Our Time*, J. M. Dent and Sons, 5.

He became a 'lively' infant . . . small toys Max Schur (1972), *Freud: Living and Dying*, International Universities Press Inc.: New York, 21, footnote 9.

The inalienable heirlooms of the royal family Simon Winder (2013/2014), *Danubia: A Personal History of Habsburg Europe*, Picador: London, 83.

Hector, Noah and even the god Saturn Ibid, 55.

it is much more likely . . . settled in Galicia Chrisfried Tögel (undated guide to the Vienna Freud Museum), 'Sigmund Freud's Path to Psychoanalysis: A Biographical Sketch', in *Freud, Berggasse 19: The Origin of Psychoanalysis*, edited by Monika Pessler and Daniela Finzi with a foreword by Siri Hustvedt, Hatje Cantz, 50.

Wilkins Micawber Ernest Jones (1953–7/1977), *The Life and Work of Sigmund Freud*, edited and abridged by Lionel Trilling and Steven Marcus, Penguin, 32.

to apply to the authorities for permission to trade Louis Breger (2000), *Freud: Darkness in the Midst of Vision*, John Wiley & Sons, 8.

a woman called Rebecca Ronald W. Clark (1980), *Freud: The Man and the Cause*, Jonathan Cape: London, 5.

tornado Martin Freud (1957), *Glory Reflected: Sigmund Freud – Man and Father*, Angus and Robertson, 11.

'card parties at an hour . . . ' Ernest Jones (1953–7/1977), *The Life and Work of Sigmund Freud*, edited and abridged by Lionel Trilling and Steven Marcus, Penguin, 32.

'A bad reproduction . . . ' Ibid, 32.

many wool merchants were prospering Louis Breger (2000), *Freud: Darkness in the Midst of Vision*, John Wiley & Sons, 16.

These flames made him think Ernest Jones (1953–7/1977), *The Life and Work of Sigmund Freud*, edited and abridged by Lionel Trilling and Steven Marcus, Penguin, 41.

'libido towards matrem . . . *seeing her* nudam' Sigmund Freud (1897/1977), *The Origins of Psychoanalysis: Letters to Wilhelm Fliess*, with an introductory essay by Steven Marcus, Basic Books, 219.

a universal phenomenon of early childhood Ibid, 223.

'Every member of the audience . . . his present state' Ibid, 223–4.

separated by a chalk line on the floor Louis Breger (2000), *Freud: Darkness in the Midst of Vision*, John Wiley & Sons, 23.

carried into the kitchen by porters Ernest Jones (1953–7/1977), *The Life and Work of Sigmund Freud*, edited and abridged by Lionel Trilling and Steven Marcus, Penguin, 45.

counterfeit rubles Frederick Crews (2017), *Freud: The Making of an Illusion*, Profile, 10.

'One evening before going to sleep . . . while they were present' Sigmund Freud (1900/1991), *Sigmund Freud. 4. The Interpretation of Dreams*, the Penguin Freud Library, Vol. 4, Penguin, 309.

'The boy will come to nothing' Ibid, 309.

'a frightful blow to my ambition' Ibid, 309.

His school record was blemished only once Chrisfried Tögel (undated guide to the Vienna Freud Museum), 'Sigmund Freud's Path to Psychoanalysis: A Biographical Sketch', in *Freud, Berggasse 19: The Origin of Psychoanalysis*, edited by Monika Pessler and Daniela Finzi with a foreword by Siri Hustvedt, Hatje Cantz, 51.

heard an essay on Nature Sigmund Freud (1925/1993), *Sigmund Freud. 15. Historical and Expository Works on Psychoanalysis. An Autobiographical Study*, the Penguin Freud Library, Vol. 15, Penguin, 191.

'there ran a premonition of a task ahead' Freud: 'Schoolboy Psychology', p. 242, cited in Ronald W. Clark (1980), *Freud: The Man and the Cause*, Jonathan Cape: London, 19.

'People who fear nothing . . . being mediocre?' Freud – Emil Fluss, 16 June 1873, in Sigmund Freud (1961), *Letters of Sigmund Freud 1873–1939*, edited by Ernst L. Freud, translated by Tania and James Stern, Hogarth Press, 23.

cherry brandy William M. Johnston (1972/1983), *The Austrian Mind: An Intellectual and Social History 1848–1938*, University of California Press, 224.

'treatment, that is nothing' Ibid, 228.

Their duties included selling coffee Ibid, 228.

eighty-five thousand autopsies Ibid, 224.

'phenomena are a visible expression . . .' Eric R. Kandel (2012), *The Age of Insight: The Quest to Understand the Unconscious in Art, Mind, and Brain from Vienna 1900 to the Present*, Random House, 27.

Gustav Klimt observed Emil Zuckerkandl Ibid, 32.

His solution was . . . Sigi's half-brother Emmanuel Ernest Jones (1953–7/1977), *The Life and Work of Sigmund Freud*, edited and abridged by Lionel Trilling and Steven Marcus, Penguin, 51–2.

'much might have been different in our world' Ibid, 52.

'in spite of fog and rain . . .' Freud – Silberstein, 9 September 1875, cited in Ronald W. Clark (1980), *Freud: The Man and the Cause*, Jonathan Cape: London, 37–8.

The last time he used Sigismund Peter Gay (1988), *Freud: A Life for Our Time*, J. M. Dent and Sons, footnote on p. 5.

the dupe or stooge Ronald W. Clark (1980), *Freud: The Man and the Cause*, Jonathan Cape: London, 36.

'I have never been able to see why I should feel ashamed . . .' Sigmund Freud (1925/1993), *Sigmund Freud. 15. Historical and Expository Works on Psychoanalysis. An Autobiographical Study*, the Penguin Freud Library, Vol. 15, Penguin, 191.

observing beautiful Italian women Freud – Silberstein, 15 April 1876, cited in Ronald W. Clark (1980), *Freud: The Man and the Cause*, Jonathan Cape: London, 40.

'terrible blue eyes' Sigmund Freud (1900/1991), *Sigmund Freud. 4. The Interpretation of Dreams*, the Penguin Freud Library, Vol. 4, Penguin, 550.

he was arrested Ernest Jones (1953–7/1977), *The Life and Work of Sigmund Freud*, edited and abridged by Lionel Trilling and Steven Marcus, Penguin, 71.

'The turning point came . . .' Sigmund Freud (1925/1993), *Sigmund Freud. 15. Historical and Expository Works on Psychoanalysis. An Autobiographical Study*, the Penguin Freud Library, Vol. 15, Penguin, 192.

peeling an apple Ernest Jones (1953–7/1977), *The Life and Work of Sigmund Freud*, edited and abridged by Lionel Trilling and Steven Marcus, Penguin, 112.

sent her a copy of his favourite Charles Dickens novel Ibid, 113.

a slightly delirious letter Freud – Martha Bernays, 19 June 1882, in Sigmund Freud (1961), *Letters of Sigmund Freud 1873–1939*, edited by Ernst L. Freud, translated by Tania and James Stern, Hogarth Press, 25–7.

carrying an engagement ring in a matchbox https://www.freud.org.uk/2019/05/20/sigmund-freuds-wedding-ring/

'*The Development of the Hero*' Freud – Martha Bernays, 28 April 1882, in Sigmund Freud (1961), *Letters of Sigmund Freud 1873–1939*, edited by Ernst L. Freud, translated by Tania and James Stern, Hogarth Press, 151–3.

Chapter 2: Love and Madness

expressed his frustration Freud – Minna Bernays, 21 February 1883, in Sigmund Freud (1961), *Letters of Sigmund Freud 1873–1939*, edited by Ernst L. Freud, translated by Tania and James Stern, Hogarth Press, 52–4.

'*It is well known . . . even among civilized peoples*' Sigmund Freud (1913/2005), *Totem and Taboo: Some correspondences between the psychical lives of savages and neurotics*, the New Penguin Freud, in *On Murder, Mourning and Melancholia*, general editor Adam Phillips, translated by Shaun Whiteside, with an introduction by Maud Ellmann, Penguin: London, 16.

'*through so many common features . . . precious to him*' Ibid, 17.

'*Outside there is fog and drizzle*' Freud – Martha Bernays, 27 June 1882, in Sigmund Freud (1961), *Letters of Sigmund Freud 1873–1939*, edited by Ernst L. Freud, translated by Tania and James Stern, Hogarth Press, 28.

'*people around me think I am computing my analysis*' Ibid, 28.

'*two-thirds of chemistry . . . same with life*' Ibid, 28.

her daughter intervened Ernest Jones (1953–7/1977), *The Life and Work of Sigmund Freud*, edited and abridged by Lionel Trilling and Steven Marcus, Penguin, 108.

Wahle declared that if Freud failed to make Martha happy Ibid, 117.

he would settle the affair finally Ibid, 120.

*he wanted to '*destroy the whole world*'* Ibid, 119.

'*going aside to pull up your stockings*' Cited by Ernest Jones (1953–7/1977) in *The Life and Work of Sigmund Freud*, edited and abridged by Lionel Trilling and Steven Marcus, Penguin, 129.

weren't enough gas lamps Ronald W. Clark (1980), *Freud: The Man and the Cause*, Jonathan Cape: London, 54.

'*light and exhilarated*' Sigmund Freud, 'Über Coca', p. 11, cited in Ronald W. Clark (1980), *Freud: The Man and the Cause*, Jonathan Cape: London, 59.

'*Woe to you, my Princess . . .* ' Freud – Martha Bernays, 2 June 1884, cited in Ronald W. Clark (1980), *Freud: The Man and the Cause*, Jonathan Cape: London, 59.

until the end of the century Frederick Crews (2017), *Freud: The Making of an Illusion*, Profile, 70.

employed only pretty housemaids Ronald W. Clark (1980), *Freud: The Man and the Cause*, Jonathan Cape: London, 65.

an ulterior motive George Makari (2008/2010), *Revolution in the Mind: The Creation of Psychoanalysis*, Duckworth, 26.

arranged his earnings into piles Christopher G. Goetz, Michel Bonduelle and Toby Gelfand (1995), *Charcot: Constructing Neurology*, 151.

pet monkey Ibid, 271.

a few days being a tourist Freud – Minna Bernays, 19 October 1885, in Sigmund Freud (1961), *Letters of Sigmund Freud 1873–1939*, edited by Ernst L. Freud, translated by Tania and James Stern, Hogarth Press, 182–6.

'disgraceful pigeon-hole boxes . . . behind the curtain' Ibid, 183.

'Elegant ladies walk here . . . carriages drawn by goats' Ibid, 184.

He was impressed . . . far too loud. Ibid, 186.

Eventually he would discover 'Chocolat Marquis' . . . 'that you shall have' Ibid, 200 (Letter: Freud – Minna Bernays, 3 December 1885).

he found Parisian women to be very ugly Louis Breger (2000), *Freud: Darkness in the Midst of Vision*, John Wiley & Sons, 75.

his first impression of Charcot Freud – Martha Bernays, 21 October 1885, in Sigmund Freud (1961), *Letters of Sigmund Freud 1873–1939*, edited by Ernst L. Freud, translated by Tania and James Stern, Hogarth Press, 187.

'He sat down . . . he took in everything' Ibid, 187.

'I gave my card to the Chef *. . . asked where I was'* Ibid, 187.

'a worldly priest . . . good living' Ibid, 187.

trimmed in the French style Freud – Martha Bernays, 20 January 1886, in Sigmund Freud (1961), *Letters of Sigmund Freud 1873–1939*, edited by Ernst L. Freud, translated by Tania and James Stern, Hogarth Press, 207.

'a small dose of cocaine' Ibid, 207.

'smoked like a chimney' Ibid, 208.

Charcot's 'buxom' daughter Ibid, 209.

a tricky moment when Gilles de la Tourette Freud – Martha Bernays, 2 February 1886, in Sigmund Freud (1961), *Letters of Sigmund Freud 1873–1939*, edited by Ernst L. Freud, translated by Tania and James Stern, Hogarth Press, 216.

'looked quite attractive' Ibid, 216.

'showed no interest in my first outline of the subject' Sigmund Freud (1925/1993), *Sigmund Freud. 15. Historical and Expository Works on Psychoanalysis. An Autobiographical Study*, the Penguin Freud Library, Vol. 15, Penguin, 202.

'Napoleon head' See A. Lubimoff (1894), *Le Professeur Charcot*, translated by L. Rostopchine, Paris.

On returning to Vienna, Freud announced Ernest Jones (1953–7/1977), *The Life and Work of Sigmund Freud*, edited and abridged by Lionel Trilling and Steven Marcus, Penguin, 142.

over 1,000 florins Ronald W. Clark (1980), *Freud: The Man and the Cause*, Jonathan Cape: London, 87.

'We continually play at war' Freud – Josef Breuer, 1 September 1886, in Sigmund Freud (1961), *Letters of Sigmund Freud 1873–1939*, edited by Ernst L. Freud, translated by Tania and James Stern, Hogarth Press, 231.

'my value written on my collar' Ibid, 232.

'ice-cream, newspapers and good pastry' Ibid, 232.

tutored by Martha's Orthodox uncle Ronald W. Clark (1980), *Freud: The Man and the Cause*, Jonathan Cape: London, 88.

On the table were napkin rings . . . roast goose and compote Undated/unattributed guide to the Vienna Freud Museum, in *Freud, Berggasse 19: The Origin of Psychoanalysis*, edited by Monika Pessler and Daniela Finzi with a foreword by Siri Hustvedt, Hatje Cantz, 64.

House of Atonement Ronald W. Clark (1980), *Freud: The Man and the Cause*, Jonathan Cape: London, 89.

she must abandon all Jewish ritual Ibid, 89.

he didn't have enough chairs Ibid, 89.

In 1928, Fliess's widow sold Freud's letters Frank J. Sulloway (1979/1980), *Freud: Biologist of the Mind*, Fontana: Great Britain, 136–7.

In due course, the letters were packaged . . . heavily mined Mai Wegener (undated guide to the Vienna Freud Museum), 'On Freud's Project of 1895', in *Freud, Berggasse 19: The Origin of Psychoanalysis*, edited by Monika Pessler and Daniela Finzi with a foreword by Siri Hustvedt, Hatje Cantz, 99.

Perhaps he'd destroyed them, or lost them Frank J. Sulloway (1979/1980), *Freud: Biologist of the Mind*, Fontana: Great Britain, 137.

They have been described as 'a farrago of nonsense' Ronald W. Clark (1980), *Freud: The Man and the Cause*, Jonathan Cape: London, 96.

'downright silly' Raymond E. Fancher (1973), *Psychoanalytic Psychology: The Development of Freud's Thought*, W. W. Norton & Company, 26.

Darwin, for example, had commented Frank J. Sulloway (1979/1980), *Freud: Biologist of the Mind*, Fontana: Great Britain, 170.

Fliess seems to have anticipated . . . Hermann Knaus Max Schur (1972), *Freud: Living and Dying*, International Universities Press Inc.: New York, footnote on p. 85.

impressed by his breadth of knowledge Frank J. Sulloway (1979/1980), *Freud: Biologist of the Mind*, Fontana: Great Britain, 135.

His letters contain affectionate salutations Frederick Crews (2017), *Freud: The Making of an Illusion*, Profile, 422.

homoerotic Frank J. Sulloway (1979/1980), *Freud: Biologist of the Mind*, Fontana: Great Britain, 232.

Chapter 3: Hysteria

Aristocrats close to the Emperor . . . Schönbrunnerdeutsch Nicholas Parsons (2009), *Vienna: A Cultural History*, Oxford University Press, 188.

holding his whip Martin Freud (1957), *Glory Reflected: Sigmund Freud – Man and Father*, Angus and Robertson, 29.

Any Habsburg subject . . . *apply for an audience* Ingrid Haslinger and Katrin Unterreiner (2000), *The Residence of Empress Elisabeth: Imperial Apartments, Sisi Museum, Imperial Silver Collection*, translated by Ingrid Haslinger and Sophie Kidd, Schloss Schönbrunn Kultur-und Betriebsges m.b.H.: Vienna, 43.

'And dress correctly!' Martin Freud (1957), *Glory Reflected: Sigmund Freud – Man and Father*, Angus and Robertson, 30.

In 1885, he had to attend an oral examination wearing a top hat Ronald W. Clark (1980), *Freud: The Man and the Cause*, Jonathan Cape: London, 64.

black ties from Hamburg Freud – Martha Bernays, 20 January 1886, in Sigmund Freud (1961), *Letters of Sigmund Freud 1873–1939*, edited by Ernst L. Freud, translated by Tania and James Stern, Hogarth Press, 207.

'and English soles' Freud – Martha Bernays, 21 October 1885, in Sigmund Freud (1961), *Letters of Sigmund Freud 1873–1939*, edited by Ernst L. Freud, translated by Tania and James Stern, Hogarth Press, 188.

'he could go in a redingote' Freud – Martha Bernays, 20 January 1886, in Sigmund Freud (1961), *Letters of Sigmund Freud 1873–1939*, edited by Ernst L. Freud, translated by Tania and James Stern, Hogarth Press, 207.

'This happened when I was six years old' Martin Freud (1957), *Glory Reflected: Sigmund Freud – Man and Father*, Angus and Robertson, 25.

visited the barber every day Sigmund Freud (1897/1977), *The Origins of Psychoanalysis: Letters to Wilhelm Fliess*, with an introductory essay by Steven Marcus, Basic Books, 171.

Arriving at a patient's house . . . *professional suicide* Martin Freud (1957), *Glory Reflected: Sigmund Freud – Man and Father*, Angus and Robertson, 24.

elimination of Jews from the medical profession Dennis B. Klein (1981), *Jewish Origins of the Psychoanalytic Movement*, Praeger Publishers, 11.

'no choice, but to band together' Joseph Wortis (1963), *Fragments of an Analysis with Freud*, Indianapolis: Bobbs-Merrill. NB: Comment made in 1935 interview with Wortis.

He referred educated, affluent patients . . . *their own patients* Frederick Crews (2017), *Freud: The Making of an Illusion*, Profile, 259.

'Almost simultaneously with her birth . . . *medical profession'* Freud – Emmeline and Minna Bernays, 21 October 1887, in Sigmund Freud (1961), *Letters of Sigmund Freud 1873–1939*, edited by Ernst L. Freud, translated by Tania and James Stern, Hogarth Press, 236.

He had translated the British philosopher John Stuart Mill into German Ernest Jones

(1953–7/1977), *The Life and Work of Sigmund Freud*, edited and abridged by Lionel Trilling and Steven Marcus, Penguin, 71.

he had discovered . . . gold chloride solution Frederick Crews (2017), *Freud: The Making of an Illusion*, Profile, 58–9.

'an assembly of psychiatrists and several colleagues . . . attract the many' Freud – Martha Bernays, 14 February 1884, in Sigmund Freud (1961), *Letters of Sigmund Freud 1873–1939*, edited by Ernst L. Freud, translated by Tania and James Stern, Hogarth Press, 114.

He also accepted a part-time appointment . . . Kassowitz Institute Henri Ellenberger (1970/1994), *The Discovery of the Unconscious: the history and evolution of dynamic psychiatry*, Fontana Press, London, 437.

His association with this clinic would last for ten years Carl E. Schorske (1961/1981), *Fin-de-Siècle Vienna: Politics and Culture*, Vintage Books: New York, 184.

a leading authority on paediatric cerebral paralyses Frank J. Sulloway (1979/1980), *Freud: Biologist of the Mind*, Fontana: Great Britain, 16–7.

and made major contributions to the extant literature Ernest Jones (1953–7/1977), *The Life and Work of Sigmund Freud*, edited and abridged by Lionel Trilling and Steven Marcus, Penguin, 198–9.

the first Freudian book Siegfried Bernfield (1944), 'Freud's earliest theories and the school of Helmholtz', *The Psychoanalytic Quarterly*, 13, 341–62 (see p. 357).

'Every large city [is] filled with nerve-specialists' Elaine Showalter (1985/1987), *The Female Malady: Women, Madness and English Culture, 1830–1980*, Virago Press: London, 121.

Hippocrates believed that hysteria Michael H. Stone (1997/1998), *Healing the Mind: A History of Psychiatry from Antiquity to the Present*, Pimlico: London, 11.

Clitorectomy was offered as a treatment until the 1860s Isaac Baker Brown (1866), *On the Curability of Certain Forms of Insanity: epilepsy, catalepsy and hysteria in females*, Robert Hardwicke: London. See https://archive.org/details/oncurabilitycer00browgoog

Charcot was fully aware . . . 'no signs of effeminacy' Christopher G. Goetz, Michel Bonduelle and Toby Gelfand (1995), *Charcot: Constructing Neurology*, 203.

up to 50 per cent . . . no 'medical' explanation Todd M. Edwards, Anthony Stern, David D. Clarke, Gabriel Ivbijaro and L. Michelle Kasney (2010), 'The treatment of patients with medically unexplained symptoms in primary care: a review of the literature', *Mental Health in Family Medicine*, Dec, 7 (4): 209–21. See https://www.ncbi.nlm.nih.gov/pmc/articles/PMC3083260/

after visiting Nancy to perfect his 'hypnotic technique' Sigmund Freud (1925/1993), *Sigmund Freud. 15. Historical and Expository Works on Psychoanalysis. An Autobiographical Study*, the Penguin Freud Library, Vol. 15, Penguin, 200.

Breuer 'objected vehemently' Ibid, 204.

Breuer had been called . . . on Liechtensteinstrasse Melinda Given Guttmann (2001), *The Enigma of Anna O: A biography of Bertha Pappenheim*, Moyer Bell: Wickford, Rhode Island & London, 26.

every day for eighteen months The period of time over which Breuer visited Anna O is reported variously as eighteen months, nearly two years (by Guttmann, p. 70) or over two years (by Breger, p. 121).

she spoke these words in English Sigmund Freud and Joseph Breuer (1895/2004), *Studies in Hysteria*, introduction by Rachel Bowlby, translated by Nicola Luckhurst, Penguin Classics, London, xi.

'hysterical phenomena disappeared . . . under hypnosis' Ibid, 38–9.

'mental balance . . . complete health' Joseph Breuer and Sigmund Freud (1895/1991), *Studies in Hysteria*, translated by James and Alix Strachey, edited by Angela Richards, 95.

her last hospital admission was in June 1887 Melinda Given Guttmann (2001), *The Enigma of Anna O: A biography of Bertha Pappenheim*, Moyer Bell: Wickford, Rhode Island & London, 96.

'the symbolic circle or cipher of feminine sexual mystery' Elaine Showalter (1985/1987), *The Female Malady: Women, Madness and English Culture, 1830–1980*, Virago Press: London, 155.

'Dr. B's child is coming' Freud – Zweig, 2 June 1932, in Sigmund Freud (1961), *Letters of Sigmund Freud 1873–1939*, edited by Ernst L. Freud, translated by Tania and James Stern, Hogarth Press, 409.

'held in his hand the key . . . but he let it drop' Ibid, 409.

'the element of sexuality was remarkably undeveloped' Sigmund Freud and Joseph Breuer (1895/2004), *Studies in Hysteria*, introduction by Rachel Bowlby, translated by Nicola Luckhurst, Penguin Classics, London, 25.

salacious rumours . . . circulated among physicians Melinda Given Guttmann (2001), *The Enigma of Anna O: A biography of Bertha Pappenheim*, Moyer Bell: Wickford, Rhode Island & London, 72.

Breuer was impressed . . . 'imaginative gifts' Sigmund Freud and Joseph Breuer (1895/2004), *Studies in Hysteria*, introduction by Rachel Bowlby, translated by Nicola Luckhurst, Penguin Classics: London, 25.

'accomplished more . . . than any previous observation' Sigmund Freud, (1925/1993), *Sigmund Freud. 15. Historical and Expository Works on Psychoanalysis. An Autobiographical Study*, the Penguin Freud Library, Vol. 15, Penguin, 202.

He did, however, develop a new way . . . Hippolyte Bernheim Chrisfried Tögel (undated guide to the Vienna Freud Museum), 'Sigmund Freud's Path to Psychoanalysis: A Biographical Sketch', in *Freud, Berggasse 19: The Origin of Psychoanalysis*, edited by Monika Pessler and Daniela Finzi with a foreword by Siri Hustvedt, Hatje Cantz, 54.

'Keep still – don't say anything – don't touch me!' Sigmund Freud and Joseph Breuer (1895/2004), *Studies in Hysteria*, introduction by Rachel Bowlby, translated by Nicola Luckhurst, Penguin Classics: London, 52.

'I am led to suspect that this intense woman . . . ' Ibid, 95.

having failed to account . . . 'more thoroughly' Ibid, 93.

'*She was in good spirits . . . health had been maintained*' Ibid, 122.

Researchers have since identified . . . on the Rax Mikkel Borch-Jacobsen (2011/2021), *Freud's Patients: A Book of Lives*, Reaktion Books: London, 83.

'*Are you a doctor, sir?*' Sigmund Freud and Joseph Breuer (1895/2004), *Studies in Hysteria*, introduction by Rachel Bowlby, translated by Nicola Luckhurst, Penguin Classics: London, 128.

She got married in 1895 . . . lived a happy life Mikkel Borch-Jacobsen (2011/2021), *Freud's Patients: A Book of Lives*, Reaktion Books: London, 87.

'*I couldn't help thinking that it was as if she were being tickled . . .* ' Sigmund Freud and Joseph Breuer (1895/2004), *Studies in Hysteria*, introduction by Rachel Bowlby, translated by Nicola Luckhurst, Penguin Classics: London, 141.

'*Now he is free again and I can become his wife*' Ibid, 160.

he gave her opportunities . . . 'accumulating for a long time' Ibid, 161.

she continued to experience leg pain . . . for the rest of her life Frederick Crews (2017), *Freud: The Making of an Illusion*, Profile, 316.

'*[Freud] was just a young, bearded nerve specialist . . . that wasn't really so*' Mikkel Borch-Jacobsen (2011/2021), *Freud's Patients: A Book of Lives*, Reaktion Books: London, 81.

'*negative aspects*' Sigmund Freud and Joseph Breuer (1895/2004), *Studies in Hysteria*, introduction by Rachel Bowlby, translated by Nicola Luckhurst, Penguin Classics: London, 267.

'*hysterical misery into common unhappiness*' Ibid, 306.

'*interpretations and conjectures do not always coincide*'. Ibid, 2.

'*shrank from recognizing the sexual aetiology of the neuroses*' Sigmund Freud (1925/1993), *Sigmund Freud. 15. Historical and Expository Works on Psychoanalysis. An Autobiographical Study*, the Penguin Freud Library, Vol. 15, Penguin, 209.

the 'most powerful source' of the neuroses Sigmund Freud and Joseph Breuer (1895/2004), *Studies in Hysteria*, introduction by Rachel Bowlby, translated by Nicola Luckhurst, Penguin Classics: London, 203.

'*I do not believe that I am exaggerating . . . in the marital bed*' Ibid, 246.

They also had differences of opinion . . . treatment length Louis Breger (2000), *Freud: Darkness in the Midst of Vision*, John Wiley & Sons, 119–21.

the mere sight of Breuer . . . a chance encounter Frank J. Sulloway (1979/1980), *Freud: Biologist of the Mind*, Fontana: Great Britain, 99.

'*excavating a buried city*' Sigmund Freud and Joseph Breuer (1895/2004), *Studies in Hysteria*, introduction by Rachel Bowlby, translated by Nicola Luckhurst, Penguin Classics: London, 143.

'*May 1, 1889 . . .* ' Ibid, 51.

'*the serious stamp of science*' Ibid, 164.

'*the story of the patient's suffering and the symptoms of their illness*' Ibid, 165.

Alfred von Berger ... wrote a glowing review Henri Ellenberger (1970/1994), *The Discovery of the Unconscious: the history and evolution of dynamic psychiatry*, Fontana Press: London, 773.

'*We dimly conceive the idea ...* ' Ernest Jones (1953–7/1977), *The Life and Work of Sigmund Freud*, edited and abridged by Lionel Trilling and Steven Marcus, Penguin, 224.

being discussed by writers such as Hermann Bahr and Hugo von Hofmannsthal Henri Ellenberger (1970/1994), *The Discovery of the Unconscious: the history and evolution of dynamic psychiatry*, Fontana Press: London, 773.

Eight hundred copies ... only 626 had been sold Ernest Jones (1953–7/1977), *The Life and Work of Sigmund Freud*, edited and abridged by Lionel Trilling and Steven Marcus, Penguin, 224.

In 1924, Freud wrote ... severe criticism Sigmund Freud (1925/1993), *Sigmund Freud. 15. Historical and Expository Works on Psychoanalysis. An Autobiographical Study*, the Penguin Freud Library, Vol. 15, Penguin, 206. NB: the *Autobiographical Study* was written in 1924 and published in 1925.

'*For more than ten years ...* ' Ibid, 231.

The eminent Swiss psychiatrist Eugen Bleuler ... in recent years Henri Ellenberger (1970/1994), *The Discovery of the Unconscious: the history and evolution of dynamic psychiatry*, Fontana Press: London, 772.

In 1893, his name was included in a Viennese Who's Who Ibid, 444.

Chapter 4: Dark Glamour

When his engagement ... was announced in the Wiener Zeitung Brigitte Hamann (1982/1986), *The Reluctant Empress: A Biography of Empress Elisabeth of Austria*, Ullstein IP: Berlin, 21.

Her grandfather was a feeble-minded 'cripple' ... after a brawl Ibid, 21.

Her bridal trousseau ... every conceivable occasion Ibid, 30–2.

A famous portrait of Sisi ... diamond stars See *The Empress Elisabeth of Austria* (1865), artist: Franz Xavier Winterhalter.

Even after having four children ... twenty inches Sabine Wieber (2012), 'Vienna's Most Fashionable Neurasthenic: Empress Sisi and the Cult of Size Zero', in *Journeys into Madness: Mapping Mental Illness in the Austro-Hungarian Empire*, edited by Gemma Blackshaw and Sabine Wieber, Berghahn Books: Oxford, 97.

eating nothing but oranges (and occasionally ice flavoured with violet) Ibid, 98.

Her hair had to be combed ... morning till night Ibid, 96.

like a vampire countess, she remained youthful by drinking blood Ibid, 98 and 107 (footnote 24).

described the Empress as resembling 'a creature somewhere between snake and bird' Ibid, 97.

she had an anchor tattooed on her shoulder – like a 'common' sailor Ibid, 103.

requested introductions to Arab snake charmers, conjurors and soothsayers Brigitte Hamann (1982/1986), *The Reluctant Empress: A Biography of Empress Elisabeth of Austria*, Ullstein IP: Berlin, 354.

When the imperial yacht . . . tied to a chair on deck Ibid, 356.

Contemporary posters . . . sunlit uplands in the distance Nicola Imrie and Leslie Topp (2009), 'Modernity follows madness? Viennese architecture for mental illness and nervous disorders', in *Madness and Modernity: Mental Illness and the Visual Arts in Vienna 1900*, edited by Gemma Blackshaw and Leslie Topp, Lund Humphries in association with the Wellcome Collection, Surrey: UK, see p. 90 for colour plate reproduction.

Freud informed his patient . . . 'treated only poor people' Frederick Crews (2017), *Freud: The Making of an Illusion*, Profile, 263.

It has been estimated that three quarters of his patients were wealthy Ibid, 263.

Moser's body was disinterred . . . Fanny's name was cleared Ronald W. Clark (1980), *Freud: The Man and the Cause*, Jonathan Cape: London, 132.

'Her fear of strangers . . . persecutions of her family' Sigmund Freud and Joseph Breuer (1895/2004), *Studies in Hysteria*, introduction by Rachel Bowlby, translated by Nicola Luckhurst, Penguin Classics: London, 82.

Later in life . . . substantial part of her fortune Mikkel Borch-Jacobsen (2011/2021), *Freud's Patients: A Book of Lives*, Reaktion Books: London, 60.

She died in 1925 . . . heinously fleeced Ibid, 61.

he was unable to expand upon her case details due to 'personal circumstances' Sigmund Freud and Joseph Breuer (1895/2004), *Studies in Hysteria*, introduction by Rachel Bowlby, translated by Nicola Luckhurst, Penguin Classics: London, 101.

He provides only a sketchy account . . . 'took a variety of different forms' Ibid, 102.

A professional chess player . . . an unsociable hour Frederick Crews (2017), *Freud: The Making of an Illusion*, Profile, 281–2.

Fine fabrics were a passion Mikkel Borch-Jacobsen (2011/2021), *Freud's Patients: A Book of Lives*, Reaktion Books: London, 35.

When staying at her family villa . . . delivered every morning from the city Frederick Crews (2017), *Freud: The Making of an Illusion*, Profile, 282.

Anna visited 'slimming spas' . . . caviar and champagne Ibid, 282.

'a beautiful and clever girl of eighteen' Sigmund Freud (1920/1990), *The Psychogenesis of a Case of Homosexuality in a Woman*, in *Sigmund Freud: Case Histories II*, the Penguin Freud Library, Vol. 9, edited and translated from the German under the general editorship of James Strachey, the present volume compiled and edited by Angela Richards, 371.

a scandalous affair with a nude dancer Mikkel Borch-Jacobsen (2011/2021), *Freud's Patients: A Book of Lives*, Reaktion Books: London, 212.

spent time in a cell . . . trying to poison him. Ines Rieder and Diana Voigt (2000/2019), *The Story of Sidonie C. Freud's famous 'Case of female homosexuality'*, translated by Jill Hannum and Ines Rieder, Helena History Press, Nevada: USA, 69

She is hiding a crooked finger Anne-Marie O'Conner (2012/2015), *The Lady in Gold: The Extraordinary Tale of Gustav Klimt's Masterpiece, Portrait of Adele Bloch-Bauer*, Vintage Books: New York, 58.

In reality, she was moody . . . nebulous ailments Ibid, 68–9.

entertained a former chancellor . . . Café Central Ibid, 68.

Art historians have interpreted its overt sexuality as incriminating evidence Ibid, 52.

He saw in Klimt's Judith . . . *'silk petticoats'* Ibid, 52.

Viennese slang for the vagina was 'jewellery box' Sigmund Freud (1905/2006), *Fragment of an Analysis of Hysteria (Dora)*, in Sigmund Freud, *The Psychology of Love*, translated by Shaun Whiteside with an introduction by Jeri Johnson, Penguin Classics: London, 60.

The journalist and author Ludwig Hevesi . . . 'bejewelled lust' Anne-Marie O'Conner (2012/2015), *The Lady in Gold: The Extraordinary Tale of Gustav Klimt's Masterpiece, Portrait of Adele Bloch-Bauer*, Vintage Books: New York, 58.

'Truth is fire; and to tell the truth means to glow and burn' Ibid, 26.

The shapes on her dress . . . the ovals represent eggs Eric R. Kandel (2012), *The Age of Insight: The Quest to Understand the Unconscious in Art, Mind, and Brain from Vienna 1900 to the Present*, Random House, 4.

The inspiration for Adele's portrait . . . Empress Theodora Anne-Marie O'Conner (2012/2015), *The Lady in Gold: The Extraordinary Tale of Gustav Klimt's Masterpiece, Portrait of Adele Bloch-Bauer*, Vintage Books: New York, 45–6.

'Send for Emilie' Ibid, 64.

the boutique employed eighty seamstresses Susanna Partsch (2006), *Gustav Klimt: Painter of Women*, translated by Michael Robinson, Prestel: Berlin, 22.

The walls were lacquered white . . . without getting cold feet Ibid, 22.

Furniture was geometric . . . stylistically consistent Ibid, 22.

Stefan Zweig described the process in his autobiography Stefan Zweig (1943/undated), *The World of Yesterday*, introduction by Harry Zohn, University of Nebraska Press: Lincoln and London, 72.

A future husband had no idea . . . revealed on the wedding night Ibid, 72–3.

The idea of modelling garments in a landscape was an innovation Susanna Partsch (2006), *Gustav Klimt: Painter of Women*, translated by Michael Robinson, Prestel: Berlin, 45.

his symbol for the vulva Frank Whitford (1990/2001), *Klimt*, Thames and Hudson World of Art: London, 140.

'Much too much,' Klimt replied, Anne-Marie O'Conner (2012/2015), *The Lady in Gold: The Extraordinary Tale of Gustav Klimt's Masterpiece, Portrait of Adele Bloch-Bauer*, Vintage Books: New York, 62.

Schiele was given permission . . . to attend his clinic Eric R. Kandel (2012), *The Age of Insight: The Quest to Understand the Unconscious in Art, Mind, and Brain from Vienna 1900 to the Present*, Random House, 173.

the painter and stage performer Erwin Osen . . . Am Steinhof asylum Luke Heighton (2012), 'Reason Dazzled: Klimt, Krakauer and the eyes of the Medusa', in *Journeys into Madness: Mapping Mental Illness in the Austro-Hungarian Empire*, edited by Gemma Blackshaw and Sabine Wieber, Berghahn Books: Oxford, 147.

'an attempt at full disclosure . . . Interpretation of Dreams' Eric R. Kandel (2012), *The Age of Insight: The Quest to Understand the Unconscious in Art, Mind, and Brain from Vienna 1900 to the Present*, Random House, 166.

'When nervousness becomes completely liberated . . . return to art' Hermann Bahr (1891), *The Overcoming of Naturalism*, in *The Vienna Coffeehouse Wits 1890–1938* (1993/1995), translated, edited and with an introduction by Harold B. Segel, Purdue University Press: West Lafayette, Indiana, 51.

He stresses his thesis . . . 'nerves, nerves, nerves' Ibid, 51.

where he unwisely bribed . . . large quantities of alcohol Peter Altenberg (1919), 'Afternoon Visit', in *The Vienna Coffeehouse Wits 1890–1938* (1993/1995), translated, edited and with an introduction by Harold B. Segel, Purdue University Press: West Lafayette, Indiana, 162.

'Fool of Vienna' Gemma Blackshaw (2009), 'Gustav Jagerspracher, Portrait of Peter Altenberg, 1909', in *Madness and Modernity: Mental Illness and the Visual Arts in Vienna 1900*, edited by Gemma Blackshaw and Leslie Topp, Lund Humphries in association with the Wellcome Collection, Surrey: UK, 67.

'Gentlemen, I am very ill' Peter Altenberg (1911), 'Episode', in *The Vienna Coffeehouse Wits 1890–1938* (1993/1995), translated, edited and with an introduction by Harold B. Segel, Purdue University Press: West Lafayette, Indiana, 135.

He lived in hotels . . . when practised by women Peter Altenberg (1906), from 'Prodromos', in ibid, 154–5.

'aristocratically delicate hands' of a female cashier Peter Altenberg (1911), from 'So Should it Always Be', in ibid, 132.

'For a long time now . . . minute details' Peter Altenberg (1909), 'Little Things', in ibid, 126.

Igor Stravinsky . . . the twentieth century Ibid, 121.

Chapter 5: The Royal Road

The Bedouin asked, 'Are the monkeys all right?' Martin Freud (1957), *Glory Reflected: Sigmund Freud – Man and Father*, Angus and Robertson, 25.

'several steps at a stride' / 'Very inadequately dressed . . . ' Sigmund Freud (1899/2006),

Interpreting Dreams, translated by J. A. Underwood with an introduction by John Forrester, Penguin Books: London, 254.

When he shook hands, he pulled people closer A. Kardiner (1977), *My Analysis With Freud: Reminiscences*, W. W. Norton & Company: New York, 18.

People felt that he could read their minds Martin Freud (1957), *Glory Reflected: Sigmund Freud – Man and Father*, Angus and Robertson, 39.

he once dreamed . . . The Marriage of Figaro Sigmund Freud (1899/2006), *Interpreting Dreams*, translated by J. A. Underwood with an introduction by John Forrester, Penguin Books: London, 223.

He thought that it looked like Martha Michael Molnar (undated guide to the Vienna Freud Museum), 'Freud as a Collector', in *Freud, Berggasse 19: The Origin of Psychoanalysis*, edited by Monika Pessler and Daniela Finzi with a foreword by Siri Hustvedt, Hatje Cantz, 253–4.

Further purchases . . . were made in December 1896 Lynn Gamwell (1989), 'The Origin of Freud's Antiquities Collection', in *Sigmund Freud and Art: His Personal Collection of Antiquities*, edited by Lynn Gamwell and Richard Wells, the Freud Museum, 25.

he 'threw aside all his professional worries . . . laughter and contentment' Martin Freud (1957), *Glory Reflected: Sigmund Freud – Man and Father*, Angus and Robertson, 27.

the first indication . . . appears in a letter to Minna Sigmund Freud and Minna Bernays (2005), *Briefwechsel 1882–1938*, letter dated 27 April 1893, edited by Albrecht Hirschmüller, Tübingen: Diskord, 237.

She liked music . . . pet names Undated/unattributed guide to the Vienna Freud Museum, in *Freud, Berggasse 19: The Origin of Psychoanalysis*, edited by Monika Pessler and Daniela Finzi with a foreword by Siri Hustvedt, Hatje Cantz, 161.

Minna developed the unusual habit . . . tolerated without complaint Andrew Nagorski (2022), *Saving Freud: A life in Vienna and an escape to freedom in London*, Icon Books: London, 106–7.

Gossip about the nature . . . in an interview John Kerr (1993/2012), *A Dangerous Method*, Atlantic Books: London, 135–6.

Less compelling evidence . . . Freud's contemporaneous writing Ibid, 138.

in 2006, an 1898 Swiss hotel register . . . husband and wife Frederick Crews (2017), *Freud: The Making of an Illusion*, Profile, 571.

'The "double standard" . . . possible to comply with them' Sigmund Freud (1908/2002), *'Civilized' Sexual Morality and Modern Nervous Illness*, in *Civilization and Its Discontents*, the New Penguin Freud, General Editor Adam Phillips, translated by David McLintock with an introduction by Leo Bersani, Penguin: London, 96.

'requirements of civilization' Ibid, 97.

'sense of duty' Ibid, 97.

'the cure for nervous illness . . . might be 'medicinal' Sigmund Freud (1921/1991), *'Civilized'*

Sexual Morality and Modern Nervous Illness, in *Civilization, Society and Religion*, Vol. 12, the Penguin Freud Library, translated by James Strachey, edited by James Strachey and Albert Dickson, Penguin Books: Harmondsworth, 47.

He suspected that Jacob . . . several younger sisters Frederick Crews (2017), *Freud: The Making of an Illusion*, Profile, 520.

He had found that making eye contact . . . would-be seductresses Ronald W. Clark (1980), *Freud: The Man and the Cause*, Jonathan Cape: London, 119.

The couch that Freud used in Berggasse 19 . . . by a patient Élisabeth Roudinesco (2014/2016), *Freud: In his Time and Ours*, translated by Catherine Porter, Harvard University Press: London, 70.

Between 1892 and 1895 . . . 'free association' Ernest Jones (1953–7/1977), *The Life and Work of Sigmund Freud*, edited and abridged by Lionel Trilling and Steven Marcus, Penguin: Harmondsworth, 214.

The English translation . . . somewhat misleading Frank J. Sulloway (1979/1980), *Freud: Biologist of the Mind*, Fontana: Great Britain, 95.

Freud claimed that he had discovered free association by 'following an obscure intuition' Ernest Jones (1953–7/1977), *The Life and Work of Sigmund Freud*, edited and abridged by Lionel Trilling and Steven Marcus, Penguin: Harmondsworth, 218.

Börne had suggested . . . 'without any falsification or hypocrisy' Ibid, 218–9.

He famously called dream interpretation . . . the life of the mind' Sigmund Freud (1899/2006), *Interpreting Dreams*, translated by J. A. Underwood with an introduction by John Forrester, Penguin Books: London, 623.

when he was a young man, he kept a dream diary Frank J. Sulloway (1979/1980), *Freud: Biologist of the Mind*, Fontana: Great Britain, 321.

Freud's first complete analysis . . . 24 July 1895 Élisabeth Roudinesco (2014/2016), *Freud: In his Time and Ours*, translated by Catherine Porter, Harvard University Press: London, 93.

'not entirely well' Sigmund Freud (1899/2006), *Interpreting Dreams*, translated by J. A. Underwood with an introduction by John Forrester, Penguin Books: London, 118.

Irma (in the dream) . . . painful periods Mikkel Borch-Jacobsen (2011/2021), *Freud's Patients: A Book of Lives*, Reaktion Books: London, 88–9.

Emma remained in Freud's care . . . first student of psychoanalysis Ibid, 92.

Freud asked Fliess . . . a marble tablet Sigmund Freud (1897/1977), *The Origins of Psychoanalysis: Letters to Wilhelm Fliess*, with an introductory essay by Steven Marcus, Basic Books: New York, 322.

Many years later, while dining with Ernest Jones . . . discussed again Ernest Jones (1953–7/1977), *The Life and Work of Sigmund Freud*, edited and abridged by Lionel Trilling and Steven Marcus, Penguin: Harmondsworth, 301.

German readers in Freud's day . . . Die Traumdeutung Frank J. Sulloway (1979/1980), Freud: Biologist of the Mind, Fontana: Great Britain, 323.

'Father, can't you see I'm burning?' Sigmund Freud (1899/2006), Interpreting Dreams, translated by J. A. Underwood with an introduction by John Forrester, Penguin Books: London, 526.

Freud suggested that the manifest content . . . fully understood Ibid, 293.

However, it should be noted . . . the importance of symbols' Ibid, 373.

'The dream of having sexual intercourse . . . outraged amazement' Ibid, 277.

'None of the findings of psychoanalytic research . . . ' Sigmund Freud (1899/1991), Sigmund Freud. 4. The Interpretation of Dreams, the Penguin Freud Library, Vol. 4, translated by James Strachey, edited by James Strachey assisted by Alan Tyson, the present volume edited by Angela Richards, Penguin: Harmondsworth, 365.

A ladder is ascended . . . quickly 'back down' again Sigmund Freud (1899/2006), Interpreting Dreams, translated by J. A. Underwood with an introduction by John Forrester, Penguin Books: London, 414.

For example, in 1893 . . . 'serious, intelligible message' James Sully (1893), 'The Dream as a Revelation', Fortnightly Review 59: 354–65.

In 1861, the psychiatrist Wilhelm Griesinger . . . 'the imaginary fulfilment of wishes' Frank J. Sulloway (1979/1980), Freud: Biologist of the Mind, Fontana: Great Britain, 324.

'one can try reversing specific portions . . . immediately clear' Sigmund Freud (1899/2006), Interpreting Dreams, translated by J. A. Underwood with an introduction by John Forrester, Penguin Books: London, 342.

The philosopher Ludwig Wittgenstein . . . logically inconsistent Ludwig Wittgenstein (1966), Lectures and Conversations on Aesthetics, Psychology and Religious Belief, Oxford: Basil Blackwell, 43–4.

'dreaming is a unique form . . . unexplored weak associations' Antonio Zadra and Robert Stickgold (2021), When Brains Dream: Exploring the science and mystery of sleep, W. W. Norton & Company: New York, 108.

'novel, creative, insightful . . . in our dreams' Ibid, 109.

'dreams are froth' Sigmund Freud (1899/2006), Interpreting Dreams, translated by J. A. Underwood with an introduction by John Forrester, Penguin Books: London, 144.

During the 1970s new physiological evidence . . . Freud's theory was undermined Mark Solms and Oliver Turnbull (2002/2018), The Brain and the Inner World: An Introduction to the Neuroscience of Subjective Experience, foreword by Oliver Sacks, Routledge: London and New York, 190.

These relate to visual perception . . . autobiographical memory and emotion Matthew Walker (2017), Why We Sleep: The New Science of Sleep and Dreams, Allen Lane, an imprint of Penguin Books, 195.

At the same time, regions controlling rational thought are deactivated Ibid, 195–6.

Subjects taught how to play . . . after the onset of sleep R. Stickgold, A. Malia, D. Maguire, D. Roddenberry and M. O'Conner (2000), 'Replaying the Game: Hypnagogic Images in Normals and Amnesics', *Science* 290: 350–3, 353.

real incidents are probably not repeated . . . marked emotional continuities Matthew Walker (2017), *Why We Sleep: The New Science of Sleep and Dreams*, Allen Lane, an imprint of Penguin Books, 204.

Sleep researchers have found convincing evidence for a dream rebound effect Daniel M. Wegner, Richard M. Wenzlaff and Megan Kozak (2004), 'Dream Rebound: the return of suppressed thoughts in dreams', *Psychological Science*, April: 15(4): 232–6.

Zadra and Stickgold . . . but only rarely Antonio Zadra and Robert Stickgold (2021), *When Brains Dream: Exploring the science and mystery of sleep*, W. W. Norton & Company: New York, xi.

Solms concludes: 'It is also the circuit that drives dreaming' Mark Solms (2021), *The Hidden Spring: A Journey to the Source of Consciousness*, Profile Books: London, 28.

Animals rehearse predatory behaviours in dreams Anthony Stevens (1995/1996), *Private Myths: Dreams and Dreaming*, Penguin: Harmondsworth, 93.

humans have a very high incidence . . . escape from an aggressor Michael Schredl (2010), 'Nightmare Frequency and Nightmare Topics in a Representative German Sample', *European Archives of Psychiatry and Clinical Neuroscience* 260, no. 8, 565.

Men have elevated levels of testosterone . . . ejaculate while dreaming Rafel Luboshitzky, Paula Herer, Michael Levi, Zila Shen-Orr and Peretz Lavie (1999), 'Relationship Between Rapid Eye Movement Sleep and Testosterone Secretion on Normal Men', *Journal of Andrology*, Vol. 20, No. 6, 731–7.

Galen described erections during sleep in the first century Antonio Zadra and Robert Stickgold (2021), *When Brains Dream: Exploring the science and mystery of sleep*, W. W. Norton & Company: New York, 43.

Women exhibit clitoral swelling . . . nocturnal orgasms Barbara L. Wells (1986), 'Predictors of Female Nocturnal Orgasms: a multivariate analysis', *Journal of Sex Research*, Vol. 22, Issue 4, 421–37.

'The Freudian proposition . . . critics would acknowledge' Sidarta Ribeiro (2019/2021), *The Oracle of Night: The History and Science of Dreams*, Penguin Random House UK, 253.

'The involvement of the dopaminergic reward system . . . is testable, definitely' Ibid, 254.

When asked which book . . . Freud nominated two Ernest Jones (1953–7/1977), *The Life and Work of Sigmund Freud*, edited and abridged by Lionel Trilling and Steven Marcus, Penguin: Harmondsworth, 299.

Where else could you find . . . blue stones? Sigmund Freud (1899/2006), *Interpreting Dreams*, translated by J. A. Underwood with an introduction by John Forrester, Penguin Books: London, 216.

He had developed a boil . . . 'as large as an apple' Ibid, 246.

he still put in 'a hard day's work' Ibid, 246.

his mother asleep . . . laid upon a bed Ibid, 598.

One of Freud's patients . . . a childhood memory Ibid, 213.

In her summer holidays . . . reflected in the surface Ibid, 409.

'we are then promised a glimpse . . . the accidents of life' Ibid, 565.

By analysing dreams . . . man's mind' Ibid, 565.

'Every dream . . . linking it to the unknown' Ibid, 135, footnote 14.

'Seldom,' Jones laments . . . no echo whatever' Ernest Jones (1953–7/1977), *The Life and Work of Sigmund Freud*, edited and abridged by Lionel Trilling and Steven Marcus, Penguin: Harmondsworth, 307–8.

Busy colleagues . . . his weighty tome Frank J. Sulloway (1979/1980), *Freud: Biologist of the Mind*, Fontana: Great Britain, 349.

'That's what my fiction is about . . . whatever the cost' J. G. Ballard (1992), interview originally published in *Hardcore 8*, in *Extreme Metaphors: Interviews with J. G. Ballard 1967–2008* (2012), edited by Simon Sellers and Dan O'Hara, Fourth Estate: London, 270.

'Well, I've always thought of Freud really as a great novelist' Ibid, 270.

Chapter 6: Dora

Freud's response was measured NB: The introductory dialogue between Freud and Ida Bauer is my own merging of two translations: the standard translation by Alix and James Strachey and the more recent translation by Shaun Whiteside. I chose to do this because I felt that by combining the two translations I could produce a blend that, although not being absolutely consistent with the German original, flows more naturally. Sigmund Freud (1905/2006), *Fragment of an Analysis of Hysteria (Dora)*, in Sigmund Freud, *The Psychology of Love*, translated by Shaun Whiteside with an introduction by Jeri Johnson, Penguin Classics, London; Sigmund Freud (1905/1990), *Fragment of an Analysis of Hysteria (Dora)*, translated by James and Alix Strachey, in *Sigmund Freud: Case Histories*, the Penguin Freud Library, Vol. 8, edited by Angela Richards and Albert Dickson.

Ida's true identity, which remained a well-kept secret until 1978 Arnold A. Rogow (1978), 'A Further Footnote to Freud's "Fragment of an Analysis of a Case of Hysteria"', *Journal of the American Psychoanalytic Association*, 26: 331–56.

As usual, Freud is completely aware of the literary qualities of his material Sigmund Freud (1905/2006), *Fragment of an Analysis of Hysteria (Dora)*, in Sigmund Freud, *The Psychology of Love*, translated by Shaun Whiteside with an introduction by Jeri Johnson, Penguin Classics: London, 47.

'vigorous anti-syphilitic cure' Ibid, 14–5.

'housewife's psychosis' Sigmund Freud (1905/1990), *Fragment of an Analysis of Hysteria*

(Dora), translated by James and Alix Strachey, in *Sigmund Freud: Case Histories*, the Penguin Freud Library, Vol. 8, edited by Angela Richards and Albert Dickson, 49.

'to be nice to him' because 'he got nothing from his wife' Sigmund Freud (1905/2006), *Fragment of an Analysis of Hysteria (Dora)*, in Sigmund Freud, *The Psychology of Love*, translated by Shaun Whiteside with an introduction by Jeri Johnson, Penguin Classics: London, 91.

Hans made 'a declaration of love' Ibid, 19'

'You know I get nothing from my wife' Ibid, 87.

Soon after, Hans was promoted . . . to the capital Mikkel Borch-Jacobsen (2011/2021), *Freud's Patients: A Book of Lives*, Reaktion Books: London, 113.

'In view of my own state of health . . . friendship and sympathy' Sigmund Freud (1905/2006), *Fragment of an Analysis of Hysteria (Dora)*, in Sigmund Freud, *The Psychology of Love*, translated by Shaun Whiteside with an introduction by Jeri Johnson, Penguin Classics: London, 19–20.

'delightful whiteness' Ibid, 49.

'He that has eyes to see . . . ' Sigmund Freud (1905/1990), *Fragment of an Analysis of Hysteria (Dora)*, translated by James and Alix Strachey, in *Sigmund Freud: Case Histories*, the Penguin Freud Library, Vol. 8, edited by Angela Richards and Albert Dickson, 114.

'played with it as she lay there . . . and so on' Sigmund Freud (1905/2006), *Fragment of an Analysis of Hysteria (Dora)*, in Sigmund Freud, *The Psychology of Love*, translated by Shaun Whiteside with an introduction by Jeri Johnson, Penguin Classics: London, 66.

'the task of making conscious . . . possible to accomplish' Sigmund Freud (1905/1990), *Fragment of an Analysis of Hysteria (Dora)*, translated by James and Alix Strachey, in *Sigmund Freud: Case Histories*, the Penguin Freud Library, Vol. 8, edited by Angela Richards and Albert Dickson, 114.

'Women take a special pride in the state of their genitals' Sigmund Freud (1905/2006), *Fragment of an Analysis of Hysteria (Dora)*, in Sigmund Freud, *The Psychology of Love*, translated by Shaun Whiteside with an introduction by Jeri Johnson, Penguin Classics: London, 71.

'I knew you'd say that' Ibid, 60.

'A very common way . . . arising from the repressed' Ibid, 80, footnote 11.

'One can talk to girls and women . . . ' Ibid, 37.

'the whole world would be a bordello, and marriage and the family unthinkable' Peter Gay (2002), *Schnitzler's Century: The Making of Middle-Class Culture 1815–1914*, W. W. Norton & Company: New York/London, 82.

At precisely the same time . . . on a regular basis Ibid, 86–7.

'If I finally bring together all these clues . . . ' Sigmund Freud (1905/2006), *Fragment of an Analysis of Hysteria (Dora)*, in Sigmund Freud, *The Psychology of Love*, translated by Shaun Whiteside with an introduction by Jeri Johnson, Penguin Classics: London, 64.

He wrote, she 'left me . . . abandoned by him' Ibid, 106.

'I can only repeat it over and over again . . . ' Ibid, 102.

'Often she would go to a bring-your-own-food dinner party . . . satisfy her lust' Procopius (1966/2007), *The Secret History*, translated by G. A. Williamson and Peter Sarris with an introduction and notes by Peter Sarris, Penguin Books: London, 38.

he is reputed to have been a 'playboy' Mikkel Borch-Jacobsen (2011/2021), *Freud's Patients: A Book of Lives*, Reaktion Books: London, 115.

Ida met Ernst on a tennis court at an expensive holiday resort Ibid, 115.

They married on 6 December 1903 . . . in central Vienna Hannah S. Decker (1991/1992), *Freud, Dora, and Vienna 1900*, The Free Press: A Division of Macmillan Inc.: New York, 151–2.

Filipp gave Ernst a job . . . hear his own music Ibid, 152.

Eventually he became a conductor . . . Georg Solti Mikkel Borch-Jacobsen (2011/2021), *Freud's Patients: A Book of Lives*, Reaktion Books: London, 115–6.

He spent a great deal of time . . . significant debts Ibid, 116.

In 1923, Ida's otolaryngologist . . . one of Freud's disciples NB: This date is sometimes reported as 1922; for clarification, see *The Histography of Psychoanalysis* by Paul Roazen.

Men were 'selfish, demanding, and ungiving' Frederick Crews (2017), *Freud: The Making of an Illusion*, Profile, 613.

She dismissed the suggestion . . . finished her game Mikkel Borch-Jacobsen (2011/2021), *Freud's Patients: A Book of Lives*, Reaktion Books: London, 117.

Ida was taken to a public building . . . her ransacked apartment Hannah S. Decker (1991/1992), *Freud, Dora, and Vienna 1900*, The Free Press: A Division of Macmillan Inc.: New York, 188.

'a famous case in psychiatric literature' Mikkel Borch-Jacobsen (2011/2021), *Freud's Patients: A Book of Lives*, Reaktion Books: London, 116.

She has inspired novels and an opera See, for example, *The Fig Eater* (2000), a novel by Jody Shields, and *Dora* (2002), an opera composed by Melissa Shiflett (with libretto by Nancy Fales Garrett).

Chapter 7: Secrets and Lies

He told his friends and relatives . . . murderous intent Janet Malcom (1984/1986), *In the Freud Archives*, Flamingo, 133, footnote.

Without mentioning Fliess by name . . . scientific ideas' Sigmund Freud (1901/2002), *The Psychopathology of Everyday Life*, translated by Anthea Bell with an introduction by Paul Keegan, the New Penguin Freud, Penguin Books: London, 138.

'Over the next week . . . remind me of it' Ibid, 138.

A contrite Freud . . . write a book together Frank J. Sulloway (1979/1980), *Freud: Biologist of the Mind*, Fontana: Great Britain, 223.

Fliess refused ... their correspondence ceased Ibid, 223.

Besides, the whole incident was 'a trivial matter' Ibid, 226.

Reflecting on Freud's behaviour ... 'completely straightforward' Ernest Jones (1953–7/1977), *The Life and Work of Sigmund Freud*, edited and abridged by Lionel Trilling and Steven Marcus, Penguin, 272.

In 1912, Freud was lunching at the Park Hotel ... Franz Riklin Ibid, 274.

'How sweet it must be to die' Ibid, 274.

'There is some piece of unruly homosexual feeling at the root of the matter' Ibid, 274.

'it was necessary for me to love you in order to enrich my life' Frederick Crews (2017), *Freud: The Making of an Illusion*, Profile, 422.

'No one can replace ... demands' Ibid, 422.

He described Mr Y ... psychological questions' Sigmund Freud (1899/2003), *Screen Memories*, translated by David McLintock with an introduction by Hugh Haughton, in *The Uncanny*, the New Penguin Freud, Penguin Books: London, 9.

In the 1940s ... Mr Y never existed Frederick Crews (2017), *Freud: The Making of an Illusion*, Profile, 527.

'The scene seems to me fairly inconsequential ... ' Sigmund Freud (1899/2003), *Screen Memories*, translated by David McLintock with an introduction by Hugh Haughton, in *The Uncanny*, the New Penguin Freud, Penguin Books: London, 10.

The two boys 'fall upon her' and 'snatch her flowers' Ibid, 11.

'to take away a girl's flower – that means to deflower her' Ibid, 15.

His paper contained nothing ... Freud suggests Frank J. Sulloway (1979/1980), *Freud: Biologist of the Mind*, Fontana: Great Britain, 38 & 41.

only a year and a half after his male hysteria presentation he was elected as a member Ibid, 42.

He was suffering from facial neuralgia ... for a consultation Peter Gay (1988), *Freud: A Life for Our Time*, J. M. Dent and Sons: London, 160; and Élisabeth Roudinesco (2014/2016), *Freud: In his Time and Ours*, translated by Catherine Porter, Harvard University Press: London, 111.

In Introductory Lectures on Psychoanalysis ... with an analogy' Sigmund Freud (1916–17/1987), Lecture 3: *Parapraxes (continued)*, in *Introductory Lectures on Psychoanalysis*, translated by James Strachey, edited by James Strachey and Angela Richards, the Pelican Freud Library, Vol. 1, Penguin: Harmondsworth, 72.

Ordinary English terms ... the German original Bruno Bettelheim (1983/1991), *Freud and Man's Soul*, Penguin Books: London, 86–7.

Freud's favourite example ... a president of the Austrian Parliament Sigmund Freud (1901/2002), *The Psychopathology of Everyday Life*, translated by Anthea Bell with an introduction by Paul Keegan, the New Penguin Freud, Penguin Books: London, 58.

'The study of the female genitals ... experiments ... ' Ibid, 77.

Posing as a bacteriologist . . . a biological institute Sigmund Freud, (1916–17/1987), Lecture 4: *Parapraxes (concluded)*, in *Introductory Lectures on Psychoanalysis*, translated by James Strachey, edited by James Strachey and Angela Richards, the Pelican Freud Library, Vol. 1, Penguin: Harmondsworth, 97.

'My inkstand was a slab of Untersberg marble . . . ' Sigmund Freud (1901/2002), *The Psychopathology of Everyday Life*, translated by Anthea Bell with an introduction by Paul Keegan, the New Penguin Freud, Penguin Books: London, 160.

'You ought to have a prettier one' Ibid, 160.

'Did I perhaps conclude from my sister's words . . . ' Ibid, 160.

'I don't like the look of your wife' Sigmund Freud (1901/2002), *The Joke and its Relation to the Unconscious*, translated by Joyce Crick with an introduction by John Carey, the New Penguin Freud, Penguin Books: London, 30.

But he is only scowling because he didn't like being photographed Peter Gay (1988), *Freud: A Life for Our Time*, J. M. Dent and Sons: London, 159.

When lecturing . . . witty remarks Ibid, 159.

Woody Allen, in his film Annie Hall *. . . accept him as a member.* See http://www.16-9.dk/2007-02/side11_inenglish.htm

During the First World War . . . to cheer himself up Peter Gay (1988), *Freud: A Life for Our Time*, J. M. Dent and Sons: London, 371.

'somewhat greyer and a good deal thinner than before the war' Ernest Jones (1953–7/1977), *The Life and Work of Sigmund Freud*, edited and abridged by Lionel Trilling and Steven Marcus, Penguin, 489.

'I told him I believed the first half,' said Freud to Jones Ibid, 489.

There may have been thousands . . . the First World War Brigitte Hamann (1999/2000), *Hitler's Vienna: A Dictator's Apprenticeship*, translated from the German by Thomas Thornton, Oxford University Press: Oxford, 152.

Chapter 8: Cabal

Freud's assertion that he was 'completely isolated' . . . is largely untrue Sigmund Freud (1925/1993), *Sigmund Freud. 15. Historical and Expository Works on Psychoanalysis. An Autobiographical Study*, the Penguin Freud Library, Vol. 15, Penguin, 231.

'a beautiful heroic era' Ernest Jones (1953–7/1977), *The Life and Work of Sigmund Freud*, edited and abridged by Lionel Trilling and Steven Marcus, Penguin, 311.

The time had come to 'break with strict virtue . . . just like other mortals' Peter Gay (1988), *Freud: A Life for Our Time*, J. M. Dent and Sons, 137.

Baroness Marie von Ferstel (one of his patients and a distant relative of his wife) Mikkel Borch-Jacobsen (2011/2021), *Freud's Patients: A Book of Lives*, Reaktion Books: London, 105.

On 22 February 1902 . . . Professor Freud Peter Gay (1988), *Freud: A Life for Our Time*, J. M. Dent and Sons, 137.

The minister is said to have been irritated by the Baroness's interference Mikkel Borch-Jacobsen (2011/2021), *Freud's Patients: A Book of Lives*, Reaktion Books: London, 107.

The two men probably met . . . one of his patients George Makari (2008/2010), *Revolution in the Mind: The Creation of Psychoanalysis*, Duckworth, 131.

to debate the psychological significance of smoking Ronald W. Clark (1980), *Freud: The Man and the Cause*, Jonathan Cape: London, 213.

Every member of the society was provided with an ashtray Peter Gay (1988), *Freud: A Life for Our Time*, J. M. Dent and Sons, 169.

Martin Freud recalled . . . able to breathe Ibid, 110.

Thus, the writer Hermann Bahr . . . early attendees Ronald W. Clark (1980), *Freud: The Man and the Cause*, Jonathan Cape: London, 214.

'A spark seemed to jump . . . like a revelation' Peter Gay (1988), *Freud: A Life for Our Time*, J. M. Dent and Sons, 174.

'There was an atmosphere of the foundation of a religion in that room . . . ' Ibid, 174.

'brothers of an order' Frederick Crews (2017), *Freud: The Making of an Illusion*, Profile, 623.

Occasionally he would take one of his 'idols' . . . channelling spirits David Bakan (1958/1965), *Sigmund Freud and the Jewish Mystical Tradition*, Schocken Books: New York, 134–5.

As Freud read the quotation . . . he became agitated Ernest Jones (1953–7/1977), *The Life and Work of Sigmund Freud*, edited and abridged by Lionel Trilling and Steven Marcus, Penguin, 316.

Jones naively attributed Freud's reticence to his exceptional modesty Ibid, 316.

An enterprising individual . . . the coming apocalypse Larry Wolff (1988/1989), *Postcards from the End of the World: An Investigation into the Mind of Fin-de-Siècle Vienna*, Collins, London, 3.

A third possibility . . . 1867 Law on Associations Mag. Dr Otto Fritsch, Grand Lodge of Austria, personal communication to author dated 17.12.2004.

Von List and his companions . . . 'hook cross' Guido von List (1908/1988), *The Secret of the Runes*, edited, introduced and translated by Stephen E. Flowers, Destiny Books: Rochester, Vermont, 3–4.

Von List established a 'magical' lodge . . . High Arman's Revelation Brigitte Hamann (1999/2000), *Hitler's Vienna: A Dictator's Apprenticeship*, translated from the German by Thomas Thornton, Oxford University Press: Oxford, 209.

It represented the 'invincible' . . . people to victory Ibid, 209.

the deliverance of the German peoples . . . the 'master man' Ibid, 216.

'Theozoology, or the News about the Little Sodom Monkeys and the Electron of the Gods' Author's translation of title. Ibid, 217.

Lanz was particularly preoccupied . . . pan-German paradise Ibid, 218.

He borrowed a copy . . . and carried it around with him for weeks Ibid, 210.

He also visited Lanz to scrounge some missed issues of Ostara Ibid, 221.

One of the speeches he delivered . . . The Names of Germania's Tribes Ibid, 211.

'Through purity to unity' Ibid, 242.

'Handsome Karl' Richard S. Geehr (1990) *Karl Lueger: Mayor of Fin-de-Siècle Vienna*, Wayne State University Press: Detroit, 210.

'It is I who decide who is a Jew' William M. Johnston (1972/1983), *The Austrian Mind: An Intellectual and Social History 1848–1938*, University of California Press, 66.

Himmler authorised expeditions to Iceland in order to find pagan relics Peter Levenda (1995/2006), *Unholy Alliance: A History of Nazi Involvement with the Occult*, with a foreword by Norman Mailer, Continuum: New York, 189.

In the medieval castle of Wewelsburg . . . Teutonic ancestors Ibid, 176.

The SS emblem was a double rune Chris McNab (2013), *Hitler's Elite: The SS 1939–45*, Osprey, 82.

as soon as Hitler transplanted . . . 'threatened civilization' William M. Johnston (1972/1983), *The Austrian Mind: An Intellectual and Social History 1848–1938*, University of California Press, 332.

'We failed to see the writing on the wall . . . ' Élisabeth Roudinesco (2014/2016), *Freud: In his Time and Ours*, translated by Catherine Porter, Harvard University Press: London, 112

Orthodox sects would have been assembling . . . God and community Harry Freedman (2019), *Kabbalah: Secrecy, Scandal and the Soul*, Bloomsbury Continuum: London, 193.

Freud's ancestry was Orthodox . . . volumes of Kabbalah David Bakan (1958/1965), *Sigmund Freud and the Jewish Mystical Tradition*, Schocken Books: New York, xx.

Chapter 9: Uncomfortable Truths

'I stand for an infinitely freer sexual life' Freud – Putnam, 19 August 1915, in Sigmund Freud (1961), *Letters of Sigmund Freud 1873–1939*, edited by Ernst L. Freud, translated by Tania and James Stern, Hogarth Press, 314.

'Surely he never wrote his "sexy" books' Lisa Appignanesi and John Forrester (1992/2000), *Freud's Women*, Penguin: Harmondsworth, 52.

psychoanalysis wasn't a science, but rather a matter for the police Peter Gay (1988), *Freud: A Life for Our Time*, J. M. Dent and Sons: London, 195.

a 'form of pornography' Ibid, 61; and Ronald W. Clark (1980), *Freud: The Man and the Cause*, Jonathan Cape: London, 51.

He planned to offer him $100,000 for 'a really great love story' Stephen Farber and Marc Green (1993), *Hollywood on the Couch: A candid look at the overheated love affair between psychiatrists and moviemakers*, William Morrow and Company Inc.: New York, 21.

'FREUD REBUFFS GOLDWYN . . . ' Peter Gay (1988), *Freud: A Life for Our Time*, J. M. Dent and Sons: London, 454.

'I do not intend to see Mr. Goldwyn' Stephen Farber and Marc Green (1993), *Hollywood on the Couch: A candid look at the overheated love affair between psychiatrists and moviemakers*, William Morrow and Company Inc.: New York, 21.

The manuscripts were placed . . . how he felt on the day Ernest Jones (1953–7/1977), *The Life and Work of Sigmund Freud*, edited and abridged by Lionel Trilling and Steven Marcus, Penguin: Harmondsworth, 315.

'fantastic and ridiculous' / *'shockingly wicked'* / *'universally unpopular'* / *'Odium' was 'brought down on him'* / *'evil'* Ibid, 315.

'filled his cup of turpitude' Ibid, 316.

Almost all of the ideas . . . preceding twenty-five years Frank J. Sulloway (1979/1980), *Freud: Biologist of the Mind*, Fontana: Great Britain, 277.

As early as 1867 . . . Henry Maudsley asserted Peter Gay (1988), *Freud: A Life for Our Time*, J. M. Dent and Sons: London, 144.

An illustration in an 1879 publication . . . shows a very young girl Frank J. Sulloway (1979/1980), *Freud: Biologist of the Mind*, Fontana: Great Britain, 278.

In 1926, Freud wrote . . . the name of "Triebe"' Sigmund Freud (1926/1993), *Sigmund Freud. 15. Historical and Expository Works on Psychoanalysis. The Question of Lay Analysis*, the Penguin Freud Library, Vol. 15, Penguin, 300.

Somewhat mischievously . . . modern languages' Ibid, 300.

'If we see a child . . . sexual satisfaction in later life' Sigmund Freud (1905/2006), *Three Essays on Sexual Theory*, in Sigmund Freud, *The Psychology of Love*, translated by Shaun Whiteside with an introduction by Jeri Johnson, Penguin Classics: London, 160.

He supposed that unconscious memories . . . tendencies in adulthood Sigmund Freud (1938/1993), *Sigmund Freud. 15. Historical and Expository Works on Psychoanalysis. An Outline of Psychoanalysis*, the Penguin Freud Library, Vol. 15, Penguin, 385.

the 'Oedipus complex' (a term that he did not use before 1910) Sigmund Freud (1910/1991), *A Special Type of Choice of Object Made by Men (Contributions to the Psychology of Love I)*, in *On Sexuality*, the Penguin Freud Library, Vol. 7, translated by James Strachey, edited by James Strachey and Angela Richards, Penguin Books: Harmondsworth, 238.

They have not endowed their daughters . . . genital mutilation Sigmund Freud (1931/2006), *On Female Sexuality*, in Sigmund Freud, *The Psychology of Love*, translated by Shaun Whiteside with an introduction by Jeri Johnson, Penguin Classics: London, 317.

The Oedipus complex is now the Electra complex . . . rejected by Freud Ibid, 312.

'serious abnormalities' Sigmund Freud (1905/2006), *Three Essays on Sexual Theory*, in Sigmund Freud, *The Psychology of Love*, translated by Shaun Whiteside with an introduction by Jeri Johnson, Penguin Classics: London, 137.

The only perversion that Freud condemns in his three essays is paedophilia Ibid, 127.

Freud's defence of homosexuals is expansive Ibid, 121.

Homosexual men frequently seek cross-dressing partners Ibid, 125.

heterosexual men frequently engage in anal sex Ibid, 126.

Although books on child rearing . . . behaviour rather than experience Graham Richards (1996), *Putting Psychology in its Place: An introduction from a critical historical perspective*, Routledge: London, 131.

'We know less about the sexual life of little girls than of boys' Sigmund Freud (1926/1993), *Sigmund Freud. 15. Historical and Expository Works on Psychoanalysis. The Question of Lay Analysis*, the Penguin Freud Library, Vol. 15, Penguin, 312–13.

'a dark continent' for psychology Ibid, 313.

his suggestion that a clitoral orgasm . . . a vaginal orgasm Sigmund Freud (1905/2006), *Three Essays on Sexual Theory*, in Sigmund Freud, *The Psychology of Love*, translated by Shaun Whiteside with an introduction by Jeri Johnson, Penguin Classics: London, 198.

'just as a piece of kindling can be used to light the harder logs' Ibid, 198–9.

When Freud stopped at coffee houses . . . changing hands under tables Stefan Zweig (1943/undated), *The World of Yesterday*, introduction by Harry Zohn, University of Nebraska Press: Lincoln and London, 76.

when he visited urinals . . . explicit drawings Ibid, 75.

'for sale at every hour . . . or a newspaper' Ibid, 83.

Nannies, for example, calmed children by stroking their genitals Sigmund Freud (1905/2006), *Three Essays on Sexual Theory*, in Sigmund Freud, *The Psychology of Love*, translated by Shaun Whiteside with an introduction by Jeri Johnson, Penguin Classics: London, 182.

When the sons of bourgeois families . . . the art of seduction

Stefan Zweig (1943/undated), *The World of Yesterday*, introduction by Harry Zohn, University of Nebraska Press: Lincoln and London, 81.

Around 75 per cent of medical students lost their virginity with a sex worker George Makari (2008/2010), *Revolution in the Mind: The Creation of Psychoanalysis*, Duckworth, 142.

It has been alleged . . . when he married Lisa Appignanesi and John Forrester (1992/2000), *Freud's Women*, Penguin: Harmondsworth, 340.

Viennese young men . . . sexual favours Stefan Zweig (1943/undated), *The World of Yesterday*, introduction by Harry Zohn, University of Nebraska Press: Lincoln and London, 82.

Ernest Jones believed . . . an underlying neurosis Frederick Crews (2017), *Freud: The Making of an Illusion*, Profile, London, 45.

He suggested that ardour cools . . . his own experience Ibid, 419.

In a letter he wrote to Fliess . . .'impotence' Peter Gay (1988), *Freud: A Life for Our Time*, J. M. Dent and Sons: London, 162.

'successful coitus Wednesday morning' Ibid, 163.

the rejuvenating effect . . . in her company Freud – Guilbert, 24 October 1938, in Sigmund Freud (1961), *Letters of Sigmund Freud 1873–1939*, edited by Ernst L. Freud, translated by Tania and James Stern, Hogarth Press, 448.

Devotion to one man was, for her, spiritual bondage Stanley A. Leavy (1964), *The Freud Journal of Lou Andreas-Salomé*, translated and with an introduction by Stanley A. Leavy, Basic Books: USA, 8.

'I have never known a more gifted and understanding creature' Ibid, 8.

he frequently escorted her ... a degree of 'romantic' enchantment Élisabeth Roudinesco (2014/2016), *Freud: In his Time and Ours*, translated by Catherine Porter, Harvard University Press: London, 307.

'If I saw you in a brothel, you are certainly not the one I would pick' Andrew Nagorski (2022), *Saving Freud: A life in Vienna and an escape to freedom in London*, Icon Books: London, 148.

'in a short, brutal gesture' Ibid, 149.

She was close to suicide when Freud accepted her as a patient Élisabeth Roudinesco (2014/2016), *Freud: In his Time and Ours*, translated by Catherine Porter, Harvard University Press: London, 311.

she opted for a surgical procedure ... as ineffective as the first Lisa Appignanesi and John Forrester (1992/2000), *Freud's Women*, Penguin: Harmondsworth, 343.

'no prudishness whatsoever' Andrew Nagorski (2022), *Saving Freud: A life in Vienna and an escape to freedom in London*, Icon Books: London, 153.

'My dear friend,' she said, 'no, I will not disappoint you' Celia Bretin (1982), *Marie Bonaparte: A Life*, Harcourt Brace: San Diego, 7.

It seems unlikely ... John Lennon Craig Brown (2020), *One Two Three Four: The Beatles in Time*, Fourth Estate: Dublin, 29.

Chapter 10: Secession

Licences were required to produce books or sell newspapers William M. Johnston (1972/1983), *The Austrian Mind: An Intellectual and Social History 1848–1938*, University of California Press, 49.

contentious articles were frequently suppressed by the state censor Ibid, 49.

police officers interfered with publishing activities Ibid, 49.

Twenty-seven officials were needed to process a single tax payment Ibid, 48.

In 1906, an Italian worker ... 'King' Ibid, 48.

In the late 1870s ... the Constitutional Party Carl E. Schorske (1961/1981), *Fin-de-Siècle Vienna: Politics and Culture*, Vintage Books: New York, 212.

Originally they were known as Die Jungen ...'The Vienna Secession' Ibid, 213.

not just 'doctors', but 'young doctors' Sigmund Freud (1914/1993), *Sigmund Freud. 15. Historical and Expository Works on Psychoanalysis. On the History of the Psychoanalytic Movement*, the Penguin Freud Library, Vol. 15, Penguin, 82.

'Do you think it gives me such great pleasure to stand in your shadow my whole life long?' Ibid, 111.

'Difficult case ... ill for six years' Sigmund Freud and Carl Gustav Jung (1974/1991), *The Freud/Jung Letters*, preface by Alan McGlashan, introduction by William McGuire, 4J, Penguin: Harmondsworth, 46.

They imagined that they could read each other's minds John Kerr (1993/2012), *A Dangerous Method*, Atlantic Books: London, 164.

Spielrein became convinced that she was destined to bear Jung a son Ibid, 165.

'love-gods' Ibid, 165.

they saw blood on her hand and arm Ronald Hayman (1999/2002), *A Life of Jung*, Bloomsbury: London, 106.

'a large measure of friendship' Sigmund Freud and Carl Gustav Jung (1974/1991), *The Freud/Jung Letters*, preface by Alan McGlashan, introduction by William McGuire, 144J, Penguin: Harmondsworth, 150.

She had wanted to seduce him ... spreading rumours Ibid, 150.

He too had only narrowly escaped seduction Ibid, 152.

'Everyone knows ... forgive me for this' John Kerr (1993/2012), *A Dangerous Method*, Atlantic Books: London, 470.

'Freud was the first man of real importance I had encountered ... ' C. G. Jung (1961/1982), *Memories, Dreams, Reflections*, Collins Fount Paperbacks: Great Britain, 172.

Jung found Freud's face 'enormously likeable, particularly around the ears' John Kerr (1993/2012), *A Dangerous Method*, Atlantic Books: London, 171.

Binswanger wanted to marry ... take his place Ronald Hayman (1999/2002), *A Life of Jung*, Bloomsbury: London, 88.

'the large Jewish penis' John Kerr (1993/2012), *A Dangerous Method*, Atlantic Books: London, 132.

'Well, now you have seen the gang' Ibid, 134.

'Crown Prince' Sigmund Freud and Carl Gustav Jung (1974/1991), *The Freud/Jung Letters*, preface by Alan McGlashan, introduction by William McGuire, 139F, Penguin: Harmondsworth, 144.

the two men exchanged photographs Ibid, 79 & 81.

'It looks marvellous' Ibid, 95.

a crush with an undeniable 'erotic undertone' Ibid, 84.

Freud's letter to Jung ... torn apart' Ibid, 110.

'If you still love him ... hatred he deserves' Christopher Hampton (2002), *The Talking Cure*, Faber and Faber: London, 78.

'catalytic exteriorisation phenomenon' C. G. Jung (1961/1982), *Memories, Dreams, Reflections*, Collins Fount Paperbacks: Great Britain, 179.

'sheer bosh' Ibid, 179.

'spookery' Sigmund Freud and Carl Gustav Jung (1974/1991), *The Freud/Jung Letters*, preface by Alan McGlashan, introduction by William McGuire, 138J, Penguin: Harmondsworth, 143.

a 'great dream' Ibid, 143.

Freud had appeared . . . customs official John Kerr (1993/2012), *A Dangerous Method*, Atlantic Books: London, 213.

Sándor Ferenczi . . . what clothes he should bring Élisabeth Roudinesco (2014/2016), *Freud: In his Time and Ours*, translated by Catherine Porter, Harvard University Press: London, 150.

Freud said that he thought Jung's talk of corpses showed that he wanted him dead Ronald W. Clark (1980), *Freud: The Man and the Cause*, Jonathan Cape: London, 265.

a dream featuring two skulls on the floor of a cave C. G. Jung (1961/1982), *Memories, Dreams, Reflections*, Collins Fount Paperbacks: Great Britain, 183.

Jung probed Freud's private life John Kerr (1993/2012), *A Dangerous Method*, Atlantic Books: London, 267. NB: there are different versions of this story. As told, for example, by Jung to Kurt Eissler in August 1953, and as recorded by Jung in his autobiography *Memories, Dreams, Reflections*.

'But I cannot risk my authority!' C. G. Jung (1961/1982), *Memories, Dreams, Reflections*, Collins Fount Paperbacks: Great Britain, 181–2.

Yet Jung and Freud . . . argument about ambition Ronald W. Clark (1980), *Freud: The Man and the Cause*, Jonathan Cape: London, 265–6.

Freud and Ferenczi saw moving images for the first time in a cinema Ibid, 266.

Freud detested American food and he refused to drink iced water Élisabeth Roudinesco (2014/2016), *Freud: In his Time and Ours*, translated by Catherine Porter, Harvard University Press: London, 157.

'American colitis' John Kerr (1993/2012), *A Dangerous Method*, Atlantic Books: London, 235.

'plump, jolly, good natured and extremely ugly' Ronald W. Clark (1980), *Freud: The Man and the Cause*, Jonathan Cape: London, 266.

Mrs Hall, overwhelmed by heat, fanned herself by an open window Ronald Hayman (1999/2002), *A Life of Jung*, Bloomsbury: London, 114.

The Europeans were astonished by American affluence Ronald W. Clark (1980), *Freud: The Man and the Cause*, Jonathan Cape: London, 266.

The anarchist Emma Goldman . . . disruptive behaviour John Kerr (1993/2012), *A Dangerous Method*, Atlantic Books: London, 242.

Freud was unflappable . . . a helpful analogy Sigmund Freud (1910/1962), *Two Short Accounts of Psycho-Analysis. Five Lectures on Psycho-Analysis. Second Lecture*, Penguin: Harmondsworth, 50–1.

'a giant among pygmies' Emma Goldman (1931/1970), *Living My Life*, Knopf: New York, 1:455.

When a medium was produced . . . extracting a confession John Kerr (1993/2012), A Dangerous Method, Atlantic Books: London, 242.

In the evenings, Jung sang songs Élisabeth Roudinesco (2014/2016), Freud: In his Time and Ours, translated by Catherine Porter, Harvard University Press: London, 157.

Freud and Ferenczi learned how to play a board game Ronald W. Clark (1980), Freud: The Man and the Cause, Jonathan Cape: London, 275.

he kept the gift on his desk for the rest of his life Ibid, 275.

Freud and Ferenczi stayed on in Berlin, where they investigated a psychic Ibid, 276.

William James . . . just to meet him Ibid, 270.

'Oh, he thought I was crazy' A. Kardiner (1977), My Analysis With Freud: Reminiscences, W. W. Norton & Company: New York, 88.

'I confess . . . a most dangerous method' James to Théodore Flournoy, 28 September 1909, in Henry James (ed.), The Letters of William James, 2 vols, Atlantic Monthly Press: Boston, 1920, 2:327–8.

James still conceded . . . Freud and his disciples John Kerr (1993/2012), A Dangerous Method, Atlantic Books: London, 244.

'a man of great refinement' Ronald W. Clark (1980), Freud: The Man and the Cause, Jonathan Cape: London, 272.

'a gigantic mistake' Ibid, 278.

Tobacco was the only excuse for 'Columbus's misdeed' Ernest Jones (1953–7/1977), The Life and Work of Sigmund Freud, edited and abridged by Lionel Trilling and Steven Marcus, Penguin, 434.

By the 1930s . . . lax social attitudes Ronald W. Clark (1980), Freud: The Man and the Cause, Jonathan Cape: London, 279.

Three years later he reminded Freud of the incident in a letter Sigmund Freud and Carl Gustav Jung (1974/1991), The Freud/Jung Letters, preface by Alan McGlashan, introduction by William McGuire, 330J, Penguin: Harmondsworth, 286.

in 1925 . . . his subsequent relations with Freud Ibid, 286 (see footnote 101).

'Freud was placing personal authority above truth' C. G. Jung (1961/1982), Memories, Dreams, Reflections, Collins Fount Paperbacks: Great Britain, 182.

Freud accused Jung of making fun of him Sigmund Freud and Carl Gustav Jung (1974/1991), The Freud/Jung Letters, preface by Alan McGlashan, introduction by William McGuire, 334F, Penguin: Harmondsworth, 290.

Jung accused Freud . . . his own faults Ibid, 293.

'I propose that we abandon our personal relations entirely' Ibid, 295.

'My personal relationship . . . His behaviour was too bad' John Kerr (1993/2012), A Dangerous Method, Atlantic Books: London, 448.

Spielrein . . . the death instinct Ibid, 501.

In fact, her writing . . . the sex drive Sabina Spielrein (1912/1994 translation), 'Destruction as the cause of coming into being', *Journal of Analytical Psychology* 39, 155–186.

pronounced psychotic features C. G. Jung (1961/1982), *Memories, Dreams, Reflections*, Collins Fount Paperbacks: Great Britain, 213.

'Psychoanalysis will survive this loss . . . ' Sigmund Freud (1914/1993), *Sigmund Freud. 15. Historical and Expository Works on Psychoanalysis. On the History of the Psychoanalytic Movement*, the Penguin Freud Library, Vol. 15, Penguin, 128.

exposing himself to two 'mentally defective' girls on one occasion Andrew Nagorski (2022), *Saving Freud: A life in Vienna and an escape to freedom in London*, Icon Books: London, 55.

talking inappropriately about sex to a ten-year-old 'hysteric' Ibid, 57.

Jones tried to silence another 'hysteric' . . . by giving her $500 Ibid, 64.

'how much have you guessed . . . We'll tell you about it someday' Brenda Maddox (2006), *Freud's Wizard: The Enigma of Ernest Jones*, John Murray: London, 142.

'I know there is a boyish and perhaps romantic element . . . the necessities of reality' Ernest Jones (1953–7/1977), *The Life and Work of Sigmund Freud*, edited and abridged by Lionel Trilling and Steven Marcus, Penguin, 416.

They met for the first time in Vienna on 25 May 1913 George Makari (2008/2010), *Revolution in the Mind: The Creation of Psychoanalysis*, Duckworth, 284.

It had functioned 'perfectly' . . . 'a happy band of brothers' Ernest Jones (1953–7/1977), *The Life and Work of Sigmund Freud*, edited and abridged by Lionel Trilling and Steven Marcus, Penguin, 423.

Jones was rumoured . . . Jones expelled George Makari (2008/2010), *Revolution in the Mind: The Creation of Psychoanalysis*, Duckworth, 349.

Soon after, Freud stopped attending Ibid, 349-350.

Rank started to develop ideas . . . blacklisted heretic Louis Breger (2000), *Freud: Darkness in the Midst of Vision*, John Wiley & Sons, 325.

Chapter 11: Games of Love and Death

On 13 October 1899 . . . the Vienna woods Larry Wolff (1988/1989), *Postcards from the End of the World: An Investigation into the Mind of Fin-de-Siècle Vienna*, Collins: London, 9.

'I have loved you till my unhappy end' Ibid, 10.

'Murder and Suicide' Ibid, 10.

By 1900 . . . duelling was rare in most European countries Kevin McAleer (1994), *Dueling: The Cult of Honor in Fin-de-Siècle Germany*, Princeton University Press: Princeton, New Jersey, 3.

It was suggested to Schnitzler that a scar would look good on him Ibid, 149.

Duellists often wore shirts . . . sleeves rolled up Ibid, 53.

Arthur Schnitzler's friend Felix Salten fought a sabre duel in 1896 Peter Gay (2002), *Schnitzler's Century: The Making of Middle-Class Culture 1815–1914*, W. W. Norton & Company: New York/London, 102.

'stupid and bestial' Ibid, 102.

Four years earlier . . . a Viennese exhibition See https://en.wikipedia.org/wiki/ Pauline_von_Metternich.

On 23 August 1892, subscribers of the Pall Mall Magazine . . . See https://www.dailymail. co.uk/femail/article-3460930/Nobles-gone-wild-moment-Princess-Countess-took-topless-sword-fight-settle-dispute-flowers-1892-detailed-fascinating-video-duels.html

the majority of serious duels . . . the honour of a woman Kevin McAleer (1994), *Dueling: The Cult of Honor in Fin-de-Siècle Germany*, Princeton University Press: Princeton, New Jersey, 161.

A form of duel . . . the so-called American duel Ibid, 80.

Gerstl and Mathilde were 'discovered' . . . they subsequently ran away See http://www. richardgerstl.com/mathildes-letters/after-denouement

'I am afraid, that, if one discovers the reason . . . ' Arnold Schoenberg to Alois Gerstl, probably c. 7–9 November 1908; see http://www.richardgerstl.com/mathildes-letters/ post-suicide/schonberg-to-alois-gerstl-november-1908

He felt a sudden surge of patriotism . . . 'another chance' Ronald W. Clark (1980), *Freud: The Man and the Cause*, Jonathan Cape: London, 364.

'It has generally been decided not to regard you as an enemy!' Brenda Maddox (2006), *Freud's Wizard: The Enigma of Ernest Jones*, John Murray: London, 117.

'England is on the wrong side' Peter Gay (1988), *Freud: A Life for Our Time*, J. M. Dent and Sons: London, 350

'Until now they had been mutually separated . . . Habsburg subjects together' Frederic Morton (1989/2001), *Thunder at Twilight: Vienna 1913–1914*, Methuen: London, 330.

Writers such as Rainer Maria Rilke . . . were equally excited Ibid, 332–3.

'a purification, a liberation, an enormous hope' Ibid, 333.

'It is too hideous . . . knowledge of psychoanalysis' Ronald W. Clark (1980), *Freud: The Man and the Cause*, Jonathan Cape: London, 367.

'Hippic psychoanalysis' Ernest Jones (1953–7/1977), *The Life and Work of Sigmund Freud*, edited and abridged by Lionel Trilling and Steven Marcus, Penguin: Harmondsworth, 433.

Winter came . . . numb fingers Ibid, 440.

A few patients trickled back, only three Ibid, 441.

'The Habsburgs have left nothing but a pile of crap' Louis Breger (2000), *Freud: Darkness in the Midst of Vision*, John Wiley & Sons, 250.

After being detained . . . a hero's welcome Martin Freud (1957), *Glory Reflected: Sigmund Freud – Man and Father*, Angus and Robertson, 188.

'Sunday child' Élisabeth Roudinesco (2014/2016), *Freud: In his Time and Ours*, translated by Catherine Porter, Harvard University Press: London, 203 (Freud to Oskar Pfister, 27 January 1920).

'It is a brutal, absurd act of fate . . . ' Ibid, 204 (Freud to Max Halberstadt, 1 January 1920).

'Do not be concerned about me . . . ' Ernest Jones (1953–7/1977), *The Life and Work of Sigmund Freud*, edited and abridged by Lionel Trilling and Steven Marcus, Penguin, 492.

For the rest of his life . . . his watch chain Peter Gay (1988), *Freud: A Life for Our Time*, J. M. Dent and Sons: London, 392.

Recalling the event in his autobiography . . . sixteen years later Martin Freud (1957), *Glory Reflected: Sigmund Freud – Man and Father*, Angus and Robertson, 189.

Chapter 12: The Rat Man

He is twenty-nine years old . . . shorter than his doctor Patrick J. Mahony (1986), *Freud and The Rat Man*, with a foreword by Otto F. Kernberg, MD, Yale University Press: New Haven and London, 16.

'We had a pretty governess called Fräulein Rudolf . . . ' NB: I have based the dialogue in this chapter on translations by Louise Adey Huish and Strachey. All of the dialogue is derived from these texts, but I have not followed either translation precisely. Real names are given (See Patrick J. Mahony (1986)) as opposed to Freud's substitutes. As Freud's original German is partly invention, I have given myself more licence than usual in the service of clarity and ease of reading.

Ernst's first consultation with Freud was on 1 October 1907 Patrick J. Mahony (1986), *Freud and The Rat Man*, with a foreword by Otto F. Kernberg, MD, Yale University Press: New Haven and London, 16.

Ernst's case was presented . . . in Salzburg Ernest Jones (1953–7/1977), *The Life and Work of Sigmund Freud*, edited and abridged by Lionel Trilling and Steven Marcus, Penguin, 332.

He mixed up the meanings of words . . . scatological expletives Patrick J. Mahony (1986), *Freud and The Rat Man*, with a foreword by Otto F. Kernberg, MD, Yale University Press: New Haven and London, 4.

'You lamp, you towel, you plate.' Sigmund Freud (1909/2002), *Some Remarks on a Case of Obsessive-compulsive Neurosis [The 'Ratman'],* in *The 'Wolfman' and Other Cases*, translated by Louise Adey Huish with an introduction by Gillian Beer, General Editor Adam Phillips, Penguin Books: London, 163.

'This boy will either be a great man one day, or a great criminal!' Ibid, 163.

'a most excellent man' Ibid, 160.

Rosa didn't like baths . . . due to an illness Patrick J. Mahony (1986), *Freud and The Rat Man*, with a foreword by Otto F. Kernberg, MD, Yale University Press: New Haven and London, 6.

Ernst responded . . . by growing up exceedingly clean Ibid, 6.

Ernst was sexually attracted to Olga . . . among the servants Ibid, 41.

'If Olga has a baby in nine months' time . . . ' Ibid, 41.

'better loved' Sigmund Freud (1909/2002), *Some Remarks on a Case of Obsessive-compulsive Neurosis [The 'Ratman']*, in *The 'Wolfman' and Other Cases*, translated by Louise Adey Huish with an introduction by Gillian Beer, General Editor Adam Phillips, Penguin Books: London, 147.

'see something interesting' Ibid, 148.

'How could I possibly have done that?' Ibid, 148.

'folly' Ibid, 147.

'numerous little attentions' Ibid, 151.

Although, in actuality, all he did was go on a strict diet Ibid, 151.

If Heinrich were to die . . . Ernst's inheritance Ibid, 144.

'I must tell father that' . . . 'That will be my father' Ibid, 140.

Bizarrely, his lapses . . . Poetry and Truth Ibid, 162.

Between midnight and one o'clock . . . his father waiting outside Ibid, 163.

'This is a glorious feeling! . . . murder one's own father, for instance.' Patrick J. Mahony (1986), *Freud and The Rat Man*, with a foreword by Otto F. Kernberg, MD, Yale University Press: New Haven and London, 11.

He is described in his military dossier as a very competent soldier Ibid, 8.

'At this point he breaks off . . . torment him' Sigmund Freud (1909/2002), *Some Remarks on a Case of Obsessive-compulsive Neurosis [The 'Ratman']*, in *The 'Wolfman' and Other Cases*, translated by Louise Adey Huish with an introduction by Gillian Beer, General Editor Adam Phillips, Penguin Books: London, 134.

Ernst was so distressed . . . 'Captain' Patrick J. Mahony (1986), *Freud and The Rat Man*, with a foreword by Otto F. Kernberg, MD, Yale University Press: New Haven and London, 102.

'horror at the pleasure he does not even know he feels' Sigmund Freud (1909/2002), *Some Remarks on a Case of Obsessive-compulsive Neurosis [The 'Ratman']*, in *The 'Wolfman' and Other Cases*, translated by Louise Adey Huish with an introduction by Gillian Beer, General Editor Adam Phillips, Penguin Books: London, 134.

'he panics, jumps, writhes . . . torn and bleeding flesh' Octave Mirbeau (1898/2015), *The Torture Garden*, Olympia Press: Kindle edition, 111.

The Torture Garden . . . until the 1960s Élisabeth Roudinesco (2014/2016), *Freud: In his Time and Ours*, translated by Catherine Porter, Harvard University Press: London, 464 (footnote 48).

How can anybody, he reasoned, know anything about the afterlife? Sigmund Freud

(1909/2002), *Some Remarks on a Case of Obsessive-compulsive Neurosis [The 'Ratman']*, in *The 'Wolfman' and Other Cases*, translated by Louise Adey Huish with an introduction by Gillian Beer, General Editor Adam Phillips, Penguin Books: London, 136–7.

He drew Ernst's attention . . . usually well preserved Ibid, 142.

he indulged in elaborate revenge fantasies . . . begged him for mercy Ibid, 155.

On one occasion, he sexually assaulted a servant girl with kisses Patrick J. Mahony (1986), *Freud and The Rat Man*, with a foreword by Otto F. Kernberg, MD, Yale University Press: New Haven and London, 115–16.

He imagined, for example, Freud's wife performing anilingus Ibid, 117.

His most surreal fantasy . . . Freud's wife's anus Ibid, 122–3.

'Most honoured professor . . . I don't deserve any better' Sigmund Freud (1909/2002), *Some Remarks on a Case of Obsessive-compulsive Neurosis [The 'Ratman']*, in *The 'Wolfman' and Other Cases*, translated by Louise Adey Huish with an introduction by Gillian Beer, General Editor Adam Phillips, Penguin Books: London, 164.

In fact, he was putting himself beyond Freud's reach Ibid, 165.

'Let me remind anyone . . . indulges his imagination' Ibid, 177 (footnote 36).

Ernst is frequently likened to literary protagonists in stories by Dostoevsky John Kerr (1993/2012), *A Dangerous Method*, Atlantic Books: London, 183.

Schnitzler and Zweig Élisabeth Roudinesco (2014/2016), *Freud: In his Time and Ours*, translated by Catherine Porter, Harvard University Press: London, 190.

'He was hungry and was fed' Patrick J. Mahony (1986), *Freud and The Rat Man*, with a foreword by Otto F. Kernberg, MD, Yale University Press: New Haven and London, 120.

'a handful of interesting deviations' Peter Gay (1988), *Freud: A Life for Our Time*, J. M. Dent and Sons: London, 262.

'I cannot provide . . . my patient's circumstances' Sigmund Freud (1909/2002), *Some Remarks on a Case of Obsessive-compulsive Neurosis [The 'Ratman']*, in *The 'Wolfman' and Other Cases*, translated by Louise Adey Huish with an introduction by Gillian Beer, General Editor Adam Phillips, Penguin Books: London, 125.

He laments the fact that the reader is being offered 'distortions' Ibid, 125.

A few pages later, he declares that his case study is 'imperfect and incomplete' Ibid, 127.

He is supplying only 'fragments of understanding' Ibid, 127.

In Freud's mind . . . 'other investigators' Ibid, 127.

It is of some note that Freud's nemesis . . . 'momentous insights' Patrick J. Mahony (1986), *Freud and The Rat Man*, with a foreword by Otto F. Kernberg, MD, Yale University Press: New Haven and London, 213.

He praises Freud's 'graphic imagination . . . intrapsychic life' Ibid, 223.

'The patient's mental health . . . the Great War' Sigmund Freud (1909/1990), Notes Upon a Case of Obsessional Neurosis (The 'Rat Man'), in Sigmund Freud: Case Histories II, Vol. 9, the Penguin Freud Library, James Strachey and Angela Richards, Penguin: Harmondsworth, 128.

Freud fed Ernst . . . even sent Ernst a postcard Patrick J. Mahony (1986), Freud and The Rat Man, with a foreword by Otto F. Kernberg, MD, Yale University Press: New Haven and London, 116.

We can easily reposition Ernst . . . vaudevillian repartee Samuel Beckett (1955/1967), Waiting for Godot, a tragicomedy in two acts, Faber and Faber: London.

Pierre Latour . . . resisted this direction Deidre Bair (1978/90), Samuel Beckett, Vintage: London, 452.

Not only was it necessary . . . completely to the ankles Ibid, 453.

Beckett was very reluctant . . . many other changes Ibid, 476.

Chapter 13: The Architecture of the Mind

It does not 'progress' towards a goal . . . but many Stephen Jay Gould (1995/1997), 'Ladders and Cones: Constraining Evolution by Canonical Icons', in Hidden Histories of Science, edited by Robert B. Silver, Granta Books: London, 44.

His intention . . . Wilhelm Fliess for criticism Sigmund Freud (1895/1977), The Origins of Psychoanalysis: Letters to Wilhelm Fliess, with an introductory essay by Steven Marcus, Basic Books, 125.

'psychology for neurologists' Ibid, 118.

He was about to see something 'unpleasant', something he wouldn't like Ronald W. Clark (1980), Freud: The Man and the Cause, Jonathan Cape: London, 439.

A grim conversation followed . . . euthanasia Ibid, 439.

After the operation . . . 'an imbecile dwarf' Ibid, 440.

Freud described the days after Heinz Rudolf's death as 'the blackest' in his life Ibid, 441.

It was the first time that Freud had ever been seen crying Ernest Jones (1953–7/1977), The Life and Work of Sigmund Freud, edited and abridged by Lionel Trilling and Steven Marcus, Penguin: Harmondsworth, 550.

He told Ernest Jones . . . killed something inside of him, for good Ibid, 550.

'the beginning of the end' George Makari (2008/2010), Revolution in the Mind: The Creation of Psychoanalysis, Duckworth, 350.

'a very sneaky way' Ibid, 351.

In fact, the basic concept of the id . . . 'Romantic' philosophers Henri Ellenberger (1970/1994), The Discovery of the Unconscious: the history and evolution of dynamic psychiatry, Fontana Press: London, 516.

'We approach the id with analogies . . . ' Sigmund Freud (1932/1991), Lecture 31: The

Dissection of the Psychical Personality, in *New Introductory Lectures on Psychoanalysis*, Vol. 2, the Penguin Freud Library, translated by James Strachey, edited by James Strachey assisted by Angela Richards, Penguin Books: Harmondsworth, 105–6.

'*The logical laws of thought* . . . ' Ibid, 106.

'*There is nothing in the id . . . the idea of time*' Ibid, 106.

'*Wishful impulses . . . are virtually immortal*' Ibid, 106.

'*archaic inheritance*' Sigmund Freud (1899/2006), *Interpreting Dreams*, translated by J. A. Underwood with an introduction by John Forrester, Penguin Books: London, 565.

Little has changed . . . regulating social behaviour Mark Solms (2021), *The Hidden Spring: A Journey to the Source of Consciousness*, Profile Books: London, 110.

'*unassuming sketch*' Sigmund Freud (1932/1991), Lecture 31: *The Dissection of the Psychical Personality*, in *New Introductory Lectures on Psychoanalysis*, Vol. 2, the Penguin Freud Library, translated by James Strachey, edited by James Strachey assisted by Angela Richards, Penguin Books: Harmondsworth, 111.

'*a monumental contribution . . . mental activity that we have*' Eric R. Kandel (2012), *The Age of Insight: The Quest to Understand the Unconscious in Art, Mind, and Brain from Vienna 1900 to the Present*, Random House, 47.

It has been suggested . . . the ventral frontal cortex Ibid, 376.

For example, the dorso-frontal and posterior sensory cortices Ibid, 376.

The most recent candidate is the default mode network R. Carhart-Harris and K. Friston (2010), 'The default-mode, ego-functions and free-energy: a neurobiological account of Freudian ideas', *Brain* 133(4): 1265–83.

The current brain model . . . is the 'predictive brain' See Thomas Parr, Giovanni Pezzulo and Karl Friston (2022), *Active Inference: The Free Energy Principle in Mind, Brain, and Behaviour*, MIT Press: London; and Andy Clark (2016), *Surfing Uncertainty: Prediction, action and the embodied mind*, Oxford University Press: Oxford.

Since Friston published . . . in 2006 Karl J. Friston, James Kilner and Lee Harrison (2006), 'A Free Energy Principle for the Brain', *Journal of Physiology-Paris* 100 (1): 70–87.

The free energy principle . . . scientifically informed individuals Anil Seth (2021), *Being You: A New Science of Consciousness*, Faber and Faber: London, 196.

'*mathematical philosophy*' Ibid, 202.

Cohesion is accomplished . . . average energy minus entropy Mark Solms (2021), *The Hidden Spring: A Journey to the Source of Consciousness*, Profile Books: London, 171.

identify formal similarities . . . Freudian formulations R. Carhart-Harris and K. Friston (2010), 'The default-mode, ego-functions and free-energy: a neurobiological account of Freudian ideas', *Brain* 133: 1265–83.

'*psychical apparatus*' Sigmund Freud (1895/1977), *The Origins of Psychoanalysis: Letters to Wilhelm Fliess*, with an introductory essay by Steven Marcus, Basic Books, 185.

'*Freud has the best theories so far . . . to make a mind*' See https://blogs.scientificamerican.
com/cross-check/the-many-minds-of-marvin-minsky-r-i-p/ – John Horgan (26 January
2016), 'The Many Minds of Marvin Minsky (R.I.P.)'. Marvin Minsky, a pioneer of
artificial intelligence, was a paradoxical figure, who once said Freud was his favourite
theorist of mind.

'*have never thirsted after truth*' Sigmund Freud (1921/1991), *Group Psychology and the
Analysis of the Ego*, in *Civilization, Society and Religion*, Vol. 12, the Penguin Freud
Library, translated by James Strachey, edited by James Strachey and Albert Dickson,
Penguin Books: Harmondsworth, 107.

'*Where id was, there ego shall be*' Sigmund Freud (1932/1991), Lecture 31: *The Dissection
of the Psychical Personality*, in *New Introductory Lectures on Psychoanalysis*, Vol. 2, the
Penguin Freud Library, translated by James Strachey, edited by James Strachey assisted
by Angela Richards, Penguin Books, Harmondsworth, 112.

Chapter 14: Coffee and Conversation

'*a sort of democratic club*' Stefan Zweig (1943/undated), *The World of Yesterday*,
introduction by Harry Zohn, University of Nebraska Press: Lincoln and London, 39.

'*You have troubles of one sort or another – To the COFFEEHOUSE! . . . *' Peter Altenberg
(1993/1995), *Coffeehouse*, in *The Vienna Coffeehouse Wits 1890–1938*, translated, edited
and with an introduction by Harold B. Segel, Purdue University Press: West Lafayette,
Indiana, 1.

'*Sometimes the coffee house resembled a winter encampment of nomads . . . *' Ibid, 16.

Georg Franz Kolschitsky was offered a reward for his services Ibid, 7.

In fact, the first coffee houses in Vienna were opened by two Armenians Ibid, 8–9.

Friedrich Torberg . . . 'by far the most complicated of these legends' Ibid, 9.

One of the founding members . . . Theodor Herzl Dennis B. Klein (1981), *Jewish Origins of the
Psychoanalytic Movement*, Praeger Publishers, 14.

Schnitzler and Herzl had known each other as students Arthur Schnitzler (1968/1970), *My
Youth in Vienna*, Weidenfeld & Nicolson: London, 129.

Schnitzler liked posing in wide-brimmed Rembrandt hats and showy cravats Ibid, 116.

resettlement in Palestine . . . had no appeal whatsoever Peter Gay (2002), *Schnitzler's Century:
The Making of Middle-Class Culture 1815–1914*, W. W. Norton & Company: New York/
London, 116.

'*Hofmannsthal! I am Loris*' Stefan Zweig (1943/undated), *The World of Yesterday*,
introduction by Harry Zohn, University of Nebraska Press: Lincoln and London, 47.

'*We had never heard verses . . . since Goethe*' Ibid, 48.

even its waiters were reputed to be discerning littérateurs See *The Vienna Coffeehouse Wits
1890–1938* (1993/1995), translated, edited and with an introduction by Harold B. Segel,
Purdue University Press: West Lafayette, Indiana, 22–3.

Café Central . . . 'a world view' Ibid, 267.

he had intercourse with 'Jeanette' 326 times Peter Gay (2002), *Schnitzler's Century: The Making of Middle-Class Culture 1815–1914*, W. W. Norton & Company: New York/London, 64.

'wild women' . . . when he was fifteen years old Arthur Schnitzler (1968/1970), *My Youth in Vienna*, Weidenfeld & Nicolson: London, 43.

'neutral ground' / 'usually some coffee-house . . . Tambour' Ibid, 82.

'the much-courted cashier . . . billiards at night' Ibid, 125.

'After I had participated . . . ' Ibid, 165.

'Around noon I would put in an appearance at the polyclinic . . . ' Ibid, 165.

'fat Baron Flotow' . . . 'musical clowns' Ibid, 86.

a chance encounter . . . sexual excesses Ibid, 97.

'I have often asked myself . . . I had admired' Freud – Schnitzler, 19 August 1906, in Sigmund Freud (1961), *Letters of Sigmund Freud 1873–1939*, edited by Ernst L. Freud, translated by Tania and James Stern, Hogarth Press, 261.

he feared that Schnitzler was his double Freud – Schnitzler, 14 May 1922, in ibid, 344.

'psychic twin' William M. Johnston (1972/1983), *The Austrian Mind: An Intellectual and Social History 1848–1938*, University of California Press, 242.

ensuring that they would never meet Ibid, 241.

He explained to his prospective guest . . . 'There will be no one else with us.' Correspondence with the Doppelganger – letter (8 June 1922) and information displayed at Vienna Freud Museum.

They discussed ageing and dying Ibid.

All of their 'literary implements' . . . rarified nerves' See *The Vienna Coffeehouse Wits 1890–1938* (1993/1995), translated, edited and with an introduction by Harold B. Segel, Purdue University Press: West Lafayette, Indiana, 81.

'Psychoanalysis is the mental illness for which it claims to be a cure' William M. Johnston (1972/1983), *The Austrian Mind: An Intellectual and Social History 1848–1938*, University of California Press, 250.

'Civility and politeness . . . daily relationships' Frederic Morton (1989/2001), *Thunder at Twilight: Vienna 1913–1914*, Methuen: London, 4.

He also honed his oratory skills in Café Central Ibid, 95.

Trotsky relaxed by reading books in French . . . dissenting voices Ibid, 49.

The interior was clean . . . the bourgeoisie Ibid, 50.

'Vienna is not a particularly moral city . . . ' Ibid, 51.

'so juicy and tasty' Martin Freud (1957), *Glory Reflected: Sigmund Freud – Man and Father*, Angus and Robertson, 33.

The sweet 'was always a work of supreme culinary art' Ibid, 33.

'Oysters, lobster . . . 'It was a terrific blow-out' Alma Mahler-Werfel (1997/1998), *Diaries 1898–1902*, selected and translated by Antony Beaumont, 349.

'He belongs in the gugelhupf*' was a local insult* Nicholas Parsons (2009), *Vienna: A Cultural History*, OUP: Oxford, 188–9.

Pravda means 'truth' Frederic Morton (1989/2001), *Thunder at Twilight: Vienna 1913–1914*, Methuen: London, 3.

'The truth', Freud wrote . . . the absolute aim of science' Peter Gay (1988), *Freud: A Life for Our Time*, J. M. Dent and Sons: London, xvii.

For Karl Kraus . . . a chamber pot' Frederic Morton (1989/2001), *Thunder at Twilight: Vienna 1913–1914*, Methuen: London, 294.

Chapter 15: Excavating the Soul

Doolittle showed him examples of her work in the British Museum tea-room Francesca Wade (2020/2021), *Square Haunting: Five women, freedom and London between the wars*, Faber and Faber: London, 36.

She was briefly hailed as a genius Ibid, 34.

and even suffered from hallucinations Lisa Appignanesi and John Forrester (1992/2000), *Freud's Women*, Penguin: Harmondsworth, 387.

'an old owl in a tree' H.D. (1956/2012), *Tribute to Freud*, with an introduction by Adam Phillips, New Directions: New York, 22.

'treasures' / 'pricelessly lovely objects' Ibid, 96.

'You are the only person who has ever come into this room . . . ' Ibid, 97.

They talked informally about Egypt, excavations and mythology Ibid, 119.

'This is my favourite . . . ' Ibid, 68-9.

She could feel chilly . . . remove the folds. Ibid, 17.

'The trouble is – I am an old man – you do not think it worth your while to love me' Ibid, 16.

like a 'child hammering a porridge-spoon on the table' Ibid, 17.

Doolittle wasn't 'cured' by Freud Lisa Appignanesi and John Forrester (1992/2000), *Freud's Women*, Penguin: Harmondsworth, 393.

'as Eternity contains him now' H.D. (1956/2012), *Tribute to Freud*, with an introduction by Adam Phillips, New Directions: New York, 101.

'He is midwife to the soul' Ibid, 117.

'Life at my age is not easy, but spring is beautiful and so is love.' Ibid, 197.

'Sigmund Freud is like the curator of a museum' Ibid, 116.

sold at Sotheby's in London for £8 10s Alexandra Villing, J. Lesley Fitton, Victoria

Donnellan and Andrew Shapland (2019), *Troy: Myth and Reality*, Thames and Hudson: The British Museum: London, 157.

it had been weighed and sold for the value of its metal Lynn Gamwell (1989), 'The Origins of Freud's Antiquities Collection', in *Sigmund Freud and Art: His Personal Collection of Antiquities*, introduction by Peter Gay, edited by Lynn Gamwell and Richard Wells, State University of New York: Binghamton, Freud Museum: London, 23.

'strange secret yearnings' Peter Gay (1988), *Freud: A Life for Our Time*, J. M. Dent and Sons: London, 172.

He would bring the new figure to the dinner table Ellen Handler Spitz (1989), 'Psychoanalysis and the Legacies of Antiquity', in *Sigmund Freud and Art: His Personal Collection of Antiquities*, introduction by Peter Gay, edited by Lynn Gamwell and Richard Wells, State University of New York: Binghamton, Freud Museum: London, 155.

One was a small jade screen depicting the Chinese character for 'long life' Vanessa Thorpe, 'How a jade ornament from China casts new light on Freud's psyche', *Observer*, 16 January 2022.

He didn't feel that he was truly free . . . Europe to London See https://www.freud.org.uk/2020/04/07/home-is-where-the-heart-is-part-two

'despite my much vaunted frugality . . . more archaeology than psychology' Freud – Stefan Zweig, 7 February 1931, in Sigmund Freud (1961), *Letters of Sigmund Freud 1873–1939*, edited by Ernst L. Freud, translated by Tania and James Stern, Hogarth Press, 402.

'There were Assyrian Kings . . . ' Freud – Martha Bernays, 19 October 1885, in ibid, 185.

Freud was taught Latin and Greek . . . the age of nine Ronald W. Clark (1980), *Freud: The Man and the Cause*, Jonathan Cape: London, 17.

his earliest heroes were military giants such as Alexander the Great Ibid, 18.

and Hannibal Sigmund Freud (1900/1991), *Sigmund Freud. 4. The Interpretation of Dreams*, the Penguin Freud Library, Vol. 4, Penguin, 285.

more an 'adventurer' than a 'man of science' Peter Gay (1988), *Freud: A Life for Our Time*, J. M. Dent and Sons: London, xvi.

he treated himself . . . archaeological reports See https://www.freud.org.uk/collections/library/highlights-of-freuds-library

He was so awestruck he was unable to introduce himself Ernest Jones (1953–7/1977), *The Life and Work of Sigmund Freud*, edited and abridged by Lionel Trilling and Steven Marcus, Penguin: Harmondsworth, 322.

Schliemann wrote . . . when he was only seven Leonard Cottrell (1953/1992), *The Bull of Minos*, Efstathiadis: Athens, 37.

'for a life of quite another kind' Peter Gay (1988), *Freud: A Life for Our Time*, J. M. Dent and Sons: London, 172.

'Have you read that the English have excavated . . . ' Sigmund Freud (1897/1977), *The Origins*

of Psychoanalysis: Letters to Wilhelm Fliess, with an introductory essay by Steven Marcus, Basic Books: New York, 333.

'I doubt if even you could do that' H.D. (1956/2012), *Tribute to Freud*, with an introduction by Adam Phillips, New Directions: New York, 175.

His thinking was greatly influenced . . . social organisation Henri Ellenberger (1970/1994), *The Discovery of the Unconscious: the history and evolution of dynamic psychiatry*, Fontana Press: London, 218–20.

'supplies the thread . . . his own unconscious' Charlotte Higgins (2018/2021), *Red Thread: On mazes & labyrinths*, Vintage: London, 81.

'a constant pilgrim' Sigmund Freud (1900/1991), *Sigmund Freud. 4. The Interpretation of Dreams*, the Penguin Freud Library, Vol. 4, Penguin, 282 (footnote).

He dreamed that he was in a railway carriage Ibid, 282.

that he was surveying the mist-shrouded capital Ibid, 282.

that he was standing on a Roman street Ibid, 284.

'My longing for Rome is deeply neurotic' Sigmund Freud (1897/1977), *The Origins of Psychoanalysis: Letters to Wilhelm Fliess*, with an introductory essay by Steven Marcus, Basic Books: New York, 236.

Once, he got as far as Lake Trasimeno . . . and turned back Peter Gay (1988), *Freud: A Life for Our Time*, J. M. Dent and Sons: London, 132.

'in which nothing . . . beside the most recent' Sigmund Freud (1930/2002), *Civilization and Its Discontents*, the New Penguin Freud, General Editor Adam Phillips, Penguin: London, 8.

'the observer would perhaps need only to shift his gaze' Ibid, 9.

'endo-psychic myths' Sigmund Freud (1897/1977), *The Origins of Psychoanalysis: Letters to Wilhelm Fliess*, with an introductory essay by Steven Marcus, Basic Books: New York, 237.

'the wishful phantasies . . . of young humanity' Ibid, 237. NB: A slightly different translation of this in PFL *Creative Writers and Day-Dreaming*: 'the secular dreams of youthful humanity', 140.

'literary masterpiece' Sigmund Freud (1913/1990), *Totem and Taboo*, in *The Origins of Religion*, the Penguin Freud Library, Vol. 13, translated by James Strachey, edited by James Strachey and Albert Dickson, Penguin Books: Harmondsworth, 47.

it should always be in reach when travelling the Greek islands Lawrence Durrell (1978/2021), *The Greek Islands*, Faber and Faber: London, 64.

'impossible to prove' Sigmund Freud (1913/2005), *Totem and Taboo: Some correspondences between the psychical lives of savages and neurotics*, in *On Murder, Mourning and Melancholia*, the New Penguin Freud, General Editor Adam Phillips, translated by Shaun Whiteside, with an introduction by Maud Ellmann, Penguin: London, 39.

'fantastic' Ibid, 141.

'creating an unsuspected unity' Ibid, 141.

the 'mass' unconscious Ibid, 154.

'a just so story' Ronald W. Clark (1980), *Freud: The Man and the Cause*, Jonathan Cape: London, 355.

'Oh, don't take that too seriously . . . Sunday afternoon' A. Kardiner (1977), *My Analysis With Freud: Reminiscences*, W. W. Norton & Company: New York, 75.

'Reading this book . . . in his childhood' Élisabeth Roudinesco (2014/2016), *Freud: In his Time and Ours*, translated by Catherine Porter, Harvard University Press: London, 168.

'a source of the Nile' Peter Gay (1988), *Freud: A Life for Our Time*, J. M. Dent and Sons: London, 93.

'The heritable id . . . previous egos . . . ' Sigmund Freud (1923/2003), *The Ego and the Id*, in *Beyond the Pleasure Principle and Other Writings*, the New Penguin Freud, General Editor Adam Phillips, translated by John Reddick, with an introduction by Mark Edmundson, Penguin: London, 128.

'a reincarnation of previous ego forms' Ibid, 139.

'mass psyche' Sigmund Freud (1913/2005), *Totem and Taboo: Some correspondences between the psychical lives of savages and neurotics*, in *On Murder, Mourning and Melancholia*, the New Penguin Freud, General Editor Adam Phillips, translated by Shaun Whiteside, with an introduction by Maud Ellmann, Penguin: London, 154.

Jung believed . . . outside the brain Richard Noll (1993/1996), *The Jung Cult: Origins of a charismatic movement*, Fontana Press: London, 102.

Almost all contemporary biologists . . . Lamarckian Frank J. Sulloway (1979/1980), *Freud: Biologist of the Mind*, Fontana: Great Britain, 274 (footnote 30).

Even Darwin accepted Lamarck's mechanism as a supplement to his own Ibid, 274.

Haeckel was a major figure . . . the nineteenth century Richard Noll (1993/1996), *The Jung Cult: Origins of a charismatic movement*, Fontana Press: London, 47.

'phylogenetic psychology' Ibid, 52.

Ancestral humans . . . performed rituals Chris Gosden (2020), *The History of Magic: From Alchemy to Witchcraft, from the Ice Age to the Present*, Penguin: London, 43–4.

women with paternal grandmothers . . . heart disease Lars O. Bygren, Peter Tinghög, John Carstensen, Sören Edvinsson, Gunnar Kaati, Marcus E. Pembrey and Michael Sjöström (2014), 'Change in paternal grandmothers' early food supply influenced cardiovascular mortality of the female grandchildren', *BMC Genetics* 15:12.

On the subject . . . the authors write . . . Brian Dias and Kerry Ressler (2014), 'Parental olfactory experience influences behavior and neural structures in subsequent generations', *Nature Neuroscience*, vol. 17 (89–96); see https://www.ncbi.nlm.nih.gov/pmc/articles/PMC3923835

the 'transgenerational curse' Simon Critchley (2019/2020), *Tragedy, the Greeks and Us*, Profile Books: London, 48.

So this all really does exist, just as we learned in school! Sigmund Freud (1913/2005), *Letter to Romain Rollan (A Disturbance of Memory on the Acropolis)*, in *On Murder, Mourning and Melancholia*, the New Penguin Freud, General Editor Adam Phillips, translated by Shaun Whiteside, with an introduction by Maud Ellmann, Penguin: London, 237.

none of us really believe in our own demise Sigmund Freud (1921/1991), *Thoughts for the Times on War and Death*, in *Civilization, Society and Religion*, Vol. 12, the Penguin Freud Library, translated by James Strachey, edited by James Strachey and Albert Dickson, Penguin Books, Harmondsworth, 77.

'feeling of estrangement' Sigmund Freud (1913/2005), *Letter to Romain Rollan (A Disturbance of Memory on the Acropolis)*, in *On Murder, Mourning and Melancholia*, the New Penguin Freud, General Editor Adam Phillips, translated by Shaun Whiteside, with an introduction by Maud Ellmann, Penguin: London, 240.

'an ancient cycle or circle, wise-man, woman, lioness' H.D. (1956/2012), *Tribute to Freud*, with an introduction by Adam Phillips, New Directions: New York, 117.

Chapter 16: False Gods

In fact, no statue had ever moved him in quite the same way Sigmund Freud (1927/1990), *The Moses of Michelangelo*, in *Art and Literature*, the Penguin Freud Library, Vol. 14, translated by James Strachey, edited by James Strachey and Albert Dickson, Penguin Books: Harmondsworth, 255.

'three lonely weeks' Freud – Eduardo Weiss, 12 April 1933, in Sigmund Freud (1961), *Letters of Sigmund Freud 1873–1939*, edited by Ernst L. Freud, translated by Tania and James Stern, Hogarth Press, 412. NB: In this letter Freud mistakenly dates his three lonely weeks to 1913 when they were in fact in 1912.

'How often have I mounted . . . where the deserted church stands . . . ' Sigmund Freud (1927/1990), *The Moses of Michelangelo*, in *Art and Literature*, the Penguin Freud Library, Vol. 14, translated by James Strachey, edited by James Strachey and Albert Dickson, Penguin Books: Harmondsworth, 255.

'personally known' Ibid, 253.

'psychoanalytic circles' Ibid, 253.

'mode of thought' Ibid, 253.

'the methodology of psychoanalysis' Ibid, 253.

'the lines of the face . . . ' Ibid, 273.

'and he will now remain seated . . . with contempt' Ibid, 273.

a psychoanalytic alternative was tantamount to blasphemy Ibid, 274.

'To deprive a people . . . carelessly undertaken' Sigmund Freud (1939[1934–38]/1990), *Moses and Monotheism: Three Essays*, in *The Origins of Religion*, the Penguin Freud Library, Vol. 13, translated by James Strachey, edited by James Strachey and Albert Dickson, Penguin Books: Harmondsworth, 243.

'*a typical little Jew with sly features*' Frederick Crews (2017), *Freud: The Making of an Illusion*, Profile, 19.

'*I stepped into the road and picked up my cap*' Peter Gay (1988), *Freud: A Life for Our Time*, J. M. Dent and Sons: London, 12.

'*godless Jew*' Letter from Freud to Pfister, 9 October 1918, cited in ibid, 602.

Martin had never heard . . . 'kindly tones' Martin Freud (1957), *Glory Reflected: Sigmund Freud – Man and Father*, Angus and Robertson, 70.

'*the faces of these crusaders in racial hatred*' Ibid, 71.

'*He never recalled the incident . . . family or friends*' Ibid, 71.

'*private religion*' Sigmund Freud (1907/1990), *Obsessive Actions and Religious Practices*, in *The Origins of Religion*, the Penguin Freud Library, Vol. 13, translated by James Strachey, edited by James Strachey and Albert Dickson, Penguin Books: Harmondsworth, 33.

'*a universal obsessional neurosis*' Ibid, 40.

Freud supposed . . . three phases Sigmund Freud (1913/2005), *Totem and Taboo: Some correspondences between the psychical lives of savages and neurotics*, in *On Murder, Mourning and Melancholia*, the New Penguin Freud, General Editor Adam Phillips, translated by Shaun Whiteside, with an introduction by Maud Ellmann, Penguin: London, 81.

Freud concluded . . . humanity's oldest wishes Sigmund Freud (1927/1991), *The Future of an Illusion*, in *Civilization, Society and Religion*, the Penguin Freud Library, Vol. 12, translated by James Strachey, edited by James Strachey and Albert Dickson, Penguin Books: Harmondsworth, 212.

'*In the course of centuries . . . hands of science*' Sigmund Freud, (1917[1916–17]/1987), Lecture 18: *Fixation to Traumas – The Unconscious*, in *Introductory Lectures on Psychoanalysis*, Vol. 1, the Pelican Freud Library, translated by James Strachey, edited by James Strachey and Angela Richards, Penguin Books: Harmondsworth, 326.

'*a tiny fragment of a cosmic system of scarcely imaginable vastness*' Ibid, 326.

'*destroyed man's supposedly privileged place . . . ineradicable animal nature*' Ibid, 326.

'*most wounding blow*' Ibid, 326.

'*not even master . . . in its mind*' Ibid, 326.

"*If I were to find myself . . . a man not easily satisfied*' Ernest Jones (1953–7/1977), *The Life and Work of Sigmund Freud*, edited and abridged by Lionel Trilling and Steven Marcus, Penguin: Harmondsworth, 58.

He compared psychoanalysis to electricity Sigmund Freud (1927/1993), *Sigmund Freud. 15. Historical and Expository Works on Psychoanalysis. The Question of Lay Analysis*, postscript, the Penguin Freud Library, Vol. 15, translated by James Strachey, edited by James Strachey and Albert Dickson, Penguin, 357.

'*Psychoanalysis is a part of psychology . . . simply of psychology*' Ibid, 356–7.

'It is a part of science . . . Weltanschauung' Sigmund Freud (1932/1991), Lecture 35: *The Question of a Weltanschauung*, in *New Introductory Lectures on Psychoanalysis*, Vol. 2, the Penguin Freud Library, translated by James Strachey, edited by James Strachey assisted by Angela Richards, Penguin Books: Harmondsworth, 219.

Erich Fromm . . . '*Western man's' spiritual crisis* Erich Fromm (1957[1960]/2013), *Zen Buddhism and Psychoanalysis II Values and Goals in Freud's Psychoanalytic Concepts*, Open Road Integrated Media: New York (e-book), see https://www.google.co.uk/books/edition/Psychoanalysis_and_Zen_Buddhism/6Q9c_91VzoUC?hl=en&gbpv=1&dq=Zen+Buddhism+and+psychoanalysis&printsec=frontcover

'*because nearly all his many references . . . excised in translation*' Bruno Bettelheim (1983/1991), *Freud and Man's Soul*, Penguin Books: London, 4.

'*in fact, it is what is so essentially human about us . . . Freud had in mind*' Ibid, 78.

'*latent tendencies*' Padmasiri de Silva (1973/2010), *Buddhist and Freudian Psychology*, 4th Edition, Shogam Publications: Carlton North, Victoria, 71.

*motivated by desires that arise from '*physical*' dispositions* Ibid, 7.

Thus, human beings pursue . . . '*pleasure principle*' Ibid, 128.

'*cravings' for self-annihilation . . . Freud's death instinct* Ibid, 149–150.

In Beyond the Pleasure Principle *. . . Barbara Low* Sigmund Freud (1923/2003), *Beyond the Pleasure Principle*, in *Beyond the Pleasure Principle and Other Writings*, the New Penguin Freud, General Editor Adam Phillips, translated by John Reddick, with an introduction by Mark Edmundson, Penguin: London, 95.

'*a conscious mind . . . past lives*' Padmasiri de Silva (1973/2010), *Buddhist and Freudian Psychology*, 4th Edition, Shogam Publications: Carlton North, Victoria, 8.

'*previous ego forms*' Sigmund Freud (1923/2003), *The Ego and the Id*, in *Beyond the Pleasure Principle and Other Writings*, the New Penguin Freud, General Editor Adam Phillips, translated by John Reddick, with an introduction by Mark Edmundson, Penguin: London, 139.

'*the archaic heritage . . . earlier generations*' Sigmund Freud (1939[1934–38]/1990), *Moses and Monotheism: Three Essays*, in *The Origins of Religion*, the Penguin Freud Library, Vol. 13, translated by James Strachey, edited by James Strachey and Albert Dickson, Penguin Books: Harmondsworth, 345.

The first noble truth of Buddhism states that life is suffering The Dalai Lama (2004/2018), *An Introduction to Buddhism*, translated by Thupten Jinpa, Shambhala: Boulder, 12–13.

Freud described . . . '*common unhappiness*' Sigmund Freud and Joseph Breuer (1895/2004), *Studies in Hysteria*, introduction by Rachel Bowlby, translated by Nicola Luckhurst, Penguin Classics: London, 306.

'*All worldlings are deranged*' Padmasiri de Silva (1973/2010), *Buddhist and Freudian Psychology*, 4th Edition, Shogam Publications: Carlton North, Victoria, 31.

'*distorted perceptions*' Beth Jacobs (2017), *The Original Buddhist Psychology: What the*

Abhidarma tells us about how we think, feel, and experience life, North Atlantic Books: Berkeley, California, 23–24.

Buddhism lays special emphasis on attachment as a cause of unhappiness The Dalai Lama (2004/2018), *An Introduction to Buddhism*, translated by Thupten Jinpa, Shambhala: Boulder, 14.

Similarly, narcissism . . . impossible Ibid, 26.

Erich Fromm . . . form of salvation Erich Fromm (1957[1960]/2013), *Zen Buddhism and Psychoanalysis II Values and Goals in Freud's Psychoanalytic Concepts*, Open Road Integrated Media: New York (e-book), see https://www.google.co.uk/books/edition/Psychoanalysis_and_Zen_Buddhism/6Q9c_91VzoUC?hl=en&gbpv=1&dq=Zen+Buddhism+and+psychoanalysis&printsec=frontcover

describes how he would sometimes creep . . . Moses' gaze Sigmund Freud (1927/1990), *The Moses of Michelangelo*, in *Art and Literature*, the Penguin Freud Library, Vol. 14, translated by James Strachey, edited by James Strachey and Albert Dickson, Penguin Books: Harmondsworth, 255.

Chapter 17: The Wolfman

'*I don't give interviews*' Karin Obholzer (1982), *The Wolf-Man: Sixty Years Later, Conversations with Freud's Controversial Patient*, translated by Michael Shaw, Routledge & Kegan Paul: London, Melbourne and Henley, 4.

'*In Vienna, hardly anyone is interested in psychoanalysis*' Ibid, 4.

'*but I had expected more*' Ibid, 6.

who urged him not to cooperate Mikkel Borch-Jacobsen (2011/2021), *Freud's Patients: A Book of Lives*, Reaktion Books: London, 172.

'*It seems that I want you to write something after all . . . after my death*' Karin Obholzer (1982), *The Wolf-Man: Sixty Years Later, Conversations with Freud's Controversial Patient*, translated by Michael Shaw, Routledge & Kegan Paul: London, Melbourne and Henley, 7.

peasants with shoes made of rags Ibid, 75.

an uncle who lived like King Ludwig II of Bavaria Ibid, 55.

travelling to a seaside resort in a horse-drawn carriage Ibid, 68.

He hunted wolves . . . 'native' dances Muriel Gardiner (1971), *The Wolf-Man by the Wolf-Man: The double story of Freud's most famous case*, with *The Case of the Wolf-Man* by Sigmund Freud, *A Supplement* by Ruth Mack Brunswick and a foreword by Anna Freud, edited with notes, an introduction and chapters by Muriel Gardiner, Basic Books: New York, 12.

'*Her blue-black hair . . . chiselled by a sculptor*' Ibid, 49.

'*Never to meet again*' Ibid, 60.

cabarets and one-night stands Ibid, 61.

Early thirties . . . reddish beard Ibid, 79.

He was also the only person in Odessa who had heard of Sigmund Freud Ibid, 79.

whose principal duty . . . card games Ibid, 84.

'Up to now . . . your chamber pot' Ibid, 139.

'weird male figures' Ibid, 84.

'incapable of autonomous existence' Sigmund Freud ([1914]1918), *From the History of an Infantile Neurosis [The 'Wolfman'],* in *The 'Wolfman' and Other Cases,* translated by Louise Adey Huish with an introduction by Gillian Beer, General Editor Adam Phillips, the New Penguin Freud, Penguin Books: London, 205.

he took fencing lessons from a former Italian officer Karin Obholzer (1982), *The Wolf-Man: Sixty Years Later, Conversations with Freud's Controversial Patient,* translated by Michael Shaw, Routledge & Kegan Paul: London, Melbourne and Henley, 38.

A photograph of Pankejeff taken in 1910 – in Muriel Gardiner (1971), *The Wolf-Man by the Wolf-Man: The double story of Freud's most famous case,* Basic Books: New York.

James Strachey described it . . . case histories Sigmund Freud ([1914]1918), *From the History of an Infantile Neurosis,* in Sigmund Freud (1979/1990), *Case Histories II,* the Penguin Freud Library, Vol. 9, translated from the German under the general editorship of James Strachey, compiled and edited by Angela Richards, Penguin: Harmondsworth, 228.

'assuredly the best of the series' . . . 'every reader's admiration' Muriel Gardiner (1971), *The Wolf-Man by the Wolf-Man: The double story of Freud's most famous case,* Basic Books: New York, vii.

inhibitions have been dissolved . . . curious and incredible Sigmund Freud ([1914]1918), *From the History of an Infantile Neurosis [The 'Wolfman'],* in *The 'Wolfman' and Other Cases,* translated by Louise Adey Huish with an introduction by Gillian Beer, General Editor Adam Phillips, the New Penguin Freud, Penguin Books: London, 209.

'I could not do otherwise . . . our philosophy' Ibid, 209.

'like a savage' Ibid, 212.

frightened him so much he would scream Ibid, 213.

he pressed his body . . . rejected his advances Karin Obholzer (1982), *The Wolf-Man: Sixty Years Later, Conversations with Freud's Controversial Patient,* translated by Michael Shaw, Routledge & Kegan Paul: London, Melbourne and Henley, 37.

the night before his fourth birthday Sigmund Freud ([1914]1918), *From the History of an Infantile Neurosis [The 'Wolfman'],* in *The 'Wolfman' and Other Cases,* translated by Louise Adey Huish with an introduction by Gillian Beer, General Editor Adam Phillips, the New Penguin Freud, Penguin Books: London, 233, 243.

'I dreamed that it is night . . . I screamed and woke up' Ibid, 227.

'It looked as if they had turned their full attention on me' Ibid, 227.

Freud didn't arrive . . . Pankejeff's treatment Ibid, 230–1.

his mother and father having sex Ibid, 234.

Freud called this the 'primal scene' Ibid, 238.

'coitus a tergo' . . . repeated three times Ibid, 235.

he resembled a wolf in a picture book standing on its hind legs Ibid, 236.

intercourse from behind . . . sexual pleasure Ibid, 238.

'It is not fear of the father *. . . but fear of the* wolf*'* Ibid, 311.

a form of infantile seduction Ibid, 225.

'The whale and the polar bear . . . cannot meet' Sigmund Freud ([1914]1918), *From the History of an Infantile Neurosis*, in Sigmund Freud (1979/1990), *Case Histories II*, the Penguin Freud Library, Vol. 9, translated from the German under the general editorship of James Strachey, compiled and edited by Angela Richards, Penguin: Harmondsworth, 281.

Modern memory research suggests . . . two and a half years Louis Breger (2000), *Freud: Darkness in the Midst of Vision*, John Wiley & Sons, 274; and E. F. Loftus (1993), 'Desperately seeking memories of the first few years of childhood: The reality of early memories', *Journal of Experimental Psychology: General*, 122(2), 274–7.

Pankejeff's depression intensified around five o'clock Sigmund Freud ([1914]1918), *From the History of an Infantile Neurosis [The 'Wolfman']*, in *The 'Wolfman' and Other Cases*, translated by Louise Adey Huish with an introduction by Gillian Beer, General Editor Adam Phillips, the New Penguin Freud, Penguin Books: London, 234–5.

'The seduction of my patient . . . his parents' coitus, too?' Ibid, 295.

emotional blackmail Louis Breger (2000), *Freud: Darkness in the Midst of Vision*, John Wiley & Sons, 274.

Pankejeff continued to mention Terese in every session Muriel Gardiner (1971), *The Wolf-Man by the Wolf-Man: The double story of Freud's most famous case*, Basic Books: New York, 85.

a private detective agency to discover her whereabouts Ibid, 86.

'scarcely more than a skeleton' Ibid, 86.

'never again to leave this woman' Ibid, 86.

Freud 'demanded' . . . infection and sterility Mikkel Borch-Jacobsen (2011/2021), *Freud's Patients: A Book of Lives*, Reaktion Books: London, 164.

he praised her serious-mindedness . . . Pankejeff's plan to marry her Muriel Gardiner (1971), *The Wolf-Man by the Wolf-Man: The double story of Freud's most famous case*, Basic Books: New York, 90.

might reduce . . . 'consequent dependence' Ibid, 149–50.

'I can't remember . . . it was of no consequence' Karin Obholzer (1982), *The Wolf-Man: Sixty Years Later, Conversations with Freud's Controversial Patient*, translated by Michael Shaw, Routledge & Kegan Paul: London, Melbourne and Henley, 42.

Freud recommended a short 'reanalysis' Muriel Gardiner (1971), *The Wolf-Man by the Wolf-Man: The double story of Freud's most famous case*, Basic Books: New York, 111.

to treat Pankejeff's constipation . . . a psychological cause Karin Obholzer (1982), *The Wolf-Man: Sixty Years Later, Conversations with Freud's Controversial Patient*, translated by Michael Shaw, Routledge & Kegan Paul: London, Melbourne and Henley, 47.

Pankejeff was indifferent . . . forty crowns an hour Mikkel Borch-Jacobsen (2011/2021), *Freud's Patients: A Book of Lives*, Reaktion Books: London, 165.

prudent to go home and settle his 'financial affairs' Karin Obholzer (1982), *The Wolf-Man: Sixty Years Later, Conversations with Freud's Controversial Patient*, translated by Michael Shaw, Routledge & Kegan Paul: London, Melbourne and Henley, 48.

'It was stupid of me that I listened to Freud and stayed in Vienna' Ibid, 48.

Moreover, after his reanalysis, he was still constipated Mikkel Borch-Jacobsen (2011/2021), *Freud's Patients: A Book of Lives*, Reaktion Books: London, 168.

enough to help him pay his rent Muriel Gardiner (1971), *The Wolf-Man by the Wolf-Man: The double story of Freud's most famous case*, Basic Books: New York, 142 (footnote).

probably a fiction invented by Freud's disciples Mikkel Borch-Jacobsen (2011/2021), *Freud's Patients: A Book of Lives*, Reaktion Books: London, 168.

With Martin Freud's assistance Ibid, 168.

'unsightly' nasal injuries . . . obstructed sebaceous glands Muriel Gardiner (1971), *The Wolf-Man by the Wolf-Man: The double story of Freud's most famous case*, Basic Books: New York, 264.

'small, snub, typically Russian nose' . . . 'nothing whatsoever' Ibid, 264.

had resumed his former habit . . . studied 'obscene' pictures Ibid, 272.

'During the analytic hours . . . cut off from reality' Ibid, 290.

'My God, now I can't kill him any more!' Ibid, 283.

The wolf is a substitute father . . . the 'wolves' were trying to destroy him Ibid, 290.

he compared himself to Jesus Christ Ibid, 290.

Pankejeff had dreamed . . . entwined branches Ibid, 291.

he could finally 'admire what others find beautiful – a love scene between a man and woman' Ibid, 292.

Her role had been 'negligible' Ibid, 306.

Pankejeff had simply 'worked his way through . . . persecution' Ibid, 291.

'The nose is, of course, the genital' Ibid, 300.

In 1930 . . . a younger woman Mikkel Borch-Jacobsen (2011/2021), *Freud's Patients: A Book of Lives*, Reaktion Books: London, 169.

'I had not the slightest foreboding . . . end in tragedy' Muriel Gardiner (1971), *The Wolf-Man by the Wolf-Man: The double story of Freud's most famous case*, Basic Books: New York, 115.

'The sight was so terrible that I simply cannot describe it' Ibid, 121.

'had not a lucky chance come to my help' Ibid, 125.

Mack Brunswick had arranged . . . insurance policies Muriel Gardiner (1983/2021), *Code Name Mary: Memoirs of an American Woman in the Austrian Underground*, foreword by Anna Freud, Freud Museum London Publishing, 129.

'Why did this have to happen to me? Why did my wife kill herself?' Muriel Gardiner (1971), *The Wolf-Man by the Wolf-Man: The double story of Freud's most famous case*, Basic Books: New York, 312.

Pankejeff took the opportunity . . . two further occasions Mikkel Borch-Jacobsen (2011/2021), *Freud's Patients: A Book of Lives*, Reaktion Books: London, 170.

after Pankejeff's departure, Freud was 'terribly weary' Ibid, 170.

she was very busy flushing illegal literature down lavatories Muriel Gardiner (1983/2021), *Code Name Mary: Memoirs of an American Woman in the Austrian Underground*, foreword by Anna Freud, Freud Museum London Publishing, 100.

attaching false passports to her body with adhesive tape Ibid, 108.

synchronising her watch to the second Ibid, 110.

an affair with the poet Stephen Spender ('I've never been in love with a woman before') Ibid, 66.

Gardiner . . . clothes and food packages Mikkel Borch-Jacobsen (2011/2021), *Freud's Patients: A Book of Lives*, Reaktion Books: London, 170.

Gardiner paid for Pankejeff to receive yet more psychoanalysis Ibid, 171.

'My only consolation . . . improve my mood' Ibid, 171.

Gardiner also visited Pankejeff eight times between 1960 and 1970 Muriel Gardiner (1971), *The Wolf-Man by the Wolf-Man: The double story of Freud's most famous case*, Basic Books: New York, 343.

'Thanks to his analysis . . . one might expect' Ibid, vii.

'There can be no doubt . . . tolerably healthy life' Ibid, 366.

'This is the Wolf-Man' Karin Obholzer (1982), *The Wolf-Man: Sixty Years Later, Conversations with Freud's Controversial Patient*, translated by Michael Shaw, Routledge & Kegan Paul: London, Melbourne and Henley, 4.

Pankejeff sold his paintings . . . her colleagues Muriel Gardiner (1971), *The Wolf-Man by the Wolf-Man: The double story of Freud's most famous case*, Basic Books: New York, 352

including several paintings of his wolf dream Ibid, 353.

Every member of the International Psychoanalytic Association wanted one Mikkel Borch-Jacobsen (2011/2021), *Freud's Patients: A Book of Lives*, Reaktion Books: London, 172.

It has been said . . . under its wing Élisabeth Roudinesco (2014/2016), *Freud: In his Time and Ours*, translated by Catherine Porter, Harvard University Press: London, 200–1.

'the disciples of psychoanalysis . . . a good effect' Karin Obholzer (1982), *The Wolf-Man: Sixty*

Years Later, Conversations with Freud's Controversial Patient, translated by Michael Shaw, Routledge & Kegan Paul: London, Melbourne and Henley, 137.

'they made a showpiece of me . . . a serious case' Ibid, 135.

'If you look at everything critically . . . Yet it helped me' Ibid, 32.

'big holidays' Muriel Gardiner (1971), *The Wolf-Man by the Wolf-Man: The double story of Freud's most famous case*, Basic Books: New York, 270.

'What she wrote there is stupid' Karin Obholzer (1982), *The Wolf-Man: Sixty Years Later, Conversations with Freud's Controversial Patient*, translated by Michael Shaw, Routledge & Kegan Paul: London, Melbourne and Henley, 132.

'is that fellow crazy or what, writing such nonsense' Ibid, 169.

'Freud traces everything back . . . terribly farfetched' Ibid, 35.

'The whole thing is improbable . . . anything of that sort' Ibid, 36.

he had been *'well' for eighteen months* Muriel Gardiner (1971), *The Wolf-Man by the Wolf-Man: The double story of Freud's most famous case*, Basic Books: New York, 307.

Mack Brunswick optimistically described her results (around 1940) as 'excellent' Ibid, 263.

he became locked . . . contemplate suicide Karin Obholzer (1982), *The Wolf-Man: Sixty Years Later, Conversations with Freud's Controversial Patient*, translated by Michael Shaw, Routledge & Kegan Paul: London, Melbourne and Henley, 203.

'I am in the same state as when I first came to Freud' Ibid, 172.

'Give me some advice!' Ibid, 247.

Pankejeff died in the arms of a private nurse – paid for by Gardiner Mikkel Borch-Jacobsen (2011/2021), *Freud's Patients: A Book of Lives*, Reaktion Books: London, 174.

did not invite her to the funeral Karin Obholzer (1982), *The Wolf-Man: Sixty Years Later, Conversations with Freud's Controversial Patient*, translated by Michael Shaw, Routledge & Kegan Paul: London, Melbourne and Henley, 250.

'taped protocols do not yield a readable book' Ibid, 11.

'The Wolf-Man himself . . . lifelong misery' Muriel Gardiner (1971), *The Wolf-Man by the Wolf-Man: The double story of Freud's most famous case*, Basic Books: New York, vii.

'It is as if the obsessional neurosis itself . . . keep him alive' Karin Obholzer (1982), *The Wolf-Man: Sixty Years Later, Conversations with Freud's Controversial Patient*, translated by Michael Shaw, Routledge & Kegan Paul: London, Melbourne and Henley, 246.

Chapter 18: Stranger Things

Nineteenth-century Romanticism . . . German Romantic philosophy Henri Ellenberger (1970/1994), *The Discovery of the Unconscious: the history and evolution of dynamic psychiatry*, Fontana Press: London, 202.

Anything shadowy, liminal or strange excited the Romantic imagination Ibid, 200.

The Romantics were even fascinated by the 'otherness' of animals Ibid, 200.

'Nature is visible Spirit, Spirit is invisible Nature' Ibid, 202.

'world soul' Ibid, 202.

'Unfortunately I must confess ... signs and wonders' Sigmund Freud (1901/2002), *The Psychopathology of Everyday Life*, translated by Anthea Bell with an introduction by Paul Keegan, the New Penguin Freud, Penguin Books, London, 247.

a series of telepathy experiments Stephen Frosh (2013), *Hauntings: Psychoanalysis and Ghostly Transmissions*, Palgrave Macmillan: Hampshire, 94.

'You know, of course, that you are a bit odd' Sigmund Freud/Anna Freud (2014), *Correspondence 1904–1938*, edited by Ingeborg Meyer-Palmedo, translated by Nick Somers, Polity Press: Cambridge, 62.

'try not to find yourself alone with him' Ibid, 83.

'Postpone your visits ... him alone' Ibid, 83.

had reached an 'understanding' ... two or three years Ibid, 87 (footnote).

'She is of course tremendously bound to you' Ibid, 87 (footnote).

'Recently I dreamed that you were a king ... ' Ibid, 113.

Carl Gustav Jung ... analysed their offspring Roman Krivanek (undated guide to the Vienna Freud Museum), 'Anna Freud's Work in Vienna', in *Freud, Berggasse 19: The Origin of Psychoanalysis*, edited by Monika Pessler and Daniela Finzi with a foreword by Siri Hustvedt, Hatje Cantz, 277.

Anna was 'quite an attractive girl'. Why wasn't she married? A. Kardiner (1977), *My Analysis With Freud: Reminiscences*, W. W. Norton & Company: New York, 77.

'nightlife' Lisa Appignanesi and John Forrester (1992/2000), *Freud's Women*, Penguin: Harmondsworth, 279.

'I murdered somebody or something like that ... ' Sigmund Freud/Anna Freud (2014), *Correspondence 1904–1938*, edited by Ingeborg Meyer-Palmedo, translated by Nick Somers, Polity Press: Cambridge, 170.

'Write me a long letter soon ... Your Anna' Ibid, 171.

They drove around the city ... in identical clothes Élisabeth Roudinesco (2014/2016), *Freud: In his Time and Ours*, translated by Catherine Porter, Harvard University Press: London, 249.

She installed a telephone line ... talk into the night Ibid, 250.

Freud described the living arrangements ... as symbiotic Mikkel Borch-Jacobsen (2011/2021), *Freud's Patients: A Book of Lives*, Reaktion Books: London, 224.

'to put an end ... thought transference' Sigmund Freud (1932/1991), Lecture 30: *Dreams and Occultism*, in *New Introductory Lectures on Psychoanalysis*, Vol. 2, the Penguin Freud Library, translated by James Strachey, edited by James Strachey assisted by Angela Richards, Penguin Books: Harmondsworth, 86.

'*common purpose*' Ibid, 86.

'*additions to the family*' Freud – Binswanger, 11 January 1929, in Sigmund Freud/Ludwig Binswanger (2003), *The Sigmund Freud–Ludwig Binswanger Correspondence, 1908–1938*, edited by Gerhard Fichtner, translated by Arnold J. Pomerans, Other Press: New York, 195.

he would refer to a dog as having a 'first husband' or a 'baby' H.D. (1956/2012), *Tribute to Freud*, with an introduction by Adam Phillips, New Directions: New York, 166.

always at the patient's expense Martin Freud (1957), *Glory Reflected: Sigmund Freud – Man and Father*, Angus and Robertson, 191.

Jofi was also considered an excellent judge of character Ibid, 192.

delivered by a tortoise . . . a poor substitute Michael Molnar (ed.) (1992), *The Diary of Sigmund Freud 1929–39*, London: Hogarth, 61.

'*So speaks Jo Fie . . . we are apart*' 'How did Freud celebrate his birthday?' – Freud Museum London; see https://www.freud.org.uk/2020/05/06/how-did-freud-celebrate-his-birthday

Freud enjoyed the manuscript . . . translated the book into German Martin Freud (1957), *Glory Reflected: Sigmund Freud – Man and Father*, Angus and Robertson, 203.

He asked Marie in a letter: 'Does Topsy realize she is being translated?' Andrew Nagorski (2022), *Saving Freud: A life in Vienna and an escape to freedom in London*, Icon Books: London, 225.

'*If you had been chained up all your life,' said Freud, 'you'd be vicious too*' Ronald W. Clark (1980), *Freud: The Man and the Cause*, Jonathan Cape: London, 483.

Although in 1913 . . . through an open window Stanley A. Leavy (1964), *The Freud Journal of Lou Andreas-Salomé*, translated and with an introduction by Stanley A. Leavy, Basic Books: USA, 89.

he attributed the charm of cats . . . lack of concern for others Sigmund Freud (1914/1991), *On Metapsychology. On Narcissism: An Introduction*, the Penguin Freud Library, Vol. 11, translated by James Strachey, compiled and edited by Angela Richards, Penguin Books: Harmondsworth, 83.

'*She certainly has her share . . . young kitten*' Élisabeth Roudinesco (2014/2016), *Freud: In his Time and Ours*, translated by Catherine Porter, Harvard University Press: London, 243.

Freud found monkeys extremely unnerving because they are both like us, and not like us H.D. (1956/2012), *Tribute to Freud*, with an introduction by Adam Phillips, New Directions: New York, 172.

Because of a calculation made by Wilhelm Fliess Frank J. Sulloway (1979/1980), *Freud: Biologist of the Mind*, Fontana: Great Britain, 145.

For no obvious reason . . . sixty-two Forbes Morlock (2020), 'Ghost Writing', in *The Uncanny: A Centenary 30 October 2019 – 9 February 2020*, edited by Ivan Ward, Freud Museum: London, 14.

'*a strange theoretical novel*' Hélène Cixous (2011), 'Fiction and its Phantoms: A Reading of Freud's Das Unheimliche (The "Uncanny")', in *Volleys of Humanity: Essays 1972–2009*, edited by Eric Prenowitz, translated by Robert Denommé, Edinburgh University Press: Edinburgh, 15.

Enucleation, he claims, is a symbolic substitute for castration Sigmund Freud (1919/2003), *The Uncanny*, translated by David McLintock with an introduction by Hugh Haughton, the New Penguin Freud, Penguin Books: London, 139–40.

Freud attributes this insight to the German psychiatrist Ernst Jentsch Ibid, 135.

Ernest Jones . . . in August 1902 Ernest Jones (1953–7/1977), *The Life and Work of Sigmund Freud*, edited and abridged by Lionel Trilling and Steven Marcus, Penguin: Harmondsworth, 321.

'applies to everything . . . come into the open' Sigmund Freud (1919/2003), *The Uncanny*, translated by David McLintock with an introduction by Hugh Haughton, the New Penguin Freud, Penguin Books: London, 132.

'nothing new or strange . . . being repressed' Ibid, 148.

'repetition of the same thing' Ibid, 143.

Freud points out that psychoanalysis is itself uncanny Ibid, 150.

an alchemist . . . Philosopher's Stone Graham Robb (2010), *Parisians: An Adventure History of Paris*, Picador: London, 229.

'demonological case history' Sigmund Freud (1923/1990), *A Seventeenth Century Demonological Neurosis*, in *Art and Literature*, the Penguin Freud Library, Vol. 14, translated by James Strachey, edited by James Strachey and Albert Dickson, Penguin Books: Harmondsworth, 385.

The devil (who had first appeared in the guise of an 'honest' old man) Ibid, 399.

'The delusional formation . . . a process of reconstruction' Sigmund Freud (1911/1990), *Psychoanalytic Notes on an Autobiographical Account of a Case of Paranoia (Dementia Paranoides) (Schreber)*, in *Sigmund Freud: Case Histories II*, the Penguin Freud Library, Vol. 9, James Strachey and Angela Richards, Penguin: Harmondsworth, 209–10.

'Italian Faust' Sigmund Freud (1910/2003), *Leonardo da Vinci and a Memory of his Childhood*, in *The Uncanny*, translated by David McLintock with an introduction by Hugh Haughton, the New Penguin Freud, Penguin Books: London, 54.

'uncanny, enigmatic character' Ibid, 87.

'demonic magic' Ibid, 81.

And the uncanniness of the smile . . . 'sinister menace' Ibid, 88.

concealed a true memory of being suckled at his mother's breast Ibid, 63.

'A strong experience . . . the creative work' Sigmund Freud (1908/1990), *Creative Writers and Day-Dreaming*, in *Art and Literature*, the Penguin Freud Library, Vol. 14, translated by James Strachey, edited by James Strachey and Albert Dickson, Penguin Books: Harmondsworth, 139.

The imaginative writer is a 'dreamer in broad daylight' Ibid, 137.

Later in life . . . greatest novel ever written Sigmund Freud (1928/1990), *Dostoevsky and Parricide*, in *Art and Literature*, the Penguin Freud Library, Vol. 14, translated by James Strachey, edited by James Strachey and Albert Dickson, Penguin Books: Harmondsworth, 441.

He also enjoyed British crime writing Peter Gay (1988), *Freud: A Life for Our Time*, J. M. Dent and Sons: London, 166.

'intensely curious' . . . performs his miracles Sigmund Freud (1908/1990), *Creative Writers and Day-Dreaming*, in *Art and Literature*, the Penguin Freud Library, Vol. 14, translated by James Strachey, edited by James Strachey and Albert Dickson, Penguin Books: Harmondsworth, 131.

The most common emotional reaction . . . is fear Anil Seth (2021), *Being You: A New Science of Consciousness*, Faber and Faber: London, 259.

'uncanny valley' Minsoo Kang (2011), *Sublime Dreams of Living Machines: The Automaton in the European Imagination*, Harvard University Press: London, England, 47.

'What makes this more than the beginnings . . . actually happen' Brian Greene (2020), *Until the End of Time: Mind, Matter, and Our Search for Meaning in an Evolving Universe*, Allen Lane: London, 298

Chapter 19: The Case of Gustav M

'It's indescribable . . . I love' Alma Mahler-Werfel (1997/2000), *Diaries 1898–1902*, selected and translated by Antony Beaumont, Faber and Faber: London, 125.

'I took his head . . . our teeth ached' Ibid, 395.

Mahler dropped one of his gloves Norman Lebrecht (2010/2011), *Why Mahler? How one man and ten symphonies changed the world*, Faber and Faber: London, 168.

'It's over' Ibid, 168.

his dealings with the palace . . . grudge-bearing aristocrat Henry-Louis De La Grange (1979/1995), *Gustav Mahler: Vienna – The Years of Challenge (1897–1904)*, Oxford University Press: Oxford, 19.

People in coffee houses would leave their tables and crowd around windows Norman Lebrecht (2010/2011), *Why Mahler? How one man and ten symphonies changed the world*, Faber and Faber: London, 12.

'Why am I so boundlessly licentious? . . . Whoever it might be' Alma Mahler-Werfel (1997/2000), *Diaries 1898–1902*, selected and translated by Antony Beaumont, Faber and Faber: London, 421.

She was a little deaf . . . during conversations Stuart Feder (2004), *Gustav Mahler: A Life in Crisis*, Yale University Press: New Haven, 88.

'It is only after fifty, sixty, seventy years . . . ' Alex Ross (2007/2009), *The Rest is Noise: Listening to the Twentieth Century*, Harper Perennial: London, 446–7.

She was suffering from depression Stuart Feder (2004), *Gustav Mahler: A Life in Crisis*, Yale University Press: New Haven, 4.

'She lay choking . . . eyes wide open' Alma Mahler (1940/1947), *Gustav Mahler: Memories and Letters*, translated by Basil Creighton, Readers Union/John Murray: London and Letchworth, 100.

'It was more than he could bear' Ibid, 100.

Arthur Schnitzler . . . the will to live Stuart Feder (2004), *Gustav Mahler: A Life in Crisis*, Yale University Press: New Haven, 144.

went to Vienna . . . in Munich in September Jens Male Fischer (2003/2013), *Gustav Mahler*, translated by Stewart Spencer, Yale University Press: New Haven, 630.

they saw each other every day . . . spectacular Stuart Feder (2004), *Gustav Mahler: A Life in Crisis*, Yale University Press: New Haven, 181.

There is some evidence to suggest . . . sexual frustration Ibid, 178.

He had told her . . . only 'suites' Ibid, 179.

diet of lettuce and buttermilk Ibid, 180.

'What's this?' Ibid, 191.

he handed the letter to his wife before he had finished reading it Ibid, 191.

'Now – at last – I was able to tell him all' Alma Mahler (1940/1947), *Gustav Mahler: Memories and Letters*, translated by Basil Creighton, Readers Union/John Murray: London and Letchworth, 144.

'overlooked' Ibid, 144.

Mahler had asked Alma to give up composing Gustav Mahler (1995/2004), *Gustav Mahler: Letters to his Wife*, edited by Henry-Louis De La Grange and Günther Weiss in collaboration with Knud Martner, first complete edition, revised and translated by Antony Beaumont, Faber and Faber: London, 82.

and to surrender herself 'unconditionally' to his every need Ibid, 84.

Alma had never stopped composing Henry-Louis De La Grange (1979/1995), *Gustav Mahler: Vienna – The Years of Challenge (1897–1904)*, Oxford University Press: Oxford, 454 (footnote).

'I kiss you a thousand times, my dearest . . . ' Gustav Mahler (1995/2004), *Gustav Mahler: Letters to his Wife*, edited by Henry-Louis De La Grange and Günther Weiss in collaboration with Knud Martner, first complete edition, revised and translated by Antony Beaumont, Faber and Faber: London, 166.

He kissed her slippers Ibid, 377.

'wondrous being' Ibid, 376.

'Almschilitzilitzilitzi!' Ibid, 377.

where it seems they shook hands before parting Stuart Feder (2004), *Gustav Mahler: A Life in Crisis*, Yale University Press: New Haven, 195.

Walter had consulted Freud . . . a psychological cause Mikkel Borch-Jacobsen (2011/2021), *Freud's Patients: A Book of Lives*, Reaktion Books: London, 124.

met at the Golden Turk Café Stuart Feder (2004), *Gustav Mahler: A Life in Crisis*, Yale University Press: New Haven, 206.

Sleep states and symbolism are recurring ideas in his compositions Ibid, 73.

although his Mozart arias were invariably painful and tuneless Peter Gay (1988), *Freud: A Life for Our Time*, J. M. Dent and Sons: London, 168.

'I am three times without a Heimat . . .' Norman Lebrecht (2010/2011), *Why Mahler? How one man and ten symphonies changed the world*, Faber and Faber: London, 24.

'My language is German . . .' From a 1926 interview conducted in English, cited by Peter Gay (1987) in *A Godless Jew: Freud, Atheism, and the Making of Psychoanalysis*, Yale University Press: New Haven, 139.

'You must come with me' Stuart Feder (2004), *Gustav Mahler: A Life in Crisis*, Yale University Press: New Haven, 69.

'the symphony is like the world . . .' Norman Lebrecht (2010/2011), *Why Mahler? How one man and ten symphonies changed the world*, Faber and Faber: London, 9.

'What is best in music is not to be found in the notes' Ibid, 9.

Freud and Mahler met in the Golden Turk at 4.30 Ibid, 208.

'How dare a man in your state ask a young woman to be tied to him?' Alma Mahler (1940/1947), *Gustav Mahler: Memories and Letters*, translated by Basil Creighton, Readers Union/John Murray: London and Letchworth, 147. NB: In the original, 'dare' is 'dared'.

even though he had difficulty pronouncing the letter 'r' Ibid, 147.

'Holy Mary complex' Stuart Feder (2004), *Gustav Mahler: A Life in Crisis*, Yale University Press: New Haven, 233.

she affirmed . . . she had 'known and loved' in her father Alma Mahler (1940/1947), *Gustav Mahler: Memories and Letters*, translated by Basil Creighton, Readers Union/John Murray: London and Letchworth, 147.

'The nightmare's dispelled . . . self-contemplation' Gustav Mahler (1995/2004), *Gustav Mahler: Letters to his Wife*, edited by Henry-Louis De La Grange and Günther Weiss in collaboration with Knud Martner, first complete edition, revised and translated by Antony Beaumont, Faber and Faber: London, 381.

'single shaft through a mysterious building' Stuart Feder (2004), *Gustav Mahler: A Life in Crisis*, Yale University Press: New Haven, 233.

'There is not one spot . . . with my tongue' Norman Lebrecht (2010/2011), *Why Mahler? How one man and ten symphonies changed the world*, Faber and Faber: London, 213.

'My love sits beside me . . . my wife at my side!' Gustav Mahler (1995/2004), *Gustav Mahler: Letters to his Wife*, edited by Henry-Louis De La Grange and Günther Weiss in collaboration with Knud Martner, first complete edition, revised and translated by

Antony Beaumont, Faber and Faber: London, 382.

'Freud is quite right . . . ' Ibid, 387.

'But just as love always engenders love . . . ' Ibid, 387.

Gropius was sitting in the audience Fiona MacCarthy (2019), *Gropius: The Man who Built the Bauhaus*, Belknap Press: Cambridge, Massachusetts, 59.

'a long period of mental and spiritual agony' Susanne Keegan (1991), *The Bride of the Wind: The Life of Alma Mahler*, Secker & Warburg: London, 167.

Kokoschka had to make do with a life-size replica of Alma Stuart Feder (2004), *Gustav Mahler: A Life in Crisis*, Yale University Press: New Haven, 293.

The Alma doll . . . a bloody murder scene Information card displayed next to a replica of the doll in the Leopold Museum, Vienna.

Mahler had told her . . . Brahms Alma Mahler (1940/1947), *Gustav Mahler: Memories and Letters*, translated by Basil Creighton, Readers Union/John Murray: London and Letchworth, 91.

He suggested that impotence arises . . . sister fixations Sigmund Freud (1912/1991), *On the Universal Tendency to Debasement in the Sphere of Love*, in *On Sexuality*, the Penguin Freud Library, Vol. 7, translated by James Strachey, edited by James Strachey and Angela Richards, Penguin Books: Harmondsworth, 248.

'Where they love they do not desire and where they desire they cannot love' Ibid, 251.

'To live for you! To die for you! Almschi!' Jens Male Fischer (2003/2013), *Gustav Mahler*, translated by Stewart Spencer, Yale University Press: New Haven, 646.

'From all who looked at this showpiece . . . ' Ibid, 647.

Chapter 20: Thanatos

threadbare blue check suit was crawling with lice Ian Kershaw (1998/1999), *Hitler 1889–1936: Hubris*, Penguin: Harmondsworth, 52–3.

He tried to earn money . . . the cold was intolerable. Ibid, 53.

a cavalcade of limousines Ian Kershaw (2000/2001), *Hitler 1936–1945: Nemesis*, Penguin: London, 81.

'The whole city . . . as Hitler entered her' George Clare (1980/1982), *Last Waltz in Vienna: The Destruction of a Family 1842–1942*, Macmillan: London, 195.

The mob outside were shouting . . . 'We want to see our Führer!' *Hitler 1936–1945: Nemesis*, Penguin: London, 81.

'At least I burn in the best of company' Theodor Reik (1942), *From Thirty Years with Freud* (Chapter II: Last Visit to Freud), Hogarth Press: London, 24 (e-book edition).

he addressed . . . in the Hero's Square Ian Kershaw (2000/2001), *Hitler 1936–1945: Nemesis*, Penguin: London, 81.

'shabbily dressed' Martin Freud (1957), Glory Reflected: Sigmund Freud – Man and Father, Angus and Robertson, 207.

'Won't the gentlemen help themselves?' Ernest Jones (1953–7/1977), The Life and Work of Sigmund Freud, edited and abridged by Lionel Trilling and Steven Marcus, Penguin: Harmondsworth, 636.

'He had a way of frowning . . .' Ibid, 636.

'I never got so much for a single house call' Mark Edmundson (2007), The Death of Sigmund Freud: Fascism, Psychoanalysis, and the Rise of Fundamentalism, Bloomsbury: London, 72. NB: Language changed slightly, 'for a single visit' becoming 'for a single house call' – which probably reflects the meaning of Freud's original German more accurately.

Draped in a black mink coat Andrew Nagorski (2022), Saving Freud: A life in Vienna and an escape to freedom in London, Icon Books: London, 240.

She was oddly composed . . . members of the SS Martin Freud (1957), Glory Reflected: Sigmund Freud – Man and Father, Angus and Robertson, 212.

Anna was taken to . . . Morzinplatz Roman Krivanek (undated guide to the Vienna Freud Museum), 'Anna Freud's Work in Vienna', in Freud, Berggasse 19: The Origin of Psychoanalysis, edited by Monika Pessler and Daniela Finzi with a foreword by Siri Hustvedt, Hatje Cantz, 277.

deposited in a corridor . . . and shot Martin Freud (1957), Glory Reflected: Sigmund Freud – Man and Father, Angus and Robertson, 212.

Both Anna and Martin . . . supply them with the drug Max Schur (1972), Freud: Living and Dying, International Universities Press Inc.: New York, 498.

Freud was never informed . . . Schur's acquiescence Andrew Nagorski (2022), Saving Freud: A life in Vienna and an escape to freedom in London, Icon Books: London 242.

The Gestapo seemed to think . . . political subversives Martin Freud (1957), Glory Reflected: Sigmund Freud – Man and Father, Angus and Robertson, 213.

This was the second and final time . . . crying Andrew Nagorski (2022), Saving Freud: A life in Vienna and an escape to freedom in London, Icon Books: London, 243.

'Look how poverty-stricken . . . sixty-five millions have . . .' Theodor Reik (1942), From Thirty Years With Freud (Chapter II: Last Visit to Freud), Hogarth Press: London, 24 (e-book edition).

Devotion to Hitler's ideals . . . a death's head ring Chris McNab (2013), Hitler's Elite: The SS 1939–45, Osprey, 98–9.

Ferdinand Raimund set an early precedent William M. Johnston (1972/1983), The Austrian Mind: An Intellectual and Social History 1848–1938, University of California Press, 175.

Eduard van der Nüll Ibid, 176.

Nathan Weiss Ibid, 176.

Viktor Tausk Ibid, 178.

Herbert Silberer Ibid, 178.

Stekel Ibid, 178.

Freud's niece, Martha Gertrud Michael Molnar (2015), *Looking Through Freud's Photos*, from the History of Psychoanalysis series, editors Brett Kahr and Professor Peter L. Rudnytsky, Routledge Taylor & Francis Groups: London, 133.

Kurt Wittgenstein Ray Monk (1990/91), *Ludwig Wittgenstein: The Duty of Genius*, Vintage, Random House: London, 11.

Rudolf Wittgenstein Ibid, 12.

Hans Wittgenstein Ibid, 12.

Freud's patient Sergei Pankejeff . . . *Jewish suicides* Muriel Gardiner (1971), *The Wolf-Man by the Wolf-Man: The double story of Freud's most famous case*, with *The Case of the Wolf-Man* by Sigmund Freud, *A Supplement* by Ruth Mack Brunswick and a foreword by Anna Freud, edited with notes, an introduction and chapters by Muriel Gardiner, Basic Books: New York, 119.

Egon Friedell William M. Johnston (1972/1983), *The Austrian Mind: An Intellectual and Social History 1848–1938*, University of California Press, 178.

His mother rubbed her hands . . . *'dust of which we are made'* Sigmund Freud (1899/2006), *Interpreting Dreams*, translated by J. A. Underwood with an introduction by John Forrester, Penguin Books: London, 220.

'You owe nature a death' Ibid, 220.

Freud believed that the composer's demise . . . *death wish* Stuart Feder (2004), *Gustav Mahler: A Life in Crisis*, Yale University Press: New Haven, 240.

'have not fallen . . . *as we imagined'* Sigmund Freud (1915/2005), *Timely Reflections on War and Death*, in *On Murder, Mourning and Melancholia*, the New Penguin Freud, General Editor Adam Phillips, translated by Shaun Whiteside, with an introduction by Maud Ellmann, Penguin: London, 179.

'If you want to endure life, prepare yourself for death' Ibid, 194.

'daemonic' Sigmund Freud (1932/1991), Lecture 32: *Anxiety and Instinctual Life*, in *New Introductory Lectures on Psychoanalysis*, Vol. 2, the Penguin Freud Library, translated by James Strachey, edited by James Strachey assisted by Angela Richards, Penguin Books: Harmondsworth, 140.

'At this point we cannot help thinking . . . *'* Sigmund Freud (1923/2003), *Beyond the Pleasure Principle*, in *Beyond the Pleasure Principle and Other Writings*, the New Penguin Freud, General Editor Adam Phillips, translated by John Reddick, with an introduction by Mark Edmundson, Penguin: London, 76.

'the goal of all life is death' Ibid, 78.

'a step' in Freud's reasoning . . . *much misgiving'* Ernest Jones (1953–7/1977), *The Life and Work of Sigmund Freud*, edited and abridged by Lionel Trilling and Steven Marcus, Penguin: Harmondsworth, 507-8.

'the most bizarre monster of all his gallery of monsters' Frank J. Sulloway (1979/1980), *Freud:*

Biologist of the Mind, Fontana: Great Britain, 393.

'*And now the instincts that we believe in . . .* ' Sigmund Freud (1932/1991), Lecture 32: *Anxiety and Instinctual Life*, in *New Introductory Lectures on Psychoanalysis*, Vol. 2, the Penguin Freud Library, translated by James Strachey, edited by James Strachey assisted by Angela Richards, Penguin Books: Harmondsworth, 140.

'*the eternal current*' From the first of the *Duino Elegies* by Rainer Maria Rilke, cited in Carlo Rovelli (2017/2019), *The Order of Time*, translated by Erica Segre and Simon Carnell, Penguin Random House: London, 19.

'*the whole temple . . . a universe in ruins*' Bertrand Russell (1957), *Why I am Not a Christian*, Simon & Schuster: New York, 107.

'*The Entropic Two-Step*' Brian Greene (2020), *Until the End of Time: Mind, Matter, and Our Search for Meaning in an Evolving Universe*, Allen Lane: London, 41.

it is now generally accepted that this was Rilke Stuart Feder (2004), *Gustav Mahler: A Life in Crisis*, Yale University Press: New Haven, 314.

whose eternal current of time '*Draws all the ages with it*' From the first of the *Duino Elegies* by Rainer Maria Rilke, cited in Carlo Rovelli (2017/2019), *The Order of Time*, translated by Erica Segre and Simon Carnell, Penguin Random House: London, 19.

All that he loved and admired . . . was its doom' Sigmund Freud (1916/1990), *On Transience*, in *Art and Literature*, the Penguin Freud Library, Vol. 14, translated by James Strachey, edited by James Strachey and Albert Dickson, Penguin Books: Harmondsworth, 287.

'*Transience value is scarcity value over time*' Ibid, 288.

*He once described the steeple of St Stephen's Cathedral as '*detestable*'* Freud – Bernays, 10 March 1886, in Sigmund Freud (1961), *Letters of Sigmund Freud 1873–1939*, edited by Ernst L. Freud, translated by Tania and James Stern, Hogarth Press, 224.

Jones suggested a superior analogy Ernest Jones (1953–7/1977), *The Life and Work of Sigmund Freud*, edited and abridged by Lionel Trilling and Steven Marcus, Penguin: Harmondsworth, 637.

the famous 'couch' . . . stored in readiness for shipping Brenda Maddox (2006), *Freud's Wizard: The Enigma of Ernest Jones*, John Murray: London, 233.

worked as a script editor . . . Paramount Pictures Andrew Nagorski (2022), *Saving Freud: A life in Vienna and an escape to freedom in London*, Icon Books: London 133.

his novel It's Not Done *sold more copies than its now greatly admired contemporary* The Great Gatsby Ibid, 135.

collaborated on . . . published until 1967 Ibid, 139.

*he permitted his American friend to call him '*Freud*' instead of '*Professor*'* Ibid, 120.

'*to die in freedom*' Freud – Ernst Freud, 12 May 1938, in Sigmund Freud (1961), *Letters of Sigmund Freud 1873–1939*, edited by Ernst L. Freud, translated by Tania and James Stern, Hogarth Press, 438. NB: words written in English in the letter.

Yet, incredibly, Sauerwald developed an interest in Freud's writing Andrew Nagorski (2022), *Saving Freud: A life in Vienna and an escape to freedom in London*, Icon Books: London, 246.

chose to withhold . . . beyond Nazi jurisdiction Ibid, 249.

Paula Fichtl . . . reported by Jones Ibid, 253.

Bonaparte presented Freud . . . for his collection Ibid, 256.

as well as his favourite statue of Athena . . . smuggled out of Austria Max Schur (1972), *Freud: Living and Dying*, International Universities Press Inc.: New York, 504 (footnote 2).

The much-loved statue . . . the mad inferno!' Ibid, 504 (footnote 2).

'Heil Hitler!' Brenda Maddox (2006), *Freud's Wizard: The Enigma of Ernest Jones*, John Murray: London, 235. NB: Also reported as 'I am almost tempted to cry out, "Heil Hitler!"'[Jones, 644]

'We thank our Führer' Edmund Engelman (1998), *Sigmund Freud: Berggasse 19, Vienna*, with an introduction by Inge Scholze-Strasser, Verlag Christian Brandstatter: Wien, 102–3.

That evening Freud wrote to the psychoanalyst Max Eitingon Freud – Eitingon, 6 June 1938, in Sigmund Freud (1961), *Letters of Sigmund Freud 1873–1939*, edited by Ernst L. Freud, translated by Tania and James Stern, Hogarth Press, 440.

'Everything is still unreal, as in a dream' Ibid, 440.

'friendly lines of welcome' . . . 'All kinds of fuss' Freud – Eitingon, 6 June 1938, in Sigmund Freud (1961), *Letters of Sigmund Freud 1873–1939*, edited by Ernst L. Freud, translated by Tania and James Stern, Hogarth Press, 441.

'The feeling of triumph . . . I have been released' Ibid, 441–2.

'We have become popular in London overnight' Ibid, 442.

'Affectionate regards to you and Mirra. Yours, Freud' Ibid, 442.

'living vertically' Brenda Maddox (2006), *Freud's Wizard: The Enigma of Ernest Jones*, John Murray: London, 236.

'he even came home with me once . . . the Hotel Sacher' Salvador Dalí (1942/1993), *The Secret Life of Salvador Dalí*, Alkin Books: Great Britain, 23.

'Freud's cranium . . . is a snail!' Ibid, 23.

The sketch was the prototype of a pen and ink drawing . . . too upsetting Information leaflet issued at the Freud Museum (1998).

'a kind of dandy of universal intellectualism' Salvador Dalí (1942/1993), *The Secret Life of Salvador Dalí*, Alkin Books: Great Britain, 24.

'I have never seen a more complete example of a Spaniard. What a fanatic!' Ibid, 25.

the 'young Spaniard' . . . his opinion of surrealism Freud – Stefan Zweig, 20 July 1938, in Sigmund Freud (1961), *Letters of Sigmund Freud 1873–1939*, edited by Ernst L. Freud, translated by Tania and James Stern, Hogarth Press, 444.

'a half extinct volcano' Mark Edmundson (2007), *The Death of Sigmund Freud: Fascism, Psychoanalysis, and the Rise of Fundamentalism*, Bloomsbury: London, 194.

'alert' with a 'monkey's light eyes' Ibid, 195.

Sir Albert Seward, Professor A. V. Hill and J. D. Griffith Davies Ibid, 158.

nothing stronger than aspirin . . . ability to think Ernest Jones (1953–7/1977), *The Life and Work of Sigmund Freud*, edited and abridged by Lionel Trilling and Steven Marcus, Penguin: Harmondsworth, 655–6.

He still wanted to discuss what was happening in psychoanalytic circles Ibid, 655.

'New light is thrown . . . new developments . . . ' Sigmund Freud (1940/1993), *Sigmund Freud. 15. Historical and Expository Works on Psychoanalysis. An Outline of Psychoanalysis*, the Penguin Freud Library, Vol. 15, translated from the German under the general editorship of James Strachey, the present volume by Albert Dickson, Penguin, 373.

Freud speculates about . . . advances in psychopharmacology Ibid, 416.

A biopsy was performed . . . a malignant epithelioma Max Schur (1972), *Freud: Living and Dying*, International Universities Press Inc.: New York, 518.

'a small island of pain' Mark Edmundson (2007), *The Death of Sigmund Freud: Fascism, Psychoanalysis, and the Rise of Fundamentalism*, Bloomsbury: London, 214.

Schur's account . . . necrosis of the bone' Max Schur (1972), *Freud: Living and Dying*, International Universities Press Inc.: New York, 526.

Hitler would be defeated . . . the ultimate outcome Ernest Jones (1953–7/1977), *The Life and Work of Sigmund Freud*, edited and abridged by Lionel Trilling and Steven Marcus, Penguin: Harmondsworth, 656.

'Every suicide is a sublime poem of melancholy' Honoré de Balzac (1831/2012), *The Wild Ass's Skin*, a new translation by Helen Constantine, edited with an introduction and notes by Patrick Coleman, Oxford University Press: Oxford, 9.

'Night, the hour of death, had suddenly arrived' Ibid, 21.

'Now it's nothing but torture . . . no sense any more' Max Schur (1972), *Freud: Living and Dying*, International Universities Press Inc.: New York, 529.

Subsequent research . . . Josefine Stross Lacoursiere, Roy B. (2008), 'Freud's Death: Historical Truth and Biographical Fictions', *American Imago* 65 (1):107–28.

placed in his favourite 2,300-year-old Grecian urn Viktor Mazin (undated guide to the Vienna Freud Museum), 'Arts, Dreams and Revolution', in *Freud, Berggasse 19: The Origin of Psychoanalysis*, edited by Monika Pessler and Daniela Finzi with a foreword by Siri Hustvedt, Hatje Cantz, 93.

Chapter 21: Magus

'down to the last man' Sigmund Freud (1930/2002), *Civilization and Its Discontents*, the New Penguin Freud, General Editor Adam Phillips, Penguin: London, 81.

'*And now it is to be expected . . . immortal adversary*' Ibid, 81–2.

'*But who can foresee the outcome?*' Ibid, 82.

'*The replacement of the power of the individual . . . step towards civilization*' Ibid, 32.

'*Much of mankind's struggle . . . claims of civilization*' Ibid, 33.

*Freud preferred '*malaise*' or '*discomfort*' to '*discontent*'* Bruno Bettelheim (1983/1991), *Freud and Man's Soul*, Penguin Books: London, 100.

The increasing demands . . . evolutionary time lags David M. Buss (2019), *Evolutionary Psychology: The New Science of the Mind*, sixth edition, Routledge: London, 18.

'*episodic phenomenon*' Sigmund Freud (1930/2002), *Civilization and Its Discontents*, the New Penguin Freud, General Editor Adam Phillips, Penguin: London, 14.

'*We are,*' *as Freud pointed out,* '*restricted by our constitution*' Ibid, 15.

'*hysterical misery into common unhappiness*' Sigmund Freud and Joseph Breuer (1895/2004), *Studies in Hysteria*, introduction by Rachel Bowlby, translated by Nicola Luckhurst, Penguin Classics: London, 306.

Today, someone, somewhere . . . trillions of dollars Frank Tallis (2021), *The Act of Living: What the great psychologists can teach us about surviving discontent in an age of anxiety*, Little, Brown: Great Britain, 6–8.

'*I'm glad you ask . . . therapeutic problems*' A. Kardiner (1977), *My Analysis With Freud: Reminiscences*, W. W. Norton & Company: New York, 68.

'*great analyst*' Ibid, 69.

'*I am much too much occupied with theoretical problems*' Ibid, 69.

'*My interest, after making a lifelong* détour *through the natural sciences . . .* ' Sigmund Freud (1914/1993), *Sigmund Freud. 15. Historical and Expository Works on Psychoanalysis. An Autobiographical Study*, the Penguin Freud Library, Vol. 15, Penguin, 257.

Homo homini lupus Sigmund Freud (1930/2002), *Civilization and Its Discontents*, the New Penguin Freud, General Editor Adam Phillips, Penguin: London, 48.

'*Who . . . would be so bold as to dispute this proposition?*' Ibid, 48.

'*love thine enemies*' Ibid, 47

'*Aggression was not created by property . . . its original anal form*' Ibid, 50.

'*nurse maids seek to mitigate with their lullaby about heavens*' Ibid, 58.

'*the sleep of the world*' Sigmund Freud (1914/1993), *Sigmund Freud. 15. Historical and Expository Works on Psychoanalysis. On the History of the Psychoanalytic Movement*, the Penguin Freud Library, Vol. 15, Penguin, 79.

'*For the space of a few quickened heart-beats . . . he is alive*' Theodor Reik (1942), *From Thirty Years With Freud* ('Preface: A Portrait Comes to Life'), Hogarth Press: London, 8 (e-book edition).

'More than Einstein . . . profound and long lasting' J. F. Kihlstrom (2009), 'Freud is a Dead Weight on Psychology', in *Atkinson and Hilgard's Introduction to Psychology*, edited by R. Atkinson, R. C. Atkinson, E. E. Smith, D. J. Bem and S. Nolen-Hoeksema, Harcourt Brace Jovanovich, 497; see also 'Is Freud Still alive? No, not really' – https://www.ocf. berkeley.edu/~jfkihlstrom/freuddead.htm

Acknowledgements

I would like to thank Richard Beswick, my UK editor at Little, Brown, for urging me to write this book. It wouldn't have been written without his confidence and enthusiasm. I would also like to thank Michael Flamini, my US editor at St Martin's Press, for helpful comments provided after I'd completed my first draft. Ivan Ward, head of learning emeritus at the Freud Museum London (where he worked for over thirty years), read what I incorrectly assumed was my final draft and supplied me with outstanding additional notes. Naturally, we didn't always agree; but when we disagreed, we managed to do so with mutual respect, courtesy and good humour. Karl Friston very kindly read my summary of the links between Freudian ideas and the free energy principle. Any errors in the text are of course entirely my responsibility. Thanks also to Nithya Rae and Daniel Balado for an excellent copy-edit. Finally, I would like to thank Nicola Fox for being my constant first reader and literary critic.

FRANK TALLIS
London, 2023

Index

Page numbers in italic refer to images